Crisis and Contradiction

Historical Materialism Book Series

The Historical Materialism Book Series is a major publishing initiative of the radical left. The capitalist crisis of the twenty-first century has been met by a resurgence of interest in critical Marxist theory. At the same time, the publishing institutions committed to Marxism have contracted markedly since the high point of the 1970s. The Historical Materialism Book Series is dedicated to addressing this situation by making available important works of Marxist theory. The aim of the series is to publish important theoretical contributions as the basis for vigorous intellectual debate and exchange on the left.

The peer-reviewed series publishes original monographs, translated texts, and reprints of classics across the bounds of academic disciplinary agendas and across the divisions of the left. The series is particularly concerned to encourage the internationalization of Marxist debate and aims to translate significant studies from beyond the English-speaking world.

For a full list of titles in the Historical Materialism Book Series
available in paperback from Haymarket Books, visit:
www.haymarketbooks.org/category/hm-series

Crisis and Contradiction

Marxist Perspectives on Latin America in the Global Political Economy

Edited by
Susan J. Spronk and Jeffery R. Webber

Haymarket Books
Chicago, IL

First published in 2015 by Brill Academic Publishers, The Netherlands
© 2015 Koninklijke Brill NV, Leiden, The Netherlands

Published in paperback in 2015 by
Haymarket Books
P.O. Box 180165
Chicago, IL 60618
773-583-7884
www.haymarketbooks.org

ISBN: 978-1-60846-552-1

Trade distribution:
In the US, Consortium Book Sales, www.cbsd.com
In Canada, Publishers Group Canada, www.pgcbooks.ca
In the UK, Turnaround Publisher Services, http://www.turnaround-uk.com
In all other countries, Publishers Group Worldwide, www.pgw.com

Cover design by Ragina Johnson.

This book was published with the generous support of
Lannan Foundation and the Wallace Global Fund.

10 9 8 7 6 5 4 3 2 1

Library of Congress Cataloging-in-Publication data is available.

Contents

Acknowledgements

Susan Spronk would like to thank the Social Science and Humanities Research Council (Canada) and the University of Ottawa for financial support for this project. Both editors would also like to thank Eva Mascolo Fortin, Rebecca McMillan, Adrian Murray and Calais Caswell for research assistance, as well as Ruth Felder and Yael Shubs for translating Claudio Katz's essay. Our gratitude also goes to the contributing authors for their patience.

List of Figures and Tables

List of Abbreviations

AD	Acción Democratica (Democratic Action)
AR	Absolute Rent
BNDES	Banco Nacional de Desenvolvimento Econômico e Social (Brazilian Development Bank)
CAP	Carlos Andrés Pérez
CC	Communal Council
CCL	Consejos Consultivos Locales (Local Consultative Councils)
CP	Convertability Plan
CEPAL	Comisión Económica para América Latina y el Caribe (United Nations Economic Commission for Latin America and the Caribbean, ECLAC)
CFK	Cristina Fernández de Kircher
CGT	Confederación General del Trabajo (General Labour Confederation)
COB	Bolivian Workers' Central (Central Obrera Boliviana)
CODAEC	Comité para la Defensa del Agua y la Economía Familiar (Committee for the Defense of Water and the Family Economy)
CONTAG	Confederação Nacional dos Trabalhadores Agrícola (National Confederation of Rural Workers)
CTA	Central de los Trabajadores Argentinos (Central of Argentine Workers)
CTERA	Confederación de Trabajadores de la Educación de la República Argentina (Confederation of Education Workers of Argentina's Republic
CUT	Central Unica dos Trabalhadores (Unitary Workers Union)
CVG	Corporación Venezolana de Guyana
CVG-Alcasa	Corporación Venezolana de Guyana-*Aluminio del Caroní S.A.*,
DR	Differential Rent
ECLAC	Comisión Económica para América Latina y el Caribe (United Nations Economic Commission for Latin America and the Caribbean, CEPAL)
EPS	Empresas Productivas Sociales (social production companies)
FDI	Foreign Direct Investment
FDPS	Frente Popular Darío Santillán (Popular Front Darío Santillán)
Fabriles	Federación de Fabriles de Cochabamba (Federation of Manufacturing Workers of Cochabamba)

FEDECOR   Federación Departmental de Regantes y Sistemas Comunales
            del Agua Potable (Federation of Irrigator's Associations from
            the Department of Cochabamba)
FEJUVE   Federación de Juntas Vecinales de El Alto (the Federation of
            Neighborhood Councils of El Alto)
FTV   Federación Tierra y Vivienda (Land and Housing Federation)
JyJDH   Plan Jefes y Jefas de Hogar (Heads of Household Program)
IIRSA   Initiative for the Integration of the Regional Infrastructure of
            South America
IMF   International Monetary Fund
INDEC   Instituto Nacional de Estadísticas y Censos (National Institute
            of Statistics and the Census)
IPC   International Petroleum Cartel
ISI   Import Substitution Inudstrialisation
MAS   el Movimiento al Socialismo (Movement towards Socialism)
MIBAM   Ministerio del Poder Popular para las Industrial Básicas y la
            Mineria (Ministry of Basic Industry and Mines)
MNR   *Movimiento Nacionalista Revolucionario* (Revolutionary
            Nationalist Movement)
MST   Movimento dos Trabalhadores Rurais Sem Terra (Landless
            Rural Workers' Movement)
MTD   Movimiento de Trabajadores Desocupados Anibal Verón
            (Movement of Unemployed Workers Anibal Verón)
MVR   Movimiento Quinto República (Fifth Republic Movement)
NEP   New Economic Policy
NIDL   New International Division of Labour
NPM   New Productive Model
OCC   Organic Composition of Capital
OPEC   Organisation of Petroleum Exporting Countries
PB   Participatory Budget
PDVSA   Petróleos de Venezuela, S.A. (Petroleum of Venezuela)
PJ   Partido Justicialista (Justicialist Party)
PNPB   Programa Nacional de produção e Uso de Biodiesel (the
            National Programme of Production and Use of Biodiesel)
PPT   Patria Para Todos (Fatherland for all Party)
PSDB   Partido da Social Democracia Brasileira (Brazilian Social-
            democratic Party)
PSUV   Partido Socialista Unida de Venezuela (the United Socialist
            Party of Venezuela)

PT	Partido dos Trabalhadores (the Workers Party)
RER	Real Exchange Rate
SEMAPA	Servicio municipal de agua potable, alcantarillado y desagües Pluviales
Sidor	Siderúrgica de Orinoco
STR	Sindicato dos Trabalhadores Rurais (Rural Workers' Union)
TNCS	Transnational Corporations
TIPNIS	Territorio Indígena del Parque Nacional Isiboro-Sécure
UNT	Unión Nacional de Trabajadores y Trabajadoras (National Worker's Union)

Note on Contributors

Dario Azzellini
is an author, filmmaker, and assistant professor at the Johannes Kepler University in Linz, Austria. He has published several books on Latin America, popular movements and workers' control.

Emilia Castorina
is a researcher at the National Council of Scientific and Technical Research of Argentina (CONICET) and professor at the University of Buenos Aires, Argentina. Her work has appeared in *Socialist Register*.

Mariano Féliz
is a researcher at the National Council of Scientific and Technical Research of Argentina (CONICET) and professor at the National University of La Plata, Argentina. He is co-author of *Proyecto neodesarrollista en la Argentina: ¿Proyecto nacional-popular o nueva etapa en el desarrollo capitalista?* (Herramienta ediciones, 2012).

Juan Grigera
is a postdoctoral fellow at the National Council of Scientific and Technical Research of Argentina (CONICET) and teaches in the Universities of Quilmes and La Plata in Argentina.

Nicolas Grinberg
is a Research Fellow at the Consejo Nacional de Investigaciones Científicas y Técnicas (National Scientific and Technical Research Council, CONICET, Argentina) and with the Facultad Latinoamericana de Ciencias Sociales (Latin American Faculty of Social Sciences, FLACSO, Argentina).

Gabriel Hetland
is a doctoral candidate in sociology at the University of California, Berkeley. His research examines popular participation, politics, labour and social movements in Latin America and the United States.

Claudio Katz
is a Professor of Economics at the University of Buenos Aires and a researcher with the National Council of Science and Technology of Argentinas (CONICET). His latest book is *Bajo el Imperio del Capital* (Ediciones Luxemburg, 2011).

Thomas F. Purcell
is the sub-director of the National Center for Advanced Research in Socio-Spatial Justice at the *Instituto de Altos Estudios Nacionales* (IAEN) in Quito, Ecuador. His research interests are in the political economy of development and critical social theory.

Ben Selwyn
teaches and researches International Development at the University of Sussex. His most recent book is *The Global Development Crisis* (Polity Press, 2014).

Susan J. Spronk
is an associate professor in the School of International Development and Global Studies at the University of Ottawa. She is a researcher with the Municipal Services Project, an international project that focuses on alternatives to privatization.

Guido Starosta
is Professor of Economics at the National University of Quilmes (Argentina) and member of the National Council of Scientific and Technical Research (CONICET). His work has appeared in *New Political Economy, Capital and Class*, and *Science and Society*.

Leandro Vergara-Camus
is lecturer at the School of Oriental and African Studies at the University of London. His book *Land and Freedom*, on peasant struggles in Brazil and Mexico, is forthcoming with Zed Books in 2014.

Jeffery R. Webber
is Senior Lecturer in the School of Politics and International Relations at Queen Mary University of London. He is the author of *Red October* (Haymarket, 2012) and *From Rebellion to Reform in Bolivia* (Haymarket, 2011).

CHAPTER 1

Introduction – Systemic Logics and Historical Specificity: Renewing Historical Materialism in Latin American Political Economy

Susan J. Spronk and Jeffery R. Webber

Writing at the height of neoliberalism in the mid-1990s, the eminent Marxist theorist Ellen Meiksins Wood laments that the 'critique of capitalism is out of fashion. Capitalist triumphalism on the right is mirrored on the left by a sharp contraction of socialist aspirations'.[1] This decline in the ambitions of the left found its intellectual expression in the marginalisation of Marxist theory across the academic disciplines. 'Left intellectuals', Wood observes, 'if not embracing capitalism as the best of all possible worlds, hope for little more than a space in its interstices and look forward to only the most local and particular resistances'.[2] Ironically, this intellectual retreat occurred at precisely the time when an understanding was most desperately needed of capitalism's historical specificities and systemic logics. As Wood argues, in the 1990s 'large sections of the intellectual left, instead of developing, enriching and refining the required conceptual instruments, show every sign of discarding them altogether'.[3]

Latin America was no exception to this trend.[4] The much-cited book by Jorge Castañeda, *Utopia Unarmed: The Latin American Left after the Cold War*, is representative of the many texts by left intellectuals who relinquished revolutionary possibilities and embraced 'the market', as if it was possible to create capitalism with a human face through state regulation.[5] Forrest Colburn's *Latin America at the End of Politics* similarly pronounced the end of History, surmising that the debate between socialism and capitalism had been settled, and that the popular forces were now resigned to participate in projects of technocratic liberal governance.[6]

---

1 Wood 1995, p. 1.
2 Ibid.
3 Ibid.
4 See Petras 1990.
5 Castañeda 1994.
6 See Colburn 1992.

How times have changed. In the context of the ideological crisis of ortho-dox neoliberalism emerging out of the 1998–2002 economic crisis in Latin America, the consolidation of left- and centre-left governments, and the recent global financial meltdown of 2008, Latin American Marxism has experienced an uneven but tangible intellectual revival.[7] Journals such as Argentina's *Herramienta: debate y crítica marxista*, and, more recently, *Crítica y Emancipación* have contributed to this revitalisation. Important sociological journals such as *Observatorio Social de América Latina* (OSAL), although never identifying as Marxist, have begun to feature a growing number of Marxists in their pages. Even mainstream journals that have historically been hostile to Marxism, such as *Nueva Sociedad*, are taking Marxist debates much more seri-ously. Marxist intellectuals have been able to influence public and academic debate in a manner that exceeds what was possible in recent periods across the region.

Thus far, the revival of Marxism is marked more in the Spanish- than English-language literature since Marxism is again animating debates on pub-lic policy in the New Left governments such as Bolivia, Ecuador and Venezuela, and still remains central to debates within the popular movements of Mexico, Argentina and Brazil, amongst others.[8] This volume aims to contribute to the debates within Marxism in the English language, by including both vet-eran observers and a host of Latin American and North American scholars representing newer voices in Latin American studies. Capturing in detail the dynamics of Latin America in its entirety would have produced a book of unmanageable size. In focusing on the cases of Argentina, Bolivia, Brazil, and Venezuela, as well as reflecting theoretically on themes that reverberate across the region as a whole, we are able to develop fine-grained, multidimensional analyses of some of the biggest, most politically and economically influential countries in the region (Brazil and Argentina), as well as those which have been host to the most radical forms of social struggle in the recent period (Bolivia and Venezuela). While the contributors to this volume represent diverse ten-dencies within Marxism, they all self-identify as 'historical materialist'; that is, they adhere to an analytical approach which is both *materialist* – the tenet that the mode of production and the behaviour of actors determined by the rules of reproduction play a major role in configuring society – and *historicist* – the tenet that there are no universal, transhistorical definitions of human

---

7 Orthodox neoliberalism refers to the principles of the Washington Consensus as articulated by Williamson 1993.

8 See Castorina 2012; Antunes 2013; Roman and Velasco Arregui 2013.

thought and action, but rather that these activities must be understood in their historical context.

In this introduction, we provide an overview of the historical factors that explain the decline of Marxism in Latin America since the authoritarian period and its recent tentative revival in the context of the commodities boom and the erosion of the legitimacy of orthodox neoliberalism, followed by a summary of the contributions to two thematic areas that frame the volume: the ways that neoliberalism has changed class formation in Latin America and the way that the relationship between state and market under capitalist social relations has been conceptualised in mainstream political economy, and Marx's critique of political economy.

The Decline of the Left (1970s–1990s): State Terror and Neoliberalism

The decline of the intellectual left was in part the result of the physical annihilation of left leaders, activists, and sympathisers over more than two decades of state-sponsored violence, beginning with the overthrowing of Brazilian president João Goulart in 1964. By 1970, 18 countries of Latin America were governed by non-constitutional regimes. 'With a few important exceptions', historian Greg Grandin points out, throughout Latin America 'state- and elite-orchestrated preventive and punitive terror was key to ushering in neoliberalism'.[9] Mass murder of activists, sympathisers, and bystanders at the hands of the state prepared the ground for neoliberalism, a new ideology and mode of economic management that emerged from the secret meetings of the Mont Pellerin society, and eventually climbed its way up from South America to the Central American Isthmus. As Grandin explains, the onset of neoliberalism in the 1980s 'had as much to do with the destruction of mass movements as it did with the rise of new financial elites invested in global markets'.[10] The memory of the loss of entire layers of left leadership, and the psychological trauma of those who survived, long reverberated through the rhythm of politics in following decades.

Argentina illustrates the trends in the Southern Cone countries. An anti-communist military junta assumed power through a 'Gentlemen's Coup' in 1976 and 'disappeared' 30,000 individuals before electoral democracy was

---

9   Grandin 2004, p. 14.
10   Ibid.

restored in 1983. 'The generals arrived with a plan', notes Marguerite Feitlowitz, citing the junta's Process for National Reorganisation:

> By meeting its 'sacred responsibility' to forever rid the earth of subversion, Argentina 'would join the concert of nations'. Argentina was the theatre for 'World War III', which had to be fought against those whose activities – and thoughts – were deemed 'subversive'. Intellectual, writer, journalist, trade unionist, psychologist, social worker became 'categories of guilt'.[11]

Regimes of comparable character were established in Chile, Brazil, Paraguay, Uruguay, and Bolivia, unified geopolitically through Operation Condor, a US-sponsored military operation that aimed to eradicate the influence of communism in the region.[12]

Meanwhile, in Central America, the 'pacification' of mass guerrilla insurgencies was a necessary prerequisite for the installation of neoliberalism across the Isthmus.[13] In El Salvador, 30,000 civilians died between 1980 and 1981; the vast majority were murdered by Reagan-backed Salvadoran security forces.[14] As Grandin comments on the genocidal war waged against indigenous people of neighbouring Guatemala over the same period:

> Beginning in 1981, the army executed a scorched earth campaign that murdered over one hundred thousand Mayans and completely razed more than four hundred indigenous communities. Anti-communist zeal and racist hatred were refracted through counterinsurgent exactitude. The killings were brutal beyond imagination. Soldiers murdered children by beating them on rocks as their parents watched. They extracted organs and foetuses, amputated genitalia and limbs, committed mass and multiple rapes, and burned some victims alive. In the logic that equated indigenous culture with subversion, army units destroyed ceremonial sites and turned sacred places such as churches and caves into torture chambers. By the time the war ended in 1966, the state had killed two hundred thousand people, disappeared forty thousand, and tortured unknown thousands more.[15]

---

11   Feitlowitz 1998, p. 7.
12   See McSherry 2005.
13   Dunkerley 1998; Robinson 2003.
14   Lafeber 1993, p. 269.
15   Grandin 2004, p. 3.

As the Argentine Marxist Claudio Katz (featured in this volume) argues, the correlation of forces is determined in Latin America 'by the positions that are won, threatened, or lost by three sectors: the local capitalist class, the mass of the oppressed, and u.s. imperialism'.[16] The reign of repression unleashed by domestic ruling classes and the imperial powers that supported them, terrorised communities from the Southern Cone to Central America and contributed decisively to a political shift in social forces in favour of the right by the early 1990s.[17]

A series of major ideological setbacks accompanied the state-sponsored violent repression of the left. In the wake of the collapse of the Soviet Union and its client states in the Eastern bloc, political confusion enveloped wide swathes of the left, including those currents who had always criticised 'really existing socialism' for its bureaucratic authoritarian rule.[18] The Cuban revolution was economically and politically isolated after the implosion of its principal benefactor, and ushered in a series of market reforms and austerity known as the Special Period in the early 1990s. The Sandinista revolution in Nicaragua was, in this same world-historical conjuncture, defeated by the right in the 1990 elections, after 11 years of counter-revolutionary destabilisation and violence conducted by the Contras at the behest of the United States. Talk of immediate socialist revolutionary change in Latin America assumed an increasingly romantic aura, disconnected from local realities, as radical social movements retreated from localised concerns at the neighbourhood and community levels. To speak of social justice and redistribution of resources sounded heretical in the context of the ideological shift of most of the extant left and centre-left political parties, as traditional labour parties in Europe and North America embraced Third Way social democracy and the Latin American left sought to accommodate itself to the principles of the Washington Consensus.[19]

Finally, the secular tendencies of capitalist development, exacerbated by neoliberal policy changes, further decomposed the working classes of Latin America, attacking both the structural and associational power of organised labour. As with other regions, capitalist production in the region has been reorganised along the lines of 'flexible accumulation', facilitated by the introduction of new labour-saving technologies, such as digital inventory systems that allow for just-in-time production. Rather than the full-time, stable employment that characterised work in the formal sector in the 'Golden Age' of

---

16　Katz 2007, p. 29.
17　Ibid.
18　For a critical historical materialist analysis of Cuba, see Farber 2006.
19　Webber and Carr 2012, p. 2.

post-WWII, new forms of employment are more precarious. Changes to labour law throughout the region also compounded these trends, such as in Bolivia, where the neoliberal 'shock therapy' programme introduced in 1985 made it illegal to organise workplaces with fewer than 10 employees. Many manufacturers have preferred to employ putting-out systems based upon a network of subcontractors – small, decentralised producers who cheapen the cost of production by lowering the wage bill.[20]

Rather than a set of policies that can simply be reversed, as David Harvey and David McNally, among others, have observed, neoliberalism must be understood as a project of class rule that aims to restore the power of capital over labour and break all forms of collective resistance to its accumulation project.[21] As Emilia Castorina puts it succinctly:

> The main target of neoliberal restructuring has ... been attacking workers' capacity to influence accumulation. Based on new mechanisms of 'accumulation by dispossession', broadly understood as efforts to privatize key aspects of the reproduction of social relations, neoliberal restoration established a different kind of social control (or form of domination), where financial instability and economic insecurity replaced class compromises of the previous era of capitalism.[22]

In sum, after the military, ideological, political, and economic assault on organisational bases of the left, by the 1990s Latin America became a paradigmatic case of the trend Wood identified on an international scale – the breakdown of the material and intellectual forces undergirding Marxism and the anti-capitalist left more generally. There was little reason to believe an about-face was possible in the near future.[23] But since the late 1990s, three politico-economic developments reopened the terrain of the possible and contributed to the resurgence of the left: (1) the 1998–2002 economic crisis in South America; (2) the subsequent successes, however uneven, of extra-parliamentary and electoral expressions of the region's left over the course of the 2000s; and (3) the steepest crisis of global capitalism since the 1930s, beginning in earnest in 2008.

---

20   Garza Toledo and Almaraz 1998; Iranzo and Patrayo 2002.
21   Harvey 2005, McNally 2006.
22   Castorina, this volume.
23   Chilcote 1990; Petras 1990.

Three Moments: Towards a Resurgence of the Left

Neoliberal economic growth patterns have been extremely volatile. Over the course of the 1980s and 1990s – the core neoliberal epoch of Latin America's 'silent revolution' – there was a modest boom (1991–7), positioned between the 'lost decade' of the 1980s and the 'lost half-decade' between 1997 and 2002. The neoliberal policy era progressed through the 'deep recession' of 1982–3, the 'false dawn' of a temporary and meagre recovery in positive per capita growth from 1984 to 1987, the increasing depth and breadth of neoliberal policy implementation between 1988 and 1991, and a thorough attempt to consolidate the model throughout the 1990s and early 2000s in the midst of increasing contradictions and crises – the Mexican Peso Crisis in 1994–5, Brazil's financial breakdown in 1998 in the wake of the Asian and Russian crises, and, most dramatically, the Argentine collapse, which reached its apogee in December 2001.[24]

While neoliberalism was successful at putting the brakes on inflation, economic data reveals the fact that it was a complete failure in terms of alleviating poverty and reducing sovereign debt. Following twenty years of debt rescheduling, the region's total debt was approximately US$725 billion by 2002, twice the figure at the onset of the debt crisis.[25] Poverty rates between 1980 and 2002 increased from 40.5 percent of the population in 1980 to 44 percent in 2002. In absolute figures, this translated into an increase of 84 million poor people, from 136 million in 1980 to 220 million in 2002.[26] Latin America continued to be the most unequal part of the world, such that in 2003 the top 10 percent of the population earned 48 percent of all income.[27] It is now widely understood that during the 'twenty five years of the Washington Consensus, the Latin American economies have experienced their worst quarter century since the catastrophic second quarter of the nineteenth century'.[28] Measured by gross domestic product per capita, improvements to life expectancy and literacy indicators over the course of the twentieth century showed their best results in Latin America between 1940 and 1980, the era of import-substitution industrialisation (ISI). In the region's six largest economies, annual GDP growth in the ISI period was over four-and-a-half times greater than between 1980 and 2000, the years of orthodox neoliberalism.[29]

---

24   Green 2003, pp. 72–118.
25   Ibid., p. 117.
26   Damián and Boltvinik 2006, p. 145.
27   Reygadas 2006, p. 122.
28   Coatsworth 2005, p. 137.
29   Love 2005, p. 107.

The false promise of neoliberalism crashed violently against the recession of 1998–2002 – the first decisive moment in the (at least partial) unravelling of neoliberal hegemony – in which most economies in Latin America sunk into stagnation or recession. For this entire period the region as a whole entered into negative per capita growth, with spikes in poverty and unemployment augmenting the already-existing social crisis flowing from the beleaguered economic performance of the neoliberal project in the preceding decades.[30] An apparent fissure between, on the one hand, the ruling class sophistry of short term gain for long term pain and, on the other, the observable social realities of unemployment, poverty, inequality, and dispossession across the region metamorphosed into a wide gap over this period. Sixty percent of families in 2002 reported that at least one adult member of their household was unemployed in the previous year. By 2004, 70 percent of the region's population registered their dissatisfaction with the performance of the market.[31] Soon enough this expressed itself in an explosion of extra-parliamentary movements in the early 2000s – capable of overthrowing heads of state in Argentina, Bolivia, and Ecuador – and a tidal electoral shift to the left and centre-left, with governments describing themselves in these terms coming to office in Venezuela (1999–), Chile (1993–2010), Brazil (2002–), Argentina (2003–), Uruguay (2004–), Bolivia (2006–), Honduras (2006–2009), Nicaragua (2006–), Ecuador (2007–), Paraguay (2008–2012), El Salvador (2009–), and Peru (2011–) over the next decade.

The post-2002 export commodities boom was the second moment which helped call into question the ideological appeal of orthodox neoliberalism. Aggregate growth rates across Latin America and the Caribbean averaged 5.4 percent between 2004 and 2007, and while faltering slightly in 2008, still hit 4 percent that year.[32] 'For the first time in decades', Steven Levitsky and Kenneth M. Roberts note, 'left-of-center governments were able to offer material benefits to popular constituencies – and to do so, moreover, without challenging property rights or adopting highly polarising redistributive measures'.[33] In other words, in the last decade, improved trade balances, budget surpluses, and the rent skimmed from royalties and taxes in the booming mining, oil and gas, and agro-industrial mono-cropping sectors have allowed states governed by these new governments to engage in a modest degree of wealth redistribution, social service expansion, and poverty alleviation without seriously encroach-

---

30   ECLAC 2003.
31   Levitsky and Roberts 2011, p. 10.
32   ECLAC 2011, p. 96.
33   Levitsky and Roberts 2011, p. 11.

ing upon, much less expropriating, the economic power of the domestic ruling classes. Rates of profit remained high. The growth rates achieved across much of the region between 2003 and 2008, especially compared to the preceding 25 years of orthodox neoliberalism, contributed to the consolidation of the centre-left, especially, and the further ideological de-legitimation of laissez-faire capitalism. When contending elections in the region over the last several years, even conservative parties have deemed it necessary to bend over backwards in ritual demonstrations of how distant their contemporary incarnations are vis-à-vis the hated epoch of 1990s privatisation and liberalisation.

The third moment arrived in 2008, as the global economic crisis internationalised, extending and mutating rapidly from its 2007 origins in the American sub-prime mortgage market. By April 2008, the International Monetary Fund (IMF) suggested that we were witnessing the largest financial crisis in the United States since the Great Depression of the 1930s. However, as David McNally observes, this seriously underestimated the scale of the crisis. First, while originating in the United States, the integrated international mechanisms of the Great Recession ensured that it rapidly assumed a global scope. Second, the crisis very quickly escaped the narrowly financial realm, and began its assault on the 'real economy'. 'Having started in the construction-, auto- and electronics-sectors', McNally notes in 2009, 'the slump is now sweeping through all manufacturing industries and spilling across the service-sector'.[34] By this point, bankruptcies, factory-closures, and layoffs – responses to over-accumulation – meant 250,000 layoffs in the North American automobile industry alone. Waves of downsizing in non-financial corporations fed the under-consumption component of the crisis. 'As world-demand and world-sales dive', McNally points out, 'the effects of overcapacity (factories, machines, buildings that cannot be profitably utilised), which have been masked by credit-creation over the past decade, will kick in with a vengeance'.[35] As is typical for the world capitalist system, we increasingly witnessed the 'geographical displacement of crisis: attempting to offload the worst impacts onto those outside the core'.[36]

In Latin America and the Caribbean taken as a whole, however, the crisis has been relatively muted thus far, particularly when compared to the economic tailspins evident in some regions of the United States and the Eurozone. The United Nation's Economic Commission for Latin America and the Caribbean (ECLAC) reports that a deceleration in growth occurred in 2009, but this was followed by a recovery of six percent growth in 2010. Although there was a

---

34   McNally 2009, p. 36.
35   Ibid., p. 37.
36   Hanieh 2009, p. 61.

decline in the rate of growth in 2011, the end of year figures still clocked in at 4.3 percent, with (optimistic) projections of 3.2 percent for 2012.[37] The attenuation of the crisis thus far can be traced to a number of different factors, including: relatively sustained high commodity prices; influxes of foreign direct investment (FDI) from capital that could not find profitable returns in the core of the world economy, particularly in 'emerging markets' such as Brazil; counter-cyclical spending facilitated by the accumulation of international reserves and primary surpluses over the boom period of 2003–8; and the relative autonomy achieved by states from the International Monetary Fund (IMF) and other international financial institutions in terms of economic policy over the last decade.[38] But no one knows, of course, for how long the region will be able to avoid a more serious downturn, given the uncertain character of the trajectory of the crisis elsewhere in the world market.

Moreover, an aggregate snapshot of the regional dynamics can be misleading insofar as it conceals significant heterogeneity across countries and sub-regions within Latin America and the Caribbean. Interestingly, this heterogeneity in terms of the fallout from the crisis elsewhere seems to suggest that there is relatively little connection to particular national policies stemming from the different political characters of different governments and economic growth rates. For example, high rates of growth have been maintained in Nestor Kirchner and Cristina Fernández de Kirchner's relatively heterodox Argentina, while much the same has occurred in relatively orthodox Peru under the direction of Alan García (replaced by Lula-inspired Ollanta Humala in 2011). Conversely, the steepest recessions in 2009 in the area hit Venezuela, under the most radical government of Hugo Chávez, and Mexico, under the right-wing presidency of Felipe Calderón (replaced by Enrique Peña Nieto in the 2012 elections).

South America as a whole has been the least affected part of the region given the delayed slowdown in China and an initially dilatory rollout of the crisis in the Eurozone, whereas Mexico, Central America, and the Caribbean were quite devastated early on due to the depth of their integration into the US economy, the initial epicentre of the crisis. The mechanisms of transmission, in these latter cases, included the collapse of their principal export market, a curtailment in investment, and rapid reduction in remittances received.[39]

For these reasons, the electoral shift to the left remains tenuous at best; much depends on the way that the popular forces re-organise in the face of inevitable economic turbulence. Despite the gloomy global forecasts, ECLAC remains

---

37   ECLAC 2012a, p. 11.
38   Katz 2011; Ugarteche 2012.
39   Ibid.

stubbornly optimistic about continuing economic growth in the region. They project a rate of growth of 4.4 percent in 2012 and 4 percent in 2013 for Central America, 2.8 percent and 4.1 percent in South America, and 3.2 percent and 4.0 percent for Latin America and the Caribbean as a whole.[40] Despite these high rates of growth, poverty alleviation efforts have stagnated. According to a 2012 study, by year end, 167 million people will be living in poverty (or 28.8 percent of the population), which is one million fewer people than in 2011. The number of people in extreme poverty or indigence will remain stable in 2012 at 66 million people (the same as in 2011).[41] These optimistic predictions for growth, however, are premised on extremely unlikely world events that deny the extent of the integration of the world market and the contradictions at the core of world capitalism: the ability of Europe to stem its recession, the United States to restructure its economy, China to stage a recovery, and oil prices to remain stable. Should the Latin American economies make a turn for the worse, the number of people living in poverty will increase substantially.

New Directions in the Marxist Political Economy of Latin America

Against this backdrop of uneven regional shifts to the left and an ongoing global economic slump, the chapters in this volume contribute to debates within Marxism in two thematic areas: how to understand changes to class formation in Latin America, particularly the role of working-class organisations in the transition to socialism, and how to understand the state-form in countries endowed with incredible natural resource wealth – particularly, how to understand the relationship between state and market in late capitalist development.

The authors of this volume are materialists with respect to the fact that they conceive of the power of the organised working class as connected to the rhythms of capital accumulation. That is, the process of capitalist development is conceived as inherently conflictive and contradictory, and to the extent that political and economic outcomes are 'determined', they are determined by the class struggle. That is, when the working classes gain power, they wrest concessions from capital that lead to an improvement in living and working conditions. When they suffer defeat, the pendulum swings back in favour of capital. Within these rhythms, some regional patterns emerge despite the tremendous variation in levels of development and traditions of working-class organisation in Latin America.

---

40   ECLAC 2012a, p. 11.
41   ECLAC 2012b.

The 'New' Working Class: Decomposition and Re-Composition
under Neoliberalism

One of the recurring themes that runs through the chapters is that this phase
of capitalist development (aka neoliberal globalisation) has posed major challenges to popular class organisations in Latin America, particularly peasant
and workers' unions. The rolling out of neoliberal economic restructuring in
the region over the course of the 'first wave' of reforms of the 1980s, and particularly the 'second wave' of the 1990s, set in motion a rapid and extensive
decomposition of the historical organisational forms of working-class and
peasant organisations, through the unions. In the urban world of work, part-
time, unprotected, and informal work proliferated.[42] At the same time, rapid
trade liberalisation and the elimination or drastic reduction of state subsidies to, and access to easy credit for, the agriculture sector led to an intensification of rural-urban migration, as growing numbers of peasants and small
commodity producers were dispossessed of their lands and transformed into
landless agrarian proletarians, swelling the reserve army of labour in the
cities.[43] While novel configurations of worker- and peasant-power eventually
emerged throughout the region in the following decades, the re-composition of
the debilitated infrastructures of organisation of the working classes required
strategic imagination, which could only emerge as people began to lose their
fear and regain their faith in collective projects and learned new strategies for
organising.

Based on case studies from Bolivia and Argentina, Susan Spronk and
Mariano Féliz argue that the informalisation of the economy has posed new
challenges for working-class organisations. Castorina focuses her attention on
how the restructuring of the Argentine economy can be characterised as a conservative populism, which did not entail an all-out attack on workers' unions
but a shift in the balance of power towards sectors that were favoured by the
liberalisation of markets. Selwyn argues that while neoliberal globalisation
has defeated many workers' organisations, new spaces of accumulation have
also opened in the most recent cycle of growth, creating new sites for working-
class organisation and struggle, such as the table grape export sector in Brazil.
Based upon an analysis of Venezuela since the election of Hugo Chávez, Gabe
Hetland, Dario Azzellini, and Tom Purcell offer contrasting perspectives on the
possibilities for working-class organisations within the formal and informal

---

42   Spronk 2013.
43   Petras and Veltmeyer 2002.

economies, including political parties and communal and workers' councils, to push forward socialist projects.

With regard to building capacity of the left for collective action, the degree of informality poses a political problem. As Spronk argues, informal workers are difficult to organise for at least two reasons. First, they cannot be organised into traditional workplace-based unions as collective bargaining agents because they work for themselves and therefore do not have the same antagonistic relationships to their employers as salaried or waged workers.[44] Second, informal workers tend to be scattered geographically, such as in the case of domestic servants or day-labourers who work in peoples' homes or market vendors who work on street corners. This is contrasted to the image of the 'revolutionary subject' that animated the left imaginary in the times of Marx, concentrated in hierarchical workplaces, such as office buildings, factories or mines. Indeed, the most militant sections of the proletariat in Latin American history have tended to be factory workers and miners, due to their physical concentration in small, concentrated spaces, which makes them easier to organise, and the dangerous nature of the work, which has necessitated collective action in order to survive against the abuses of negligent employers. In the case of the miners, the relatively homogenous (male) nature of the workforce has also enabled unions to draw on machismo in order to inspire revolutionary worker militancy.[45]

But the decline of the formal sector jobs associated with ISI-sponsored manufacturing over the neoliberal period has been characterised by a parallel trend that has escaped the purview of most observers of capitalist development.[46] New sites of accumulation have sprung up in the agricultural sector. Striving to earn foreign exchange to pay back the foreign debt, many Latin American countries are now producing 'non-traditional exports' such as asparagus, cut flowers and grapes, which make their way to export markets in the North at tremendous human and environmental cost. Furthermore, since the Green Revolution, capital has sought to subvert the natural rhythms of growth cycles by applying increasingly sophisticated technologies, such as bovine growth hormone, high-yield seeds, chemical inputs, genetically modified organisms and the like. With the expansion of the biofuels market since the late 1990s, investors across the planet have sought to prepare for a potential

---

44   Olivera and Lewis 2004; Parodi Solari and Conaghan 2000.

45   See Winn 1986 on factory workers and Klubock 1998 on miners in Chile; Seidman 1994 on factory workers in Brazil; Nash 1979 on miners in Bolivia, and more recently Sandor 2009.

46   See McMichael 2011 for an exception to this trend.

post-petroleum economy through a series of land and water grabs.[47] Given the dominance of extractivism in the Latin American economies, these new sites of accumulation deserve the increasing attention of scholars.

Féliz's account of the shift from ISI-sponsored industrialisation in the 1940s and 1950s to orthodox neoliberalism in the 1980s and 1990s to neo-developmentalism in the 2000s also explains that such shifts are in part the result of the resistance of the working class, whose self-activity through strikes and protests occasionally puts limits on accumulation and forces the ruling class to make concessions. Similar to Selwyn, his analysis demonstrates that the connections between structural and associational power are not automatic, since the working class can find new ways to organise itself, such as in associations of unemployed workers.

Féliz argues that in Argentina, the organised, industrial working class was at the height of its structural power in 1973 when 24.2 percent of GDP was produced by the industrial sector. During this time, some of the profits related to increases in labour productivity were shared with labour in the form of increases to wages and benefits through collective bargaining agreements. Neoliberalism, by contrast, broke the pact between capital and labour that sustained the positive cycle of growth in the ISI period, during which time capital was forced to invest in the reproduction of the labour force and corporatist labour unions did their part to shore up accumulation efforts by disciplining the labour force. Neoliberalism, by contrast, has been characterised by 'jobless growth'. Even though the return to capital on investment was at a record high between 1993 and 1998, it was also a period of 'jobless growth' as domestic and international investors turned their attention to the primary export sector. The de-industrialisation that accompanied this process thoroughly decomposed the Argentine working class, as increasing numbers of workers found themselves within the ranks of the unemployed or facing more precarious forms of employment. This trend was compounded by the unprecedented economic meltdown of 2001–2, which created a social crisis when unemployment levels jumped to 25 percent.

According to Féliz, the emergence of the *piquetero* movement represented a recomposition of the working class, 'which weakened the possibility of the further advancement of the neoliberal project', as workers took to the streets in displays of discontent.[48] As yet, he notes, these new social actors have not been able to restore the gains of the previous era of capitalist expansion: 'in 2007 real wages for formal-sector workers in the private sphere were only

47   Borras et al. 2011.
48   Féliz, this volume.

6.7 percent over their 2001 levels, while for precarious workers real wages were still 22.4 percent lower and state employees were 28.4 percent below their 2001 levels'.[49] Given such data, Féliz concludes that the neo-developmentalist project promoted by the Kirchner regimes in Argentina remains thoroughly neoliberal with respect to two structural elements: the plundering of the commons given the extractive mode of development and the super-exploitation of labour.

Castorina challenges the notion that the new left in Argentina represents a form of 'post-neoliberalism', arguing instead that the Kirchner regimes have instituted a form of 'democratic neoliberalism'. That is to say, this form of neo-liberalism has eased off the brutal repression and stripping the state of its regulatory capacities, as it did in the rollout stage in the 1990s, but remains neoliberal in its form. She points to one of the central contradictions of liberal democracy under capitalism that has been similarly observed by Ellen Meiksins Wood, arguing that 'there is a constitutive tension within capitalist democracy as a system of power that exists to uphold and enforce exploitative relations while granting universal civic and political rights at the same time'.[50] Under democratic neoliberalism, the Kirchner regimes have been forced to make some concessions to the militant *piquetero* movements, but given the long-standing politics of clientelism in Argentina, Castorina argues that most factions of this social movement were quickly neutralised politically when they entered into relationships with the Peronist government, accepting the terms of the work programmes. Such social policies, in Castorina's view, remain thoroughly neoliberal compared to the previous economic era when welfare was viewed as a set of universal rights. Welfare is now seen as a low-cost way to enhance individual opportunities while nurturing the Peronist political machine. As such, the working classes in Argentina have yet to launch an offensive that can reverse the losses of neoliberalism.

Based upon a case study of women grape workers in the São Francisco Valley of Northeast Brazil, Selwyn argues that new sites of accumulation also create new labour forces, which under certain conditions can increase their bargaining power with capital. Building on the work of Erik Olin Wright and Beverly Silver, Selwyn argues that labour's power depends on two sources: (1) structural power, which refers to the position of workers in the production process and their ability to disrupt it; and (2) associational power, which refers to workers'

---

49   Ibid.
50   Castorina, this volume.

collective organisation, more often than not via trade unions.[51] Associational power is related to, but not determined by, structural power. As Selwyn notes,

> Whilst workers' associational power is often based upon some aspects of their structural power and their ability to disrupt work via, for example, strikes, go-slows, work to rule, and thus disruption of the generation of profits, it is not the case that workers' structural power is necessarily or automatically transformed into effective associational power. Quite often factors such as the lack of trade union capacity, employer intimidation, state control of trade unions, and lack of confidence within the trade union movement contribute to situations where despite significant structural power, and the (formal and actual) existence of trade union organisations, workers possess very little effective associational power.[52]

Selwyn further finds that women constitute a majority of the labour force in the table grape export sector. While in the 1990s the majority of these women were initially employed on full-time, permanent contracts, as work in the sector has intensified, more and more women are being employed on temporary contracts as employers increasingly prefer to hire men for the 'hard work' that grape picking entails. Nonetheless, women continue to play a central role in the Sindicato dos Trabalhadores Rurais (Rural Workers' Union, STR), which has successfully fought to provide benefits specific to women workers such as maternity leave and childcare, given the gendered division of labour in the home. Selwyn's case study presents a labour-centred version of development studies that challenges the biased perceptions that trade unions are doomed to be male-dominated and the gendered perceptions of employers that the female labour force represents a 'nimble-fingered', docile workforce willing to be exploited without a fight.[53]

With the growing weight of the 'informal proletariat' in working-class politics throughout the region, left political parties in office have favoured this constituency in their social policies. As other scholars have observed, this shift in the class formation has also meant the decline of old ISI-style corporatism and labour-based parties throughout the region and a rise in what Ruth Berins Collier and Samuel Handlin have called 'popular associations'.[54] There are crucial questions that need to be asked, however, about what effect these changes

---

51   Wright 2000; Silver 2003.
52   Selwyn, this volume.
53   Alexander and Mohanty 1997.
54   Berins Collier and Handlin 2009.

to the working-class formation have on the possibilities for advancing 'Twenty-First Century Socialism'. The decline of trade unions, which have traditionally been the working-class organisations that politicise class relations at the point of production, has also meant the decline of class consciousness (in the traditional sense) and political demand-making for socialist projects that place the capital-labour relation at the centre of the analysis. Even in Venezuela, where the project of 'socialism' is most advanced, the 'right' to private property is guaranteed under the new constitution. As Gabe Hetland observes in this volume, however, there is growing awareness at the local level that if socialism is 'going to be more than a slogan, institutions must be constructed – or expropriated – which allow for popular control to be extended from *political* decision-making to *economic* production'.[55]

Based on a case study of participatory budgeting in the municipality of Torres, Venezuela's first 'socialist' city, Hetland argues that under a left mayor, the local government is engaged in a project of building 'socialism' at the municipal level. He finds that in the case of Torres, the Patria Para Todos, (Fatherland for all Party, PPT) has played a crucial role in building socialism due to its internal democracy, links to working-class organisations and civil society, its leadership role in fostering the ideology of socialism, and the fact that it has maintained a critical distance from the national state.[56] In these conditions, argues Hetland, the party has managed to avoid what sociologist Michels characterised as the 'iron law of oligarchy' by which hierarchical party structures inevitably become bureaucratic organisations.[57] He acknowledges, however, that the local experiments in Torres with socialist production models in the electric meter factory and with decision-making models such as participatory budgeting are unlikely to survive if they are not generalised to a broader scale. Nonetheless, Hetland emphasises the importance of such experiments for building working-class capacity for self-management and constructing 'socialist hegemony'.

Dario Azzellini offers a similar account of the social transformation in Venezuela. Since the election of Hugo Chávez in 1998, argues Azzellini, a dialectical relationship has developed between what autonomist Marxists

---

55   His emphasis.

56   The PPT was founded in 1997. The party decided not to join Hugo Chávez's Partido Socialista Unida de Venezuela (the United Socialist Party of Venezuela, PSUV) but has been part of the coalition that supports the PSUV since the founding of the latter in 2006.

57   Michels 1962. For an alternative account, see Charlie Post's brilliant essay on Ernest Mandel's theory of bureaucracy as grounded in the division of manual and intellectual labour under capitalism. Post 2005.

such as Antonio Negri have termed 'constituent' versus 'constituted' power.[58] Constituent power refers to popular power based on the self-activity of working-class organisations, while constituted power refers to the alien form of power embodied in the capitalist state. As Azzellini argues, '[t]he central question ... should not be whether Venezuela has already built a socialist society (which is obviously not the case), or whether the state is putting into praxis the right socialist politics, but rather how social relations and collective popular experiences have evolved in the past 12 years'.[59] On this score, Azzellini finds much room for optimism given the blossoming of popular power initiatives at the local level in Venezuela. The first Communal Council (CC) – a local body of self-government at the neighbourhood level that is supported financially by the national state – was established in 2005; now there are more than 40,000 across the country. Since 2008, the Bolivarian government has been promoting the transformation of CCs into communes, which seek to integrate mechanisms of socialist planning of production, consumption and distribution.[60] He also provides an in-depth account of the complicated internal politics that have frustrated the construction of workers' councils at the factory level, such as in the CVG-Alcasa aluminium plant. Although CVG-Alcasa represents one of the most advanced experiences of workers' control, deep ideological divisions amongst workers at the plant and the uncooperative stance of state bureaucrats have thwarted attempts to socialise production. Azzellini concludes that while the experiment might have 'failed' for the moment, 'at least there is class struggle where there was none before'.[61] As such, socialism remains on the horizon.

With regard to the relationship between the material (political economy) and ideational (socialist hegemony) in socialist politics, Purcell offers a diametrically opposed view to Hetland and Azzellini. Purcell's materialist analysis challenges 'voluntarist' accounts of social transformation. In his view, such analysts do not take seriously enough the material constraints of political economy as a limit to political possibilities. For Purcell, there is no escaping the fact that, in terms of the world market, the aluminium sector in Venezuela is a 'backwards' capital that cannot compete with more efficient producers in

---

58   Negri 1999.

59   Azzellini, this volume.

60   See interview with Rosangela Orozco for an account of Comune 'El Panal' in the barrio 23 de enero of Caracas, available at: <http://upsidedownworld.org/main/venezuela-archives-35/3809–honey-of-the-revolution-an-interview-with-rosangela-orozco-member-of-the-alexis-lives-foundation-fundacion-alexis-vive>.

61   Azzellini, this volume.

other countries. In this sense, the project for workers control is a means by which the state can wrest efficiency gains from the workers through the use of cooperative labour, and provide subsidies to the sector without seriously investing in plant upgrading. He notes that the Bolivarian government promotes experiments with workers' control in these 'backwards' capitals but not in the petroleum industry, since the latter supplies the Venezuelan state with the majority of its rents. Purcell thus raises thorny questions about the impossibility of building socialism in one country, particularly in an oil state where the majority of social wealth accumulates in the hands of the state.

Relationship between State and Market in Late Capitalist Development

One of the key tenets of mainstream political economy is that the state and market are diametrically opposite forms of organising capitalist social relations. On this view, neoliberalism is defined as a set of policies that aim to reduce the intervention of the state in the economy in favour of the market. As such, neoliberalism is also identified as a set of policies that can easily be reversed: public utilities that were privatised can simply be returned to state control; contracts that allowed multinational corporations to exploit mines and oil and gas fields can be renegotiated in favour of state control; finance can be regulated again by restoring capital controls, and so on. Some have therefore argued that as states have resumed their protagonist role in creating optimal conditions for capitalist growth, we are witnessing a shift to 'post-neoliberalism' in Latin America.[62] The contributors to this volume take a different view, arguing that under capitalist social relations, the state and market are not dichotomies but complementary forms of class power. By depicting neoliberalism as a simple shift from market back to state, mainstream political economy fails to address the vexing questions of gross inequality, class relations and social structures, instead trying to buy off grassroots militancy through a series of investments in human capital. As such, the many variations of mainstream political economy are about 'social management', not 'social liberation'.[63] By contrast, the authors in this collection draw on Marx's critique of political economy, which argues that the state-market dichotomy that underpins neo-structuralist thought obfuscates key components of class relations under capitalism, reifies the state as a neutral 'institution' rather than

---

62   Macdonal and Ruckert 2009; Lievesley and Ludlam 2009.

63   Bello 2008.

a form of class power, and is wholly inadequate as a means to theorise either the form of state in Latin America's rent-dependent economies or working-class emancipation from exploitation by capital.[64]

Grigera subjects the concepts of state and market within structuralist and neo-structuralist thought to critical review, analysing the key tenets put forward by the United Nations Economic Commission for Latin America and the Caribbean (ECLAC). Grinberg and Starosta compare the different varieties of centre-leftism in Argentina and Brazil by uncovering the material basis of different political regimes based on an analysis of ground rent. Vergara-Camus and Purcell also draw on theories of ground rent to analyse the dynamics of state-sponsored accumulation strategies in the sugar-cane export sector in Brazil and the aluminium sector in Venezuela, respectively. Given the contradictions of capitalist development, Webber and Katz argue that truly revolutionary projects require a rethinking of the very basis of 'development' itself. By exposing the contradictory dynamics of the Morales administration in the TIPNIS project, Webber points to the insights of new theoretical vistas in the Latin American literature, including work on the new extractivism, compensatory states, and the latest rounds of stratification within and dispossession of resilient peasantries. Katz argues that given such contradictions, the eco-socialist alternative provides the only way out of the current economic and ecological crises.

Grigera provides a piercing critique of one of the central tropes of progressive development studies – that state-market interactions within developing countries provide the focus for assessing the prospects for just growth. Grigera argues that while the structuralists' concept of state and market that informed the state-led development project of the import-substitution industrialisation (ISI) era is preferable to the neoclassical view that the relationship between the two is a zero-sum game, it rests on similar liberal foundations that cannot adequately conceive of the logic of accumulation under capitalism or the class nature of the state. In the liberal conception, the 'state' is represented as a neutral institution that aims to serve the 'general interest' of the population, while 'the market' is seen as the outcome of the natural tendency of humans to 'truck, barter, and trade'. Grigera argues to the contrary that since the central rôle of the state in capitalism is to facilitate capital accumulation, the much celebrated notion of 'state capacity' is 'not a function of the extent of interven-

---

64   For an important theorisation and critique of the statist literature in development stud-
      ies from a Marxist perspective, see Selwyn 2009. For examples of recent writings that still
      avidly endorse the orthodox neoliberal framework, see Stallings and Peres 2011; Edwards
      2010.

tion in the economy, nor its regulatory power; rather from a classist viewpoint, the strength/weakness of a state is measured against the extent of its command over the working class'.[65] He finds that the neo-structuralist synthesis that was pioneered in the 1980s by Brazilian economist Fernando Faynzylber has since integrated some of the main tenets of neoliberalism into structuralist analysis. Rather than focusing on building a robust domestic economy, neo-structuralists place more emphasis on 'structural competitiveness' and increasing productivity, which puts increasing pressure on labour to accept increasingly precarious forms of employment.

As Grinberg and Starosta note, most mainstream analyses of the left turn in Latin America distinguish countries where a 'responsible left' governs from countries where old-style 'populism' is in control of the national state. Most left-wing commentators, on the other hand, conceive of that distinction as one between formally centre-left but substantively 'neo-liberal' governments, and more genuinely 'progressive' ones. The first group includes countries like Brazil, Chile, Peru and Uruguay. The second group includes Argentina, Venezuela, Ecuador and Bolivia. Grinberg and Starosta challenge these distinctions on the grounds that they fail to uncover the essential material basis of those apparently different political-economic regimes. Most positions in the debate fail to offer foundations for the comparative analysis of the economic structure of these national processes of capital accumulation. Instead, they posit the different political forms that mediate the economic structure as the basis for the comparison between the 'varieties of centre-leftism' in Latin America. Their chapter offers a materialist inquiry into the historical development of capitalism in Argentina and Brazil, arguing that capital has been accumulating in these countries under the same specific form, namely, through the appropriation of the extraordinary mass of social wealth existing there under the form of ground rent.

Ground rent, defined simply, is a form of income that results from production processes involving scarce natural resources (that is, natural conditions that are non-renewable or non-substitutable, like land and mineral and oil deposits). In its absolute form it derives from the monopoly of property rights over such resources; this form of rent tends to accrue more in the mining sector than the agrarian sector, since stopping production does not hamper the prospects for profitability. In its differential form, rent accrues to the owners of land whose 'natural productivity' allows for the production of certain commodities at particularly low costs. In contrast with all other goods and services, agrarian and mining commodities thus circulate in the world markets at prices

---

65   Grigera, this volume.

which contain not only the costs involved in their production and the normal profit of individual capitals but also a portion of value in the form of differential ground rent. For example, as the price of oil increases, the amount of rent appropriated by producers in the Venezuelan state increases exponentially.[66] According to the theory elaborated by the Argentine political economist Nicolás Iñigo Carrera, these natural endowments affect the formation of the capitalist class. In such economies where natural resources are 'cheap' (since production is taking place on marginal lands that are less accessible or less fertile), there is little incentive for producers to invest in the state-of-the-art technology necessary to create more advanced forms of production. This is not to say, however, that countries rich in natural resources are forever doomed to what liberal scholars have termed the 'Dutch disease' or the 'natural resource curse' since:

> Underdevelopment ... is not a product of dependence on natural resource wealth, but rather the other way around – dependence on natural resource wealth is a product of underdevelopment. Venezuela's oil dependence is a *symptom* of underdevelopment, not its cause. And just as dependency and world-systems theorists have been criticized for ignoring the internal class structural causes for the development of underdevelopment, these oil-centered approaches have also sought to explain underdevelopment as the result of factors largely unrelated to class relations.[67]

In other words, the natural resource endowments combined with the history of the development of land as property affect the formation of the capitalist class. Producers that have been able to depend almost exclusively on the exploitation of ground rent tend to be more 'backward' compared to their counterparts in countries where industrialisation is more advanced.

Theories of ground rent are also a central theme in the Vergara-Camus and Purcell chapters on Brazil and Venezuela. The theoretical inspirations of the two authors are slightly different. Similar to Grinberg and Starosta, Purcell situates his analysis in the work pioneered by Iñigo Carrera. He finds that in the case of Venezuela, the heavy dependence on oil wealth has created a 'landlord state', whose central role is to 'sow the oil' and to redistribute the social wealth through investments in human capital (i.e. health, education, housing, etc.). As Purcell puts it, 'the social power of capital ... is not embodied in the capitalist class, but in the power of oil-money concentrated in the form of

---

66   The editors thank Mariano Féliz for providing this definition. See also Iñigo Carrera 2007a.
67   Carlson 2012, p. 2.

the landlord state'.[68] Efforts to socialise production relations that have been sponsored by the landlord state, such as the experiments in the aluminium smelters in Guayana, have been fraught with contradictions and tensions. Self-congratulatory revolutionary statements also mask the real effects of these efforts, which primarily encourage workers' self-exploitation rather than their self-emancipation.[69]

For his part, Vergara-Camus is concerned with the way that material relations, grounded in the political economy, are reflected in the symbolic sphere, including the self-representations of state managers. Drawing on the work of the late Venezuelan-American historian Fernando Coronil, Vergara-Camus argues that Lula's government has drawn from a similar ideological frame of the 'magical state' that has characterised state-society relations in twentieth-century Venezuela. Similar to Coronil, Vergara-Camus recounts the way that Brazil was transformed from a poor, agrarian country in the mid-nineteenth century to one of the emerging markets of the twenty-first century by studying the way the dialectical relationship between agents and structures have influenced the development of the sugarcane ethanol industry. The current drive to make ethanol derived from sugarcane the 'golden egg' is the outcome of the conservative modernisation that took place 50 years before, which 'eliminated non-capitalist social relations and triggered another round of land concentration allowing for the fully capitalist development of agriculture in which accumulation became much more capital-intensive than before'.[70] Drawing from Marx and the work of historian Robert Brenner, Vergara-Camus argues that through this process of primitive accumulation property in land and access to labour-power became less based on 'politically-constituted' property and more on economic forms of extraction.[71] As such, the capitalist production relations that characterise farm-owner and farmhand relations in the sugarcane

---

68   Purcell, this volume.

69   Ibid.

70   Vergara-Camus, this volume.

71   Here Vergara-Camus's interpretation of Marx's 'Trinity Formula' differs slightly from that of Coronil 1997. Coronil argued that the 'Trinity Formula', which described the different forms of revenue generation in agrarian capitalism – landowners-rent; capital-profit; workers-wages – offers a way to insert 'Nature' into the analysis of capitalist development and to criticise 'Eurocentric' conceptions of the development of capitalism that do not take this 'triadic dialectic' into account. By emphasising that the landowning class was replaced by the capitalist class as capitalist social relations have further penetrated the agrarian sector, however, Vergara-Camus's analysis is closer to that of George Comninel, who makes the argument that Marx's 'Trinity Formula' described the historically-specific form of class structure on the eve of the transition to capitalism in eighteenth-century England. In short, while Coronil folds a tripartite class structure into his analysis, Marx's

ethanol industry represent a maturing of the (capitalist) industrialisation of agriculture in Brazil. Despite rhetorical emphasis on the Brazilian 'miracle', the prospects that this industry will create a 'green' and worker-friendly economy remain a fairy tale.

Dominant currents of socialism in the twentieth century stressed the 'development of the productive forces' as necessary for the advancement of socialism. The crudest Stalinist versions of this idea focused on the stages of development whereby communism was impossible before passing through the phase of fully developed capitalism. The ecological crisis has moved some of these ideas to the backburners, but they remain central to the practice (if not the rhetoric) of twenty-first century socialism.

As Webber has highlighted in his other work, similar to transitions to more democratic forms of capitalism elsewhere, the transition away from 'informal apartheid' in Bolivia has been successful in ending some of the most egregious forms of racial discrimination. Similar to South Africa under the African National Congress, the end of the formal racial discrimination of apartheid does not mean liberation for the majority of citizens. Similar to early discussions about South Africa, such debate about the 'revolutionary' impact of the racialised transition have thus far overshadowed discussions about the limited and reformist character of Morales's development policies. With new forms of class struggles coming to the fore, however, the literature on Bolivia has taken a more critical turn in the past couple of years.

It is undeniable that the Morales government has accomplished some mild forms of social redistribution. According to Webber, these reforms go nowhere near far enough, however, in raising the living standards of the majority of the population – most of whom are workers or peasants who self-identify as indigenous. Given the racist history of post-colonial Latin America, Webber further argues that these indigenous movements, such as the movement that emerged to defend the TIPNIS territory against the construction of a highway, challenge the very foundations of 'the development project' being advanced by the Morales administration. As such, only eco-socialist alternatives that focus on the re-orientation of production priorities to produce for human need and environmental sustainability rather than profit have the potential to unmoor the meaning of socialism from the productivist logic that dominated nineteenth- and twentieth-century understandings. To accomplish this task requires something different than 'state-capitalism'. Eco-socialists must ultimately have the abolishment of the capital-labour relation in their sights.

---

conception of the class structure under capitalism, for Comninel, is clearly binary: the labour-capital relation. See Comninel 1987, pp. 95–102.

Claudio Katz considers the prospects for such an anti-capitalist popular project rooted in an eco-socialist perspective in the concluding sections of his contribution to this volume. He situates the crisis of global warming within a wider set of destructive tendencies inherent to capitalism which threaten contemporary civilisation. Katz traces the short-term conjunctural contradictions of financialisation, overaccumulation, and trade imbalances that have fed into the dynamics of the global crisis over the last few years, and lays them over the top of longer term structural transformations in the neoliberal epoch of global capitalism, such as specific developments in the sphere of demand and the rate of profit.

Conclusion

This chapter has sought in part to historicise the decomposition and partial recomposition of Marxist intellectual life in Latin America since the early 1990s by positioning it within a mapping of the key political, economic, social, and ideological developments across the last quarter of the twentieth century and the opening decade of the twenty-first. The social weight of the political left and Marxist theory reached a simultaneous nadir in the early 1990s. However, the crisis of neoliberal legitimacy precipitated by the 1998–2002 economic downturn in South America, the subsequent rising wave of social and electoral lefts, the commodities boom of the 2000s, and the mutations of the global crisis since 2008, have together set in motion a new dynamic terrain upon which Marxist intellectual currents have experienced something of a renewal in Latin America.

The purpose of this volume is to introduce for the first time to the English-speaking world some of these intellectual developments in the field of Latin American political economy, and simultaneously to contribute to the debates themselves through novel theorisations of the composition, de-composition, and re-composition of the region's working classes and peasantries, as well as the specificities of states and markets within the uneven and combined development of capitalism today. We have sought to ground our theoretical explorations within concrete analyses of social formations, including those of Brazil, Argentina, Bolivia, and Venezuela. Our hope is that these initial forays into the latest in Latin America's Marxist political economy will spur further investigation and radical scholarship that shares a commitment to understanding Latin American realities in order to better build the capacities of the exploited and oppressed to realise their own emancipation from the resilient structures and processes of capitalist power.

PART 1

The 'New' Working Class: Decomposition and Recomposition under Neoliberalism

∵

Roots of Resistance to Urban Water Privatisation in Bolivia: The 'New Working Class', the Crisis of Neoliberalism, and Public Services[1]

Susan Spronk

> While you can't drink the rhetoric of anti-globalisation, struggles like the water war are vital, and the only hope for rebuilding a progressive agenda.
> THOMAS KRUSE, *Investigator on labour issues in Bolivia*[2]

On 18 December 2005, Bolivia hit the international news with the announcement that the country had elected its first indigenous president, Evo Morales. Winning an unprecedented 54 percent of the popular vote, Morales' party, el Movimiento al Socialismo (Movement towards Socialism, henceforth the MAS) rode into office on a wave of protests that rocked the small Andean country for more than five years. The Cochabamba Water War is widely credited as the event that started it all. In April 2000, residents of the Cochabamba Valley successfully expelled a powerful multinational corporation that had been given monopoly control over the urban water supply. After fifteen years of ineffective resistance against neoliberal structural adjustment policies, the Water War opened a new cycle of protest that forced the resignation of two Bolivian presidents within two years and helped to define a new era in Bolivian politics.

Locally, the Water War and the events that followed have inspired much theorising about the new social subjects which have successfully contested neoliberalism in Bolivia. At the heart of the resistance struggle in the Cochabamba Valley was a rural-urban, multi-class alliance called the Coordinadora de

---

1 This article is based upon personal interviews and participant observation conducted in Bolivia between July 2004 and August 2005. The research was funded by grants from the Social Sciences and Humanities Research Council and the International Development Research Centre. The author would like to thank Étienne Cantin, Jennifer Klein, Liisa North, Jeffery R. Webber, and an anonymous reviewer for comments. All translations from Spanish are by the author.

2 Cited in Postero 2005b, p. 133.

Defensa del Agua y de la Vida (Coalition for the Defense of Water and Life, henceforth the Coordinadora), which appeared to overcome some of the problems associated with 'old' forms of social movements, particularly trade unions. Bolivian sociologist (and now Vice President) Álvaro García Linera argues that organisations such as the Coordinadora 'do not create a border between members and nonmembers in the way that the unions used to do'.[3] According to this view, trade unions with their struggles over legal contracts, closed membership, and hierarchical leadership structures no longer represent the interests of the majority of the population, especially those engaged in informal types of work. In contrast, the Coordinadora, which fights for the right to water, 'the source of all life', is a better vehicle for organising the working class because the only criterion for membership was active participation in the daily struggles.

While most evaluations of the Cochabamba Water War have rightly stressed the importance of building coalitions amongst different groups in the struggle against neoliberalism, this investigation focuses on the inherent tensions that emerge within such coalitions and the manner and degree to which these tensions can limit their effectiveness in raising living standards for all. More specifically, five years after the Water War, tension emerged within the Coordinadora between consumers, who lobbied to lower the costs of goods and services, and the workers who produce those services, who sought to improve, or at least preserve, their wages and working conditions. I argue that while consumption issues such as access to potable water are an essential part of the broader working-class struggle, organisations that focus on lowering the price of wage goods at the expense of workers' struggles for better wages and working conditions risk contributing to the decline of the working class as a whole.

The following begins by placing the resistance struggles against the privatisation of urban water utilities in their historical context, providing a synthetic account of the recent changes to the Bolivian political economy under neoliberalism. The second section explains why territorially-based organisations such as the Coordinadora came to replace class-based organisations in Bolivia with the rise of the so-called new working class. The third and fourth sections describe the social composition of the coalitions that emerged to contest water privatisation in Cochabamba in 2000 and El Alto in 2005, followed by a specific analysis of the Cochabamba case five years after the Water War.

---

3   García Linera 2004, p. 73.

From State Capitalism to Neoliberalism, 1952 to 2005

The high level of resistance to neoliberalism in the past decade in Bolivia relates in part to the severity of its impact in the country. Bolivia was widely heralded as a star reformer that pursued one of the most ambitious – and harshest – structural adjustment programmes on the continent.

The neoliberal structural adjustment policies introduced in 1985 aimed to systematically dismantle the policies and practices of the developmental state established after the national-popular revolution of 1952. The revolutionary government embarked on an ambitious plan to develop the economy along state-capitalist lines. The tin mines, which were previously controlled by three men known as the 'tin barons', were placed under national control and direct foreign investment was limited. During the revolutionary period, the tin mines provided the Bolivian state with the bulk of its hard currency and formed the base for a radical, highly-centralised trade union movement headed by the Bolivian Workers' Central (*Central Obrera Boliviana*, henceforth COB). The COB brought together unions from the proletarian, peasant, and middle class sectors, but its leadership has always been drawn from the militant miners' unions, which played a leading role in the popular class struggle in the post-revolutionary period.

After a post-revolutionary period of military rule that began in 1964, the leftist coalition government elected in 1982 after the restoration of democracy came to office under extremely unfortunate circumstances. The government inherited an unmanageable debt-load, largely accrued by an unaccountable elite who preferred to transfer their earnings overseas rather than invest in Bolivia. In an attempt to redistribute the social wealth after decades of hardship and repression, the government adopted an expansive wage policy. The economic situation quickly spiraled out of control when the price of commodities, particularly tin, crashed in the mid-1980s. The low level of capital formation, and the consequent government inability to collect revenue while being held to unsustainable social expenditures led to spiraling hyperinflation, wiping out overnight what little savings people had managed to scrape together.[4]

The response to the crisis was an orthodox shock therapy programme designed by the International Monetary Fund and implemented by the Bolivian state. The 'New Economic Policy' (NEP) was much more than an economic policy. It was, in fact, nothing less than a new ideological and philosophical framework to redefine Bolivia's future economic, social, and political choices. Under

---

4 Dunkerley 1993, 121–38; Veltmeyer and Tellez 2001, pp. 67–94.

the NEP, the government closed down the majority of its mines, reducing the workforce from 30,000 in 1985 to around 7,000 in 1987, hence demolishing the base of the organised labour movement. While the miners' union accused the government that it 'was bent on destroying their economic power in order to crush [their] political power', the closing of the mines was also a quick solution to the 'problem' posed by the unprofitable state mining company and the militant unions, whose wages placed a heavy strain on the government budget.[5] The government also dismissed another 31,000 public service workers (out of more than 200,000) and 35,000 manufacturing jobs were lost by the end of the decade due to economic contraction.[6] In this early stage of the process, the government could not yet muster the political support needed to shed all state enterprises – a task that was taken up during the second stage of neoliberal restructuring.

One of the original architects of the NEP, Gonzalo Sánchez de Lozada, was elected president in 1993. Although he only won 34 percent of the popular vote, he formed a pact with two other traditional political parties, which together pushed a controversial privatisation programme through Congress. The programme, which was designed by a small group of technocrats working closely with Sánchez de Lozada, intended to limit social opposition to the sale of what had long been considered by Bolivian citizens to be their national patrimony. Euphemistically called 'capitalisation', half of the shares in public companies in the major sectors of the economy – energy, transportation, and public services – were to be sold to foreign companies and the other half to private companies in Bolivia. The proceeds from the sales were to be distributed to all Bolivian citizens over 65 through a partially-privatised pension programme.

The privatisation programme elicited strong criticism from across the political spectrum. The traditional left claimed that the transfer of state property to private enterprises was unconstitutional, while the right opposed the denationalisation of enterprises that it considered strategic. The military, remembering Bolivia's defeat by Chile in the War of the Pacific in 1883, took particular offence at the sale of the railway company to a Chilean firm, arguing that it was a threat to national security and an insult to the country's honour.[7]

The results of the privatisation programme were as disappointing as they were predictable. In fact, more than half of the shares were transferred to foreign companies and the newly 'capitalised' enterprises were placed under the

---

5 Cited in Sanabria 1999, pp. 535–62.
6 Farthing 1991, pp. 18–23; Grindle 2003, pp. 318–44; Jemio and Choque 2003, p. 6.
7 On the privatisation programme and the reaction in the press, see Kohl 2004, Fernández Terán 2003.

control of multinational corporations, including the municipal water utilities in La Paz-El Alto and Cochabamba in 1997 and 1999, respectively. Shortly after its privatisation, the national railway was shut down, isolating many rural communities that depended on the railway for access to essential services and markets. Despite the government's promise that the privatised enterprises would create thousands of new jobs, 14,000 workers were laid off from privatised enterprises. With little state control over the pension programme, the privatised companies diverted their revenues elsewhere instead of making the promised contributions, and the government had to borrow $44 million to make the first payments, thus deepening the debt burden.[8]

In a nutshell, two decades of neoliberalism engendered profound structural changes in the Bolivian political economy. The state, once the main employer, was no longer a provider of goods and services, and limited its role to regulation and social repression. The labour movement, once the leader of the popular struggle, has been debilitated.[9] Between 2000 and 2005, however, new actors emerged to contest the polarisation of society, such as the Coordinadora (mentioned above), and the Federación de Juntas Vecinales de El Alto (the Federation of Neighbourhood Councils of El Alto, henceforth, the FEJUVE). Unlike earlier working-class organisations in Bolivia, the Coordinadora and the FEJUVE were not organised under a trade union banner. Rather, they focused on neighbourhood issues relating to living conditions and not workers' issues relating to work and employment. To understand the nature and political saliency of these territorially-based organisations requires a more detailed examination of the factors that have created the 'new working class'.

The 'New Working Class' and the Challenge of Mobilisation

The deepening of neoliberal capitalism has engendered two trends that have introduced new dynamics in working-class politics – accelerated urbanisation and the decline of trade unions. First, from 1985 to 2005 there was a profound demographic shift. For most of its history, Bolivia has been a rural, agrarian society. During the colonial period, the majority of *'Indios'* lived in the countryside and performed servile labour duties on haciendas and in the mines established by the Spanish and their Creole descendants. The cities were divided into separate zones for the elite white minority and the *'Indio'* majority. Indians could not vote, nor set foot in the central square of

---

8 Kohl 2004, pp. 899–904.
9 On the COB and its demise, see Lazarte 1989; Arze 2000.

the capital La Paz. Liberal reforms enacted by the revolutionary government ended legal forms of discrimination, but a deep racial divide between the *k'ara* (white people) minority and the indigenous majority remains to this day.[10]

By contrast with the past, 60 percent of the Bolivian population now lives in its three major urban areas. Between 1976 and 1992 the population in urban areas grew by 4 percent per year, continuing to grow at nearly the same rate throughout the 1990s. El Alto, the satellite city of La Paz, grew from 11,000 in 1950 to almost a quarter of a million in 1985, and it reached about 650,000 in 2001 and over 800,000 in 2006, making it Bolivia's third largest city, with a population nearly the size of La Paz. Cochabamba, Bolivia's fourth largest city, had a population of 220,000 in 1976 and nearly doubled to 536,000 in 2001. While the majority of migrants to Cochabamba previously came from the surrounding region, when the mines were closed in the mid-1980s, migrants also flooded in from the *altiplano*, the high plateau where the capital La Paz and the mines are also located. Most of these migrants moved to shantytowns located at the peripheral areas of cities that lack basic infrastructure such as paved roads, water, sewerage, and garbage collection.[11]

These urban areas have become sites of an explosive mix of class, ethnic, and racial identities.[12] While space constraints do not permit the lengthy discussion that this topic deserves, the changing relationships between peasants and miners from 1952 to the present provides a partial explanation of why contemporary social struggles are no longer framed in class terms. The overwhelming majority of peasants and miners share a common indigenous heritage. The majority of the population in western Bolivia are descendants of two ancient empires. The Quechua, the dominant group in the central valleys, are descendants of the Inca, who established a colony in the Cochabamba Valley in the mid-fifteenth century. The Aymara of the Andean *altiplano* were also conquered by the Inca, but retained their languages, and autonomous social, economic, and even political structures in an area known as the Kollasuyu. Both the Quechua from the Cochabamba Valley and the Aymara from the *altiplano* joined a common struggle to oust foreign monopolists in the revolution of 1952.[13] Since the revolution, however, the relations between miners and peasants became increasingly tense. Despite their common indigenous heritage, miners tended to view peasants as 'backwards' politically. As Bolivian his-

---

10   See Reinaga 1969 for an influential work on the 'Indian question' from an *indigenista* perspective.

11   Statistics are from Arbona and Kohl 2004; Butrón Oporto and Rosales 2003.

12   Albro 2005; Lesley Gill 2000.

13   Klein 2003, pp. 1–23.

torian Silvia Rivera Cusicanqui writes, this animosity is in large part due to the fact that rural peasant unions 'were increasingly used as a basis of support for the government's anti-worker policies' as the relationships between the miners and the state deteriorated over the post-revolutionary period.[14] These tensions came to a head with the formalisation of the 'military-campesino pact' (1966–77), under which violent conflicts ensued between peasants supported by the military and the miners.

The relocation of many miners and peasants to the cities and the shared experience of racism and economic hardship have facilitated the construction of new forms of identity within the urban environment. Indeed, while '*Indios*' were traditionally thought to only live in rural areas in Bolivia, a strong process of indigenisation has taken place in towns and cities as well.[15] Since statistics have been collected on indigenous identity, the number of Bolivians reporting indigenous heritage has grown. In the official census of 2001, 62 percent of respondents over 15 years of age self-identified as 'indigenous', making Bolivia the most indigenous country in South America.[16] With the decline of class-based organisations such as the COB and the recent influx of former miners and peasants to the swelling cities, the axis around which popular struggles have been organised has slowly turned from class to racial/ethnic exclusion.

The second important trend that explains the nature and characteristics of the organisations fighting privatisation in Bolivia is the emergence of what has been dubbed the 'new working class', which is now primarily urban and engaged in informal forms of work. While the informal sector has always been sizable, it is no longer thought of as the 'backward' sector that would eventually be phased out with economic development. Indeed, it has proven to be the most dynamic sector of the economy. One study estimates that in the 1990s, 9 out of 10 new jobs that were created in Bolivia were informal jobs. Most individuals employed in the informal economy, however, are highly vulnerable workers who lack labour and social protection such as contracts, severance pay, social welfare benefits, etc.[17]

Labour organisers face a daunting task in the neoliberal context. Changes to labour legislation ushered in with the NEP prohibited the organisation of workplaces with fewer than twenty workers into trade unions. Far more

---

14   Rivera Cusicanqui 1990, p. 105.
15   Albó 1991; Yashar 2005; García Linera 2005.
16   The first time that a question relating to indigenous identity was asked on the official census was in 1976, when respondents were asked to specify their 'maternal tongue'. The 2001 census included a question specifically about indigenous identity.
17   On the growth of the informal sector in Bolivia, see Lourdes 2001.

challenging than these legislative reforms, however, are the structural conditions that inhibit the formation of workplace organisations. As Oscar Olivera, the former shoe-factory worker and union leader who became a principal spokesperson of the Coordinadora, explains, the growing informalisation of work has seriously hampered the capacity of 'those who do not live off the labour of others' to organise *as a class*.[18] Most men and women employed in the informal economy are self-employed and therefore not in a position to join a conventional workplace-based union. The informalisation of work has also lead to the dispersal of workers, who now work as street vendors in market stalls (men and women of all ages), as casual labourers in the construction and building trades (mostly men), or in the homes of middle-class people as domestic servants (mostly women). The physical dispersal of workers has inhibited the formation of strong collective identities connected to the workplace, as was the case in the mining communities of Bolivia's recent past. Within this highly segmented labour market, tensions have emerged between full-time workers who enjoy the protection of contracts and labour legislation versus unprotected workers in the informal economy. Olivera observes that:

> The new working class has, so far, found it extremely difficult to project itself as an active social subject with sufficient personality to launch convincing mobilisations, to generate demands that motivate large numbers, or with even less success, to put forward practical proposals that incorporate the demands of other social sectors.[19]

There is wide agreement amongst scholars and activists that new organising strategies are necessary to overcome the societal fragmentation engendered by neoliberal restructuring, but few trade unions have risen to the challenge. Oscar Olivera's union of private manufacturing workers, the Federación de Fabriles de Cochabamba (Federation of Manufacturing Workers of Cochabamba, henceforth Fabriles), is a notable exception. Under Olivera's leadership, the Fabriles have looked for creative ways to overcome the barriers to working-class mobilisation, such as integrating demands for wages and working conditions as part of a broader platform for economic and social justice. Based upon his experience during the Cochabamba Water War, Olivera argues that organising multi-class alliances involving all groups negatively affected by neo-

---

18   For the purposes of this paper, the 'working class' is defined broadly as per the above
      quote in Olivera and Lewis 2004, p. 157. On the structural conditions that inhibit work-
      place organisation in contexts such as Bolivia and Peru, see Roberts 1998, pp. 67–73.
19   Olivera and Lewis 2004, p. 107.

liberalism around the basic necessities of life is a potential way to overcome the fragmentation of the working class.[20]

The Cochabamba Water War

Water was the issue that detonated two of the most effective protests in Bolivia in the pre-Morales years – the Water Wars in the cities of Cochabamba in April 2000 and in El Alto in January 2005. Both protests succeeded in pressuring the government to cancel privatisation contracts with multinational corporations.[21] Given the two trends noted above, it is not surprising that these struggles were not led by trade unions, but rather by territorially-based organisations that bring together people from different walks of life with common concerns that relate to their neighbourhood or region.

Cochabamba is the site of one of the most famous and spectacular incidences of privatisation failure that has since become an icon in the anti-neoliberal, anti-globalisation movement. In September 1999, government authorities granted a private concession to Aguas del Tunari (henceforth Tunari), a ghost company formed by a consortium in which International Water Limited (a subsidiary of the US-based multinational, Bechtel) held a majority share. A month and a half later, the government passed Law 2029, which granted monopoly rights over water sources to private companies, in order to promote privatisation in the water sector. Both the timing of the legislation and the stipulations of the contract set the stage for social conflict. The contract committed Tunari to expand the water network through the construction of an expensive dam project. It was to accomplish this task although it inherited some of the debts accrued by the former public utility, the Servicio municipal de agua potable, alcantarillado y desagües Pluviales (SEMAPA for short), and was guaranteed an average rate of return on capital of 16 percent for 40 years.[22] Since the World Bank dictated that no public funds could be channeled to the utility in Cochabamba, this money had to come from the users themselves. The Tunari contract and the new water law also granted exclusive property rights over water to concessionaires, which meant that residents within the

---

20   Ibid., pp. 117–28. Gay Seidman 1994 describes such union strategies as 'social movement unionism'.

21   The government promised to cancel the contract but has taken more than a year to follow through with the promise. Nonetheless, the 'Water War' in El Alto was effective in the sense that the government reacted quickly to meet social movement demands.

22   Lobina 2000; Crespo Flores 2002, p. 208.

concession area could be charged for collecting water from their own wells. Under the law, concessionaires could also apply to draw on water resources in the region surrounding the concession area, which raised the ire of the indigenous peasants in the Cochabamba Valley who depend on water for irrigation.

The city of Cochabamba is located in a dry, fertile valley and there is a lot of competition over water use for both domestic and productive purposes. Due to its scarcity, water has long been one of the most important political issues for all citizens in the Cochabamba Valley. As graffiti scrawled on a building in the centre of Cochabamba reads: 'I drink water, therefore I exist, therefore I vote'. At the time of privatisation, almost half of the urban population was not connected to the public water system. The problem was the most acute in the poor, southern area of the city known as the *Zona Sur* (South Zone). Since SEMAPA never extended its network into these communities, most residents in the *Zona Sur* have built their own independent water systems. In the words of Abrahan Grendydier, the president of the Asociación de los Sistemas Comunitarios de Agua en el Sur (Association of Communal Water Systems of the South, henceforth ASICA-Sur), communities in the *Zona Sur* had to dig their own wells to provide drinking water because:

> It is a zone of very few economic resources, where humble people from different departments and provinces have migrated because of drought in the *altiplano* and the relocalisation of the miners...But the government has never offered us any solutions, or the mayors, or the prefecture, or the water company.[23]

The members of these community water systems invested time and money building these independent systems with little help from the state, and they became angry when the government granted a foreign private company the right to charge them for their own well water.

The indigenous peasant farmers from the surrounding region were also angry that the government failed to respect their right to water. For several decades, conflicts over water have erupted between small farmers and government authorities. Seven years before the Water War, the government sent in the military to break blockades erected by small farmers in Quillacollo (13 km from Cochabamba), who were trying to prevent SEMAPA from drilling deep wells for the city's water supply. The conflict was resolved peacefully when the government and SEMAPA promised to find another way to solve the city's

---

23   Author interview with Abrahan Grandydier, Vinto, Bolivia, 14 July 2006.

water problem.[24] In 1997, these farmers founded Federación Departmental de Regantes y Sistemas Comunales del Agua Potable (Federation of Irrigator's Associations from the Department of Cochabamba, henceforth FEDECOR) in order to protect their water rights, or their *'usos y costumbres'* (uses and customs). The members of FEDECOR argue that these rights are inalienable because they have '[e]xisted since antiquity and come from our ancestors. Water comes from the *Pachamama* [the pre-Hispanic fertility deity], who is the earth who gives us life'.[25]

Months before the signing of the Tunari contract, a Committee for the Defense of Water and the Family Economy (Comité para la Defensa del Agua y la Economía Familiar, CODAEC), comprised of FEDECOR, various urban water committees, and an informal coalition of environmentalists who named themselves People on the Move (El Pueblo en Marcha, PUMA), warned the public that rates under a privatised company would rise by as much as 175 percent over the short term.[26] In November 1999, peasant farmers and independent water users associated with CODAEC blockaded roads around Cochabamba to protest the terms of the contract and the new water law. Later that month, groups of urban consumers and water users merged to form the Coordinadora. By December, urban water bills showed the anticipated price hikes, even though water services had not improved. Poor families, which had access to water only two or three hours a day, saw their bills increase by as much as 200 percent.[27] Some found themselves paying 20 percent of their monthly income for water, four times more than the limit recommended by the Pan American Health Organisation.

The Coordinadora found it relatively easy to mobilise people, who had already suffered recurring economic crises that many of them linked to neoliberalism. In early February 2000, the Coordinadora organised a peaceful takeover of the city (*'toma pacífica'*) to pressure the government to freeze the rate hikes and remove the monopoly provision from the contract and water legislation. Over 50,000 people participated in marches and blockades that shut down the city for 24 hours. Although the organisers assured the authorities that the protests would be peaceful, the central government sent in motorcycle police from La Paz known as 'the Dalmatians' (*las dálmatas*), famous for their black and white uniforms and their use of violent tactics. After hundreds of protestors were injured in conflicts with the police, the Coordinadora and the

---

24   Crespo Flores 1999.
25   Crespo Flores et al. 2004, p. 70.
26   The following account draws mostly from Olivera and Lewis 2004, pp. 33–49.
27   *Precensia* 1999, p. 25.

government reached an agreement, which gave the government two months to return water tariffs to their previous level and revise the contract and water legislation to recognise indigenous users' rights to water resources.

By the time the deadline expired, the government failed to fulfill its promises. Growing increasingly frustrated, the Coordinadora radicalised its demands, calling for the outright cancellation of the contract and an overhaul of the water legislation. The Coordinadora called an indefinite, city-wide strike to force the government to listen. On 4 April, the first blockades were erected by the militant peasant organisations on the main roads to the city. Protest escalated rapidly thanks to sympathetic coverage in the press, incorporating the poor and the middle classes from the urban areas. Within two days, there were over 100,000 people occupying the streets chanting, 'The water is ours, damn it!' (*'El agua es nuestra, ¡carajo!'*) and the entire centre of the city was blocked. Residents coming from the outskirts of the city also helped to reinforce the blockades. As Oscar Olivera describes, during the first days of the 'final battle', the government was careful not to provoke the protestors:

> The government learned one lesson from February: they did not bring out a single soldier or police officer. I remember people standing in the roads with bottles filled with liquid. I asked one woman what she intended to do with her bottle. 'Oh', she said, 'since February we've been making these bottles with water and oil'. 'But why?' I asked. She replied, 'To throw at the *dálmatas!*'[28]

As the protests grew larger, President Hugo Banzer, a former military dictator, declared a state of siege and dispatched riot police to control the crowds with tear gas, rubber bullets, and live ammunition. On 6 April, over a hundred people were wounded and twenty-two organisers from the Coordinadora, including Oscar Olivera, were arrested by police. The organisers were released on bail a few hours later with the help of the Archbishop of Cochabamba, who declared his support for the Coordinadora. Conflicts between protestors and police continued and on 8 April, an innocent by-stander, 17-year-old Victor Hugo Daza, was shot dead by a sniper. The arrests and the murder precipitated a furious response from the protestors, galvanising the population against the government. Sympathy blockades were also organised by campesinos in the *altiplano* and Evo Morales's powerful coca growers' association in the neighboring Chapare. Meanwhile, the government refused to negotiate with the Coordinadora, claiming that it was a small organisation led by a few individuals financed by drug trafficking.

---

28   Olivera and Lewis 2004, p. 37.

Finally, on 9 April, the government finally gave in. In the words of Vice Minister Jose Orías – who was sent by the government to negotiate with the Coordinadora – it became apparent that the Coordinadora 'was not just five vandals, but rather one hundred thousand people in the streets ready to do any-thing'. The agreement signed between the government and the Coordinadora guaranteed the withdrawal of Tunari, transferred the water utility back to the municipal government, and assured the release of detained protesters. On 11 April, Congress passed a law executing the decision and the blockades within the city were dismantled the following day. The peasant farmers, who emerged as the most militant participants in the protests, maintained block-ades for another day until the Congress passed a new water law (Law 2066) that recognised their rights to '*usos y costumbres*'.

The coalition that formed the Coordinadora brought together diverse groups from a wide array of civil society organisations in a way that 'ruptured the rural/urban dichotomy that characterises politics in many countries of the South'.[29] As has been noted in the burgeoning literature on the Water War, the coalition was also diverse with respect to gender and race. Women played an active role in the daily aspects of the struggle, although few took leadership positions. Indigenous peasants, mestizo leaders such as Oscar Olivera, and 'white' urban professionals played key roles as leaders and spokespersons. The coalition was also 'multi-class' with respect to the fact that it brought together urban professionals, unionised workers, and informal workers together with peasants from the surrounding area.[30]

At the time of the Water War, however, public sector trade unions were nota-bly absent. While the Fabriles played an important role in the Coordinadora, providing ideological leadership and office space, the union that represents the workers of the public utility played a much less visible role. Indeed, they did not even participate in the street protests of February or April. In an interview, union leader René Cardona explained that workers supported the mobilisa-tion by providing an essential service, which required that they stay at work.[31] He emphasised, however, that the leaders from the union did attend meet-ings of the Coordinadora at the time of its founding and consider themselves members of the Coordinadora. As we shall see further below, the leaders of the SEMAPA union have played an important, yet controversial role in restructur-ing the public utility.

---

29   Laurie 2005, p. 536.

30   See *inter alia* Bustamente et al. 2005; Albro 2005.

31   Author interview with René Cardona, Cochabamba, Bolivia, 5 July 2005.

Bolivia's Second Water War in El Alto

The Cochabamba Water War started a process of wider grassroots mobilisation that spread across the country, eventually inspiring the next conflict over urban water privatisation in El Alto in January 2005. In 1997, a private consortium controlled by the French company Suez named Aguas del Illimani (henceforth, Illimani) was granted a private concession to run the local water supply. Local papers report sporadic protests against Illimani at the time of privatisation and in the years that followed, but it was not until 2004 that the resistance strategies became more effective. This time there were no irrigating peasants, but similar to Cochabamba, poor, indigenous urban consumers and those who lacked access to a safe water supply were the main protagonists of the story.

El Alto is perched on the edge of the 14,000 foot high *altiplano* overlooking a steep canyon that cradles the capital city La Paz. The majority of 'white' people live in the wealthy neighbourhoods of La Paz located at the bottom of the canyon, where the climate is more moderate. The majority of the poor and overwhelmingly indigenous people live on the steep hills that climb the canyon known as 'las laderas' (literally, the ladders) or in the neighbouring city of El Alto. El Alto is the poorest city in Bolivia. By no coincidence, it is also Bolivia's most indigenous city. In the last official census, over 82 percent of respondents self-identified as indigenous, predominantly Aymara. The population of El Alto has been at the centre of the indigenous movement in Bolivia.

At the head of this struggle is the militant territorially-based organisation, Federación de Juntas Vecinales de El Alto (the Federation of Neighbourhood Councils of El Alto, henceforth the FEJUVE). The FEJUVE is the executive structure that agglutinates more than 500 grassroots associations of residents (*junta vecinales*) that have been created by residents at the neighbourhood level. To participate in a local *junta vecinal*, there is only one requirement: one must establish proof that he or she has resided in the zone for at least two years. Local committees and the city-level executive are elected every two years and all positions are voluntary.

The executive of the FEJUVE, who tend to be more moderate than the base, present their demands in terms of neighbourhood interests rather than polarised race or class terms. In an interview, Abel Mamani, President of the FEJUVE during the second Water War, described the struggle for the right to water in El Alto as follows:

> I do not see a difference between the residents of La Paz and those from the city of El Alto. I have also lived in the city of La Paz ... I have family in Villa Favón [a neighbourhood in La Paz], and in all the zones of La Paz ... Therefore I believe that we all have necessities no matter where we live or who we are.[32]

Traditionally, most of the demands of the FEJUVE have been related to basic services (education, healthcare, water, electricity, cooking gas, etc.), which by most definitions are working-class concerns. Although the FEJUVE is not formally an indigenous organisation, given the demographics of El Alto the membership and leadership of the FEJUVE are predominantly Aymara. Amongst the executive of the FEJUVE, for example, one finds many men and women named 'Mamani' and 'Quispe', the Aymara equivalents of the British 'Smith' and 'Jones'.

The tragic events during the first Gas War of 2003 put El Alto on the region's political map. In October 2003, an estimated eighty people lost their lives in a struggle to prevent the export of natural gas through Chile. The following year, new leadership elected to the FEJUVE took on the mandate to advance the October Agenda. Suddenly, not only was FEJUVE working on local issues, but also on national political demands such as the call for a Constitutional Assembly and the nationalisation of natural resources, two demands that were imprinted in the public consciousness as a result of the Cochabamba Water War. The struggle against Illimani in El Alto is therefore perceived by FEJUVE members as part of a much broader political project to restore Bolivia's economic sovereignty.[33]

The Illimani contract was considered to be pro-poor by international financial institutions because it focused on expanding the number of new connections rather than reducing tariffs. Indeed, Illimani made enough new connections to allow the government to claim that the company achieved 100 percent coverage for potable water in both La Paz and El Alto within the first four years of the contract. What was seldom mentioned, however, is that this statistic referred to a small area within the total area of the concession known as the 'served area'. The contract was a classic example of ring fencing, the practice of focusing service provision on profitable customers and removing obligation from extending service to the newest and most marginal settlements – the areas most in need of improvements. According to the FEJUVE,

---

32   Author interview with Abel Mamani, El Alto, Bolivia, 19 July 2005.
33   Postero 2005; Spronk and Webber 2007.

approximately two-hundred-thousand people in El Alto did not have access to Illimani's services because they live outside the served area defined by the contract. An additional 70,000 people without water and sewerage lived within the served area but could not afford the US$445 connection fees, the equivalent of almost nine monthly salaries. As a title of a pamphlet circulated in El Alto in November 2004 put it, these were just two of the '14 Reasons to Break the Contract with Aguas del Illimani'.

The FEJUVE started to negotiate with the government in mid-2004, asking it to change the terms of the contract. After nearly six months of fruitless negotiations, the FEJUVE called a general strike to begin on 9 January 2005. The timing of the strike turned out to be fortuitous since civic strikes were later called in the department of Santa Cruz for 11–12 January over the rising cost of gasoline. On the first day of the El Alto strike, thousands of citizens took to the streets yelling the slogan popularised during the Gas War, 'El Alto on its feet, never on its knees!' On 11 January, residents of Ballivian and Alto Lima, two neighbourhoods that lie outside of the served area, seized several Illimani facilities, including a water tank.

That day, the beleaguered President Carlos Mesa – whose predecessor had been forced to resign by popular protests – sent the FEJUVE a letter saying he was beginning 'the necessary actions for the termination of the concession contract' with Illimani. The FEJUVE gave Mesa's government 24 hours to promulgate a decree immediately canceling the contract with the water company or protestors would seize the company's central offices in El Alto. The next day, Mesa issued a Presidential Decree which formalised the government's decision. After consulting with neighbourhood councils, the FEJUVE called an end to the strike, but warned the government that it would continue pressing other demands over the price of electricity and fuel.[34]

Similar to events five years earlier in Cochabamba, the workers directly affected by privatisation were conspicuously absent from the protests in El Alto. Indeed, the union has played a marginal role in the privatisation process from start to finish. Local activists consider the union untrustworthy, since any opposition to the privatisation on the part of the leaders quickly evaporated when Illimani offered workers one percent of shares in the new private water company.[35] Jhonny Vasquez, the Secretary General of the Illimani workers' union, explained that the company's offer turned out to be a trick:

34 Nicaragua Solidarity Network of Greater New York 2005; *Bolpress* 2005.
35 Crespo Flores 2001.

> When they told us that we would be able to buy 'preferential shares' we thought that we would have special treatment . . . To the contrary, the preferential shares are not very preferential. The ordinary shares gain more interest than our shares. They are owned by Suez, an Argentinean company, the World Bank, and the Banco Mercantil . . . With my shares, I only make about 5 bolivianos [under US$1] per year.[36]

The company also failed to keep the promise it made to the union that it would not lay-off workers, and fired 205 out of 600 workers within four years, subcontracting many services to micro enterprises.[37] In 2004, the government regulator announced that Illimani had the lowest number of permanent workers (1.7) per thousand connections of any water utility in the country. The experience of privatisation in La Paz-El Alto therefore confirms many workers' fears that the principal mechanism of private enterprises to increase profits and enhance competitiveness is to reduce the price of labour, and set a dangerous precedent for 'efficiency' amongst Bolivian water utilities.

Cochabamba: Five Years after the Water War

The importance of the Water Wars for the Bolivian left cannot be understated. In the words of Oscar Olivera, the Water Wars were about a lot more than water; they were a struggle for a new form of democracy from below. Protestors' demands for a Constituent Assembly and for nationalisation have since been taken up by the new MAS government. Since the Water War, Oscar Olivera of the Coordinadora also became an important figure in the international campaign for public water. The Coordinadora was therefore successful in scaling up its demands to the national and international levels.

The concrete results of the Cochabamba Water War at the local level, on the other hand, have been disappointing. Attempts to expand the water network – the key demand of the poor in the *Zona Sur* – have been frustrated by a lack of capital. For those who were already customers of SEMAPA, service has not improved either; water continues to be supplied to many areas of the city for only a few hours a day. Five years after the Water War, local activists associated with the Coordinadora acknowledged that the work of building a truly democratic public water company was a more difficult task than first imagined.

---

36 Author interview with Jhonny B. Vasquez, La Paz, Bolivia, 21 April 2005. At the time of the interview, 5 bolivianos was the equivalent of about US$0.60.

37 Crespo Flores 2001.

Under a series of neoliberal administrations between April 2000 and December 2005, the Bolivian state did little to help the ailing public utility. While many of the previous debts accumulated by SEMAPA were scheduled to be forgiven under the privatisation contract with Tunari, the reconstituted public company was saddled with all of its previous debts that it had accumulated over 30 years of service, which amounted to about US$18 million. Other state institutions have also added to the debt burden, demanding the payment of back debts, among them the Bolivian Internal Revenue Service and the City of Cochabamba. To make a difficult situation worse, Minister Mario Galindo threatened to make city residents pay US$25 million in damages to Tumari's shareholders in a lawsuit launched in an international court.[38] As a consequence, promises to bring water to the poor neighbourhoods of the *Zona Sur* have been delayed repeatedly.[39]

The public utility faced enormous challenges of an external nature since its re-founding, but unraveling the story of what went wrong also requires an analysis of the structure of mobilisation. The coalition that formed the Coordinadora was a temporary organisation that mobilised around a particular issue – the privatisation of the region's water supply and water supply services. The surge of local energy that erupted in April 2000 largely ebbed when the government called off the troops and gave in to protestors' demands. The fracturing of the coalition was a result of this process, which can be explained as the results of the tensions that exist within territorially-based organisations composed by disparate social groups with conflicting concerns.

In Cochabamba, the Coordinadora aimed to democratise the water utility by exerting social control 'from below' and within the management structure.[40] The board of directors, formerly constituted only by professionals and municipal politicians, was expanded to include three elected members from each macro district of Cochabamba. More controversially, the union was also granted a vote on the board of directors at the insistence of Oscar Olivera. This partially elected board saw the public utility through the process of institutionalisation through which a new management structure was implemented, and executives have been appointed through an open and competitive process. As Philip Therhorst and former elected board member Luis Sánchez describe, however, the project to exert social control over the utility remains a 'work in progress'.[41]

---

38   *Los Tiempos* 2004.
39   Sánchez Gómez 2004.
40   Sánchez Gómez and Terhorst 2005.
41   Ibid.

Since the decision to include the union on the board of directors, the leadership of the SEMAPA union has created a lot of problems. First, the union reportedly put pressure on the management to increase the number of personnel. Before its privatisation in 1997, SEMAPA had 6.38 employees per thousand connections.[42] By the end of 2003, the government regulator reported that the number of workers had nearly doubled to 11.5 per thousand connections. The management argued that these new personnel were needed to build the networks in the *Zona Sur*, but the perception of most consumers was that the increase in the number of personnel could not be justified without improving the utility's performance.

Second, the union leadership has been accused of corruption.[43] There are a large number of illegal connections creating commercial losses within the company. Local activists suspect that much of this illegal activity takes place with the explicit consent of a few SEMAPA workers high up within the union hierarchy who have also secured positions within the utility's management. For example, the union representative on the board of directors (2004–6), Jorge Ortíz, was also head of the Financial Division, which made it difficult to identify the source of the problem.

Third, the union is not democratic. Rank-and-file activists who want to expose corrupt practices face a chilly climate. Internal elections within the union have not been contested for the past six years. A worker that I met in the union office argued that the leadership has been uncontested because the current leadership 'does a good job', but those who do not agree with the union's practices have been fired. In April 2005, leaders of FEDECOR joined four SEMAPA workers in a hunger strike to protest against the firing of a worker who was accused of nepotism and fired without just cause.[44] A relationship of mistrust between the union leadership and other members of the Coordinadora has developed, which has made it difficult for the latter to take a pro-worker stance in negotiations regarding the restructuring of the utility.

The roots of this conflict go even deeper, however, than problems with corruption and the bureaucratisation that pervades the SEMAPA union. At base, it is also a conflict amongst workers at different ranks within a segmented labour market. When I asked how the tensions between other members of the Coordinadora and the SEMAPA workers developed, Oscar Olivera responded:

---

42   Crespo Flores 2002, p. 112

43   For reasons of confidentiality, these individuals remain unnamed.

44   *Opinión* 2005a.

First, unions in the public sector are very different from the private sector. Unionisation in the public sector is completely impregnated with a type of co-management and there are many deals between the union and the management to maintain the status quo of an enterprise that mean that they have certain privileges. I would say that the ideal salary for a Bolivian is 3000 Bolivianos per month. In SEMAPA, the average salary is 2200 Bolivianos per month. It is a reasonable salary. But it is much higher than whatever salary in the private sector. It is a right. But it is a privileged sector that has salaries much higher than the rest of the population.[45]

Olivera's comments require some clarification. When the mines were under national control, the public sector mining unions were at the forefront of the popular struggle and fiercely resisted the privatisation of the mines, although their efforts were ultimately unsuccessful. The public sector workers who deliver basic services such as potable water, electricity and telephone, however, have played a marginal role in the more recent struggles against privatisation. Olivera also acknowledges that there has been a decline in wages and salaries in all sectors, a trend that cannot be solved by cutting workers' wages at the top of the pay scale.[46] Nonetheless, the income differentials among various members of the Coordinadora have exacerbated the tensions between the public sector workers that produce water services and people who buy these services.

These tensions amongst the different fractions of the Coordinadora came to a head in late 2005. Given SEMAPA's disappointing performance from 2000 to 2005, the threat of privatisation returned in a new guise: sub-contracting. The Inter-American Development Bank (IADB) demands that SEMAPA meet certain conditions such as reducing the number of permanent workers per connection in order to receive all the installments of an US$18 million loan. The last installments of the loans are supposed to be used to expand the network in the *Zona Sur*. In the struggles over how to accomplish these reforms, a major fault line opened between the consumers of water services, who want to see the costs of services lowered to allow for expansion, and the leaders of the union, who want to protect workers from being fired. In the end, the consumers 'won'. In October 2005, the representative of the SEMAPA union was dismissed from the board of directors and has not been replaced. Within two

---

45   When the interview was conducted, 3000 bolivianos was about US$375 and 2200 about
      US$275. Author interview with Oscar Olivera, Cochabamba, Bolivia, 28 September, 2004.
46   See Olivera and Lewis 2004, pp. 118–25.

weeks, the board fired 164 SEMAPA workers, promising to buy back their services on a contractual basis if they formed their own micro-enterprises.[47]

The issue of sub-contracting in Cochabamba raises a hairy dilemma that faces all water justice activists and managers of public services. Difficult questions arise in deciding how far reforms should go such as, how many workers are truly required to provide quality public services? And, what is to be considered a fair wage for public service workers in the context of the pauperisation of the working class as a whole? A delicate balance must be struck between the need for quality public sector employment and consumers' rights to affordable public services. In Cochabamba, however, the principal task of the Coordinadora from the start was to defend the rights of the urban and rural consumers of water, and not the rights of the workers who produce water services. Since these rights are viewed as being in conflict in SEMAPA, which is facing pressure from the IADB, it is not surprising that the board of directors made a decision to improve services in a way that shifts the costs of restructuring onto workers.

Conclusion: The Future of Public Services and the MAS

Neoliberal restructuring in Bolivia has weakened trade unions, which have traditionally been the only working-class organisations with a specific mandate to improve wages and working conditions. Given the stripping of state supports for the working class in terms of subsidies for water, shelter, and food, workers without stable employment have found themselves increasingly engaged in battles with workers with stable employment who produce these basic goods and services. Under these conditions, unionised workers in the public sector face pressure to bear the brunt of cost-saving measures implemented in the name of efficiency, even from their allies. The result has been a downward spiral that affects all workers, both formal and informal, as both working and living conditions have deteriorated.

The Cochabamba experience provides several lessons for the struggle in El Alto in their struggle to define a new public water company, where activists face the same dilemmas mentioned above. There have been strong organisational links between the activists in Cochabamba and El Alto, and the latter have resolved not to repeat the mistakes of the Coordinadora. It has been difficult for the Coordinadora to sustain the level of grassroots mobilisation needed to build a democratic municipal water utility. By contrast, the FEJUVE

---

47   *Los Tiempos* 2005; *Opinión* 2005b.

of El Alto, while a territorially-based organisation, has a more formal structure with elected representatives, which may be more likely to sustain the social energy needed to build participatory institutions at the local level. The FEJUVE also has over twenty-five years of experience with local forms of democracy that may facilitate effective community participation in the management of the municipal utility and provide an important check on the union and the management. The FEJUVE faces the same dilemma, however, of how efficient service delivery can be achieved without sacrificing workers' rights to self-representation and participation within the workplace, and decent wages and working conditions. As a private corporation driven by the profit motive, Illimani found its answer easily: it lowered the cost of production by contracting out to micro enterprises that hire workers at lower wages without social benefits. Will the FEJUVE support or reverse these trends? Given the social composition of the FEJUVE, the lead anti-privatisation organisation in Bolivia's largest informal city, and the relationship of mistrust that has developed with the workers' union, this problem will not be resolved easily.

The difficult transition from public to private and back again in Cochabamba also suggests that the tension between workers and consumers in struggles over public services is not irresolvable but rather calls for a social transformation much greater than organisations such as the Coordinadora, the FEJUVE, or trade unions can accomplish in isolation. Indeed, a fundamental restructuring of society is required such that the social wealth is used to satisfy human needs rather than private profit. As Oscar Olivera argues, 'the true opposite of privatisation is the social re-appropriation of wealth by working-class society, itself self-organised in communal structures of management, in neighbourhood associations, and in the rank and file'.[48]

The MAS (Movement Towards Socialism), the leftist party which won the 2005 national elections for president and congress, has taken a few steps to remodel the economy, but Olivera's more radical vision is far from being realised. On 1 May 2006, President Evo Morales announced that his government planned to 'nationalise' the country's hydrocarbon resources. Most of the country appeared to welcome the news, but the government's announcement that it planned to purchase shares of the oil and gas companies fell short of the demands of the FEJUVE and the Coordinadora, whose members took to the streets in May–June 2005 calling for expropriation without compensation on the grounds that the contracts signed under Sánchez de Lozada were unconstitutional. The MAS also followed through on its promise to form a Constituent Assembly. In the elections for delegates held on 2 July 2006, the

---

48   Olivera and Lewis 2004, pp. 156–7.

MAS won 134 of the 255 seats. Controversy has also erupted over how the MAS designed the elections, which made it impossible for the party to win the two-thirds majority needed to make deep changes to the Constitution.

On a more positive note, the MAS government has signaled its commitment to public water. The government appointed former president of the FEJUVE, Abel Mamani as the head of the newly created Water Ministry. Since Mamani's appointment, the government announced that SEMAPA will be forgiven for US$12 million of the debt that it owes to the central government, providing more room in the budget for expansion to the *Zona Sur*.[49] As of the time of writing (mid-August 2006), there is no final decision about how Illimani will be replaced and whether the new water utility in La Paz-El Alto will be fully publicly-owned and operated. The proposal for the new water utility includes the sub-contracting of some services, which as the Cochabamba experience demonstrates, may eventually become the next frontier in the struggle against privatisation of public services in Bolivia.[50]

---

49   *Los Tiempos* 2006.
50   Pérez 2006.

CHAPTER 3

The Neo-Developmentalist Alternative: Capitalist Crisis, Popular Movements, and Economic Development in Argentina since the 1990s

Mariano Féliz

After the economic meltdown of 2001 Argentina appeared to enter a new period of sustainable economic growth and relative political stability. After the crisis, changes in public policies were so far-reaching that several authors have argued that Argentina underwent a transition from neoliberal rule to an altogether new period of neo-developmentalism.[1] This chapter argues that while neo-developmentalism represents a break with neoliberalism in some respects, the changes in macroeconomic policies also express profound continuities with past neoliberal policies. Furthermore, any changes must be understood as the result of shifts in the correlation of political forces in the broader regional and international context, rather than a conscious policy 'choice' per se.

The chapter is structured as follows. The first section discusses the dynamics of neoliberal rule and its crisis in Argentina between 1991 and 2001. The second section presents the main structural continuities of the current process in relation to earlier periods of neoliberal orthodoxy. The third section analyses the new political foundations of neo-developmentalism, while the following section discusses changes in public policies, showing how they manifest the particular articulation of continuity and change. We finish our discussion with a few preliminary conclusions.

Neoliberal Transformations: Structural Adjustment, Class Struggle and Crisis

Neoliberalism has been a worldwide process meant to restore capitalist class power over society.[2] In this sense, neoliberalism implies a regime shift: a process that puts into action a set of policies intended to alter the balance

---

1   Curia 2007.

2   Harvey 2009.

of forces in favour of capital instead of labour.[3] In general terms, the transition to neoliberalism from Fordism (the so-called 'golden years' of capitalism between the 1940s and the 1960s) began to materialise in Chile in 1973, followed by Argentina in 1976, the UK under Thatcher in the late 1970s, and the US under Reagan in the early 1980s.

In Argentina, the dominant classes had been trying to regain uncontested social control of production since the 1970s.[4] Since the 1940s, organised labour in Argentina had been able to gain considerable social power as the economy passed through several phases of industrialisation led by a developmentalist ideology.[5] By 1973 industrial GDP had peaked at 24.2 percent of total GDP.[6] Thus, even the dictatorship of 1976–83 (the first stage of the neoliberal era) was not enough to undermine the power of the labour movement.[7] While the military government kidnapped and killed several thousand political activists, relatively low unemployment levels prevented an all-out attack on labour.[8] Even if political repression weakened the labour movement, low unemployment rates helped it to maintain its structural power and continue the struggle for better working conditions.[9]

All of this changed in the 1980s. During the second stage of neoliberalism, capital fled from production into the financial sector, while advancing in its concentration and centralisation by means of stagnation.[10] According to the Instituto Nacional de Estadísticas y Censos (National Institute of Statistics and the Census, INDEC) GDP per capita fell 23 percent between 1980 and 1989.[11] Gross investment in fixed capital fell 1.7 percent per year between 1984 and 1990. Industrial employment fell 26.6 percent between 1984 and 1993.[12] The contribution of industry as a proportion of GDP fell from 27.2 between 1970–9 to 18.1 percent in 1991.[13] The precarisation of labour also intensified as

3   Jessop 2010.
4   Féliz and Pérez 2004; James 1990.
5   Basualdo 2006a; Peralta Ramos 2007; Neffa 2008.
6   Ferreres 2005.
7   Pozzi and Schneider 1993; Bonnet and Glavich 1993.
8   Canitrot 1981.
9   See Selwyn in this volume for a definition of 'structural power'. See Pozzi 2008; Basualdo, no date, on the Argentine case.
10   Basualdo 2006a; Féliz and Pérez 2004.
11   All data provided in the chapter comes from the National Institute of Statistics and the Census (Instituto Nacional de Estadísticas y Censos, INDEC) unless noted otherwise.
12   Azpiazu 1998.
13   Ferreres 2005.

the unemployment rate grew from 2.5 percent in 1980 to 7.6 percent in 1989.[14] Eventually, after two hyperinflationary episodes in 1989 and 1990, capital had set the scene for its final strike: the Convertibility Plan (CP) of April 1991.

The year 1991 was a milestone in the neoliberal structural adjustment of Argentina's capitalist economy. The implementation of the CP, which lasted until early 2002, completed the plan of Argentina's dominant classes for a successful capitalist restructuring of society. The CP was the Washington Consensus translated into policy, which entailed the following measures: fixing the nominal exchange rate to the US dollar through a currency board (the Argentine Currency Board); liberalising both trade and capital accounts of the balance of payments; privatising most public companies and social security, as well as health and education services; deregulating most economic activities; and introducing greater flexibility to the labour market through modifications in labour law.[15]

We must stress that although in terms of the usual standards (i.e. growth, income distribution, social indicators, etc.) the CP might appear as a failure, in terms of the objectives of the dominant classes the plan was highly successful. Most public enterprises, as well as social security, were privatised. The labour market was effectively liberalised, as well as most economic activities.[16]

The CP also allowed foreign corporations to gain control over some of the largest firms in the economy, which at first was to the advantage of local firms. Early privatisation programmes required their inclusion, particularly in the formation of public-private partnerships. However, in the late 1990s most local partners were displaced from those partnerships.[17] Big local corporations remained significant but subordinated actors in the economy. Exceptions to this rule were those large local corporations that had been able to succeed in their own trasnationalisation, such as the steel producer Techint and the food-stuffs manufacturer Arcor. Of the top 500 corporations in Argentina, in 1993 foreign capital controlled 32 percent, while the figure reached 48 percent in

---

14   For some authors, neoliberal rule was led in Argentina by a process of (unproductive) financial valorisation that displaced productive accumulation. For this view, see Basualdo 2006a. While we agree that the growing leverage of financial capital on the economy is important, we understand it as the result of difficulties faced by productive investment. As such, financialisation was an integral component of the final stage of restructuring during the 1990s. Without the participation of financial capital in the process of privatisation and in the reorganisation (concentration and centralisation) of capital, both transformations would have been much more difficult to achieve.

15   Lindenboim and Danani 2003.

16   Peralta Ramos 2007.

17   Basualdo 2006a.

1998 and 66 percent in 2007. The CP succeeded in creating a new, more competitive productive structure based on the export of agricultural and mining commodities (both primary products such as soybeans and basic manufactures such as soybean oil).[18] For the first time in many decades, every year since 2002 has shown for Argentina a positive result in the trade balance as well as in the balance of payments. Taken as a whole, the CP represented a frontal attack on labour's rights as well as the consolidation of a new transnational coalition of export-oriented agro-industrial and mining capitals.[19]

This programme was pushed forward through the better part of the 1990s by the traditionally labour-oriented Peronist party with the critical support of the government-allied trade unions affiliated with the Confederación General del Trabajo (General Labour Confederation, CGT). In a highly corrupt process, many union leaders and congressional members with ties to the labour movement benefited from the privatisation of state-owned enterprises. Unions were given responsibility for the administration of a portion of the shares of the privatised companies, thus obtaining economic and political gains for many of their leaders.[20] Unions were also allowed to participate in the newly privatised pension system, as well as in the healthcare and insurance businesses. As Novick puts it, the privatisation process gave birth to a new trade union movement with entrepreneurial interests.[21] Without the CGT's support, the CP could not have advanced as it did in its objectives.

While the CP was successful in achieving the objective of the dominant classes to restore profitability, it also created contradictions that led eventually to the economic meltdown of 2001. This crisis became evident in the second half of 1998 and reached its pinnacle in the final quarter of 2001.[22] Rapid GDP growth between 1990 and 1998 – more than 57.9 percent according to the INDEC – was built on an important increase in the ratio of fixed capital stock to living labour, otherwise known as the organic composition of capital (OCC). Between 1992 and 1998, the OCC increased by 16 percent, with a further increase of 12.7 percent by 2001.[23] This ratio expresses two combined

---

18   Arceo 2006.
19   Ibid.; Basualdo 2006b.
20   Peralta Ramos 2007.
21   Novick 2001.
22   Féliz 2011.
23   Following Saad-Filho's 1993 interpretation, we approximate the OCC as the ratio between real fixed capital stock and total hours worked. See Iñigo Carrera 2007a. Empirically this allows us to analyse changes in the OCC.

processes.[24] On the one hand, at a more fundamental level, the OCC represents the displacement of the source of surplus value (living labour) in relation to dead labour, that is, the replacement of human labour by machines.[25] On the other hand, higher OCC also implies greater labour productivity. In Argentina, labour's productivity in manufacturing jumped 44.5 percent between 1991 and 1998, and a further 16 percent between 1998 and 2001. Indeed, as demonstrated elsewhere,[26] the rising OCC is the original source of crisis tendencies in capitalism that were exacerbated by Argentina's CP, for it created the structural forces that led towards the eventual destruction (devalorisation) of capital in all its forms and manifestations (i.e. falling profitability, decreasing investment, lack of demand, excess relative supply).[27] Increasing labour exploitation, growing foreign markets, and rising luxury consumption staved off, at least temporarily, the tendencies posed by the rising OCC.[28] But most importantly, capital's restructuring also implied the flexibilisation of labour and an increase in the rate of exploitation. According to one calculation, between 1990 and 2001 the ratio of exploitation rose by 40 percent.[29]

The process of labour flexibilisation was only possible because Argentina's labour movement had been beaten and/or co-opted into accepting reforms. This co-optation was possible because the main labour unions affiliated with the Peronist CGT adopted a defensive position within the context of the extreme disciplinary effect of hyperinflation and the increasing precariousness of labour due to the restructuring of capitalist relations. According to the National Institute of Statistics and the Census (*Instituto Nacional de Estadísticas y Censos*, INDEC), unemployment had jumped from an average 3.6 percent in the 1970s to 10.5 percent in 1993–4. Real wages fell by 39.9 percent between 1974 and 1993. The combination of these political transformations and economic reforms created new rules of the game in which workers

---

24   Saad-Filho 1993; Weeks 1981.

25   As accumulation progresses this relative displacement tends to limit the possibilities of further expansion. For further discussion of this process see Saad-Fiho 2003; Weeks 1981; Mandel 1968; Shaikh 1992; and Moseley 1991.

26   See Féliz 2007; Féliz 2009a; and Féliz 2011.

27   As OCC grows and relative surplus-value production falters, the difficulties for further expanded valorisation of capital tend to appear as devaluation of capital (failing enterprises, growing unused production capacity, falling profitability, etc.). See Weeks 1981.

28   Ibid.

29   The ratio of exploitation was measured as the ratio of net surplus value and the mass of variable capital. Net surplus value was estimated as gross GDP minus consumed fixed capital and direct and indirect wages while direct and indirect wages were used as equivalent to the mass of variable capital. See Iñigo Carrera 2007a.

found it harder to defend their interests vis-à-vis capital. Finally, while neo-liberal reforms entailed the shrinking of the domestic market, increasing luxury consumption by dominant classes and growing markets in new centres of accumulation overseas made it possible to displace the contradictions of accumulation into the future, at least temporarily.[30] The participation of non-workers in total income rose from 53.3 percent in 1974 to 64.2 percent in 1997.[31] On the other hand, exports went from 3.5 percent of GDP in 1974 to 10 percent in 1997.

By the late 1990s, however, things began to change. After several years of disorganisation, Argentina's working class began to regain momentum.[32] The CGT no longer had a monopoly on the trade union movement with the establishment of the Central de los Trabajadores Argentinos (Central of Argentine Workers, CTA), which was formed when several important unions, such as the national teacher's union Confederación de Trabajadores de la Educación de la República Argentina (Confederation of Education Workers of Argentina's Republic, CTERA) and one of the main associations of public employees, Asociación de Trabajadores del Estado (Association of State Employees, ATE), left the CGT to create a new organisation in 1992. The new CTA, the growing *piquetero* movement, growing uneasiness within the 'middle classes' (in particular, students and small entrepreneurs), and even disgruntled sectors within the bureaucratic CGT, all came together to form a multi-pronged movement of opposition to the harsh consequences of the Convertibility Plan. The first *puebladas* (popular uprisings) by the unemployed in Cutral-có and Plaza Huincul (in the southern provinces of the country) broke out in 1996. After two decades of ineffective resistance, the CGT and the CTA organised several general strikes between 1996 and 2001.[33] Direct action protests (local and regional strikes, picket lines, road blocks, mobilisations) by workers also increased significantly.[34] Between 2000 and 2001 the unemployed became the cornerstone of social protests, leading numerous mobilisations that included roadblocks.[35] This progressive re-composition of the working class weakened the possibility of further advancement of the neoliberal project, as the available options for displacing the contradictions inherent in the neoliberal model of accumulation were narrowing.

---

30   Féliz 2011.
31   Graña 2007.
32   Bonnet 2002; Piva 2001; Lucita 2001.
33   Piva 2006.
34   Gómez 2000.
35   Bonnet 2002.

By 1998 the world market began to contract and international financial conditions turned gloomy. Flagging export demand led to economic stagnation; valorisation and accumulation faltered. The aforementioned contradictions went from being potential constraints for expanded reproduction to actual limits. Capitalist consumption fell as financing grew dearer and expectations for future growth bleaker.[36] With rising levels of public and private debt,[37] surplus value was increasingly channelled towards paying interest rather than productive investment.[38] Profit rates for big corporations plummeted: the profit rate for big firms fell from an average 10 percent from 1993 to 1998 to only 7 percent from 1997 to 2001, while absolute profits fell every year between 1997 and 2001. These structural limits combined with the contraction in the world economy culminated in a devastating economic crisis. The rate of growth of global imports fell from an annual average of 6.4 percent in the period 1991 and 1997 to only 3.1 percent annually between 1997 and 2002 while the price index of Argentina's exports fell 12.3 percent between 1991 and 1997 and 1998 and 2002.

Political conditions worsened for capital as the different branches of the recomposed working class confronted the government's attempts to deepen neoliberal structural adjustment. In the elections of 1998, the strong neoliberal alliance led by the Peronist Party, which had governed since 1989, was displaced by a weak coalition called Alliance (Alianza) that tried to overcome the mounting crisis by addressing its symptoms rather than its causes. To reduce the public deficit, the government increased taxes on the upper middle classes (its own political base); to cope with the public foreign debt it took measures to refinance but at a much higher interest rate; finally, it reduced public employees' wages and pensions by 13 percent and tried to impose a zero-deficit policy.[39] Eventually, as the crisis reached its final stages in December 2001, the government imposed a strict limit on the extraction of cash from banks in an attempt to stop the staggering reduction in bank deposits: during 2001 bank deposits fell by 20 percent. Social and political opposition to these policies weakened the government's support.[40]

---

36   Astarita 2001.
37   Damill, Frenkel, and Rapetti 2005.
38   Duménil and Lévy 2006.
39   Damill, Frenkel, and Maurizio 2003.
40   Bonnet 2002.

Potential over-production became a reality: capacity utilisation in industry fell to 64 percent in 2001, the lowest level since 1989.[41] Under-consumption (the flip side of over-production) became a problem as real wages fell due to policy choices and recession. Capital flight increased as the political situation deteriorated: between December 2000 and December 2001 capital flight reached US$12 trillion. Deflationary pressures and then the devaluation of the exchange rate were progressively the outcome of a process that had created the conditions for commodity devaluation across the board.[42]

The crisis of the CP appeared to most analysts as a typical stop-go process, perhaps mediated by a sudden stop in capital inflow.[43] However, under the appearance of the archetypical exchange rate crisis produced by the lack of finance for deficit in the external accounts, this time the fleeing capital was nothing more than the paradoxical manifestation of the successful restructuring of capitalist production in Argentina.[44] In fact, financial capital only began to abandon Argentina in late 2000 while, according to the Centro de Economía Internacional (Centre of International Economy, CEI), country risk had begun rising as late as the first quarter of 2001. Deflationary tendencies were the partial result of the increasing productivity combined with the parallel contraction of foreign and domestic demand. Given the fact that increases to productivity in Argentina's industry outstripped that of the United States (the country that holds the world currency, the US dollar) and that real wages had also fallen substantially in relative terms to the US between 1991 and 2001, falling unit costs were manifest in pressures for currency devaluation or price deflation in dollar terms.[45] In short, given falling relative unit labour costs and increasing competitive pressures in a situation of falling demand, local prices as measured in US dollars had to fall. They began to do so as between 1998 and 2001 the producer price index fell by 5.3 percent. However, the Argentine Currency Board made these processes extremely complicated. Currency devaluation thus appeared to be the most feasible option to restore profitability given the increasing productivity of local capital and falling relative unit

---

41   Fundación de Investigaciones Económicas Latinoamericanas (Foundation of Latin American Economic Research, FIEL), available at: <www.fiel.org>.

42   See Féliz 2007; Féliz 2009a.

43   See Calvo et al. 2003. For example, Kalantzis 2004 explains that flagging exports caused the crisis. While sluggish exports are one of the elements behind the crisis, they are not their cause. See Féliz 2007.

44   See Féliz 2009a; Féliz 2011.

45   See Féliz 2009a.

labour costs compared with the rest of the world.[46] The nominal exchange rate
was devalued by 40 percent in January 2002 but then entered into an uncon-
trollable spin, reaching 200 percent nominal devaluation by the end of the first
quarter of 2002, after which it stabilised.

How Neoliberal Restructuring Created the Structural Foundations of Neo-Developmentalism

Without changing Argentina's peripheral position within the circuit of global
capital,[47] this process did allow dominant fractions within the capitalist class,
such as the export-oriented, transnational, and concentrated capitals in the
mining and agricultural sectors, to place themselves in a hegemonic position.[48]
This position would allow them to control and orient the process of valorisation and accumulation of capital in the local economy.[49]

---

46   See Shaikh 1991; Féliz 2009a. Rising productivity was the other side of the coin of increas-
     ing OCC (Féliz 2011) since as Marx explained rising OCC is the expression of such a pro-
     cess. See Marx 2000.

47   Argentina's capitalist economy can be characterised as peripheral and dependent. This
     implies at least two elements. First, the economy has a low level of development of its
     productive forces in comparison with the main economies (such as those of the G8).
     Second, the development of capitalist relations in such an economy creates particular
     relations in production and circulation of value giving way to especially high levels of
     dependence on foreign capital in different forms. See Marini 1973; 1979.

48   According to Ortiz and Schorr, the leading industrial conglomerates and enterprises
     organised in the Unión Industrial Argentina (Argentine Industrial Union, UIA) began to
     demand an exit from the CP already by 1998. Together with Basualdo, they stress the fact
     that the UIA with other business groups related to export and import competing activities
     constituted a bloc within the dominant class. They confronted the privatised enterprises
     and foreign banks and corporations who preferred the alternative of dollarisation of the
     economy. While we agree that interests within the dominant classes grew more divergent
     as the crisis deepened, we think that the resulting alternative (devaluation) was forced
     by the structural tendencies: falling relative real unit labour costs, fleeing capital, falling
     demand, and plummeting profitability. The main beneficiaries of the exit from the CP
     were the same sectors that grew during the neoliberal phase. For more information, see
     Ortiz and Schorr 2007; Basualdo 2006.

49   In the process that had begun in the seventies, big local and foreign capitals, especially
     those tied to the agro-industrial and mining export-oriented complex, displaced local,
     industrial, mid-sized firms from control of the process of capital accumulation. See
     Basualdo 2006.

The fall of the CP came about as the result of the contradictory tendencies of capitalist development in Argentina. The convergence of the successful model of capital accumulation (GDP growth based upon rising labour productivity and increasing OCC) with political developments (the recomposition of labour) created the material preconditions for the crisis. However, while the crisis of the CP presented itself as the exhaustion of neoliberalism in Argentina,[50] it did not in fact lead to its definitive end but rather its recomposition.[51] From 2002 onwards, neo-developmentalism has allowed the dominant classes to recreate their hegemony by building on the foundations laid during the neoliberal phase.[52] In particular, the neo-developmentalist project retains two major structural elements of neoliberalism: the plundering of common goods via an extractivist model of development and the super-exploitation of labour.

First, in the post-2002 era, the exploitation and export of primary products from the mining and agricultural sectors became one of the main sources of surplus value in the form of absolute and relative rent.[53] Rent appropriated by landowners jumped from 6,514 million constant pesos in 1991 to 21,600 million constant pesos in 2004. Primary production grew 31 percent between 1993 and 2003, coming to represent 9.9 percent of nominal GDP by 2003. Exports of primary commodities (such as soya bean) and manufactured commodities (such as soya oil) reached 10.8 percent of GDP and 74 percent of total exports that same year, becoming the main source of foreign currency. In particular, soya exports have grown exponentially. Between 2002 and 2010 they averaged 220 percent more tonnes than in 1991–2000, according to the Ministry of Agriculture, Stockbreeding and Fishing (Ministerio de Agricultura, Ganadería y Pesca). Total exports grew 123 percent in the same period.

Second, precarious employment remained the source of a significant portion of surplus-extraction. In other words, the new capitalist strategy after the crisis of the CP retained super-exploitation of labour as a means of its valorisation. In 2009, 35 percent of the salaried workforce remained informal

---

50   See Lascano 2001.

51   See Castorina in this volume.

52   Azpiazu and Schorr 2010b, p. 229 state that the year 2002 expressed the breaking point of the hegemony of the pre-eminence of financial valorisation and structural adjustment, beginning the transition towards a new, imprecise, and uncertain regime of accumulation.

53   See definition of absolute and differential rent in the introduction to this volume, based on Iñigo Carrera 2007a. For further discussion see the review by Campbell 2002 and chapters by Grinberg and Starosta and Purcell in this volume.

workers, more than 20 percent of the working class lived below the poverty line.[54] Average wages have remained at their lowest levels in 30 years.[55]

These two elements of continuity between neoliberalism and neo-developmentalism have produced new economic dynamics in the first decade of the twenty-first century, expressed in higher profit rates and a devalued real exchange rate. On the one hand, the orientation of capital towards production in rent-producing export commodities together with the persistence of historically low levels of wages has meant even higher profit rates. In 2006–7, for example, profit rates were 16.6 percent compared to 10.4 percent in 1993.[56] Today, profit rates are even higher for export-oriented capital. On the other hand, the combination of a higher level of relative productivity obtained during the 1990s and the persistence of high levels of labour flexibility (and thus low relative real unit labour costs) has allowed for the real exchange rate (RER) to remain at relatively competitive values: the RER was 78.9 percent more competitive (devalued in real terms) during 2009 than in the mid-nineties (1998).[57] In fact, RER competitiveness is the other face of a relatively high ratio of productivity to real wages. Based on these structural conditions capital's ability to expand has remained strong since mid-2002, even if challenged by the dynamics of class struggle.

Neo-developmentalism not only advanced due to changes to the structural conditions at the domestic level but to significant changes in the world market. Two of these changes were particularly important for Argentina. First, China became a major trading partner. In fact, Argentina's trade with China jumped from a yearly average 2.2 percent of total exports between 1990 and 2001 to 7.7 percent of total exports between 2002 and 2008, while during the same period imports from China surged from an average 3.3 percent of total imports to 8 percent. This evolution was in line with the evolution of China's trade: while China's exports went from 1.8 percent of total world exports in 1990 to 4.3 percent in 2001 and 9.5 percent in 2009, imports to China from the rest of the world went from 1.4 percent of total world imports in 1990 to 3.8 percent in 2001 and 8 percent in 2009.[58]

---

54   Féliz, López and Fernández 2010.

55   We understand super-exploitation of labour in the sense of Marini 1973.

56   Profit rates are estimated as the ratio of net profits of the top 500 corporations to their total circulating capital (total sales minus net profits). See the INDEC's National Survey of Big Enterprises.

57   See Féliz 2009a on the higher rate of relative productivity. The RER was estimated as the ratio of the nominal rate for the US dollar (pesos per US dollar) to the ratio between the producer price indexes of both the US and Argentina.

58   CEI.

Second, the growing weight of soya and mineral exports allowed Argentina's capitalist class to profit from growing commodity prices: in 2009 Argentina's terms of trade were 40 percent higher than the average of the period 1990–2001. This change allowed Argentina's economy to find a significant space for exports in the neo-developmentalist phase: total exports of goods and services grew from 6.9 percent of GDP in 1993 to more than 21.3 percent in 2009, while net exports (exports minus imports) of goods and services went from a deficit of 2.4 percent of GDP in 1993 to a surplus of over 5.3 percent in 2009.

The Political Foundations of Argentina's Neo-Developmentalism

The transition from neoliberalism to neo-developmentalism in Argentina was no easy task for the dominant classes. During the first months of 2002, it was not at all clear for anyone (not even for the dominant fractions of capital) which direction the development process would take in the context of extreme economic and political uncertainty. The progressive unfolding of a neo-developmentalist strategy was in fact not the result of a planned transition but rather the outcome of an articulation of the new structural restrictions and political challenges posed by the popular movement. In a sense, in the unfolding of the neo-developmentalist project dominant classes have recognised the renewed composition of the working class, the need to accommodate, albeit partially, some of its demands, and the limits they pose on their strategic goals. The successful consolidation of the neo-developmentalist strategy is an indication of the hegemonic construction of the dominant classes.

In the last years of the CP, the succession of misplaced attempts to solve the severe economic and political crisis led to increasing social unrest that resulted in the resignation of the Minister of the Economy on 19 December 2001, followed by the president, De la Rúa, the next day. The social mobilisation during the second semester of 2001 not only ended the CP but also displaced four presidents in 15 days. The interim president, elected by Congress in January 2002, Peronist Eduardo Duhalde, was able to resolve the financial and exchange rate crisis with little cost to the biggest corporations that were the main beneficiaries of the new policies.[59] The policy package included currency devaluation, imposition of export taxes, partial public debt default, a price freeze on privatised public services, and 'asymmetric pesification'. This last element implied that the dollar debts of big private debtors within the financial system were turned into peso debts (avoiding the cost of devaluation)

---

59   IDEF-CTA 2002; Basualdo, Lozano and Schorr 2002.

while at the same time the state compensated the banks for any losses by giving them new public debt bonds.[60]

At the same time, the combination of mild political repression and the creation of new social programmes allowed the government to stay a steady course
in the midst of unprecedented social mobilisation. Duhalde's government created the most comprehensive income support programme in all of Argentina's
history: the *Plan Jefes y Jefas de Hogar* (Heads of Household Programme, JyJDH).[61]
This programme extended income support to almost two million direct beneficiaries within the first few months of 2002. A number serves to illustrate the
magnitude of the programme: in May 2003 the number of beneficiaries represented 81.6 percent of the unemployed.[62] While the amount of the benefit going
to each household was extremely low (only about US$40 a month) it provided
a minimum income in a context where real wages had fallen by 20 percent
between the last quarter of 2001 and the first quarter of 2002. Unemployment
touched 25 percent of the active population, and 40 percent within the youth.

The JyJDH sought to calm down political unrest by dismantling popular organisation and to maintain the Duhalde government's tenuous grip on
office.[63] However, the repression of a mobilisation by the *piquetero* movement
on 26 June 2002 resulted in the death of two young militants of the Movimiento
de Trabajadores Desocupados Anibal Verón (Movement of Unemployed
Workers Anibal Verón, MTD Anibal Verón) and ended the chances of continuation for Duhalde's government.[64] Presidential elections were called for early
2003; Néstor Kirchner, a member of the same party as Duhalde, the Peronist
Justicialist Party was elected. By May 2003 the pieces had been put into place
for the implementation of a new regime of accumulation.

The termination of the CP laid the basis for short-run economic growth by
adjusting the ratios of variable capital versus constant capital (thus enhancing
profitability) and productive capital versus financial capital (thus favouring
productive accumulation). Now that economic growth rates had recovered,

---

60   LASFRC 2002.

61   Féliz and Pérez 2007.

62   Ibid.

63   Dinerstein et al. 2008.

64   The MTDs were new organisations born in the 1990s. Since traditional labour unions
      and left-wing parties would not represent the mounting ranks of the unemployed, in the
      mid-1990s the MTDs multiplied as new organisational forms of struggle. The MTD Anibal
      Verón was an archetypical organisation that employed direct action (roadblocks) as a
      main means of struggle, base democracy, and class independence. Later in the decade
      several left-wing parties as well as the CTA decided to include the MTDs in their strategies.
      See Svampa and Pereyra 2003; Stratta and Barrera 2009.

the newly elected Kirchner government set out to create the conditions for the reproduction and expansion of its political power. In fact, while the Kirchner government always stressed that the recovery of economic growth was the result of their economic policy, GDP had been rising long before Kirchner was elected. By the first quarter of 2003, GDP was growing at a five percent annual rate. This meant that the state-form had to change to allow for a new correlation of social forces that was born during the neoliberal phase.[65]

Kirchner consolidated a political alliance with a fraction of the labour movement bureaucracy (mostly within the CGT, whose new leadership had participated in the struggles against privatisation in the late 1990s) and local capital's hegemonic fractions (of both national and transnational origin). Within the CGT, a new wave of grassroots activism put pressure on the bureaucratic leadership to make demands on the government.[66] This mobilisation also had an important impact on the formation of new grassroots movements. For instance, there was a rise of young activists who were involved in new social movements and organisations that had sprung up all around the country in movements of unemployed workers, movements of women, community radio stations, etc.[67] To gain the CGT's support, the government took steps to partially recover real wages that had been depressed by the devaluation's effect on domestic prices (particularly on basic consumption goods). In the first 12 months after devaluation in 2002, consumer prices jumped by 41 percent while food prices went up by 58 percent.[68] The government put forward a new labour policy that promoted the signing of collective agreements and decreed several wage hikes and increases in the minimum wage for formal workers. In 2004, the number of formal collective agreements doubled compared to the average of the previous ten years, and was 20 percent higher than the year before.[69]

The combination of demands from below, and pro-active policies from above, created the conditions for a limited amelioration of working conditions within the formal segment of the labour force.[70] While wages increased significantly from 2002 to 2007, in 2007 real wages for formal-sector workers in the

---

65   Poulantzas 1979.

66   Etchemendy and Berins Collier 2007; Basualdo 2010; Prensa de Frente 2005.

67   Lobato and Suriano 2003.

68   To avoid confusion it is important to recall that the devaluation of Argentina's currency implies the increase in the peso price of the US dollar. This means that the domestic prices of all dollar-denominated commodities (such as exported food stuffs and fuels) increase when the domestic currency is devalued.

69   Ministerio de Trabajo, Empleo y Seguridad Social 2005.

70   Neffa 2008.

private sphere were just 6.7 percent over their 2001 levels, while for precarious workers real wages were still 22.4 percent lower and state employees were 28.4 percent below their 2001 levels.[71] The official unemployment rate also fell rapidly between 2002 and 2005, but high levels of informal and precarious work continued to prevail.[72]

Regarding the local bourgeoisie, the government followed an active policy to garner the support of a significant (and politically relevant) portion of the import-competing manufacturing and export-oriented business class.[73] On the one hand, the decision to maintain a high and stable real exchange rate through the central bank's massive purchase of dollars and the unofficial policy of wage ceilings was the main instrument to preserve the profitability of the capitalist class as a whole.[74] Wage ceilings were the main macroeconomic element of the new labour policy and were aimed at containing wage growth within the growth of labour's productivity. The government proposed a limit to wage increases equal to 19 percent for the year 2006 and 16.5 percent for 2007. While the official inflation rate was 9.8 percent in 2006 (down from 12.3 percent in 2005) many observers (including workers within INDEC) claimed actual inflation to be at least twice as much.[75] In 2007, the rapid improvement in labour's income hit a ceiling.[76] The combination of successful repression of non-institutionalised conflicts, tight control (at times violent) by union leaders of grassroots movements, and the difficulties in creating political alternatives constricted the ability of workers to claim a larger share of value added. In 2008 labour's participation in value added stagnated. In addition, the state supported capital's profitability with a combination of direct and indirect subsidies and renewed impetus of public investment in infrastructure projects.[77]

The local bourgeoisie and the CGT were the strongholds of the government's societal coalition. However, Kirchner was elected by only 22 percent of eligible voters; he needed to build a wider support base. He came in second place in the first round of the 2003 elections, after the neoliberal candidate Carlos Menem (another Peronist who served as president from 1989 to 1999). However, since

---

71   It is important to clarify that super-exploitation of labour does not imply that wages
      necessarily stagnate or fall. While wages grew in the neo-developmentalist phase, the
      prevalence of labour precarisation meant that many workers were still earning below the
      minimum wage or even below the poverty line.

72   Rameri et al. 2008.

73   Azpiazu and Schorr 2010b.

74   Ministerio de Economía y Producción 2007; Frenkel 2005.

75   ATE-INDEC 2008.

76   Féliz 2008.

77   Ministerio de Economía y Producción 2007.

Menem desisted from participating in the second round, Kirchner was named president on 25 May 2003.[78] In an adequate reading of the political situation, the newly appointed president moved forward on a political programme that discursively rejected neoliberalism and allowed him to win additional constituents. In actual policy, the government rolled back some of the policies of the 1990s – particularly, trials for human rights violators during the last dictatorship, and reassertion of state ownership over some of the companies that had been privatised in the 1990s, such as the Correo Argentino (Argentine Postal Service) in 2003, Aguas Argentinas (Argentine Waters, the water and sanitation company of Greater Buenos Aires) in 2006, Aerolíneas Argentinas (Argentine Airlines, the national airline) in 2008, and so on. These changes won the government the support of wide sectors of the middle classes and of some popular organisations, particularly a significant sector of Madres and Abuelas de Plaza de Mayo (Mothers and Grandmothers of May Plaza) and some *piquetero* movements such as the Federación de Tierra y Vivienda (Federation of Land and Housing, FTV), a member of the CTA.[79]

The final element in the new government's strategy for political survival in turbulent times was to create a new generation of social policies.[80] These policies included the bifurcation of the JyJDH in 2005 into two separate programmes aimed at those deemed to be unemployable (generally, single women with children) and to those regarded as potentially employable (married men).[81] Under the *Plan Familias* (Families Plan), beneficiaries would receive a monetary incentive to return home by relinquishing work duties established under the former JyJDH and in return, send their kids to school and submit them to periodic medical check-ups. The other programme, *Seguro de Empleo y Formación* (Employment and Training Insurance) paid beneficiaries to learn trades and to look for work. In both cases, the unspoken objective was to dismantle the nationwide network of movements of unemployed workers that had been able to use the former JyJDH as a means of mobilisation and organisation.[82] The MTDs were able to reap economic resources from the government in the form

---

78   Bruschtein 2003.

79   The Madres and Abuelas de Plaza de Mayo are two of the most influential human rights organisations in Argentina. Born during the last dictatorship, they have fought for truth and punishment of those responsible for human rights violations during the period 1976– 83. FTV is one of the most important territorial organisations born in the 1980s in the struggles for living conditions in the neighbourhoods of the greater Buenos Aires. See Stratta and Barrera 2009.

80   Dinerstein et al. 2008.

81   Pérez 2005; Pérez and Féliz 2010.

82   Golbert 2004; Castorina in this volume.

of social allowances and financial assistance for socio-economic subsistence projects. These resources allowed the movements not only to improve the living conditions of their members but also worked as organisational means to increase their ability to make effective demands on the state. The JyJDH was the pinnacle of such processes. After the assassination of Kosteki and Santillán in 2002, the state begun to regain control of the socio-political situation, dividing and co-opting a significant part of the movements of the unemployed.[83]

Argentina in the Neo-Developmentalist Stage: Protected Against All Odds?

The new structure of capital has provided Argentina's economy with the means to respond effectively to changing conditions in the world market. In fact, the aforementioned changes have allowed capital in Argentina to continue its expanded reproduction almost unharmed between 2008 and 2009 in the midst of the greatest crisis in the world's capitalist economy in almost 70 years. While the GDP of developed economies plummeted by 3 percent between 2008 and 2009, and peripheral countries such as Brazil contracted by 0.2 percent in 2009, Argentina's economy grew 6.7 percent in 2008 and 0.9 percent in 2009, recovering in 2010 to a projected 11 percent GDP growth rate.[84]

Several elements have to be brought to bear in order to comprehend these new developments.[85] First, for the first time in many decades Argentina has been able to sustain a significant surplus in its external balance of payments even while growth has been significant: compared to the year before, exports fell by 20 percent in 2009 while imports were reduced by 32 percent. On average, the current account surplus has been equivalent to four percent of GDP between 2002 and 2009. This situation has turned the external sector of the economy into a buffer against the contraction of world trade during the initial stages of the crisis from 2008 to 2009. Thus, while exports fell significantly in those years, so did imports, such that the contractive impact of crippling international trade remained moderate as net exports remained stable. Besides, the foreign exchange surplus allowed the Central Bank to accumulate international reserves, which jumped to more than US$50 billion by 2008. These

---

83   Stratta and Barrera 2009; Svampa and Pereyra 2003.

84   Statistics from Economic Commission for Latin America and the Caribbean (ECLAC), various years.

85   Féliz and López 2010a; 2010b.

reserves created a cushion to offset any possible outflow of speculative capital in the months of international turmoil during 2009.

Second, the devaluation of all forms of capital during and after the crisis of 2001–2 created ample space for capital's contradictions 'to move', for it created new sources of exploitation, recreated the means for pumping up aggregate demand, and significantly diluted the drainage of surplus value towards financial capital. In 2002 the (international) value of commodity production in Argentina fell by about 30 percent, increasing the international competitiveness of local capital. Meanwhile, through a process of debt default and renegotiation the public and private stock of debt fell significantly, reducing its weight on productive accumulation. Devaluation of variable capital (wages and salaries) between 2001 and 2002 was very important and created a buffer of extraordinary surplus value for the absorption of the effects of the upcoming international crisis.

Third, the state's financial situation improved greatly after 2002, creating the means for a pro-active, counter-cyclical policy in 2008–9. National public expenditure reached 31 percent of GDP in 2009. This expansion included several infrastructure programmes as well as social policy expenditures, which worked directly to enhance profitability, or indirectly to boost domestic aggregate demand in the context of falling external sales.

As the world financial and economic crisis quickly progressed, Argentina's dominant sectors demanded that the government promote policies for the improvement of their competitive position.[86] The new president, Cristina Fernández de Kircher (CFK), wife of former president Kirchner and faithful executor of the neo-developmentalist programme, was elected in late 2007. CFK introduced a controlled devaluation of the nominal exchange rate and more explicit caps on wage negotiations.

The main result of this policy was that wages stagnated for the first time since 2002,[87] which halted the falling exchange rate competitiveness (or rising relative real unit labour costs). At the same time, in the midst of the world food crisis in 2008, agricultural sectors of the dominant classes began a series of protests to push the government to reduce export taxes. In May 2008, the government had attempted to raise export taxes to increase fiscal revenue and to absorb the inflationary effect of higher crop prices due to crisis-ridden speculation in world commodities' markets. Crop producers responded with massive demonstrations and roadblocks.[88] After several weeks of protests, the

---

86   Féliz 2009b.
87   Lozano 2009.
88   Grigera 2009; Sartelli et al. 2008.

government was forced – in a divided vote in Congress – to back down from the increased export taxes.[89] This divided vote reflected the first important fracture in the alliance between the government and the dominant classes, which as a whole still back the current economic strategy.

As the impact of the crisis advanced and with the advancement of exporting fractions of the bourgeoisie, social movements that were born in the process of resistance to neoliberal rule increased their demands for public actions to protect the working people. The creation of the political space (*'Otro camino para superar la crisis'* or 'Another road to overcome the crisis') was a step in this direction. Integrated by the Frente Popular Darío Santillán (Popular Front Darío Santillán, FPDS), the collective Economistas de Izquierda (Economists from the Left, EDI), and the Bloque Piquetero Nacional (National Piquetero Block, BPN), amongst other groups, this movement began a series of actions and mobilisations to demand lower consumption taxes, wider income support for the unemployed and higher taxation of export-oriented firms.[90] The CTA also demanded that the working people not pay the cost of the crisis through a series of mobilisations, 'national days of struggle', and strikes.[91]

To maintain political support within this context of increasing political agitation, the changes in macroeconomic policy were coupled with the implementation of several programmes to control the negative impact of falling export demand and keep a lid on social unrest.[92] First, the government created the *Programa de Recuperación Productiva* (Programme of Productive Recovery, REPRO), which allowed troubled firms to receive subsidies on their payroll if they refrained from firing workers. Under REPRO, a firm could suspend workers, and pay reduced wages, while the state would cover the difference.[93]

Second, the government re-nationalised the pension system that had been privatised in the early 1990s.[94] Nationalisation implied the transfer without

---

89   *Página/12* 2008a.

90   See Katz et al. 2008; *Página/12* 2008b. For example, see the declaration *'No votes contra el pueblo'* ('Do not vote against the People') by the space 'Another path ...' that came out before the 28 June elections (Document 1 2009) and the *'Solicitud de audiencia con la Presidenta'* ('Demand for audience with the President') requested by several social movements on 24 July 2009 (*Prensa de Frente* 2009).

91   See, for example, the National Day of Struggle (*Día Nacional de Lucha*) of 22 April 2009 (CTA *de los Trabajadores* 2009a), the National Strike of 27 May 2009 (*Página/12* 2009), the statements by the CTA on 20 July 2009 (*Agencia CTA 2009*) or the National Day of Mobilisation (*Jornada Nacional de Mobilización*) of 7 August 2009 (CTA *de los Trabajadores* 2009b).

92   Pérez and Féliz 2010.

93   Lukín 2010.

94   Cufré 2008.

pay out of all the assets of the private pension funds to the state. The state not only appropriated those assets (including stocks in almost fifty of the most important companies in the country and a sizeable share of public debt bonds) but also regained control of the social security taxation that was formerly being directed to pension funds. This move allowed the government to increase domestic demand by raising the incomes of pensioners. In addition, re-nationalisation gave the government fiscal resources to cope with mounting public deficits without having to return to the international debt markets.

Third, in late 2009 the government created the *Asignación Universal a la Niñez* (Universal Benefit for Children) a new, more universal programme that provides benefit to adults with children and low-income with informal employment (wages under US$380 per month) or unemployed.[95] As of 2010 the plan served almost four million families with children. This subsidy was meant to reach those who are ineligible for other social benefits. However, the implementation of the programme implied the elimination of several other benefits for poor families (such as the *Plan Familias*), it was not generalised to the whole population was not unconditional.[96]

By late 2009, the economy had begun to recover. A few months into 2010, employment levels had recovered to their previous peak.[97] While ten years before Argentina's neoliberal economy was hit hard by worsening international conditions due to its own internal contradictions, neo-developmentalism seems to have provided the country with a significant cushion to soften the blow of the international crisis. The combination of modified internal structural conditions and a new form of the state – ready to respond to capital's demands but able to adapt politically to a renewed class composition – provided the general conditions for a successful displacement of the contradictions of capital accumulation.[98] Argentina's economy seems to have found a new path of successful capitalist accumulation without abandoning its dependent and peripheral character.

---

95   Barrera 2009.
96   Ibid.
97   Ministerio de Trabajo, Empleo y Seguridad Social 2010.
98   External transformations – such as the aforementioned role of China – also have been important in allowing Argentina to successfully navigate this crisis. In this article, however, we wish to stress the fundamental role of internal structural transformations.

Conclusion

Neoliberal rule in Argentina ended abruptly and violently in 2002, giving way to a new mode of reproduction of capitalist social relations. The neo-developmental form of capitalist development emerged as the supersession and paradoxical continuation of the process of capitalist restructuring that began in the 1970s. New political forces in action within a renewed and consolidated structure of the cycle of capital gave birth to a seemingly stable state-form. This new form of the state does not contradict the needs of dominant fractions of capital – to the contrary – but rather absorbs and contains in a conflictive manner the new forces and demands of a working people that has achieved a new political class composition.

Neo-developmentalism repeats two trends of the previous neoliberal stage: the successful (from the point of view of local dominant classes) structural transformation of the economy (transnationalisation based on plundering of common goods), and extreme exploitation of labour as a necessary element for successful capital valorisation. Both these elements were the fundamental bases upon which the main changes that constitute a new phase of capitalist development were introduced: a new form of the state that expresses – mainly through macroeconomic policy – the competitive needs of the leading fractions within the dominant classes and a new set of public policies to contain and channel a new form of social conflict (that resulted from the constitution of a new class composition of labour).

What is most important is that we can no longer speak of neoliberalisation in Argentina as an ongoing process. As a political programme of the dominant classes looking to establish a new stable pattern of valorisation and accumulation, neoliberalism has triumphed. However, such victory came about with two limitations. First, it did not overcome class conflict but has had to contain it in new ways. Second, neoliberalism did not alter Argentina's peripheral position in the world economy and thus it has not fully met the requirements for 'successful' capitalist development.

Capitalist hegemony in Argentina appears to be stronger now than it was in the mid-1990s – before the crisis of the Convertibility Plan – due to strong and stable conditions for the production and realisation of value. But in order to maintain political stability, capital has had to give in to some of labour's demands, reflected in the reforms to labour and social policies.

CHAPTER 4

The Reproduction of Democratic Neoliberalism in Argentina: Kirchner's 'Solution' to the Crisis of 2001

Emilia Castorina

The shift in policymaking that followed from the crisis of 2001 in Argentina has been largely promoted as a fundamental departure from neoliberalism. However, while much effort has been spent wrestling over whether this new era of 'national-popular' development[1] is 'post-neoliberal', capitalist concentration increased from 2003 to 2007 as the ten largest multinational corporations that accounted for 37 percent of GDP in 1997 came to account for 57 percent of GDP in 2007.[2] Despite an extraordinary average growth rate of 8 percent since 2003, income distribution between 2003 and 2007 remained even more uneven than in the 1990s, whereas the income gap between the richest and poorest 10 percent of society was 17.3 in 1992 and 28.3 in 1999, it was 35 by 2005.[3] The persistence (and increase) of social inequality and economic concentration casts some doubts, particularly, on how neoliberalism is (or should be) defined. If seen in a narrow sense of a rigid set of macroeconomic reforms, then it is plausible to argue that Argentina has moved beyond neoliberalism after the crisis of 2001. But, if neoliberalism is conceptualised as an ambitious project of social and political disciplining beyond the level of specific policies, then it has not been overcome.

As some critical Marxist scholars[4] whose work addresses debates on state and globalisation argue, neoliberalism is not merely an economic system but more properly 'a political response to the democratic gains that have been previously achieved by subordinated classes and which had become, in a new context and from capital's perspective, barriers to accumulation'.[5] The main target of neoliberal restructuring has thus been attacking worker's capacity to influence accumulation. Based on new mechanisms of 'accumulation by

---

1 See Kirchner and Di Tella 2003.

2 These are: YPF, Shell, Cargill, Molinos, Ford, Volkswagen, Telecom, Telefonica, Esso, and Carrefour.

3 See Lozano 2005, and 2007.

4 See Panitch and Gindin 2004; Harvey 2005; Gill 1995; Rude 2005.

5 Panitch and Gindin 2004, p. 21.

dispossession',[6] broadly understood as efforts to privatise key aspects of the reproduction of social relations, neoliberal restoration established a different kind of social control (or form of domination), where financial instability and economic insecurity replaced class compromises of the previous era of capitalism. The apparent failures in the economy have acted as signs for, and been crucial instruments of, capitalism's successful restructuring by reinforcing permanent forms of organisational assaults on unions.[7] Debt crises within particular countries (two-thirds of the members of the International Monetary Fund experienced a financial crisis after 1980, some more than twice, as in the case of Argentina) have been used to reorganise the internal social relations of production in such a way as to favour the further penetration of external capitals,[8] increase capital concentration and labour exploitation. Therefore, as the social reproduction of our societies was increasingly marketised, commodified, and linked to power structures over which working classes came to have little or no control, capitalist valorisation was increasingly reproduced *through* crises. As Rude explains, financial instability and economic turmoil are functional for disciplining world capitalism and social relations by means of punishing subordinated classes and nations for the damage caused by crises, which is usually directed away from the dominant classes and the centre.[9] This way, the burdens of a crisis tend to be borne less by financial capital in the form of lower profits, bank failures, and insolvencies (at least for the branches located at the centre) than by subordinated classes in the form of unemployment, poverty, job insecurity, and lower wages. As long as subordinated classes assume much of the risks while the private sector takes most of the profits, neoliberalism can be reproduced. In the terms of Gowan, 'every financial and economic blow-out has been successfully blamed upon its victims and has been used to destroy the earlier developmental strategies of countries plunged into crisis'.[10]

In this sense, 'democratic neoliberalism' – as distinguished from authoritarian forms of neoliberalism and 'neoliberal democracy' where the neoliberal aspect is only an adjective – is an attempt at political disempowerment of the subordinated classes and an institutional mechanism to explicitly preempt either progressive/distributive reforms or revolutionary changes without

---

6   See Harvey 2005.
7   See Gindin 2001.
8   See Harvey 2003.
9   See Rude 2005.
10   Gowan 1999, p. 126.

resorting to military or political repression.[11] Contrary to received wisdom, it does not involve 'less' state intervention but a different form of intervention based on an uneven politicisation of classes: subordinated classes and their social demands are expelled from the politico-institutional realm (as democracy is defined and promoted as a 'limited' game)[12] while the concentrated fractions of capital gain privileged access to state decision-making. The institutionalisation of the corporate power of capital under neoliberalism has been best captured by George Soros when claiming that 'markets vote everyday'.

According to Boron, this means that the most powerful economic actors raise their voice every day – in the stock markets and the valorisation of the dollar as well as in the bureaucratic centres of power – whose decisions and preferences are taken more seriously into consideration than those of the subordinated classes since even progressive or social democratic governments are very well aware of the unlikely prospects of resisting the pressures and extortions of capital. Through economic blackmail, investment strikes, and threats of capital flight the market gives shape to another, and certainly more powerful, decision-making process, detached from the demands of subordinated classes.[13]

Popular sectors and their demands are to some extent reduced to struggle outside the state and ironically the new left seized this as a revolutionary opportunity to 'think without the state'.[14] Meanwhile, on the other side of the class divide, very active states and highly politicised sets of business sectors are hard at work to secure the rights and conditions of economic growth.

---

11   Placed in comparative perspective, during the 1990s Argentina combined neoliberal economic reform and democracy in a way that was virtually unparalleled in Latin America. For instance, even though Bolivia maintained a democratic regime, market reforms were implemented with harsh labour repression and a state of siege. In countries with more stable democracies, such as Uruguay, Brazil, or Venezuela, economic reforms were slower and less extensive. In other words, among full democratic cases Argentina carried out the most rapid and extensive market reforms; and among the most radical cases of market reforms (Chile, Bolivia, Mexico), it was the most democratic. See Levistky 2003.

12   Indeed, as part of the strategy of state reform and transformation of power relations, the neoliberal project of democratisation in the South involved a re-definition of democracy in which a limited and politically narrow vision of democracy as formal rules (polyarchy) prevailed over more social and distributive forms. Limited democracy was conceived as a new form of intervention to pre-empt more radical change by incorporating broad popular forces in electoral participation, while guaranteeing continuity with the restructuring policies of its military predecessors, see Gills et al. 1993.

13   See Boron 2006.

14   For example Holloway 2002a.

The specificity of democratic neoliberalism is not so much about a 'retreat' of the state as it is of labour since powerful business sectors have succeeded in warding off the intrusion or 'intervention' of subaltern classes in economic policy-making. As such, it is an attempt at locking-in the power gains of business while locking-out or depoliticising the claims for greater social rights or income distribution made by the working and popular classes.

Economic insecurity, in this context, becomes a key disciplinary mechanism within labour markets. In the terms of Harvey, the neoliberal determination to transfer all responsibility for well-being back to the individual has deleterious effects:

> As the state withdraws from welfare provision and diminishes its role in arenas such as health care, public education and social services, which were once so fundamental to embedded liberalism, it leaves larger and larger segments of the population exposed to impoverishment. The social safety net is reduced to a bare minimum in favour of a system that emphasizes personal responsibility. Personal failure is generally attributed to personal failings, and the victim is too often blamed.[15]

In Argentina, these kinds of social safety nets favoured a neo-populist integration of popular classes into the state as a new form of popular disciplining. To some extent, what changed under neoliberalism was the mechanism for absorbing and reintegrating the lower classes. While old (Peronist)[16] populism was based on a corporatist integration of social and labour rights and universal measures of distribution, neoliberal populism is based on more focused strategies of poverty alleviation. As Roberts argues, neoliberal policy adjustments may facilitate the provision of more selective, targeted material benefits to specific groups, which can be used as building blocks for local clientelist exchanges. Targeted programmes have a more modest fiscal impact than universal measures, but their political logic can be functionally equivalent, as both attempt to exchange material rewards for political support. Moreover,

---

15   See Harvey 2005, p. 76.

16   Peronism is a political movement that first emerged in the 1940s around the charismatic leadership of Peron, and probably represents the paradigmatic example of party-movement incorporation of popular and working classes into the state through the legalisation and institutionalisation of labour organisations. The General Confederation of Labour (Confederación General del Trabajo, CGT) gained monopoly of representation over preexisting, well-established anarchist, socialist, and communist-controlled trade union organisations. See Collier and Collier 1991.

Besides their lower cost, targeted programs have the advantage of being direct and highly visible, allowing government leaders to claim political credit for material gains. By allowing leaders to personally inaugurate local projects or 'deliver' targeted benefits, selective programs are highly compatible with the personalistic leader-mass relationships of populism. As ... selective incentives provide more powerful inducements to collective action than do public goods, selective benefits may create stronger clientelist bonds than universal benefits, especially politically obscure ones like permanent price subsidies and exchange controls.[17]

As Taylor argues when describing the recent shift in policymaking in Latin America, Argentina's reconstruction after 2001 does not represent a fundamental break from the political objectives of the neoliberal project given the path-dependent qualities of neoliberal structuring: 'By recasting institutional structures and the distribution of resources, neoliberalism reshaped power relations across the continent in an enduring manner that has frustrated the aims and strategies of many political movements that sought to break with the market ontology of neoliberalism'.[18] In the case of Argentina, the political viability of neoliberalism during the 1990s was facilitated by the recasting of the old populist coalition and by a series of political ('informal') institutions such as patronage politics, clientelism, and other strategies for integrating the poor into the power structures of Peronism, which were revitalised by Kirchner as key strategies to cope with the new political challenges emanating from 'below'. By resorting to the same (but reinvigorated) structures of domination that made market reforms plausible in the first half of the 1990s, Kirchner was able to avoid any significant distribution of power and wealth to the 'losers' of the crisis.

In this sense, Kirchner's reproduction of concentrated forms of accumulation, which was based on a growth strategy that differed from the orthodox policy of the 1990s at the same time that it revived the same power structures that prevented subordinated classes from effectively participating in a fairer redistribution of income, does not represent a genuine break with the neoliberal era. At best, it is similar to Joseph Stiglitz's notion of 'post-Washington Consensus', which captured the need to supersede the ideological dogmatism of the early stages of neoliberalism by means of more pragmatic policymaking. The new pragmatism had to be capable of replacing the rhetoric of state retrenchment with the notion of a proactive state able to secure

---

17   Roberts 1996, p. 91.

18   Taylor 2009, pp. 35–6.

market efficiency while incorporating social development and 'empowerment of the poor'.[19] Indeed, although capital accumulation strategies in Argentina have varied over time (in the 1990s economic growth was tied to structural indebtedness, while in the 2000s export-led growth was based on a discount of foreign debt), the nature of the current post-convertibility macroeconomic regime should not be misconstrued as 'anti'-neoliberal. Instead, it should be seen as a pragmatic – and certainly successful – strategy aimed at stabilising the economy after the collapse of the financial system and the default on the external debt within the new context of the commodities boom in the world market. Not only had some of these policies already been implemented in other export-oriented market economies, but more importantly, the structural power of the private sector and the concentrated fractions of capital (multinational corporations) remained untouched in the period 2003–7. In order to explain how democratic neoliberalism as an effective strategy of political disempowerment of subordinated classes was reproduced in the period 2003–7, it is important to understand what created the crisis in the first place.

The Contradictions of Democratic Neoliberalism in Argentina

Democratic neoliberalism is based on a contradiction not always easy to resolve between a logic of integration and a logic of exclusion; that is, between the political form of universal freedom and the anti-democratic structure of inequality in a market-based society.[20] To some extent, the historical forms of democratic capitalism are necessarily contradictory because there is a constitutive tension within capitalist democracy as a system of power that exists to uphold and enforce exploitative relations while granting universal civic and political rights at the same time. Democracy not only means the right to vote, but also, and more problematically, the right to conduct class struggle and/ or politically organise social demands, since freedom of association is, for instance, a crucial element of even the most minimalist and procedural form of polyarchy. Indeed, the period 1998–2002 in Argentina can be described as one of increasing politicisation of social demands from 'below' based on a series of new social movements (particularly, the unemployed – *piqueteros* – but also teachers, public employees, independent trade unions, and small rural producers) whose common call to resist market policies ultimately resulted in the famous slogan '*Que se vayan todos!*' ('Out with them all!') in 2001. If articu-

---

19   See Stiglitz 2002.
20   For example, Wood 1995; Boron 2006.

lating the inherent contradiction between democracy and capitalism involves, to use the classic formulation of Gramsci and Poulantzas, the state's capacity to effectively function as the factor of political organisation of dominant classes and as the factor of political disorganisation (or fragmentation) of subaltern classes, then it is key to understand why the state failed in this task in the period 1998–2001 in Argentina and how it recomposed this capacity after 2003.

The neoliberal alliance coming to power in 1990 represented the most powerful sectors of Argentina's civil society, including traditional sectors of local economic power. It was a complex intermingling of multinational and domestic capital,[21] external creditors, technocrats of the new orthodoxy, and the Peronist trade union bureaucracy. This alliance had accumulated so much decision-making authority in the period 1990–5 that it was able to suppress any opposition while 'limiting the ability of various institutions to exercise control over the government in the democratic system'.[22] In turn, 'this concentration of decision-making power allowed the executive to negotiate with all the structures of power'.[23] As extensively argued,[24] the transformation and adaptation of Peronism within the Partido Justicialista (Justicialist Party, PJ) – the traditional political expression of labour in electoral politics – was crucial for the viability of market reforms.[25] After all, it was President Carlos Menem's (1989–99) overtures to Peronism's traditional adversaries in the business community and the liberal political establishment that paved the way for a consensually-based neoliberal restructuring. The economic policy-making institutions of the Peronist government of Menem became veritable revolving doors for appointees of the economic elite.[26] As Gibson argues, after almost a

---

21   For instance, among the domestic and foreign corporations who controlled newly privatised state assets (thus appropriating and concentrating value mostly through the rent of oil, water, and communications), Argentine capital led the way with 40 percent, followed by Spain (15 percent), US (12 percent), Italy (9 percent), and France (7 percent).

22   Schvarzer 1998, p. 69.

23   Ibid.

24   See for example, Levistky 2003; Gibson 1997; Roberts 1996.

25   Indeed, through the 1980s Argentina seemed to be an unlikely case for radical and sustainable neoliberal reforms given the strong opposition by traditional Peronist unions (CGT), whose 13 general strikes made governability for Alfonsín (1983–9) very difficult. Alfonsín had to resign in the midst of a hyperinflation crisis and popular lootings triggered by the PJ.

26   For instance, in 1989, Menem appointed Miguel Roig, the former president of multinational Bunge y Born, as the first minister of economy. Bunge y Born was Argentina's sole multinational corporation, a company associated with the mainly anti-Peronist sectors of the business community. Roig was later replaced by Néstor Rapanelli, the company's

century of ruling by electoral fraud, coercion, and military governments – all
of which gave way to a long pattern of social conflict and recurrent authoritarianism – business and conservative elites came to invest seriously in electoral
politics for the first time.[27]

Some scholars correctly defined this process of the 1990s as 'conservative
populism', since neoliberal restructuring involved not the wholesale strengthening or weakening but the recasting of the old populist/industrial coalition,
shifting the balance of power within the policy coalition away from those
sectors which fostered social welfare 'towards the more concentrated and
internationally competitive sectors of business and those parts of the labour
movement that were linked to those sectors [electricity, telecommunications,
oil, natural gas and railroad] and were able to gain economic and political
benefits from the decentralisation of the labour movement and the flexibilisation of industry-labour relations'.[28] As Etchemendy argues, rather than being
unambiguous losers from market reform, some key industrial and labour
actors within the old import-substitution industrialisation coalition were
favoured by the government and brought into the liberalising coalition.[29] For
some Peronist unions affiliated with the Confederación General del Trabajo
(General Confederation of Labour, CGT), it involved granting the workers
rights to purchase shares in the privatised companies and a privileged position
in the private pension funds markets while preserving labour's role in admin-
istering the health-care system.[30] As a result, 'compensatory policies biased

---

chief executive officer. And finally, in 1991, the ministry was assigned to Domingo Cavallo,
a prominent liberal economist who became Menem's economic czar. Cavallo had also
been the military government's Central Bank president and promoted the nationalisation
of the private sector's external debt in 1982.

27   See Gibson 1997. The elite was mainly composed of capitals that benefited from the
'nationalisation' of the private debt in 1982, a process that transferred the burdens of an
illegitimate debt to Argentine citizens and institutions, including foreign banks located
in Argentina (Citibank, First Boston, Chase Manhattan, Bank of America, Banca di Italia,
Bank of London, French Bank, Deutche Bank), local banks (Río, Quilmes, Galicia), multinational companies (Esso, IBM, Ford, Mercedez Benz, Pirelli) and local businesses
(Perez Companq, Macri, Bulgueron y Bridas, Techint, Fortabath, Pez Carmona, Soldati,
Celulosa). See Basualdo 2001.

28   Gibson 1996, p. 356.

29   See Etchemendy 2005.

30   This has been broadly defined as 'neo-corporatism'. As Viviana Patroni argues, 'regardless of his assault on labour rights and his not-always-cordial relationship with the CGT,
Menem invested considerable political effort in avoiding a final breakdown in the relationship between the government and the labour sector within the party. This certainly

toward the unions and workers who remain in the formal sector cemented a strong insider/outsider divide within the working class'[31] as unemployed, laid-off workers, and urban informal workers, mostly from the retail and service sectors, were for the most part left without representation.[32]

The successful adaptation of the PJ to the neoliberal era in the 1990s was therefore based on its extraordinary capacity to redefine its relationship with organised labour by dismantling traditional mechanisms of union participation and replacing its union-based linkages with clientelist linkages. In a context of working class decline and increasing unemployment,

> The consolidation of clientelist links created new bases upon which the PJ could sustain its ties to the urban working and lower classes. Clientelist organizations are better suited than unions to appeal to the heterogeneous strata of urban unemployed, self-employed and informal sector workers generated by de-industrialization. In urban zones characterized by high structural unemployment, unions tend to be marginal or nonexistent, and corporate channels of representation are therefore ineffective. A territorial organization, and especially one based on the distribution of particularistic benefits, can be more effective in such a context.[33]

Indeed, the populist logic of democratic neoliberalism in Argentina during the 1990s was one of nurturing governors and mayors with as many state resources as possible to exchange 'favours' or loyalties with their clients as a key to governability. These *caudillos* played a key role in the policy success of the 1990s since the PJ's legislative dominance 'was the consequence of the strategic use of positive and negative agenda control'.[34] In their classic study, Gibson and Calvo demonstrate how the party bosses of the interior provinces, Peronism's 'peripheral coalition', were able to secure advantageous fiscal transfers in exchange for supporting Menem's market-oriented policies. Patronage politics and clientelism were *integral* to the political rationality and sustainability of

---

included maintaining some of the corporatist prerogatives so central to the labour leadership'. Patroni 2001, p. 270.

31   Etchemendy and Palermo 1998, p. 65.

32   Given the monopoly of representation of the CGT, alternative unions such as Argentine Workers' Central Union (Central de Trabajadores Argentinos, CTA) or other leftist ones had no legal status to bargain at any level.

33   Levitsky 2005, p. 195.

34   See Jones and Hwang 2005.

market reforms as the timing of the reforms conformed to the governing party's need to maintain winning electoral coalitions.[35] Indeed, postponing public sector employment cuts in the provincial public sector well after Menem's 1995 re-election, particularly in politically overrepresented and therefore vote rich peripheral regions where public spending and patronage are key to provide support to the governing party, while increasing subsidy flows from the central to the provincial government coffers – total federal transfers to the provinces more than doubled between 1990–5 – gave shape to a form of democratic neoliberalism based on 'another institutionalisation', as famously captured by O'Donnell. In the new institutional configuration the viability of market reforms came to depend on the PJ's capacity to sustain a system of territorial power – known as 'brown' or 'neo-feudalised' areas – in which popular sectors became integrated into systems of privatised power, the 'personalistic machines' that anxiously depend on 'the prebends they could extract from the national and the local state agencies'.[36]

As welfare was no longer seen as a set of universal rights, but rather as either individual opportunities or, in this case, 'favours' by local politicians, the strategic replacement of the socialised provision of public goods with privatised forms and targeted programmes for the poor (such as *Plan Trabajar* or *Plan Vida*), resulted in the development of a social assistance apparatus or safety net that enabled the PJ to reproduce forms of concentrated accumulation at very low 'social' costs while nurturing their political machine at the same time. As state-based material resources became the dominant currency of exchange both between local leaders and *punteros* (political brokers), and between *punteros* and brokers in poor urban zones, Peronist identities became closer to those of 'clients' than workers, ultimately pointing to the daily politics of domination in the poverty enclaves where Peronist brokers, given their privileged access to state resources as members of the governing party, emerged as key actors in the problem-solving networks of lower classes.[37]

This strategy of popular integration effectively reduced the space for lower-class mobilisations against key economic policies in the period 1990–5 and it also helped to create a popular political constituency for Menem's successful re-election. Indeed, under Menem's leadership the PJ oriented its extensive informal networks of clientelism and patronage-based relations towards the goal of maximising its share of the vote. This strategic shift resulted in an overwhelming electoral victory in 1995, which was mostly based on disproportion-

---

35   See Gibson and Calvo 2000.
36   O'Donnell 1993, p. 1360.
37   See Auyero 2000.

ate support of the less well-off sectors of society as poor households came to depend increasingly on state relief programmes and public jobs for their basic survival. But the integrative capacity of the PJ also came under increasing pressure during Menem's second term in office given the fiscal restraints of the economic recession that began in 1998, which was further aggravated by the rise of a non-Peronist party to the presidency (De la Rua 1999–2001).

The model of accumulation that underwrote economic growth during the 1990s was structurally problematic. Based on the accumulation of debt without the development of the productive capacity to meet financial commitments, it lacked any strategy for creating a productive economic base.[38] In the context of the convertibility regime, the Argentine peso had become seriously overvalued, undermining the ability of local producers to export, and, in so doing, diminishing the hard currency export earnings needed to service foreign debt. Indeed, the combination of trade opening with an overvalued exchange rate resulted in a chronic trade balance deficit along with a growing structural deficit caused by debt accumulation, making the Argentine economy completely dependent on substantial net capital inflows. The country's economy therefore became more vulnerable to the demands of the International Monetary Fund (IMF) – mainly, that debt servicing had to be met through budget adjustment, that is, through the diminution of people's welfare conditions: education, health, and salaries.

As a result, in the period 1998–2002, the neo-populist articulation of democratic neoliberalism failed to effectively cope with social conflict as the recession intensified and strategies of social control, such as clientelism and patronage, were often undercut. By the end of the 1990s, a growing number of poor individuals who had previously secured a form of dependent political integration through clientelistic structures linked to the PJ were increasingly left bereft as poverty relief programmes were undercut by decreased government finances, especially from provincial and local sources.[39] The erosion of the PJ's clientelistic and patronage networks increasingly came to express the material inability of democratic neoliberalism to cope with its own contradictions, opening up a political opportunity for subaltern classes to organise and politicise their social needs.

This was particularly the case of the *piquetero* movement, constituted by mass organisations of the unemployed, which engaged in direct action (roadblocks or pickets), community organising and popular assemblies in poor neighbourhoods. The *piqueteros* became a prominent actor on the political

---

38   See Rapoport 2000.
39   See Epstein 2003; Auyero 2005.

scene, where they were seen as a new model of social resistance against neoliberal policies in Argentina for organising outside and against the institutional frameworks of the state, traditional unions, and organised leftist parties. The consolidation of the *piqueteros* as a national movement (1999–2001), based on the increasing institutionalisation of the demands for state relief programmes (*Planes Trabajar*) throughout the country, became a real threat to De la Rua's (1999–2001) government and played a key role in destabilising his administration. For instance, the massive national road blockades that took place in 2000 proved the incapacity of De la Rua to negotiate with the *piqueteros* given the external pressure to maintain existing orthodox economic measures. There was a considerable increase in the overall number of road blockades after 1999, growing from 140 in 1997 to 252 in 1999, to 514 in 2000, and to 1,381 in 2001.[40] To some extent, the Alianza's governability project was doomed to failure from the start as it was based on a contradictory and problematic diagnosis, which was effective in attracting middle-class voters but completely flawed as a means of solving the Argentine crisis: that corruption and bad administration (rather than the macro-economic setting) created deficit and indebtedness, and so social problems like unemployment or poverty could be addressed with more orthodox policies (and fundamentally by keeping the convertibility regime). Such arguments obviously proved unrealistic and only made the initial recession that began in 1998 much worse, and, as a consequence, popular discontent began to boil over. This became clear with the 'zero deficit' plan launched in 2001, involving huge cuts in the public budget, including a 13 percent reduction of public sector wages and retirement pensions, which resulted in increasing levels of social unrest.

The catastrophic results of this policy are well known. By the end of 2001, the impossibility of maintaining the parity between the peso and the dollar became clear and so did debt servicing (external debt rose from US$7.8 billion in 1976 to US$128 billion in 2001). The increasing loss of confidence of financial investors fuelled the 'country risk', the drain of banking deposits and a massive flight of capital. In order to prevent the bankruptcy of major banks after a run against them at the beginning of December, the government of De la Rua implemented the '*corralito*' (the freezing of banking savings of the Argentinean population). This triggered social unrest and looting all over the country, leading to a massive insurrection against the government, the economic programme and the banks under the slogan '*Que se vayan todos!*' (Out with them all!), which resulted not only in the resignation of President De la Rua but a crisis of governance as the country went through five consecutive presidencies

40   Epstein 2003, p. 21.

in less than a week and defaulted on its debt. GDP fell by more than 16 percent during the first quarter of 2002 alone and manufacturing output decreased by 20 percent. Unemployment figures rose to 23 percent during the first half of the year and an additional 22 percent of the workforce was underemployed. By mid-2002, 57.7 percent of Argentines did not have sufficient income to cover their basic needs – with conditions even worse in already depressed provinces such as Tucumán, where the rate of poverty was 71 percent.

Kirchner's Solution

'Chaos', 'Anarchy', 'Social Revolt', 'Revolution' were some of the words commonly used both with fear and hope during the events of December 2001 to describe the Argentine crisis. But far from the fears of the capitalist class or the hopes of the left for a radical transformation of power relations in Argentina, democratic neoliberalism proved remarkably strong and effective in recomposing order based on one of its defining features: the uneven politicisation of the classes. Social movements, intellectuals, and activists endlessly debated about the end of the neoliberal state and the rise of the 'multitude' or 'anti-power', 'autonomy', and 'horizontalism', and the need to expand productive self-managed projects. But while this movement called for catharsis (in the Gramscian expression) in the streets, the provisional government of the Peronist leader, Duhalde (2002–3),[41] orchestrated catharsis in the supposedly vanished or exhausted institutions of the state, passing a series of laws and 'rescue plans' for the banks and the rest of the capitalist class. Just while the left debated about the end of capitalism, the capitalist class was doing business and recomposing accumulation. In fact, Duhalde's policies effectively distributed the costs of the breakdown of the convertibility regime away from the most powerful economic actors and transferred them to the entire society, reproducing neoliberal recipes that call for the 'socialisation of risks'.

This distribution of social costs was accomplished mainly through the devaluation of the currency, which resulted in an immediate depreciation of salaries as wages declined (24 percent) vis-à-vis the rising value of the US dollar and the constant increase in the costs of the family food basket. In fact, the

---

41 As former Vice President of Menem and Governor of the Province of Buenos Aires during the 1990s, Duhalde was probably the most important promoter and organiser of political clientelism and patronage-politics, particularly through the creation of *Manzaneras* (a network of largely female block-workers in charge of the food distribution programme for the poor, the *Plan Vida*).

private sector was able to take advantage of the opportunities that unfolded with devaluation and the change in relative prices. Devaluation had a positive wealth effect on the private sector's foreign assets holdings, which increased their value in relation to domestic goods, real estate, and land, and the 'pesification' of bank deposits mainly favoured big local capital, diminishing their debts. While the devaluation had an immediate negative effect over poor sectors of society, for many of Argentina's richest businesses this arrangement was highly profitable; moreover, the banking fiasco and devaluation actually made them richer than before. They could now pay their employees, their expenses and debts in devaluated pesos, but the value of their assets was still in dollars.

Duhalde aimed at controlling social unrest and alleviating poverty through 'a combination of old-school machine politics and effective social policies that included the distribution of low-cost medicine and monthly subsidies to more than two million unemployed heads of households'.[42] After declaring a 'National Occupational Emergency' in January 2002, the new *Plan Jefes y Jefas de Hogar* (Heads of Household Programme, JyJDH) launched by decree in April 2002, sought to assist male and female heads of household with children under 18. The plan offered a cash transfer of US$150 per month to the unemployed, who, in return, had to engage in four to six hours of daily work, including productive work, training, or community work.[43] Covering close to 20 percent of Argentine households, the JyJDH was larger but similar to previous welfare programmes of the 1990s, such as *Planes Trabajar*, insofar as it provided 'assistance' without social security to those in need.

The main intention behind the JyJDH, however, was to enable the PJ to recover the territory it had lost to new social forces at the grassroots level, most notably the *piqueteros*.[44] While the government argued the JyJDH would introduce new methods of collaborative decision-making at the local level in order to 'break with clientelism', the objective was actually to displace the unemployed organisations' capacities to allocate places in the programme (as was the case during De la Rua's government) towards institutions more functional to the reconstruction of the Peronist machine. This involved undermining the autonomy achieved by the *piqueteros* between 1999 and 2001 through the creation of Consejos Consultivos Locales (Local Consultative Councils, CCLs) in 1,873 out of 2,150 localities, as a way to allow local authorities and non-governmental organisations to work in partnership to distribute, implement,

---

42   Levitsky and Murillo 2005, p. 161.
43   See CELS 2004.
44   See Svampa 2008.

and monitor programmes.[45] But these CCLs often encouraged rather than avoided clientelism, as political connections and relations with local politicians and/or *punteros* became key to obtaining benefits or access to the programme. Crucial in this respect was the fact that mayors kept control of the on-the-ground administration of the programme, giving them *de facto* veto power regarding who was and who was not a legitimate welfare recipient.

The JyJDH programme became instrumental in dividing the *piqueteros*. Up to this point, the different organisations had relations of cooperation, but this massive state relief programme opened a new period of conflict and competition among them. The government and the media introduced a distinction between 'good' *piqueteros* ('moderates' or *dialoguistas*) and 'bad' *piqueteros* ('hard liners' or *combativos*) depending on their propensity towards bargaining and dialogue with the government. Critically, only the 'good' ones (such as the Federación Tierra y Vivienda [Land and Housing Federation, FTV], and the Corriente Clasista y Combativa [Classist and Combatant Current, CCC]) were chosen by Duhalde from the entire *piquetero* movement to officially participate in the Consejo Consultivo Nacional (National Advisory Council), the central body charged with managing the JyJDH.[46] Moreover, the FTV and the CCC decided to no longer participate in the *piqueteros'* National Assembly and made an agreement with the government securing a larger amount of places within the JyJDH in exchange for abandoning contentious protests. This state strategy of 'divide and conquer' definitely broke the cycle of cooperation and joint mobilisation among the different fractions of the unemployed movement.

These developments paved the way for the hegemonic construction of Néstor Kirchner's regime (2003–7). It was probably the renegotiation of the Argentine debt (2004–5) with international financial institutions, resulting

---

45   Under De la Rua's government, unemployed organisations gained unprecedented levels of autonomy because they were allowed to present their own local development projects and administer the social subsidies. This favoured the *piqueteros'* organisation and development 'on the ground' by strengthening their ties with individual members and the local community. See Wolff 2007. However, this governmental strategy was inspired less by an explicit attempt at developing autonomous and participatory forms of social activism than by the aim of disarticulating the Peronist power structures. See Svampa and Pereyra 2003. To some extent, the organisational growth of the *piqueteros* was an 'unintended consequence' of the Alianza's political strategy vis-à-vis the Peronist machine in the province of Buenos Aires.

46   See Epstein 2003.

in an unprecedented discount on foreign debt and reversing default,[47] which became the key factor explaining not only economic recovery but also the unprecedented rise in the popularity and public support of the newly elected Kirchner. He understood from the outset that moving Argentina out of the crisis had to involve a growth programme that would not be sacrificed before the interests of foreign creditors. Unlike previous presidents, Kirchner was not about to merely submit to the usual package of adjustment and austerity. He observed correctly that the IMF was on the defensive, having been criticised at home and abroad for its abandonment of Argentina as the nation plunged into crisis. Argentina's bargaining position vis-à-vis the international financial institutions was therefore much stronger than it had been in the recent past.[48]

This provided Kirchner with a simple formula for economic recovery: [(soybean + oil ground rent) x devaluation] + fall of wages and state relief programmes for the poor and unemployed.[49] Given the internationally favourable scenario of the rise in commodity prices, the Argentine recovery came to be based on the exports of soybean and soybean oil triggered mainly by the demand for primary goods in China. The government thus strongly committed itself to preserving a competitive exchange rate for exports (US$1 = 3 pesos) by Central Bank intervention in the foreign exchange market. Higher exports had a positive effect for the domestic market, which explains the high rates of growth: 8.8 percent in 2003; 9 percent in 2004; 9.2 percent in 2005 and 8.4 percent in 2006. It also explains the fiscal surplus and the increase in federal monetary reserves thanks to export taxes.[50] What is key in this equation is that the fiscal surplus allowed the state to subsidise prices of public utili-

---

47   US$21 billion owed to multilateral lending institutions was refinanced in a three-year scheme based on a reduction of interest rates, and US$9.5 billion was paid off to the IMF in 2005. Much of its outstanding debt with private creditors was also renegotiated: Argentina offered bondholders 30 cents back on each dollar face value, a write-off of 70 percent. Although bondholders were upset with the deal (as it involved bigger losses for them than those of previous debt settlements as in Russia and Ecuador), by March 2005, 76 percent of them agreed to the terms of repayment, mainly because the Argentine government did not concede more. See Epstein and Pion-Berlin 2006.

48   During this period the IMF had also undergone a structural decline in its power as creditor, only recently partially restored in the wake of the new string of bailouts since 2008 as the global crisis continues to mutate.

49   See Sartelli 2007.

50   While reserves reached their lowest point in 2002 at US$10 billion, by 2004 they were US$19 billion (similar to the pre-crisis rates), and by 2006 they rose to US$35 billion. The latter figures represent Argentina's reserves *after* the state's payment of US$9.5 billion to the IMF in 2005. See Epstein and Pion-Berlin 2006.

ties and massive state relief programmes for the poor and unemployed (JyJDH and other social programmes), giving Kirchner a remarkable space for building social and political consensus.

This macro-economic setting shaped the consolidation and expansion of an extractive, export-driven model that offered continuity with the model introduced in the late 1990s based on the extension of monoculture (genetically modified soy), open-cast mining, and mega-dam projects.[51] This 'agro-mining boom', which has turned Argentina into one of the world's leading exporters of transgenic crops, was accompanied by a process of corporate concentration, as 80 percent of soybean production is owned by multinational corporations. It is also important to mention the well-known devastating effects of single crop farming: the erosion of land, the loss of 6,000 small farms per year, the increasing migration from rural to urban areas and the rise in domestic food prices (since it is more profitable for agro-business to export soy than to produce food for the domestic market).

Despite Kirchner's 'anti-neoliberal' rhetoric, his economic policy was one of substantial support of private capital, particularly in the energy sector. While Kirchner employed a discourse in favour of the 'renationalisation' of public services that had been sold off in the 1990s – for example, the water company, the postal service, and the San Martín railway – these are better understood as 'a response to the lack of interest of foreign capital to remain in these sectors than a strategic reestablishment of the state as provider of basic public services'.[52] Except for the case of the postal service, now fully owned by the state, what came to be promoted as a 'renationalisation' of public utilities was in fact an active policy of 're-privatisation', involving merely a change in the owners of privatised companies in favour of new local capitals or new partnerships between foreign and local groups. The fact that concessions granted to foreign companies in the oil and mining sectors did not mandate an increase in the tax burden is a clear example of how little the Kirchner government has departed from the orthodox neoliberal approach to foreign direct investment in strategic areas of the economy. For instance, the creation of Energía Argentina Sociedad Anónima (ENARSA), a state company that was apparently established to regain control over the oil ground rent for the benefit of the Argentine population, was in fact no more than an office for adjudicating concessions granted to multinational corporations like Pan American Energy, Repsol, and Tecpetrol. This enthusiastic embrace of the oil sector is hardly surprising considering that Kirchner first emerged politically as a strong *caudillo* in a province rich

---

51   See Svampa 2008.
52   Azpiazu and Bonofiglio 2006, p. 49.

in oil, Santa Cruz. He actively supported the privatisation of the national oil company, Yacimientos Petrolíferos Fiscales (YPF) in the 1990s, and then promoted its re-privatisation in 2005 (20 percent of the shares were floated on the stock market and 25 percent were transferred to Argentine private groups close to Kirchner, while the rest remained in the hands of the Spanish oil and gas corporation, Repsol). This hardly represents a policy to fundamentally democratise the distribution of oil rent for the benefit of the Argentine population.

Economic recovery in the mid-2000s provided some relief. According to official data, which treats beneficiaries of unemployed programmes as 'employed', by 2004 official unemployment had decreased to 12.1 percent, continuing to drop to 10.4 percent in 2006 and to 8.4 percent in 2009. But as Patroni observes, 'economic growth can only provide a means toward the resolution of some of the most pressing problems for workers in Argentina if it is connected to state policies that aim at assuring a fairer distribution of income'.[53] So far this has not been the case. According to many observers, the true basis for economic recovery lay mostly in increased exploitation, as measured by the further fall of real wages.[54] The combination of the devaluation of the currency with inflation was immediately translated into a process of brutal erosion of income, as wages did not increase at the same pace as inflation. Between 2002 and 2006 food prices rose almost 120 percent, while wages only rose 50 percent.[55] To some extent, the structural adjustment policies of the 1990s came to be replaced by another, less visible, form of social adjustment based on the combination of inflation and devalued wages. By 2006, only a small number of formal workers in the private sector had a real income that was higher than in the pre-crisis period; the rest of the working class had a significantly lower income.[56]

Poverty also decreased according to official data, from 57 percent to 32 percent by 2007. According to Lozano, of the 2.5 million paid jobs that were created between 2003 and 2005, 1.8 million were informal.[57] The persistently high rates of unemployment and underemployment strengthened the negative conditions under which workers re-entered the world of work. This trend is indicative of the fact that post-2001 growth processes were still based on neoliberal forms of labour exploitation: Kirchner's economic model encouraged informality, illegality, and precariousness, particularly in the growing service sector, such as the small-scale enterprises connected to the agricultural sector.

---

53   Patroni 2008, p. 217.
54   See, for example, the chapter by Féliz in this volume.
55   See Kornblihtt 2006.
56   See Dinerstein 2008.
57   See Lozano 2005; 2006; and 2007.

According to Lozano, a comparison of the levels of economic activity in 1998 and 2005 shows that they are similar, suggesting that there has been significant recovery since the crisis of 2001. Yet in 2005 there were 30 percent more unemployed, the average income was 30 percent lower, and there were 5 million more poor people than in 1998.

Building 'K' Hegemony

Crucially, the economic recovery provided the material conditions for the reproduction of neoliberal forms of populism based on the centralisation of state power, patronage politics, and clientelism (particularly in the 'brown areas'). The sustainability of accumulation under Kirchner's government was facilitated by the rise of fiscal surplus, itself a result of economic growth and lower interest debt payments, which helped to institutionalise the new Peronist hegemony under Kirchner's leadership. While the PJ and the Alianza were crushed by the combined failures of increasing indebtedness and the collapse of the convertibility regime and therefore could not cope with social conflict after 1995, Kirchner was able to revive the PJ's political machine, particularly its integrative capacities towards popular classes, thanks to the growing resources available through fiscal surplus: US$8.6 billion in 2003, US$17.4 billion in 2004, US$19.6 billion in 2005 and US$23.2 billion in 2006. In relation to GDP, this rate of revenue surplus was unprecedented in the last thirty years. Such an extraordinary rise of fiscal surpluses and state resources gave shape to a system of power in which Kirchner came to have almost absolute control over the distribution and allocation of state resources to the 'neo-feudalised' areas, which are key to the hegemonic construction of the PJ. According to the Argentine system of fiscal co-participation, it is the national government and not the provinces that collects taxes. Unlike Menem and De la Rua, whose administrations were characterised by deep fiscal deficits, the new fiscal bonanza gave Kirchner the chance to create a system of political loyalties with the governors based exclusively on cash transfers. With the crisis of 2001–2, the sanction of a series of 'emergency bills' gave extraordinary powers to the National Executive to discretionally decide upon the spending of the national budget – unprecedented executive capacities known as 'superpowers'. The distribution of social spending to the provinces thus became a key disciplinary mechanism forcing governors to support Kirchner in order to guarantee governability in their own territories. Overall, it reinforced the PJ's machine politics and clientelism. The new state resources allowed Kirchner to claim control of the Peronist machine and to sideline most of his political opponents within and outside the party; or to use the

CASTORINA

terms of Romero, 'to force the big provincial barons to yield to his authority, one by one, by alternating reward and punishment, the carrot and the stick'.[58]

The persistence of social inequality, poverty, and unemployment were fundamental for reproducing neoliberal forms of social discipline, particularly in relation to popular sectors. The government's strategy of social control is evidenced by the considerable difference in the number of beneficiaries of unemployed programmes in the pre- and post-crisis periods. Indeed, the *Planes Trabajar* launched by Menem in 1996 reached an average of 100,000 beneficiaries (with a peak of 206,000 in 1997, and a low point in March 2002 of 25,000) whereas the JyJDH covered two million people on average. This means that while the *Planes Trabajar* were not enough to prevent the rise of the *piquetero* movement in a context of rising unemployment under Menem and De la Rua (18 percent and 22 percent, respectively), Kirchner was able to de-mobilise, divide, and co-opt unemployed sectors through the extension of social programmes in a context of decreasing unemployment rates (averaging 10 percent). In addition to the JyJDH, by 2004 Kirchner's government was able to provide assistance to 1,115,000 people through Food Emergency Plans and 1,900,000 through soup kitchens.

To some extent, Kirchner has been even more effective than Menem in using this form of discipline and social control by turning the massive social assistance programmes into exquisitely tuned vehicles for incorporating the poor and disciplining unemployed organisations, rewarding 'loyal' *piqueteros* with social programmes, state resources, and state offices for their leaders, and isolating (repressing and prosecuting) those who have been more critical towards the government. In significant ways, Kirchner saw the co-optation of the growing unemployed organisations as an opportunity to consolidate a greater margin of political autonomy within the PJ and to avoid or minimise eventual dissatisfactions with his government. What came to be known as '*piqueteros* K', the most salient example being the FTV, became, as it were, Kirchner's 'auxiliary private police' (to use Gramsci's term). Indeed, this cooptation effectively reshaped the map of popular organisations along the lines of 'K' and 'anti-K', a division that certainly enhanced the state strategy of divide-and-rule of the most potentially contentious actors in a context of persistent unemployment. State strategy under Kirchner was successful at neutralising the *piqueteros*' capacity to mobilise and organise as a coherent, collective network – something Kirchner's predecessors found more difficult given the fiscal restraints of the economic recession of 1998–2002.

---

58   Romero 2004, p. 38.

Kirchner mobilised the *piqueteros K* as a show of force on several occasions, not only during electoral campaigns but also at public rallies where he needed to display wide popular support. Indeed, Kirchner used the continuing inauguration of public works in the municipalities as a regular governing policy, since his popular support there was highly visible. For this reason, the *piqueteros K* became partially incorporated into the clientelistic networks of the government and very active in clientelistic practices with their own members. Despite Kirchner's 'anti-(neo)liberal' rhetoric, he revived social policy based on the increased prominence of 'social safety nets' once advocated by the 'Washington Consensus', by reproducing a decentralised, targeted social welfare policy that gave increasing power to local government officials (mayors and municipalities) in the administration of social policy. While this was presented as a way to undermine the type of patronage politics that had predominated in the 1990s, ethnographic and empirical research provides ample evidence of targeted social policies being used by local government officials for political exchanges and, moreover, to revive clientelism under Kirchner's administration.[59] Overall, in this period poor citizens were turned into political clients through a process described by Susan Stokes as 'reverse accountability'.[60] That is, citizens are held accountable to politicians for their vote choices under the risk of losing valued benefits if they do not support particular candidates or politicians. As in 1995, the Kirchners' electoral victories in 2005 and 2007 (with Cristina Fernández de Kirchner running for the Senate and for the presidency, respectively) were based on disproportionate support of the less well-off sectors of society, as 40 percent of poor households in Argentina had come to depend on state relief programmes for their basic survival. Most observers agree that clientelism, in a context of persistent poverty and unemployment, became an effective strategy for obtaining political support from poor voters after the crisis of 2001.[61]

In addition, by launching a series of new social programmes (such as Social Capital Funds and Solidarity Funds for Development) with the aim of institutionalising and de-politicising issues around poverty and unemployment, Néstor Kirchner effectively co-opted the language and material frameworks of the so-called new politics from below which had organised around ideas of 'social economy' or 'autonomous development'. According to Dinerstein, the novelty of his new policy, mirroring the World Bank's new trend of 'incorporating the poor', was to take on board the communitarian practices and

---

59   See Weitz-Shapiro 2008; Swarcberg 2007; Ketelaars 2008; Ponce 2007.

60   See Stokes 2005.

61   Brusco, Nazareno and Stokes 2004; Stokes 2005; Auyero 2005; Levistky and Murillo 2005.

solidarity expressions underpinning the implementation of productive projects and other forms of collective action of the unemployed and NGOs since
the second half of the 1990s.[62] Nestor Kirchner's government carried out this
policy shift by providing these groups with technical and financial support in
the form of social capital funds, micro-credits, and various types of technical
assistance. But contrary to the expectation that these grassroots initiatives
could transform or challenge neoliberal development, they instead became
integral to the sustainability of democratic neoliberalism. Financing such projects through NGOs not only allowed the state to withdraw from social provision at virtually no cost, it also forced unemployed organisations to compete
for funds with local politicians, which encouraged even more patronage and
clientelism. Ultimately, local political bosses had *de facto* veto power as to who
was and who was not a recipient of these resources.

In the social context of *Que se vayan todos!* – understood as a massive repu-
diation of politicians and, to a deeper extent, as an exhaustion of the links
between the citizenry and the political class – Kirchner presented himself
as an anti-party president, even alienating and infuriating some important
Peronist leaders. He understood from the outset that there was a crisis of confidence in political parties, including his own, so he was determined to act outside the party to gain public support, knowing that Peronists in general respect
their national leader once he or she has shown the ability to exercise authority. He correctly sensed there was a crisis of confidence in democratic institutions so he took aim at key components of the state apparatus, such as the
Supreme Court and the army, which had long been bastions of conservatism.[63]
This was part of Kirchner's strategy to address the long neglected demands of
progressive sectors, a central explanation for the spirit of *Que se vayan todos!*
In this sense, the 'links between the citizenship and the political class that
had almost disintegrated in the violent episodes of December 2001 began to
be reconstructed under Kirchner's leadership'.[64] Some scholars defined this as

---

62   See Dinerstein 2008.
63   Not only did Kirchner appoint a new Supreme Court and replace Menem's judges (highly
      suspected of corruption) with figures renowned for their competence and integrity, he
      also adopted an entirely new and long-expected policy towards the military, replacing its
      top ranks and unequivocally condemning the atrocities committed by the dictatorship of
      1976–83. He promoted the Congressional annulment of Alfonsín's laws of 'End Point' and
      'Due Obedience' that, for example, had allowed the military and paramilitary to evade
      trial for human rights violations. As a result, dozens of members of the armed forces were
      finally tried and prosecuted, which sharply distinguished Kirchner from Menem who had
      granted presidential pardons to the generals in 1989.
64   Llanos 2004, p. 101.

the 'K factor' as a way to refer to Kirchner's ability 'to build power by explic-itly questioning the limits that Argentine politicians had imposed on them-selves ... which pleasantly surprised a society fed up with the 1990s discourse of impossibility'.[65]

Given the extraordinary institutional (and ideological) flexibility of Peronism, under Kirchner the PJ was able to present itself as a left-of-centre force, a new space for building a 'national-popular' project that by no means involved, however, a departure from the 'old politics' of the 1990s, but rather a renewed opportunity for Kirchner to build his own populist power. Indeed, he built his leadership on the classic 'us' vs. 'them' style, targeting the neoliberal-ism of the '1990s', Menemism and the IMF, while rebuilding a new PJ coalition that included *piqueteros*, select trade unions, human rights groups, non-party leftists, and even some radicals. Bringing in progressive forces under the notion of a 'transverse alliance', that is, 'a space that goes beyond the PJ', gave him the chance to successfully play inside as well as outside the party, which was struc-turally possible given the PJ's flexible (informal) internal rules. By attacking the 'political class' (including especially rivals within his own party), Kirchner resorted to rule by decree instead of congressionally mandated laws (despite having a parliamentary majority) to promote his agenda. He used executive *Decretos de Necesidad y Urgencia* (Necessity and Urgency Decrees, DNUs) 67 times in his first year in office, surpassing Menem's record of 64, ultimately aimed at sending a clear message to other PJ bosses as to who was in charge.

Crucial for the political equation of Kirchner was the renewed privileged position of the CGT within the government. As Patroni argues, in a context of growing unemployment and devalued salaries, the safest route for Kirchner to control or prevent a reactivation of labour struggles was to support or co-opt a labour leadership committed to the government's socio-economic plans. Thus, the CGT under the leadership of Moyano repositioned itself effectively in the negotiation of salaries, a fact that has given it a new opportunity to strengthen its position as the hegemonic labour sector vis-à-vis alternative or indepen-dent unions such as the CTA which, in contrast, has lost its capacity to influ-ence in a decisive way the debate on issues that are fundamental in terms of social justice and that still remain unresolved.[66] However, this resurgence of unions' bargaining position, defined as 'segmented neo-corporatism'[67], only applies to a substantial minority of the labour force that remains in the rela-tively privileged formal sector. In the cases of subway, auto, oil, or tire workers,

65   Abal Medina 2006, p. 141.
66   Patroni 2008, p. 217.
67   See Etchemendy and Collier 2007.

for example, the labour force earns well above the average working-class income, therefore reproducing inside-outside divides within the labour market. Such divisions have long been a structural feature of neoliberal discipline.

Conclusion

Néstor Kirchner's governing strategy (2003–7) can be described as being an even more sustainable formula than the one applied in the 1990s for being able to pull the country out of the recession/crisis and, at the same time, prevent or manage more effectively social and political unrest, without fundamentally altering the structure of social inequalities and power. Indeed, the sustainability of neoliberalism under Kirchner's government was facilitated by the rise of fiscal surplus, a result of both economic growth and default and lower payments of debt interests. This was of crucial importance later on as a factor explaining the relatively reduced impact of the global financial crisis (2008–9) on Argentina's economy under Cristina Kirchner's administration. Unlike the US, Canada, and other European countries, Argentina did not enter into recession and even managed to reach positive growth rates in 2009 (0.9 percent) and a rapid acceleration in 2010 (8.4 percent). Although there was an increase in labour conflicts in 2009, particularly in the face of foreign capital's restructurings (the most salient case being Kraft Food suspending hundreds of workers), the government was able to establish bargaining channels between unions and business management based on the segmented forms of neo-corporatism explained above. In this way, Peronist unions in most cases effectively displaced and reduced the role of alternative or leftist unions attempting to radicalise the struggles.

The progressive ruptures carried on by Néstor Kirchner (a legacy arguably continued by his wife) are less a revolutionary shift or a fundamental transformation of power relations in Argentina than a pragmatic re-composition of the contradictions of neoliberalism. The Kirchner governments are best captured by notions like *Izquierda Permitida*[68] or 'pink tide', which stress the need for a greater role for the state in assistance to the poor while making explicit 'that the logic of the market must not be challenged, nor ... an open integration into global capitalism'.[69] For this reason, despite their anti-neoliberal discourses, the Kirchner governments have not engaged in 'significant redistribution of income or wealth'. Nor has there been, it must be stressed, a 'shift in basic

---

68   See Webber and Carr, 2012.
69   Ibid.

property and class relations despite changes in political blocs, in discourse in favour of the popular classes, and mildly reformist or social welfare measures'.[70]

Therefore, the reproduction of democratic neoliberalism after the crisis of 2001 may disprove any naive (leftist) presumption that the increase of poverty and social inequality undermines neoliberalism by inevitably producing a popular backlash in favour of radical transformations. On the contrary, both the 'factory of poverty', which nurtures a profitable political network of power, and the resurgence of segmented forms of Peronist unionism seem to have turned the effectiveness of democratic neoliberalism into recurrent 'Peronist solutions', ultimately disabling the effective construction of deeper social change.

---

70   Robinson 2007, pp. 144–7.

CHAPTER 5

Doubly Marginalised? Women Workers in Northeast Brazilian Export Horticulture[1]

Ben Selwyn

One of the most oft-repeated assumptions within the literature on globalisation is that not only has capital become more mobile than in the past, but that it is hyper mobile. Various authors claim frequently that we live in a 'borderless' or 'flat' world[2] and that distance has 'died'.[3] In these accounts, technological innovations and market liberalisation have freed capital from its previous territorial base. Such accounts generally also assume that relatively immobile labour is at the mercy of increasingly mobile capital. Hence firms 'race to the base' in their 'manic logic' of searching for cheap labour.[4] For example, Castells writes of

> Structural instability in the labour markets everywhere, and the requirement for flexibility of employment, mobility of labour, and constant reskilling of the workforce. The notion of the stable, predictable, professional career is eroded, as relationships between capital and labour are individualised and contractual labour conditions escape collective bargaining.[5]

The implication of this analysis is that labour is even more structurally disadvantaged in relation to capital than prior to globalisation – during the

---

1   The account that follows is based on PhD research conducted in the São Francisco valley, in the states of Pernambuco and Bahia, Northeast Brazil, in 2002 and 2003 and follow-up research in August and September 2008. I conducted open-ended semi-structured interviews in Portuguese with women workers on farms across the valley and at the trade union headquarters in Petrolina (Pernambuco). The open-ended approach enabled interviewees to introduce issues that they thought relevant, even if they were not part of my list of questions. All quotations from interviews are taken from this period.

2   Ohmae 1990; Friedman 2006.

3   Cairncross 2002.

4   Greider 1997.

5   Castells 2006, p. 9.

so-called 'golden age' of capitalism.[6] This chapter argues that whilst globalisation is characterised by new forms of capital mobility and sites of investment and accumulation, these sites are themselves also characterised by the emergence of new labour forces. This in turn raises the question of the extent to which these newly created labour forces are able to increase their bargaining power with capital. Further, and within this capital-labour dialectic, what do these new sites of accumulation offer to women workers?

One manifestation of increasing capital mobility is the unfolding retail revolution occurring over the last quarter century, first in the global North and now, increasingly, in the global South. This has pushed new technologies, production systems, and supply chains connecting geographically disparate producers with economically powerful northern supermarkets.[7] This revolution involves not just increasingly wide global sourcing, but also the setting/imposition of ever-stricter requirements on producers.[8] In tandem with the expansion of non-traditional agricultural exports to supply global retailers, the 'feminisation of agriculture' has been documented widely. Simply put, this refers to a situation where there is an absolute increase in women's participation in the agricultural wage labour force and/or where there is an increase in the percentage of women workers relative to men in the sector.[9] The double subordination of women workers – as workers and as women – is often observed in globalised export agriculture. Hence, Raynolds argues that 'employers manipulate gender ideologies and institutions to depress wages, to increase labour discipline, and to maximise labour extraction from both women and men'.[10] And 'women are seen as an apt group for the implementation of flexible and precarious kinds of work, given their higher levels of socioeconomic vulnerability'.[11]

Whilst there are numerous cases where women workers experience such a regressive double marginalisation,[12] it is also important to investigate cases where gendered working practices have given rise to more complicated, and possibly, more progressive outcomes. This chapter illustrates such a case in Northeast Brazil by investigating some gender dimensions of capital-labour relations in the São Francisco valley's export horticulture (specifically table grape) sector, where by 2008 there were around 120,000 irrigated hectares of

6   Hobsbawm 1994.

7   Reardon et al. 2001; Wrigley and Lowe 2007; Humphrey 2007.

8   Dolan and Humphrey 2000.

9   Deere 2005, p. 17; Katz 2003, p. 33.

10   Raynolds 2001, p. 25.

11   Omaira Páez Sepúlveda 2007, correspondence with Nora Ferm, in Ferm 2008, p. 23.

12   Thrupp 1995; Deere 2005.

fruiticulture.[13] By the mid-2000s, table grapes had become the region's principal export crop. Between 1997 and 2007, export volumes and earnings increased from 3,700 tonnes and US$4.7 million, to over 78,000 tonnes and over US$170 million.[14] By the mid-2000s, there were more than 50,000 workers employed in the grape sector alone.[15] Production has expanded rapidly, from approximately 4,500 hectares of vineyards in 2001, to around 12,100 hectares by 2007.[16] The valley accounts for over 90 percent of Brazilian grape exports because it is able to organise production to take advantage of periods of low supply in Europe.[17] National and international capital has located and re-located to the region to take advantages of the boom.[18]

Against this general backdrop, the chapter is structured as follows. Section two discusses how to investigate and document capital-labour relations under globalisation. Section three explains the reasons for, and extent of, women's employment in the São Francisco valley. Section four documents how women have become increasingly active in the valley's rural trade union and how this has, in turn, resulted in important changes both within the trade union and to women's working conditions in the grape sector. Section five offers some preliminary conclusions to this study.

Investigating Labour Relations within the Global Retail Revolution[19]

Labour is often understood within academic literature as if it were simply an input, reflecting a neoclassical bias,[20] but such an understanding should be resisted as it depoliticises work and marginalises the agency of workers, who, despite their subordinate position in the capital-labour relationship possess significant power that can be used to improve their positions in the accumulation process.[21] Such a perspective also obscures the social (rather than simply

---

13   VALEXPORT 2008.

14   Ibid.

15   Estimates provided by the STR and the Ministry of Labour.

16   Selwyn 2007b; VALEXPORT 2008.

17   VALEXPORT 2008.

18   Selwyn 2010.

19   In this section I discuss how to investigate labour in general under globalisation. For a specific discussion of how to think about and investigate changing gender divisions of labour, see Selwyn 2010.

20   Gereffi and Korzeniewicz 1994.

21   Wright 2000; Selwyn 2008.

technological) construction of globalisation.[22] Wright and Silver use the concepts of structural and associational power to illuminate sources of workers' power.[23] The former refers to workers' position in the production process and their ability to disrupt it. The latter refers to workers' collective organisation, more often than not via trade unions. Whilst workers' associational power is often based upon some aspects of their structural power and their ability to disrupt work via, for example, strikes, go-slows, work to rule, and thus disruption of the generation of profits, it is not the case that workers' structural power is necessarily or automatically transformed into effective associational power. Quite often factors such as the lack of trade union capacity, employer intimidation, state control of trade unions, and lack of confidence within the trade union movement contribute to situations where despite significant structural power, and the (formal and actual) existence of trade union organisations, workers possess very little effective associational power. After all, and this is perhaps the grain of truth in much of the globalisation literature, if structural power was automatically realised via associational power it is doubtful that the thesis of capital hyper-mobility versus labour immobility and weakness would have gained so much credence over the last two decades or so.

If this line of argument is accepted and if it is also accepted that progressive social scientists need to develop a greater understanding of why much organised labour around the world appears to have been forced onto the back foot despite new sources of structural power emerging from within new production systems,[24] then it seems worthwhile setting out a methodology that enables social scientists to investigate and illuminate the circumstances under which workers' structural power is transformed into effective associational power which, in turn, advances their collective work conditions and strength vis-à-vis capital. This, then, requires an investigation of class formation and class relations under capitalism.

A standard criticism of much Marxist political economy is that it imposes onto its objects of study pre-determined categories, none more so than that of class.[25] E.P. Thompson reacted strongly against this tendency within some strands of Marxism: "'It', the working class, is assumed to have a real existence, which can be defined almost mathematically ... Once this is assumed it becomes possible to deduce the class-consciousness which "it" ought to have

22   Radice 1999.
23   Wright 2000; Silver 2003.
24   Dunn 2004; 2009.
25   See Ellen Meiksins Wood's excellent discussion in Wood 1995.

(but seldom does have)'.[26] In place of such deductive and non-dialectical schemas Thompson proposed to study how working classes (in his case the English working class) were 'made'. The stress on making is important because 'it is a study of an active process, which owes as much to agency as to conditioning'. 'The notion of class entails the notion of historical relationship' and these relationships 'must always be embodied in real people and in a real context'.[27] Above all:

> Class happens when some men [and women!], as a result of common experiences (inherited or shared), feel and articulate the identity of their interests as between themselves, and as against other men whose interests are different from (and usually opposed to) theirs ... Class is defined by men as they live their own history.[28]

Thompson's emphasis on the subjective and experiential aspects of class formation, action, and consciousness, does not prevent him from observing the objective structural aspects of class formation: 'The class experience is largely determined by the productive relations into which men [and women] are born – or enter involuntarily'. Here there is an historical and materialist approach to class formation and action. Ellen Meiksins Wood, commenting on Thompson's method, makes the following observation:

> He does not proceed from a theoretical dualism which opposes *structure* to *history* and identifies the 'structural' explanation of class with the charting of objective, static class locations while reserving the process of class formation for an apparently lesser form of historical and empirical explanation ... [He] ... treats the process of class formation as a *historical* process shaped by the 'logic' of material determinations ... Class, in other words, is a phenomenon which is visible only in process.[29]

Thompson was investigating and documenting the process of working-class formation in England between roughly 1790 and 1832. This chapter attempts to utilise Thompson's historical methodology for the purposes of investigating gendered aspects of class formation over a relatively short time-frame, because these women's experiences reflect a process of the making of a new regional

---

26   Thompson 1963, p. 9.
27   Ibid., p. 8
28   Ibid., pp. 8–10.
29   Wood 1995, p. 81.

rural proletariat that simply did not exist some two decades ago. Further, and as indicated in the introduction, this is not an isolated process (which would discount any possibility of generalisation), but one intimately connected to the unfolding global retail revolution. Thus, while this case study is obviously unique (there is only one São Francisco valley), it is but one of many taking place around the world, all with their own peculiarities, but all, also, conditioned by many of the same forces.

This investigation dovetails with some other important attempts to map the changing fortunes and histories of labour under conditions of contemporary capitalist globalisation. Russo and Linkin note that '[o]ne way of putting working-class people at the centre [of research] is to make working-class voices a primary source for the study of working-class life'.[30] This approach mirrors Kabeer's earlier insistence in relation to the study of women workers' lives that:

> [a]llowing women's own accounts to inform an analysis ... has the advantage of including a set of 'voices' which are often missing from both policy and academic discussions ... [T]he 'subjective' insights provided ... offer a valuable tool for interpreting the more 'objective' hypotheses formulated by researchers and policymakers.[31]

Marcel van der Linden also recognises the value of oral histories, noting that 'oral sources are more centrally important than is generally the case' (in writing history), and further that 'if one wants to write the history of casual labour in a slum district, one usually finds that there is very little written source material'.[32] The same is true of the 'doubly marginalised' women workers in the new global zones of export horticulture. Van der Linden's work[33] represents a pioneering project of mapping the emerging global working class via a 'global labour history', which embodies 'the transnational and even the transcontinental study of labour relations and workers' social movements in the broadest sense of the word'. 'By "transnational" we mean the placing in a wider context of all historical processes, *no matter how geographically small*'.[34] And, crucially for the present study, '[t]he study of labour relations concerns the individual workers but also his/her family. Gender relations play an important part within the

---

30   Russo and Linkin 2005, p. 12.
31   Kabeer 1999, p. 262.
32   Van der Linden 2004, p. 146.
33   Van der Linden 2002; 2008.
34   Van der Linden 2002, p. 2, emphasis added.

family and in labour relations involving individual family members'.[35] Therefore, this suggests that despite limited geographical scope and a relatively narrow focus on one section of an emerging working class (women workers), that even from the worm's eye of the São Francisco valley we can potentially make connections with wider global processes (the global retail revolution) in order to achieve a more integrated bird's eye view of the emerging and changing global working class.

These observations suggest that a 'global labour history' can be written from the bottom up, that is, from the perspective of both emerging and already established (although always in transformation) working classes of the world. When conceptualised this way, geographically small-scale ethnographic studies potentially fit into a broader framework of progressive social science research, with a central objective of 'giving voice' to workers within academia through outlets such as journal articles and books. With these points in mind, and with a clear commitment to making audible the voices of workers in the global South, we can agree with Thompson that our objectives are to rescue them 'from the enormous condescension of posterity' (and the present!)[36] It is also worth noting that such a project is not simply academic. Highlighting the experience of workers in the global South (and North) potentially facilitates solidarity.

I have discussed elsewhere how the São Francisco valley's principal trade union has managed to transform workers' structural power into effective associational power.[37] This chapter is concerned primarily with illustrating how, within this transformation, women workers have become increasingly active within the rural trade union in question, and how, consequently, issues concerning specifically women workers have risen up the trade union's campaigning agenda.

Women Workers in the São Francisco Valley Grape Sector

The principal trade union in the São Francisco valley is the Sindicato dos Trabalhadores Rurais (Rural Workers' Union, STR) and the increasing importance of women workers and trade union representatives is discussed in detail below. Here it is worth noting a few basic points before proceeding further. As noted above, São Francisco valley horticulture, in particular the table-grape

---

35   Ibid.
36   Thompson 1963, p. 12.
37   Selwyn 2007b; 2012.

export sector, has emerged over the last two decades as one of Brazil's hot spots of agrarian accumulation (although relatively small, compared to soya and beef production in the south and southeast of the country). Within the grape sector, women comprise the overwhelming majority of the labour force. They are employed, increasingly, on temporary contracts. While during the mid-to-late 1990s women comprised the majority of permanently employed workers, by the early 2000s they made up only between 40 and 50 percent. This is still significantly more than in other world regions of grape production. For example, Barrientos shows that in Chile and South Africa women comprise 5 percent and 26 percent of the permanent labour force, and 52 percent and 69 percent of the temporary labour force respectively.[38]

There are several reasons for the initial gender division of labour and its change over the last decade or so. Referring specifically to the São Francisco grape sector, Collins provides four reasons why the employment of women helps farms reduce their labour costs.[39] First, managers tend to grade women's skills differently than men's: 'What would ordinarily be construed as skill, grafting of grape vines, is coded instead as manual dexterity, delicacy and nimbleness of fingers'.[40] Hence, skilled work is re-defined as 'natural' to women workers; therefore not a skill per se, but an attribute, thus reducing pressures on farms to remunerate skilled workers more favourably. Second, women are relatively easily classified as temporary workers because they are assumed to have primary responsibility for looking after their families. Third, in the 1980s and early 1990s women were perceived to be less active politically in the São Francisco valley. Fourth, women are also perceived by firms to be less bothered by the close supervision exercised by the field managers.

However, whilst large numbers of women were initially employed on permanent contracts, there are at least two reasons why they are increasingly being employed temporarily.[41] The intensity of work on exporting farms is increasing. Whereas farms initially employed workers based on daily task targets, most have moved to combining such targets with piece rate systems – thus seeking (mostly successfully) to maximise workers' productivity.[42] Under these conditions managers often consider male workers to be stronger and to

---

38   Barrientos 2001, p. 86.
39   Collins 1993.
40   Ibid., p. 105.
41   For a fuller analysis of the changing gender division of labour in the valley's export grape sector see Selwyn 2010.
42   Selwyn 2007b.

be able to work for longer periods in the heat, and have subsequently begun to employ increasing numbers of male workers on permanent contracts.

A second reason is that whilst non-wage costs for employing women may be relatively lower than for male workers under conditions of flexible labour contracts,[43] once women workers win rights, such as crèche care facilities and maternity leave, non-wage costs may become higher than for male workers.

One manager explained how:

> The problem with hiring women under Brazilian law is that they have the right to stay at home for three months per year when they are pregnant; if you add another month for holidays, then she is away from work for four months of the year... [B]ut we are changing and many men are already doing the bunch pruning process. Since they only have one month of holidays, it is better for us to hire them.

Employers on many farms thus recognise the potential disadvantages associated with hiring large number of women on permanent contracts. Consequently, many farms across the valley employ women workers neither on permanent nor temporary bases, as the former would entail higher costs, and the latter would prevent managers guaranteeing recruitment of the skilled workers necessary to carry out the detailed work in grape production. Instead, they hire women increasingly on 'permanent temporary' contracts. On the one hand, this strategy enables farms to 'retain' skilled workers for the 17-week production cycle twice a year whilst laying them off during the intervening periods. In addition, this strategy places pressures upon women workers to maintain a reputation as 'good' workers, achieving productivity objectives set by managers, and not 'causing trouble', in order to be re-employed the following season. On the other hand, it also means that they have significant experience of the grape sector, and know many of their co-workers. In addition, that the valley's rural trade union has the right to trade union representation on farms, and has a formal agreement with employers that workers cannot be disciplined for complaining about, for example, poor working conditions, means that a significant space exists for women workers to participate in the trade union, even if they are employed on seasonal contracts. That this space exists is a product of a process of learning through interaction between the trade union and its fast expanding female membership.

---

43   Standing 1999.

Rural Trade Unions and Women Workers

Some literature concerned with women's employment in developing countries observes how trade unions are often male-dominated and unresponsive to the specificity of women workers' conditions. As Prieto and Quinteros note, '[t]here is an almost total absence of women in positions of power in unions worldwide, one explanation for which appears to be male resistance'.[44] One result is often ignorance of issues that specifically concern women. For example, Razavi observes how trade union leaderships rarely recognise 'that women workers may have different priorities from male workers: some form of childcare support, for example, may be much more important for them than having a minimum wage'.[45] Similarly, Mitter argues that most trade unions in the global South focus on organising workers in the formal sector and that their cultures and procedures usually assume a male bias, by, for example, failing to take account of the real experiences and lives of women workers.[46]

Clearly there are many cases of such male bias. However, Standing provides evidence from numerous cases to show that where industries and firms are unionised the gender gap in wages tends to be narrower.[47] As Dunn notes, the 'union premium' is very important.[48] Hence, in the United States, for example, 'the pay advantages of unionising are 24 percent for men but 31 percent for women'. This raises the question of how unionisation and trade union activity can lead, under certain circumstances, to significant improvements in women workers' wages, conditions, and ability to participate in and influence trade unions. Whilst male-bias exists in many trade unions, it would be erroneous to reject *a priori* the possibilities of such organisations changing in ways that benefit women workers. Indeed, Hyman suggests that different trade unions, by definition, possess stronger or weaker organisational capacities, which can be better or worse suited to meeting the challenges faced by their membership, and which should be understood as 'the ability to assess opportunities for intervention [and] to anticipate, rather than merely react to changing circumstances'.[49]

Their effectiveness in formulating and pursuing such strategies requires 'the capacity to interpret, decipher, sustain, and redefine the demands

---

44   Prieto and Quinteros 2004, p. 155.
45   Razavi 1999, p. 670.
46   Mitter 1994.
47   Standing 1992.
48   Dunn 2009.
49   Hyman 2007, p. 198.

of the represented, so as to evoke the broadest possible consensus and approval'.[50] Hence, the leaders of trade unions' bureaucratic organisations will determine to important degrees their abilities to respond to new challenges. However, it is not just at the upper leadership levels that the ability to anticipate, interpret, and decipher changing circumstances are important. Barker et al., argue for distinguishing between authoritarian and authoritative trade union leaderships, suggesting that, for the latter, 'leadership is exercised at all manner of levels and locations . . . and not only by those obviously designated as "leaders"'.[51] Hyman observes that Gramsci's notion of the 'organic intellectual' is relevant in situations where leadership is not simply an activity performed by the formal trade union bureaucracy: 'Grass-roots activists may develop a breadth of information and analytical capacity which distinguish without distancing them from their colleagues. Hence there can, and must, be a complex dialectic between leadership and democracy'.[52]

Paulo Freire's attempts to develop an emancipatory educational praxis are particularly relevant here.[53] Like Gramsci, Freire stressed the dangers of a strong dichotomy between educators and educated, and instead argued for dynamic reciprocity in order that education might become the 'practice of freedom' and 'the means by which men and women deal critically with reality and discover how to participate in the transformation of their world'.[54] His concept of 'conscientisation' (critical consciousness or consciousness raising) stresses the ability of educators to assist the oppressed in their development of new levels of awareness, in their movement from viewing themselves as objects of broader forces, to self-determining subjects. Trade unions that aim to radically re-shape the political economic terrain on which they operate often attempt to engage in such practices in order to a) change the balance of forces between employers and employed, and b) change the way the workers view their role in the transformative process – from being recipients of benefits to being active participants in the winning of benefits.

If it is accepted that trade unions are potentially flexible and can learn and incorporate new practices into their routines, and that membership can inform these practices, then it is also possible to envision a situation where women workers, particularly in economic sectors where they predominate, may stand

---

50   Regalia 1988, p. 51.
51   Barker et al. 2001, pp. 15–17.
52   Hyman 2007, p. 199.
53   Freire 1970.
54   Freire 1970, cited in Mayo 1999, p. 5.

a chance of not just gaining better representation from such organisations, but also of playing a significant part in their evolution.

Trade Union Strategies

The STR was originally formed in 1963 to represent small-scale farmers in the São Francisco valley. The 1964 military coup and subsequent 21 years of military rule heavily influenced trade union activity until the return of democracy in the mid-1980s.[55] From the early 1990s, coterminous with the early expansion of the valley's horticulture sector, the STR began campaigning vigorously for improvements in rural workers' rights. Its leadership soon identified sources of workers' structural power on exporting grape farms. The latter employ precise scientific production practices to produce high quality fruit, including a complex harvest calendar comprising over 30 operations such as berry and bunch pruning. The intense heat of the valley accelerates plant growth, and operations must be performed at specific times to facilitate production. If they are delayed the fruit quality quickly deteriorates. The trade union leadership realised that short suspensions of work would severely reduce fruit quality. The STR was able to use strikes – and sometimes even simply the threat to strike – to disrupt fruit quality and thus to push employers to make concessions to the sector's labour force. Consequently, workers have experienced significantly improved conditions over the last two decades. Initial gains included pay rates above the minimum wage, established overtime wages, the rights for workers to protective clothing and the rights for trade union representatives to enter farms at lunch breaks to communicate with union members.

However, despite its re-orientation towards rural wage workers, Collins observed how initially the STR largely ignored women workers.[56] But this did not last long. From the mid-to-late 1990s, the trade union began campaigning for women workers' issues and began recruiting women into its leadership, conscious of the fact that women constituted the majority of the labour force. The trade union's women's officer describes how the trade union re-orientated itself towards women workers: 'We wanted to gain influence amongst the workers and help them improve their lives and working conditions, and we realised that to win their leadership we needed to appeal to women workers in a special way. How could we be considered the leaders of the valley's workers if we only fought to improve conditions for men?'

---

55   Cammack 1991.
56   Collins 1993.

Through its ability to mobilise workers, the trade union has been able to win victories and improve significantly women's working conditions. Gains include provision of crèche facilities, a paid day per month for women workers to visit doctors, the right for women with babies in the crèche to breastfeed for an hour per day, over and above the lunch hour, and a two month period of paid maternity leave, with the right to return to employment following such leave. Significantly, the union has also campaigned vigorously for improved transport conditions. Initially workers often experienced overcrowded transport to work and women complained about sexual harassment (groping) on buses. A recent gain included in the collective agreement is that all workers have sufficient seating space on company-provided transport, thus giving women workers valuable personal space and dignity. Alongside these gains, women workers have experienced changes to their lives, often seeing themselves in new ways. The following section uses interviews with women workers, most of whom were members of the STR, to provide an image of how women workers have emerged to play a central role in the trade union – the SF valley's largest civil society organisation – contributing to the amelioration of working conditions, and, simultaneously, transforming their own perceptions about their roles in domestic life and wider civil society.

Women's Backgrounds

Women workers come from a variety of backgrounds, ranging from small-scale rural farming families, to urban communities linked to the region's industrial and service sectors. For many women, working in the grape sector represents their first paid employment. Aldemira, now a rural workers' union official responsible for coordinating the trade union's campaigns to support land-less labourers, and formerly employed in the grape sector, explains: 'Before I started working as a wage worker in grape production I worked on my father's farm, where we planted beans, corn, rice, in Lagoa Grande'. However, the family farm did not generate a sufficient income for her to raise her children, so she began seeking work elsewhere:

> I started working on grape farms because it was the only option I had. I had separated from my husband, had three children to bring up, and we did not make much money on my father's farm from the crops that we were growing and selling. A friend of mine told me about a work opportunity on the farm she was working at, so I went, and started working there. Once I was there I learned how to prune, thin the bunches, deflower the plants, harvest and wrap, and all the other important operations that farms need us to carry out.

Marta is in her mid-20s and explains that:

> Before [working in the grape sector] I didn't do anything. I studied, had children, but I didn't work. But now I am proud of my profession. Here in the region there is very little opportunity to work, and if you want to look after your children then you have to work. So grapes are very important, and I'm proud to be able to support my children through my own work.

The Experience of Work

Work on grape farms is hard. Male and female workers work for around eight hours a day in temperatures often above 30°C, and are subject to increasingly scientific management, designed to raise labour productivity.[57] Managers tell of how, when visiting farms, buyers, importers, and quality inspectors from northern countries often faint from the heat. As Aldemira highlights, the conditions of work prior to and within the grape sector are often starkly different:

> We had easy working conditions on my father's farm, but we had very little income. When I started working on the grape farms, the work became much harder, but my income also increased. It was a big difference from working for my family. We [the workers] were told what to do [on the grape farm], sometimes the managers were rude to us and humiliated us. This never happened on my father's farm.

Similarly, referring to the valley's employers generally, Simone describes how:

> They make us work harder every year, and not all of them provide us with the basics that are agreed in the collective agreement. Some farms' basic standard [Daily Task Target] pruning rate is 2,000 bunches per day. Some women can prune 2,500 bunches a day, but that is too much work! If we don't achieve these targets they move us to another job and demand that we meet these targets ... If we are on temporary contracts and want to be invited back to work for the following harvest, then we have to meet these targets.

Despite tough conditions women workers are overwhelmingly proud of their work and of the opportunities it gives them. Francisca is 23, has two young

---

57   Selwyn 2007a.

children, and works on Timbauba, the largest farm in the region, with over 3,000 employees during the harvest cycle. She explains how:

> It is good to work here. We have few opportunities to work, so this is a good place for us... This is the first time I've worked here, and I like it. I study, I live alone, with my two children, and I rent the house for R\$60 per month in Novo Descoberta, near Lagoa Grande.

Women often have to negotiate their new status as wage earners with their husbands. An STR official explained how:

> We have women members who work, but their husbands do not work. When they get home they have to prepare the food and look after the house, and at the end of the month some husbands tell them 'give me the money'. Women accept this because they are scared of fighting for their rights and many of them are afraid because their husbands beat them when they complain.

However, despite many men's initial resistance to women entering the work-force, it is also often the case that the former become more accepting of their partner's role as familial breadwinner. Magda-Adriana explains how:

> In the beginning it was difficult. My husband was not happy about me working like this. He was jealous, and he thought that other men would chase after me on the grape farms. At the start he was embarrassed by my working and not having a proper job himself. But I fought against his doubts and worries and started working and earning a wage for the first time. Today he accepts my work. Men never accept that a woman has to work, because they are afraid that women will become independent of them, and will not 'remain under their thumb', but once we show them we can do it they are okay about it.

Clearly, women have different experiences of how their employment has an impact upon intra-household relations, ranging from relative empowerment through the gaining of a disposable income, to increased workload, and the double-burden of wage and domestic labour. However, that some women experience improvements in their domestic lives, and that the trade union acts as a forum for workers' interaction and communication, at least presents the possibility that women with positive domestic outcomes resulting from employment will share their experiences, and that a more assertive culture of pushing for greater equality in the home will emerge. Whether this occurs will depend partly on the actions of the women workers themselves, in conjunction with the trade union leadership and wider membership.

Women in the Rural Workers' Union

Before working in the grape sector many women had no experience of trade unions, but once employed they quickly came into contact with trade union representatives. The current salaried workers' secretary of the STR, for example, tells her story of initial encounter, increasing involvement, and eventual election to a position of influence in the trade union. Her trajectory is instructive when considering the potential for women's activity within the STR. She explains how when she started working, 'the *delegado sindical* [trade union representative] began talking to us, and organising us to go to meetings about the conditions of work in the valley and how the rural workers union had a vision of improving our lives as workers. With the campaign around the collective agreement I learned more about our rights and I joined the trade union'. She recounts how she became increasingly involved in trade union activities: 'I began working in the union when I learned about our rights in the collective agreement. Every time the employer did something wrong, or failed to implement something within the collective agreement I got in contact with the *delegado sindical*, and the trade union to try and rectify the situation'.

She distinguishes between grape production and the rest of the horticulture sector, and how women workers both fulfil important tasks at work and how, consequently, they have the possibility of engaging in collective action to improve their conditions both as workers and as women:

> We have a conception that women need to be at the front of the political process in the STR. The STR leadership at the moment is four men and three women. It wasn't always like this, but women have become more important in the STR as we have continued to represent wage workers. If you look at the other crops it is mostly men, but in grapes, women are very important. Many of the specialised operations are carried out by women, so we are central to grape production.

Simone, a *delegada sindical*, discussed the difficulties that many active trade unionists face, and why many workers do not look favourably upon trade union work. But she is also clear of the necessity of such work for the benefit of her colleagues:

> A lot of the time, workers don't want to be delegates, because they know how much work is involved, and they don't want to spend their lives arguing with the employers. They also don't want to get blacklisted, since the

employers pass around information about whom they consider to be 'troublemakers'. But this is what makes the position so important. It is about fighting with the employers to ensure that our rights are implemented, to represent workers when they are in trouble, and most importantly, to raise the consciousness of the workers about their rights, the law, the conditions of grape production, and to improve our position and lives. It is about teaching the workers that we need to struggle to achieve our rights and improve our lives.

As indicated by this quote, and as part of their continuing attempts to mobilise the rural labour force, the STR has, since the early 2000s, been engaged increasingly in the consciousness-raising of its membership. This entails STR leaders visiting farms and explaining to workers their role in the grape production process, and simultaneously encouraging STR members to become increasingly active within the trade union, in particular through the reporting of employer abuses to trade union *delegados* and/or to the union leadership. In a development in this educational work, the trade union has begun emphasising women's abilities to perform delicate tasks in grape production. As already mentioned, managers initially employed women on the basis that their ability to carry out delicate operations made them particularly suited to the job of grape production; however, as noted by Collins, this ability was considered innate rather than an acquired skill, and it therefore did not attract higher wages or special working conditions, making it easier for employers to play down the importance of women's work.[58] Employers thus attempted to preclude any claim from women workers for preferential remuneration through, for example, bonuses or better conditions. However, the trade union is attempting to subvert this ideology. The waged workers' secretary explains:

> We tell the women, 'Look at your contribution to the wealth of the SF valley. If it were not for you the farms would not be able to produce these high quality grapes, export them, and make such huge profits. In reality, the dynamism of the valley is in your hands. It is you that produce and you deserve better conditions'. In this way we educate them about the importance of their work and why it is important to become active in the trade union.

These sentiments are increasingly widespread within the trade union, and its representatives spend considerable time and energy discussing these issues with their female (and male) colleagues. They are also encouraging workers

---

58   Collins 1993.

to demand more from their trade union representatives. Sonja, for example, explains how:

> [T]he delegate plays an important role, but it is not just up to them to do it. When we have a problem we don't go and ask them 'can you do something to help me', we ask 'what are you going to do about this?', so they have to be ready to work very hard to represent us. It is a great responsibility. They have to be on top of everything, knowing what is going on, and how to respond.

Women workers complain that some farms often ignore safety standards, for example, making them prune grapes immediately after male workers have applied agro-toxins to the plants, leading to health problems such as eye, skin, and lung damage. But Flavia describes how workers respond: 'If the farm does not treat us properly we tell the trade union and it brings the Ministry of Labour here to check up on the farm and ensure that it is implementing its side of the agreement'.

There is a feedback mechanism operating here: increased awareness of their rights and employers' responsibilities enables women workers to identify abuses and mobilise the trade union, which, in turn, works in conjunction with other organisations such as the Ministry of Labour to rectify such abuses; ultimately, this dynamic leads to a situation where increasingly aware women workers are able to orientate the trade union towards campaigning around their interests. A labour inspector from the Ministry of Labour explained how:

> Today workers know a lot more than when I started here [about 20 years ago]. They all have TVs. They have access to the Internet. Their trade union tells them about their rights. They know how much grapes sell for in Europe. The trade union makes a big effort to teach them about their rights and how they have been achieved. When you have better information you are better placed to speak up for and fight for your rights. Many of them study in their spare time. So they are much more aware than previously.

In its attempts at mobilising workers and augmenting their associational power the trade union is involved in educating its members (and non-members) about how the grape sector operates, its requirements for labour, its profits, but also its potential weaknesses. The wage worker's secretary explains:

> What you have to realise is that the São Francisco valley is continually expanding and there is a lot of demand for labour. During the period of production the employers are desperate for labour, they are looking for

workers who can carry out these complex operations, and so we say to the workers, 'you don't need to be scared, the employers need you to work, and they will sooner give in to our demands than lose their export crop'. One of our biggest struggles is to ensure that workers are registered. We tell our members how important their work is.

The trade union's stress on the importance of women workers educating themselves is notable. A trade union lawyer explained how one of the important gains established and written into the collective agreement is a clause related to workers who are also students. According to the clause, workers must be free to leave farms at 5 p.m. in order to attend school. Hence, they cannot be 'forced' to do overtime:

> This was a major achievement by the trade union. Not only did we win it, we have defended it, and we impress upon the workers the importance of their studying. That is why so many of them are in education at the same time as working on the grape farms. Previously workers would work until 6, 7 or 8 p.m. in the evening. Generally, a worker who studies does so in the evening, and so they have to be free to leave work at 5 p.m. in order to get home, have a shower, and get ready for and go to school. And if there is an exam that they need to take during the day, farms are required to allow them to take the day off.

The lawyer estimates that worker literacy levels have increased over the last decade, with over 70 percent literate by the late 2000s. The impact on women workers' political consciousness was noticeable to the author throughout the interviews. This is a significant achievement, because, as Diane Elson argues, organisations seeking to represent women workers should be concerned with 'enhancing the skills and education of those workers, so that if workers lose their jobs, they have acquired something of permanence – more self-confidence, more organisational and advocacy skills, more knowledge of how their society works'.[59] The policy is also widely supported by women as it guarantees them the ability to leave farms relatively early to care for their children (farm managers also share in this tacit understanding).

Overall the STR has come a very long way from when it represented small farmers and when it began representing rural wage workers (albeit with a male bias) in the mid-1990s. Today, women play an increasingly important and influ-

---

59   Elson 1996, p. 50.

ential role in its leadership, and women's issues are held up as serious matters for all members of the trade union.

Conclusion

This chapter began by noting briefly some of the arguments advanced by proponents of the globalisation thesis of capital hyper-mobility, many of whom posit a general trend in the deterioration of labour's position in both the accumulation process specifically, and, more broadly, across national political economies. For our purposes, however, the framework developed by Moody, Silver, and Dunn is more compelling.[60] The latter framework suggests that the relocation (and formation) of capital to and in new regions of accumulation gives rise to new working classes that did not previously exist; these working classes possess the capacity, in turn, to wrest concessions from capital. Whilst these authors provide examples of new industrial working classes that emerged in the 1970s and 1980s in South Africa, Brazil, and South Korea (mostly in the auto sector), a similar, albeit smaller-scale dynamic is identifiable in the present case study. However, the problematic for this chapter has not been to assess whether a new working class is emerging, but to investigate the conditions and circumstances under which a) workers' structural power is transformed into effective associational power, and b) women workers become increasingly influential in trade union organisation and orientation.

This case study reveals a case of positive interaction between an initially male-worker orientated and run workers' union and its expanding number of (flexible and permanently employed) women workers. It reveals too how the transformation (and maintenance) of workers' structural power into effective associational power requires a continual and evolving strategy of consciousness-raising and mobilisation of union membership, as well as a strategic orientation vis-à-vis capital by the trade union. This, in turn, has provided (perhaps unexpectedly, given the literature documenting the frequent male bias of trade unions) valuable space within which women workers have been able to make their voices heard. Mobilisation, consciousness-raising, and strategic orientation in the context of a rapidly expanding export horticulture sector, and with a relatively flexible trade union leadership, has generated the positive feedback mechanisms mentioned above. These, in turn, have both boosted workers' (and women workers' in particular) position within the trade union whilst ameliorating their working conditions. As noted throughout this chapter, there

---

60   Moody 1997; Silver 2003; Dunn 2009.

are numerous cases, within agriculture, but also industry, where male-led trade unions concentrate on mobilising and representing the mostly male section of the permanently employed labour force. Indeed, there is no particular reason, given its earlier history of representing male-led family farmers, and then male wage workers, why the STR should not have gone down a similar path.

The process of re-orientation toward inclusion of women workers is, therefore, especially important. What is more, the relationship between the union leadership and the grassroots membership that allowed this re-orientation to occur is not unique to the São Francisco valley. In his discussion of the unionisation of Californian farm workers in the 1960s, for example, Ganz notes how the United Farm Workers possessed limited resources, but compensated for this through its 'resourcefulness', which derived, in part at least, from the interaction between the particularly dynamic union leadership and its internal organisational structures. He notes further that '[s]trategic thinking is reflexive and imaginative, based on how leaders have learned to reflect on the past, pay attention to the present, and anticipate the future'.[61] To be sure, the ability of trade union leaders in general, and the STR's in particular, to reflect and act on challenges faced by their membership, rests on flows of knowledge up and down the union hierarchy, and it is here that the activities of women workers have been invaluable.

This chapter also suggests that there is a continual process of strategic manoeuvre occurring in the grape sector, as farms and trade unions attempt to position themselves most favourably within the accumulation process. As soon as one side changes its strategies in order to enhance its position, the other side responds, setting off a new trajectory of class interaction (ranging from re-negotiation to outright struggle). Farms initially employed women on mostly permanent contracts, but have shifted in recent years towards employing a larger percentage of them on temporary contracts, primarily because of rising non-wage social costs. However, because of the rapid expansion of the sector, the absolute number of women workers employed in grape production has increased, which has provided a basis from which to up the campaign to improve women workers' conditions. To conclude, it is fitting to hear, once more, from one of the women working in the valley's grape sector. In an interview with the author, Elizabeth explained:

> Those beautiful grapes that you eat in your country, they are the result of our work, women's work. You've seen how nicely they are prepared. The

---

61   Ganz 2000, p. 1009.

majority of that work is done by skilled, professional women, like us. We have the delicate touch that enables us to produce these beautiful grapes.

She concluded:

We need to be more highly valued . . . in your country, who knows about how we work and live? We work on the farm, and then we get home and have another battle. We go back home and tidy it up, we get to bed at 11:30 or 12:00, and then need to get up at 4 a.m. to prepare our packed lunch and get to the collection point for around 6 a.m., to start work at 7 . . . People who eat these grapes need to know what our lives are like.

CHAPTER 6

Emergent Socialist Hegemony in Bolivarian Venezuela: The Rôle of the Party[1]

Gabriel Hetland

The rôle of political parties in processes of radical transformation is a subject of longstanding debate. High-profile leftist critics like Hardt and Negri see the party form as hopelessly outmoded, arguing that social movements are more effective in channelling the 'network power' of the 'multitude' in its struggle against 'empire'.[2] This position resonates with more anarchist and mainstream sociological critiques of parties and states (which are difficult to discuss in isolation from each other) as bureaucratic machines incapable of producing revolutionary change.[3] These critiques, which have called forth vigorous leftist defences of parties and states from authors like Tariq Ali and Gregory Wilpert, are not entirely invalid.[4] The question is whether recognising the limitations and dangers inherent to parties and states should lead to a rejection of these institutions as potentially fruitful vehicles for radical change.

The recent and ongoing wave of elections of leftist leaders across Latin America has put this question squarely on the current agenda of the left. Given that the region's 'left turn' began with Hugo Chávez's 1998 election, it should not be surprising that Venezuela has occupied a central place within this debate. Despite their differences, authors as diverse as Marta Harnecker, Michael Lebowitz, Diana Raby, George Cicariello-Maher, Dario Azzellini, Steve Ellner, Gregory Wilpert, and Sujatha Fernandes, amongst others, are relatively united on three points: (1) sympathy for what Chávez has sought to accomplish; (2) the view that Chávez's 'twenty-first century socialism' must be seen as distinct from Soviet-style 'twentieth-century' socialism; and, (3) a belief that

---

1   The author would like to acknowledge the generous readings given to this text by the editors of this volume, along with Michael Burawoy and Michael McCarthy.

2   Hardt and Negri 2000, 2004.

3   See Michels 1962; Weber 1968; Przeworski 1985; Scott 1998; Holloway 2002b; Zibechi 2010. Holloway and his followers do not necessarily consider themselves anarchist, but there are enough similarities in their position to merit making this connection. Scott openly identifies as anarchist; see Void Manufacturing 2009.

4   Ali 2004; Wilpert 2007.

the Bolivarian process necessitates a *rethinking*, but *not* a *rejection*, of parties and states as tools for radical change.[5]

This chapter takes up this challenge, examining the rôle of parties – in terms of their class character, internal structure, and relations to the state and civil society – in the construction of emergent socialist hegemony in the Venezuelan municipality of Torres. This concept refers to the largely *political* process of building popular consent for a socialist economy. The term 'emergent' highlights the incipient and unconsolidated nature of this hegemony. Socialism refers to an economic system that is explicitly geared towards meeting human needs, rather than the accumulation of capital or the expansion of the forces of production, under which economic decisions concerning the use of scarce resources are subject to democratic control by workers' and community-based councils and popular assemblies. The chapter is divided into two sections. The first section reviews the most important left and mainstream sociological critiques of parties as instruments of radical change. The following section elaborates a Gramscian theory of parties, which accepts the partial validity of these critiques but seeks to re-conceptualise rather than abandon the party as an instrument for change, and in particular for the construction of socialist hegemony. This theoretical perspective is explored empirically in the second section of the chapter, which analyses the conditions necessary for a political party of this type to be successful. Based upon a case study in the municipality of Torres, I argue that political, class, and bureaucratic based resistance faced by radical political leaders in Torres has been crucial in pushing a socialist agenda at the municipal level, since it has helped to solidify their horizontal links to popular classes and social movements. These links provided leaders with the support needed to carry out an ambitious project of political and economic transformation that, while remaining far short of the goal of constructing a socialist economy, has generated impressive levels of popular consent for continuing the struggle to reach this goal.

A Different Type of Party

Leftists who refuse to abandon the idea that parties can serve as useful tools of radical change must confront the arguments of those who are critical of this organisational form. Three critiques stand out as particularly important:

---

5   Harnecker 2008a; Lebowitz 2006, 2010; Raby 2008; Ciccariello-Maher 2007; Azzellini 2010; Ellner 2008a; Wilpert 2007; and Fernandes 2010. Of these scholars, Raby is the most critical of parties, though she agrees that states can be useful for change.

(1) parties are too rigid and hierarchical to respond effectively to the constantly changing conditions of struggle in a globalised/digitised world, with social movements seen as more effective (the Hardt and Negri argument); (2) parties seek to dominate and control social movement allies;[6] and, (3) due to electoral competition, parties cannot avoid oligarchisation, a process that leads to a growing gap between (a) leaders and bases, and (b) discourse and action (the Michels/Weber argument).

Each of these problems can be seen in the Bolivarian process, as shown by the work of various scholars and the discussion of Torres provided below. Raby and Jose Molina discuss the 'anti-party' origins of Chávez, noting how Chávez's rise was predicated on the inability of Venezuela's traditional parties – the centre-left Acción Democratica (Democratic Action, AD) and the centre-right Comité de Organización Política Electoral Independiente (Political Electoral Independent Organisation Committee, COPEI) – to effectively respond to the nation's changing reality in the 1980s and 1990s.[7] Chávez's Movimiento Quinto República (Fifth Republic Movement, MVR) and the Partido Socialista Unida de Venezuela (United Socialist Party of Venezuela, PSUV), which superseded the MVR in 2007, have also been criticised for problems of party rigidity and inability to adapt to changing circumstances.[8] Harnecker and Fernandes discuss the often-tense relationship between the MVR/PSUV and its social movement allies, noting party attempts to control grassroots Chavistas and communal councils.[9] Wilpert and Ellner examine the gap between party discourse and action, highlighting MVR leaders' efforts to circumvent a 2002 law mandating participatory budgeting, despite the MVR's rhetorical commitment to popular participation.[10]

Critics of the party can no doubt take these observations as proof that parties and revolutionary transformation do not mix. Gramsci provides an alternate way of responding, by means of a rethinking, rather than a rejection of, the party. In 'Observations on Certain Aspects of the Structure of Political Parties in Periods of Organic Crisis', Gramsci writes:

> Parties come into existence, and constitute themselves as organisations, in order to influence the situation at moments which are historically vital for their class; but they are not always capable of adapting themselves to

---

6   See, for example, Harnecker 2008a, an author who is by no means 'anti-party'.
7   Raby 2008; Molina 2004.
8   See contributions by Fernandes, Denis, and Lebowitz in Spronk and Webber 2011.
9   Harnecker 2008a; Fernandes 2010, p. 85.
10   Wilpert 2007, p. 58; Ellner 2008a, p. 183.

new tasks and to new epochs, nor of evolving *pari passu* [hand in hand] with the overall relations of force (and hence the relative position of their class) in the country in question, or in the international field. In analysing the development of parties, it is necessary to distinguish: their social group; their mass membership; their bureaucracy and general staff. The bureaucracy is the most dangerously hidebound and conservative force; if it ends up by constituting a compact body, which stands on its own and feels itself independent of the mass of members, the party ends up by becoming anachronistic and at moments of acute crisis it is voided of its social content and left as though suspended in mid-air.[11]

The passage touches directly on two of the problems noted above – the Hardt and Negri argument about party rigidity in the face of historical change and the Michels/Weber argument about oligarchisation, with Gramsci noting how the latter leads to the former. The issue of the party's relationship to civil society is not addressed, but is extensively dealt with by Gramsci elsewhere (as discussed below).

Gramsci's writings provide a means of re-conceptualising the characteristics that a party capable of generating radical/socialist transformation must have: (1) internal democracy; (2) horizontal links to the (a) urban/rural working class and (b) civil society;[12] (3) a practical and ideological commitment to the pre-figurative construction of democratic socialism; and, (4) links to, along with autonomy from, the (national) state. The first and second characteristics follow as obvious corollaries to the passage quoted above. This is not simply a matter of 'playing with democracy', as per Lenin's denunciation of those he sees as overly concerned with democratic proceduralism at the expense of effective party action.[13] As the above passage makes clear, internal democracy

---

11   Gramsci 2000, p. 219.

12   While the urban/rural working class is 'part' of civil society, I distinguish between the two to account for the specificity of the term civil society, which highlights the voluntary, non-state and non-economic nature of civil society.

13   The Gramscian theoretical perspective taken here amounts to a partial critique of Leninism. Gramsci considered himself a faithful follower of Lenin. But his insights into the links between the party and civil society (the particular details of which I do not entirely agree with, as discussed below), and his concern with internal party democracy, take Gramsci in a non-Leninist direction. It should be noted that Lenin's own writings on the party are marked by some ambiguity with respect to the question of party democracy. In *What is to be Done?* (1902) Lenin emphasises the importance of constructing a strong party leadership, made up of full-time 'professional revolutionaries' who are well steeped in Marxist theory, and openly dismisses those who are overly (in his view) concerned

and horizontal links connecting the party's leadership to its working-class base are essential for preventing bureaucrats ('the most dangerously hidebound and conservative force') from taking over and sapping the party's historic vitality. The maintenance of party vitality also requires horizontal links connecting the party to social movements. Gramsci's view of a 'totalitarian' (which like Burawoy I take to mean nothing more than 'all-encompassing')[14] party, that substitutes itself for all the ties party members previously found in a variety of social and cultural organisations, is highly problematic with respect to this. The complete subordination of social activism to party directives risks severing the party from the dynamism and creativity of social movements. Social movements must therefore remain autonomous from the party and state with respect to their operations but not necessarily with respect to their finances.

The demand that party/state leaders respect civic autonomy does not, however, negate the need for a specifically *political* leadership in order to achieve revolutionary transformation.[15] The party's rôle as the creator of a new, *socialist* culture and worldview is especially critical for the construction of an *emergent* socialist hegemony, which differs from a fully consolidated hegemonic system due to the lack of relatively automatic mechanisms for hegemonic reproduction.[16] This pedagogical work occurs through (1) the activism of organic intellectuals and (2) the construction of what Gramsci calls a 'concrete fantasy': 'a historical exemplification of the Sorelian myth – that is, of a political ideology expressed neither in the form of a cold utopia nor as learned theorising, but

---

with internal party democracy. At other times – in *State and Revolution* and the essay 'Dual Power', both written in the revolutionary ferment of 1917 – Lenin is more attentive to the potential for bureaucrats to abuse their power, and proposes concrete mechanisms, such as instant recall of elected officials, to prevent this from happening. Hal Draper's (1990) essay on Lenin's (non-) 'concept of the party' is worth consulting (I am indebted to Michael McCarthy for pointing this out). Draper's points about (1) Lenin's early reliance on Karl Kautsky, (2) his evolving thinking on the question of the party, and (3) the need to read Lenin's treatise in its particular historical context – that of autocratic Russia – are important. I do not fully agree with Draper's textual interpretation. In my view, the thrust of the text – even when allowances are made for historical context – is far from supportive of internal party democracy. It is important to note, as Draper does, that Lenin's writings have frequently been misinterpreted and used to justify practices that Lenin himself would never have supported.

14   Burawoy 2003, p. 226.
15   See, for example, Harnecker 2008a.
16   These more or less 'automatic' mechanisms of reproduction in consolidated hegemonic systems are what lead Gramsci to speak of the 'spontaneous' nature of popular consent. They include Althusser's 'ideological state apparatuses' as well as economic concessions, which Przeworksi (1985) calls the 'material bases of consent'.

rather as a creation of concrete fantasy which acts on a dispersed and shattered people to arouse and organise its collective will'.[17] In addition to their pedagogical function, concrete fantasies also have organisational and motivational value: by offering a concrete image of what socialism 'really is' (democratic control over economic decision-making), they can help dispel distorted views of socialism (that it equals state control of the economy or a lack of freedom), and convince people that it is something worth struggling for.

Being linked to state power, even at the local level, is crucial, since it provides the party with the means (i.e. financial resources, and the symbolic legitimacy that comes with state power) for constructing concrete fantasies. Having control over state resources also opens up possibilities for moving beyond distribution to *re*distribution, although having power at the local level almost always provides fewer opportunities for doing this than national power. Being part of the state, especially the national state, also brings certain dangers – of co-optation, bureaucratisation, and top-down control – as critics like Holloway, and Hardt and Negri are aware. This is why the maintenance of a certain level of party autonomy vis-à-vis the national state is so important, as a bulwark that can limit these dangers.

A theoretical basis has now been laid for this chapter's argument concerning the rôle parties (of a certain type) can play in processes of radical transformation. This argument is explored in empirical detail in the next section. The account is based upon five months of ethnographic fieldwork in Torres municipality, carried out over the course of several field visits conducted between August 2007 and May 2011. During this time, I directly observed political party (PSUV), communal council, and commune meetings, two yearly cycles of participatory budget assemblies, Chavista and opposition protests and rallies, and meetings between government officials and local communities. I also conducted several dozen interviews with Chavista and opposition neighbourhood activists, government functionaries, political and civic leaders, and workers in an electric meter factory. The account also draws upon newspapers and other primary source documents, and secondary literature.

Torres: Venezuela's First 'Socialist City'

In October 2004, Venezuelans throughout the country geared up for local and regional elections. In Torres, a largely agrarian municipality (population 185,275) in the central-western state of Lara, the race for mayor had been

---

17   See Gramsci 2000, pp. 239; Wright 2010 on 'real utopias'.

thrown into disarray in late 2003, when incumbent mayor Javier Oropeza left the ruling MVR to join the ranks of the anti-Chávez opposition. The MVR's initial decision to support Oropeza, a rising local media baron and son of one of Torres's wealthiest families, in the 2000 election had been based on the (correct) view that he could win. This strategy, in which the party set aside its revolutionary ideals for the sake of short-term electoral gain, had obviously not worked out entirely as planned, but that did not stop the same *realpolitik* logic from being used in the 2004 election. This time the party chose to support Walter Cattivelli, a medium-sized construction contractor whom locals told me 'was an Adecco [supporter of AD] his whole life' (that is, not someone with radical politics). Cattivelli faced off against Oropeza, who was supported by local commercial media, the church, and agrarian elites, and Julio Chávez, a relatively unknown candidate (of no relation to the president) with the Patria Para Todos (Fatherland for All, PPT), a small leftist party allied with the MVR at the national level that had been formed in the 1990s out of the remnants of another small leftist party, La Causa R (the Radical Cause). With little financing or institutional support, Chávez had the backing of local social movements, student activists, rural petty commodity producers (small-holding goat farmers), agricultural workers on the area's large cattle and dairy haciendas, workers from two local sugar processing plants, municipal and transport unions, and some middle-class professionals in Carora, Torres's capital (population approximately 100,000).

In a result that seemed to surprise everyone but himself, Chávez prevailed in the tight, three-way race, albeit by the thinnest of margins. One of the keys to Chávez's victory was the fact that, while the MVR leadership supported Cattivelli, many grassroots MVR members voted for Chávez. This grassroots rebellion was fuelled by the facts that (1) Cattivelli was seen as a top-down imposition, and (2) the last top-down candidate supported by MVR voters – Javier Oropeza – had gone on to betray the party. Chávez, by contrast, was seen as a grassroots candidate and his party, the PPT, was known for being significantly more internally democratic and ideologically cohesive than the MVR. The party's willingness to support relatively unknown, anti-establishment candidates bolstered these perceptions.

The MVR's regional leadership, led by Lara's governor Luis Reyes Reyes, was forced to accept Chávez's victory, but was not happy about it. According to Miguel 'Chicho' Medina, a social movement leader-cum-municipal functionary who currently heads the municipality's work-supporting communes and was an early ally of Chávez, 'Reyes Reyes never forgave Julio for beating his candidate'.[18]

---

18   This quote comes from an informal conversation with the author, November 2010. All quotations are from conversations with the author during fieldwork carried out between August 2007 and May 2011.

Despite losing the mayoralty, Reyes Reyes and the MVR had managed to retain a majority of seats on the municipal council, providing the party with a useful institutional base for continuing to challenge Chávez. Medina and others report that Reyes Reyes mounted a 'parallel City Hall', funnelling thousands of dollars to Naomi Lopez – a municipal councillor and close local confidante of Reyes Reyes – in an attempt to disrupt Chávez's ability to govern. The new mayor also faced continued opposition from the agrarian elite, who initially tried to buy him off. Chávez recounts that, 'they tried to seduce us. I received invitations to the *godarria's* exclusive clubs, to their *fincas* [plantations] for weekend retreats, offers of golden credit cards at local banks, and even invitations to the homes of high-society ladies'.[19] When seduction efforts failed, the opposition launched full-scale confrontation, which came from all sides. The opposition included local contractors upset at being excluded from municipal construction contracts; church leaders angered that Chávez had eliminated a lifetime pension previously paid to the bishop by the municipal government; and the usual suspects – the elite-controlled television, radio, and print media. Chávez even recounts that, 'the day after the election my head appeared in a frying pan on the cover of the newspaper', *El Caroreño*.[20]

Never one to back down from a fight (a quality that close supporters say can be infuriating), upon taking office in January 2005, Chávez quickly sought to make good on what he says was 'my only campaign promise: to build popular power'. The mayor's first move was to convoke a Municipal Constituent Assembly, which was modelled after the 1999 national constituent assembly that had rewritten Venezuela's constitution. For the next three months, 120 delegates – small-holding farmers, student and labour activists, social movement leaders like Chicho Medina, and many more – gathered in popular assemblies throughout Torres to rewrite the ordinances guiding their municipality. Medina, Chávez, and others say that the same institutions – the PPT, and various social movement, labour, and student organisations – that had helped elect Chávez were at the forefront of these efforts. The process was designed to be as participatory as possible: delegates were chosen in popular assemblies, and the results of the three-month process were then discussed and voted upon in community assemblies held throughout the municipality.

---

19   Agrarian elites in Torres are known as the '*godarria*'. The term is said to come from the Gothic or *Godo* region of Spain from which Torres's leading families emigrated several hundred years ago.

20   The paper, Torres's only daily, is owned by the Oropeza family, and has been edited by ex-mayor Javier Oropeza since his electoral defeat in 2004. Since then, Chávez and his successor, Edgar Carrasco (Torres's mayor from 2008 onwards), have faced a constant barrage of criticism in the paper's pages for their alleged 'ineptitude' and 'negligence'.

According to Chávez, local and regional MVR leaders viewed all this as 'anarchy' and 'said that it could never work'. The process also faced resistance from the local commercial media and national bureaucrats, with the National Electoral Council refusing to oversee a referendum on the results of the municipal constituent assembly. Ironically, this political, class, and bureaucratic resistance helped to strengthen the participatory nature of the process, since it served to solidify horizontal linkages (1) between key PPT leaders (such as Chávez) and the party's base and (2) between the party and its social movement allies. The fact that the PPT was autonomous from the MVR's regional and national leadership structure, without being seen as an outright 'enemy' of the Bolivarian process, was also an asset, since it meant that Chávez was free to put together an administration led by social movement leaders – like Chicho Medina and Eladio 'Lalo' Paez, the head of Torres's Office of Citizen Participation, and a co-founder with Medina of an important local cultural movement – rather than party bureaucrats. At the same time, it should be noted that local radicals in Torres, both inside and outside of the local state and party structures, drew heavily upon the revolutionary/socialist ideology of the MVR/PSUV. They also received important political support from a few top officials within the national state, including President Chávez, who in 2006 appointed Julio Chávez as the only mayor on his Presidential Commission on Popular Power.[21] Even Reyes Reyes eventually came around, christening Torres 'Venezuela's first socialist city' following the success of the municipality's participatory budget (see below). This highlights local radicals' highly contradictory relationship to the national state, underscoring the importance of both their political autonomy from, and their ideological (and more occasional political) links to, the Chavista establishment.

Build It Now: Prefiguring Socialism through Concrete Fantasies[22]

The chapter's next section details two examples of the construction of concrete fantasies in Torres: participatory budgeting and a 'socialist' electric meter factory. The examples are used to highlight several theoretical issues discussed above: (1) the use of concrete fantasies as a means of building popular consent

---

21   Marta Harnecker, who has worked in various capacities for the Venezuelan national state since Hugo Chávez came to power, played an important rôle in Torres, writing a 2008 book on the municipality (Harnecker 2008b) that helped to bring it positive national attention.

22   This slogan is the title of a book by Michael Lebowitz (2006) and has also been used by the South African Communist Party.

for the transition to a socialist economy; (2) the rôle played by organic intellectuals in connecting concrete issues to larger struggles; (3) the struggles waged by local political and social movement leaders and activists against regional political leaders, national bureaucrats, and local elites to construct these concrete fantasies; and (4) the way in which these struggles have helped reinforce horizontal linkages between state/party leaders and bases, and between the party and its social movement allies.

Participatory Budgeting

In terms of building popular power, the most important institutional innovation of the Julio Chávez administration was the implementation of an ambitious participatory budget (PB) that transfers decision-making power over 100 percent of the municipality's investment budget to local citizens. The first step in the municipality's yearly budget cycle is a 'participatory diagnosis' in which volunteers from each of the municipality's 550–plus communal councils map out their community's resources and needs.[23] A popular assembly is then held, with 20 percent of the communal council's members needed for a quorum, after which discussion and then voting on the community's priorities takes place. Elected delegates from each communal council then come together in two rounds of parish assemblies – held in each of the municipality's 17 parishes – to discuss and vote upon projects.[24] Although the budget requires formal approval from the Consejo Local de Planificación Popular (Local Public Planning Council), the results of these parish assemblies are binding, with Julio Chávez fond of recounting that 'the mayor cannot even veto these decisions'.

In addition to generating concrete projects – roads, schools, and sewers – Torres's PB has served as a practical arena where values associated with the idea of 'twenty-first century socialism' – participation, deliberation, and solidarity – have been implemented. The PB also served as a venue for the inculcation of socialist ideology, which functioned in a variety of ways. (It should, however, be noted that the PB includes participants with a range of political beliefs, with local officials in Torres scrupulous about maintaining this political pluralism.) Delegates in parish assemblies would often publicly identify themselves as 'socialist' and used the term to discuss the merits of particular projects (that is, by putting forth arguments about why a given project

---

23   Communal councils are civic associations, composed of 200–400 families in urban neighbourhoods, and 20–40 families in rural communities. They are fiscally dependent upon and organisationally autonomous from the state; in practice the degree of this autonomy varies greatly.

24   Parishes are the lowest political administrative units in Venezuela.

was 'socialist' and should be funded). As Gramsci's notion of concrete fantasy as 'a political ideology expressed neither in the form of a cold utopia nor as learned theorising' suggests, ideas about socialism functioned less as a fixed reference point than as an open-ended horizon of struggle that helped to both (1) facilitate discussion of practical matters (such as whether electricity, education, or transportation was the most pressing issue facing a given community) and (2) connect these practical discussions to more explicitly political questions about class, power, and strategy.[25] Organic intellectuals like Julio Chávez, Chicho Medina, Lalo Paez, and President Chávez himself, played an important rôle in helping to draw out these connections. This pedagogical work took place in a variety of venues, including communal council meetings, parish PB assemblies, community and party-run media, state-funded educational and cultural 'missions', and weekly PSUV meetings (and in PPT meetings before Julio Chávez, and most of his supporters, joined the PSUV in 2007).[26]

A fierce struggle was needed to ensure that the PB would actually be implemented. As mentioned, the MVR had retained a majority of seats on the municipal council. Given that the PPT and MVR were part of the same alli-

---

25   The following definition of socialism, given to me by the facilitator of a meeting in which
      multiple communal councils had come together for the purpose of forming a 'commune',
      could have come straight out of Gramsci's discussion of concrete fantasies in the *Prison
      Notebooks*: 'socialism isn't an abstract theory of Leninism, or Marxism, it's the practice . . .
      it's what you see here . . . it's what we do'.

26   A good example of this work is the way in which Venezuela's energy crisis of 2010 was dealt
      with in weekly PSUV meetings I attended in the spring of 2010. At the time, Venezuela was
      in the midst of a serious energy crisis, with regular blackouts in Torres and throughout the
      country. The crisis was a regular topic of discussion in PSUV meetings, with Julio Chávez
      and other party leaders discussing how factors such as global warming (nearly always
      linked to global capitalism), and the substantial increase in ordinary Venezuelans' access
      to electricity over the course of the Chávez presidency (a topic dealt with in a surprisingly
      critical manner), had helped to contribute to the current crisis. As one means of miti-
      gating the crisis, the party spearheaded a plan to distribute energy-efficient light bulbs
      to local residents, with party leaders stressing the need to explain the 'true' nature of
      the energy crisis, as opposed to the view presented in the commercial media, in which
      President Chávez was blamed for the crisis (along with everything else bad happening in
      Venezuela). PSUV meetings were also important as a venue where grassroots party mem-
      bers worked through their own understanding of what socialism was. This often occurred
      by means of discussion of the gap between socialist discourse and practice, with grass-
      roots party members frequently airing grievances about a few local 'socialist' factories
      which had failed to pay their workers on time, and were seen as 'worse than capitalist fac-
      tories'. Finally, it is worth noting how party meetings provided a regular venue for public,
      and often quite critical, discussion between party leaders and base-level members.

ance, and that this alliance (which also included the Venezuelan Communist Party) controlled eight out of the council's nine seats, there should have been little difficulty in getting the council's members, almost all of whom had to express rhetorical support for popular participation, to approve the PB. But in December 2005, when it was time for the council to do so, a majority refused. Chávez, who comments that, 'I had to fight against my own party...they thought I was crazy to give up my power', responded by mobilising hundreds of supporters, who physically occupied the council and refused to leave until the budget they had spent months discussing had been approved. Edwin Juarez, a PPT-cum-PSUV municipal councillor – who says that he was the only consistent supporter of Chávez during this time period – told me that the same tactic had been used in May 2005 when the council had refused to approve the results of the Municipal Constituent Assembly.

In terms of its impact, Torres's PB can be linked to several important local developments, including (1) a dramatic reduction in practices of clientelism and corruption, and (2) the opening up of avenues for direct citizen input into government decision-making. The most important result of Torres's PB (in terms of the present discussion) may be the way it has generated high levels of popular consent for ideas about popular power and socialism. This can be seen in the dramatic increase in the electoral support given to radical political leaders (those who actually support the construction of popular power and socialism) in Torres between 2004 and 2010. While Julio Chávez barely managed to scrape by in the 2004 mayoral election, in 2008 his successor, Edgar Carrasco, won office with 48.3 percent of the vote (an impressive achievement in Torres, given that Julio Chávez was elected with only 35.6 percent in 2004).[27] In September 2010, Chávez won a National Assembly seat with almost 56 percent of the vote, one of the highest percentages achieved by any PSUV candidate in the election. In 2013, Carrasco was re-elected with 54.7 percent.

Equally impressive is the way in which Torres's PB has altered popular consciousness. In addition to leading thousands of *Torrenses* (residents of Torres) to proudly self-identify as socialists,[28] the PB has narrowed the gap separating rulers and ruled, a gap which, as Azzellini argues, lies at the core of capitalist social relations.[29] I was able to observe this first-hand while attending numerous PB parish assemblies. Following one assembly, I provocatively asked a teacher attending why PB made sense: 'Why not just leave the

---

27   CNE 2008; CNE 2004.

28   This phenomenon is obviously also linked to President Chávez's 2005 declaration of the socialist character of the Bolivarian Revolution, and the formation of the PSUV in 2007.

29   Azzelini 2010; this volume.

budget to the mayor to decide?' His response, clearly tailored to my national identity, was immediate: 'Why not? I'm equal to the president of the United States. If he can make decisions, why can't I?' Another delegate, standing nearby, chimed in to say:

> In the past, government officials would stay in their air-conditioned offices all day and make decisions there. They never even set foot in our communities. So who do you think can make a better decision about what we need, an official in his air conditioned office who has never even come to our community, or someone who is from the community?

Both responses indicate the impressive degree to which residents of Torres have accepted the essentially socialist idea that ordinary citizens from the popular classes can be entrusted with significant decision-making power over issues that in the past would have been left to government officials, elites, and technocratic experts.

Socialist Production

As the Bolivarian process has progressed in Torres, there has been a growing sense that, if 'twenty-first century socialism' is to be more than a slogan, institutions must be constructed – or expropriated – to allow popular control to extend from *political* decision-making to *economic production*. The second example of a concrete fantasy in Torres is a socialist electric meter factory (its official name) that began production in late 2010, and addresses this issue head-on. Unfortunately, since the factory had only been in operation for three months at the time of research (December 2010), this discussion will raise as many questions as it answers. To facilitate the analysis, it is worth restating Lebowitz's three elements of the 'elementary socialist triangle': (1) social ownership of the means of production, (2) worker control over production, and, (3) production for collective needs.[30]

An agreement between the Torres municipal government and Petróleos de Venezuela, S.A. (Petroleum of Venezuela, PDVSA), Venezuela's national oil company, established the electric meter factory. The agreement was signed in May 2009, with PDVSA agreeing to construct the factory, which relies on technology from China.[31] From the beginning of its operation, the plant has been a contested space. The plant's workers – who appear to be quite united – and local community residents have been pushing for worker and community

---

30   Lebowitz 2010.
31   Escalante 2009.

control over the operation and profits of the factory. The Ministry of Electrical Energy, the de facto owner of the plant, has not, however, acceded to all of the workers' and community leaders' (many of these being the same people) demands.

As of December 2010, the all-important issue of ownership over the factory and its products, seen by workers and communities associated with the factory as key, remained unresolved. The workers of the factory have pressed the Ministry of Electrical Energy (MEE) to designate the factory as 'social property'. This would mean that instead of the state deciding (via the MEE) how to use the factory's profits, it would be the workers themselves who would do so. The workers have already put together a proposal by which the factory's profits would be given to local communities (via communal councils and communes). Under the proposal, local communities would have to meet and decide, in popular assemblies, upon project ideas. These project ideas would then be submitted to the factory's Workers' Assembly (see below), which would have final say. If enacted, the workers' proposal would effectively establish social ownership over the factory, which as Lebowitz notes must include mechanisms for *community*, as well as worker, input into economic decision-making.[32]

Unfortunately, key officials in the MEE whom workers strongly suspect are opposed to their proposal have been dragging their feet on the issue. Several delegations of workers have travelled to Caracas to pressure the MEE to make a decision. But, as of December 2010, the ministry had still failed to convene a meeting of the factory's Board of Directors, which must meet to decide the issue. The board is composed of seven members, three appointed by the MEE and four elected by the plant's workers. This seemingly democratic, pro-worker arrangement belies the fact that the board must come to a consensus for crucial decisions (such as the factory's property status), effectively giving the board's ministry-appointed members veto power. The workers, however, are aware of the struggles waged by workers elsewhere – such as at the Sidor steel plant in Ciudad Guayana which was only nationalised after a protracted fight that led to President Chávez's eventual intervention on behalf of the workers – and spoke openly of the possibility that direct action on their part might be needed to force the issue.

Somewhat more progress has been made in terms of worker control over production. The plant's 113 workers are organised into a Workers' Assembly, composed of all workers and empowered to make decisions regarding day-to-day operations, such as plant hours. Other decisions are made by a Workers' Council, made up of nine committees (health, discipline, etc.), each with two

---

32   Lebowitz 2010.

members elected by the Workers' Assembly. As one of the plant's supervisors told me, the workers determined their own schedule, a contrast – she noted – with how things work in capitalist factories: 'This isn't like a private firm, where if your boss says that you have to show up at such and such a time, you have to. It doesn't matter if you live far away, or anything. Here, this is decided by consensus'. The workers have also put together a proposal that would equalise pay amongst all of the factory's employees, including the plant director. According to workers, the Workers' Assembly will ultimately decide on the proposal, though the Board of Directors (which was still non-existent at the time of research) must consider it first. The factory's hiring system represents one of the most promising areas in terms of worker and community self-management. As a worker told me, all but six of the plant's 113 employees 'were chosen by assemblies, who took the person's situation into account, what their economic situation was, if they really needed this job, if they had kids'. The area supervisor mentioned above again noted how different this was from an impersonal capitalist firm, where 'they don't care who you are'.

The issue of whether the factory is producing for collective or individual needs remains unclear. It will depend, to a large extent, upon whether the factory is designated as social or state property; the former would clearly open up more possibility for producing for collective needs. The question of how the factory's products (electric meters) are distributed is also key, with distribution via the market, state, or some form of social exchange mechanism clearly holding out different possibilities in terms of production for collective or individual needs (with social exchange or state distribution holding out greater possibilities for producing for collective needs). Unfortunately, workers at the factory were unable to enlighten me much on this issue, possibly due to the plant's limited time in operation.

Despite these unanswered questions, and the crucial, unresolved issue of ownership, the factory can be seen as a relatively hopeful example of the potential for establishing democratic worker and community control over production. Obviously, even if the factory is designated as social property, it will have a limited impact in terms of directly challenging the still-overwhelming capitalist character of economic production in Torres. The factory is, however, of immense symbolic and political value, and has been taken as a source of inspiration by thousands of local radicals who believe that it is possible to establish socialist production. Most importantly, the factory is a concrete site where the intertwined class/political struggle to establish democratic control over production is actively taking place.

Conclusion: The Struggle Continues

Amongst certain circles in Venezuela, Torres has been seen as a model for how to construct popular power. Julio Chávez has travelled throughout the country, as well as abroad, speaking about the municipality's constituent assembly and participatory budget. And over the course of 2010, Chicho Medina travelled regularly to the municipality of Yare, in the state of Miranda, to advise local officials who had convened their own municipal constituent assembly modelled on Torres. Given this, it is important that the lessons of Torres be clearly understood. This chapter has focused on one of the key lessons of Torres, regarding the rôle that a particular type of political party can play in processes of radical transformation. As the above discussion has sought to demonstrate, this is a party that is (1) internally democratic, (2) horizontally linked to (a) the urban/rural working class and (b) civil society, (3) ideologically and practically committed to the pre-figurative construction of democratic socialism, and (4) linked to, but autonomous from, the national state.

The discussion has also examined the particular conditions under which a party with these characteristics may be found, highlighting how the contradictory nature of the relationship between local, regional, and national class and political actors helped to strengthen the hand of local forces in the PPT (and then PSUV) committed to popular power and socialism. As noted, the class, bureaucratic, and political resistance faced by political radicals in Torres helped to facilitate the construction of popular power by solidifying party leaders' horizontal links to popular classes and social movements. In dialectical fashion, these links provided leaders with the popular support they needed to overcome elite resistance to their attempts to construct concrete fantasies. These concrete fantasies, in turn, helped to generate popular consent for the idea of moving to a socialist economy, with organic intellectuals playing a key pedagogical rôle in drawing out the connections between local struggles and larger issues. The contradictory relationship that radical local political leaders had to the national state – drawing on the state's revolutionary and socialist discourse while (initially) remaining politically autonomous – was also crucial, since it provided them with important discursive and institutional tools, along with the political breathing room needed to effectively make use of these tools.

As the above discussion should have made abundantly clear, the expansion of popular power depends upon popular struggle. Successful struggles, however, can bring unintended consequences; one consequence of the success of radicals in Torres is that it has brought them *inside* the power structures they previously struggled *against*. The clearest example of this is the trajectory of Julio Chávez, who in just six years went from being a local, anti-establishment fringe candidate to a national assembly member with the ruling PSUV.[33] Chávez's rise appears (perhaps unsurprisingly) to have partially blunted his radical edge. In PSUV meetings in late 2009 and early 2010, Chávez occasionally sounded like the MVR leaders he used to rail against. Chávez spoke frequently of the need for PSUV members to avoid publicly criticising the party, alleging that public criticisms of the party (even when justified) would serve to strengthen the 'enemies of the revolution'; on a separate occasion, Chávez had told me of how MVR leaders had often used this label in their attempts to discredit him during his time as mayor. And in April 2011, Chávez was featured in a prominent, front-page piece in a leading regional newspaper, appearing to offer relatively unconditional support to Reyes Reyes as the PSUV candidate for the 2012 governor's race, following statements from President Chávez that Reyes Reyes should be the candidate (*El Informador* 2011). Chávez was upset about the article, which he claims took his words out of context, but he has not withdrawn his support for Reyes Reyes, an indication of his changed position within the party, and a sign of the distance he has travelled since his days of challenging Reyes Reyes as Torres's mayor. The fire in Chávez's belly has not been completely extinguished, as the prominent rôle he played supporting the formation of a 'radical current' within the PSUV in November 2010, despite the president's vocal opposition to the idea, shows.[34]

As is the case throughout Venezuela, Torres is a long way from socialism. This reality is underscored by the fact that the wealth and economic power of the local agrarian elite remains largely untouched. The municipality's continuing reliance upon central government transfers for the vast majority of its

---

33   Chávez's rise through the PSUV has not happened without a fight. When he tried to run for governor in the June 2008 PSUV primary, party leaders in Lara initially blocked him, since they did not want to see a challenge against their preferred candidate, Henri Falcon. They blocked him despite the fact that Falcon is alleged to have supported the 2002 coup against President Chávez (similar to Javier Oropeza) and was always seen by Julio Chávez as a 'neoliberal'. Chávez was only allowed to run in the primary after hundreds of his supporters mobilised in support of his candidacy, prompting a phone call from the president telling Chávez that he could run. Chávez lost badly to Falcon, but feels as though he has had the last laugh, with Falcon leaving the PSUV in early 2010. Ironically Falcon joined the PPT, which has moved away from its radical roots, and now seeks to present itself as a 'third way' between President Chávez and the anti-Chávez opposition. Julio Chávez was also initially blocked by regional PSUV leaders from running in the party's May 2010 primary leading up to the September 2010 National Assembly elections, although in the end he was allowed to run, this time without any need for popular mobilisation.

34   *Aporrea* 2010.

revenues highlights its dependence and fiscal vulnerability. This shows that socialism cannot be constructed in a single city (much less one as fiscally poor as Torres), and underlines the fact that the possibilities for radical change and socialist transformation in Torres are dependent on changes happening at the national (and international) level. While it is beyond the scope of this article, it is clear that to actually challenge (as opposed to symbolically discrediting) the hold of capitalist relations of production in Venezuela, or even to alter the predatory, *rentier* nature of this capitalism, would, at a minimum, require addressing: (1) the nation's continued extreme dependence on oil; (2) the fact that the United States remains the single largest importer of Venezuelan oil; (3) the continuation of widespread corruption and inefficiency within the state bureaucracy; and, (4) the almost shocking fact, given the image of the Chávez administration presented by both supporters and opponents, that the private sector's share of economic activity in Venezuela has *increased* under President Chávez.[35] While Chávez has talked repeatedly of the need to tackle these issues, and there have been promising signs (for example, the effort to form a radical current in the PSUV) that grassroots Chavistas may take their own initiative on issues like corruption and bureaucratic power, progress has been painfully slow.

Despite these limitations at the local and national level, radicals in Torres have succeeded in doing something that would have been unthinkable just fifteen years ago: generating massive popular consent for the idea of moving towards a socialist economy. This active consent, which is linked to the on-going construction of the types of concrete fantasies discussed above, provides the basis for the claim that an emergent socialist hegemony has been estab-lished in Torres. This hegemony is fragile and unconsolidated, and it is likely that elite forces will seek to re-appropriate the popular energies unleashed in Torres in order to legitimate the continuation of capitalism and their own power. It cannot, however, be denied that the 'explosion of popular power' (to use a phrase coined by President Chávez) in Torres has resulted in a thorough transformation of local politics, helping to erode the gap separating rulers and ruled. The genie of popular power is out of the bottle and, whether or not it leads to socialism, it may not be entirely easy to put back inside again.

---

35   During a November 2010 meeting, held to launch the PSUV's 'radical current', Victor Álvarez, former minister of mining and basic industry in the Chávez administration, reported this fact (that is, that the percentage of private control over the economy has risen under Chávez). See also *Aporrea* 2009, as well as Weisbrot, Ray, and Sandoval 2009 on the surprising *lack* of state control over the economy under Chávez. For an alternative view, see comments by Lebowitz in Spronk and Webber 2011.

CHAPTER 7

Venezuela's Social Transformation and Growing Class Struggle[1]

Dario Azzellini

The Venezuelan process of social transformation, commonly called the Bolivarian process, did not evolve according to pre-established leftist theories. In the beginning, it characterised itself as anti-neoliberal rather than socialist. There was no revolutionary party, strong working-class organisation, or even a newspaper functioning as a leading or orienting structure. Some traditional leftist currents, including social democrats, orthodox Marxists, and self-proclaimed revolutionaries have dismissed the Venezuelan transformation process as nationalist and reformist, while others have praised the undoubtedly great advances in social justice as constituting socialism itself. The central question, however, should not be whether Venezuela has already built a socialist society (which is obviously not the case), or whether the state is putting into practice the right socialist politics, but rather how social relations and collective popular experiences have evolved during the past 12 years.

In contrast to traditional Leninist or social democratic approaches that see the state as the central agent of change, and autonomist approaches that conceive of no role for the state in a process of revolutionary transformation, the present investigation argues that the current transformation in Venezuela is the product of a two-track approach that produces a creative tension between constituent and constituted power.[2] Constituent power is understood as the legitimate collective creative capacity of human beings expressed in movements and in the organised social base to create something new without having to derive it from something previously existing. The constituted power – the state and its institutions – must guarantee the framework and conditions of

---

1 This chapter is based on intense fieldwork in Venezuela from six to eight months a year between 2003 and 2011. I have conducted workshops for spokespeople of communal councils (a non-representative structure for local self-government based on assemblies and spokespeople) from September 2007 to April 2008 and workshops about co-research in factories, as well as more than one hundred formal interviews with activists and institutional employees. In total, I visited around 150 different communal councils and half a dozen communes.

2 Zibechi 2006, p. 226.

this process. By providing examples of how self-organisation and conflict have evolved in workplaces and communities, this chapter argues that the Chávez government has been able to uphold and deepen the process of social transformation for at least a decade. Given the two opposing logics of constituent and constituted power, however, conflict between them is likely to increase.[3] This chapter analyses how the conflicts have evolved in the communities and workplaces, focusing on the period since 2007. Finally, I draw conclusions about the emancipatory character of the transformation process.

Constituent and Constituted Power: Growing Class Struggle in Venezuela

Constituent power and constituted power are based on two antagonistic logics. Based upon a fundamental contradiction, constituent power, the growing politicisation and organisation from below, and the ongoing development of popular power, clashes automatically with constituted power, resulting in growing conflicts. The contrast between the normative orientation and declared political intentions on one side, and the inherent logic of a bourgeois and capitalist state apparatus on the other, has grown increasingly acute in Venezuela since the election of Hugo Chávez, and particularly since the radicalisation of the Bolivarian process since 2003.

Since Chávez assumed power in February 1999, and especially since the transformation project consolidated after the defeat of opposition mobilisations in 2002–3, the government has tried to diversify production in the largely oil-dependent economy, to assume control over the secondary processing of its own resources, to democratise ownership and management of the means of production, and to promote forms of local self-organisation, popular participation and self-administration. The defeat of the *coup d'état* in 2002 opened up the path for a series of laws and social practices that point toward a structural transformation of the economy, society, and political system. The government concentrated on the building of state-guided production and distribution, as well as sponsorship and promotion of cooperatives, mixed-ownership models, and the co-management of companies. Several factories that were initially closed down after the business lock-out of 2002–3 were subsequently taken over by their workers, opening space for experiments with different forms of co-management and workers' control.[4] The government started innovative

---

3   For a detailed characterisation of the transformation process see Azzellini 2010a and 2010b.
4   Azzellini 2011a; 2011b.

social programmes called 'missions' and initiated models of participatory budgeting at the local level.[5]

State institutions in many cases support these processes of autonomy and self-administration, while at the same time they attempt to control and block them. So even if top-down and bottom-up strategies have maintained themselves in the same process of transformation for 14 years, remaining in constant tension, it is doubtful that they can be compatible over the long term. Top-down logic understands the state as the agent of transformation and sees popular power as part of its administration. The bottom-up perspective, by contrast, sees the state with a progressive government as a useful setting in which to build popular power but believes that the ultimate goal is to transcend the state-form. This basic contradiction prevents dual power from prolonging itself indefinitely. Autonomous organisation and popular power will increasingly limit and overflow constituted power if it does not limit them. They can only expand over time if they get the upper hand, in which case the constituent power would profoundly transform the constituted power.

The concept of constituent power in Venezuela needs to be connected theoretically to the new political culture and different forms of resistance that have emerged through the struggles in the barrios, which constitute the most important pattern of collective identification and organisation in Venezuela and the main support base for the process of transformation.[6] The majority of the barrios were created through occupations of private or public land, since cities did not offer any housing or land for newcomers. The territorial identification that has arisen in this context is not a nostalgic localism. Since a strong territorial segregation exists, the identification with a certain community automatically contains a class dimension. Sharing the experience of daily life and both the collective and precarious dimensions of the barrio or the rural community represents a basic facet of identity for the majority of Venezuelans. But this identification with place does not necessarily connote 'community'. Social living has to be constructed and maintained, and is therefore always a process. Many Venezuelan barrios have a long history of struggles. They had to defend themselves over dozens of years against evictions, and organise offensive battles for basic services. Through these defensive and offensive struggles residents of the barrios developed collective mechanisms of mutual aid.[7]

Given the prior absence of a broad, organised grassroots in Venezuela, a base capable of pushing forward the Bolivarian Revolution has had to be built

---

5 Azzellini 2010b, pp. 184–205; compare pp. 261–300; Azzellini and Ressler 2010. See also Hetland, this volume.
6 Azzellini 2010b.
7 Antillano 2005.

simultaneously with the unfolding of the transformation itself. Consequently, many government programmes and missions have aimed to build community capacity for self-organisation. In the context of a rentier economy dominated by oil, the landlord state is the main agent that handles and distributes the social wealth. As such, class struggle in Venezuela is also mediated through the state, as is the question of who has access to the oil revenues and where and how they are invested. The dominant presence of the state is not new in Venezuela, but the deepening of social transformation has multiplied the points of confrontation between constituent and constituted power. As such, class struggle over the state form has intensified under the Chávez administration. The broadening of institutions and the expanding of the state's role has resulted in a growing bureaucratisation, which in turn impedes the opening and the transformation. The broadening of direct grassroots participation brings an increase in the conflicts between the state and its popular base, especially in the sphere of production (where the interests at stake are high) as well as within the state, which itself becomes a site of class conflict. Therefore class struggle takes place in, with and against the institutions. The different moments of class struggle – resistance, insurrection, and constituent power (similar to the struggle in, against, and beyond capitalist relations, in accordance with critical Marxism) – are not separate events in chronological order as the thinking of the revolutions and movements of the nineteenth and twentieth centuries assumed, and as they are still presented by most currents in the social sciences. Today they have to be and are simultaneous.[8]

One indication of the intensification of the class struggle in Venezuela is the increasing frequency and intensity of social protests, which have blossomed in recent years, particularly since 2007. The liberal human rights organisation Provea presents its own figures in a special survey, stating there were 1,169 non-violent, and 143 violent protests in 2000–1, compared to 3,266 nonviolent and 46 violent protests in 2009–10. And while from 2000–1 to 2007–8 the number of strikes counted every year was between 57 and 132, the number of workers' strikes rose to 214 in 2008–9 and to 222 in 2009–10.[9] From the point of view of liberals and some small leftist groups opposed to the government this is clear proof of the failure of the transformation process – a view based on a simplified conceptualisation of the state, government, and revolutionary transformation, which tend to see the state as a neutral instrument of

---

8 Hardt and Negri 2002, p. 29.
9 See Provea 2011. The numbers are problematic since Provea – in a liberal logic – does not distinguish between protests to defend privileges and protests for access to rights and basic benefits. Nevertheless, a rise in conflict is manifest.

social transformation. By contrast, from a revolutionary and Marxist point of view the rise in social conflict in Venezuela is to be welcomed, since it is still a capitalist system with a bourgeois state. It can even be considered a great achievement of the transformation process that it has fomented class struggle. And it is an even greater achievement that social conflicts are growing in a society that since 1998 became less unequal then ever before in its history.

Poverty in Venezuela decreased from 50.4 percent at the end of 1998 to 31.9 percent at the end of 2011 and extreme poverty decreased from 20.3 percent at the end of 1998 to 8.6 percent at the end of 2011.[10] The Gini index went down from 0.465 in 1999 to 0.39 in 2011, meaning Venezuela shifted, in terms of income, from being one of the most unequal countries in Latin America to being one of the most equal (after Costa Rica and Uruguay).[11] Caloric consumption in Venezuela grew 55 percent between 1998 and 2008, from 1,800 calories per kilo (kcal) per habitant to 2,800 kcal per habitant. That is 100 kcal above the optimum level established by the Food and Agriculture Organization (FAO) of the United Nations. A national survey in Venezuela in 2008–9 established that 80 percent of the population was having three meals a day and 16.2 percent even four meals a day.[12] The population has free health care and free access to education at all levels. Venezuela ranks among the top five countries in the world in terms of the percentage of students in universities. In addition, Venezuela scored sixth out of 124 countries in Gallup's global wellbeing surveys (2010), with 64 percent of its population considering itself 'thriving', the same result as Finland. Higher percentage scores were obtained only by Denmark (79), Canada (69), Sweden (69), and Australia (66), while the US scored twelfth with 59 percent.[13]

---

10   Instituto Nacional de Estadísticas (INE) March 2012, 'Resumen de indicadores sociodemo-
      gráficos', available at: <www.ine.gov.ve/documentos/Social/IndicadoresSocioeconomicos/
      Resumen_ISD.pdf>. The data is based on the same methodology employed by the United
      Nations Economic Commission for Latin America and the Caribbean, World Bank, United
      Nations Development Programme, and the national statistic institutes of other countries.
11   Ibid.
12   AVN and MinCI 2011.
13   People interviewed for the survey were asked to rate their current wellbeing and their
      expectations for the next five years based on a scale of 1–10, with 10 being the best life pos-
      sible. The ones who are rating their actual situation at 7 or higher and their future lives
      at 8 or higher were considered to be 'thriving'. Only 19 countries reached a score over 50
      percent and the worldwide median was only 21 percent (Ray 2011).

Communal Councils and Self-Government

The 1999 constitution declares that Venezuela is a 'participatory and protago-nistic democracy'. A variety of mechanisms for the participation of the popu-lation in local administration and decision-making have been experimented with since then. At the beginning they were connected to local representative authorities and integrated into the institutional framework of representative democracy. Competing on the same territory as local authorities and depend-ing on the finances authorised by those bodies, the different initiatives showed little success. But constituent power made its way between self-organised ini-tiatives and institutional ones, between autonomy and co-optation, and any new participatory structure is a result of this tension. The idea of local self-administration is connected to the socialist ideas of the commune and also inspired by the experiences of indigenous and Afro-Venezuelan people, as well as by currents of Latin American Marxist thought, not least that of the Peruvian José Carlos Mariátegui, who Chávez references frequently in his pub-lic speeches.

In 2005, what later came to be called Communal Councils (CC) began form-ing parallel to the elected representative bodies of constituted power. Their construction began as an initiative from below. In January 2006, Chávez adopted this initiative and began to promote it formally. In April 2006, when already approximately 5,000 CCs existed, the National Assembly approved the Law of Communal Councils, which was reformed in 2009 after intense dis-cussions with CC spokespeople.[14] To support the community self-organising processes the government created the Ministry of Popular Economy in 2004, which was transformed into the Ministry of Communal Economy in 2007 and then the Ministry of Communes in 2008. The CCs are the smallest unit of con-struction of direct democracy and self-government in Venezuela. In urban areas they encompass some 150–400 families, in rural zones, at least 20 fami-lies, and among indigenous people, at least 10 families. The heart of the com-munal councils and its decision-making body is the Assembly of Neighbours.

CCs are financed directly by the central state and its institutions, thus avoiding major interference from other representative bodies, such as offi-cial municipalities. It is difficult to quantify the exact amount of finances transferred to CCs every year, since they get support from all institutions on a

---

14 Among other changes the minimum number of households forming a CC in urban areas was reduced from 200 to 150, a coordinating body among the spokespeople was intro-duced, and the financial body does not have to assume the legal form of a cooperative any more.

local, regional, and national level. But if we consider only the finances flowing through the central financial fund created exclusively for CCs and the Ministry of Communes, it is clear that the state allotted US$2.79 billion in 2007 and US$3 billion in 2008 to CCs and communes under construction.[15] The law does not give any entity the authority to reject proposals presented by CCs, but the relationship between CCs and established institutions is not exactly harmonious.

Opinions differ as to whether or not CCs can be defined as instances of popular power. Liberal analysts tend to see them as an extension of the state. Since the CCs tend to transcend the division between political and civil society (i.e., between those who govern and those who are governed), liberal analysts who support that division view the CCs in a negative light, arguing that they are not an independent civil society organisation, but rather are linked to the state.[16] In fact, however, they constitute a parallel structure that gradually draws power and control away from the state in order to govern on their own. Conceptually they should form the foundation of what since 2007 has been discussed as a communal state (*el Estado Comunal*). The main idea is to form council structures of all kinds (CCs, communes, and communal cities) that coordinate and will gradually supplant the bourgeois state. The future communal state would be subordinate to popular power,[17] which would replace bourgeois civil society. This would overcome the rift between the economic, social, and political – between civil society and political society – which underlies capitalism and the bourgeois state.[18] It would also prevent, at the same time, the over-centralisation that characterised the countries of 'real socialism', where civil society was underdeveloped or non-existent and the state became everything.[19]

The CCs are best seen, however, as a mechanism of self-government designed to maintain the pressure of constituent power over constituted power.[20] Since the CCs are community-based and not part of the representative institutional framework, they are better situated to organise parallel to the constituted power and confront it. The CCs are particularly important in advancing a 'new geometry of power'. Existing 'power geometries', or the formal geography of power

15   Azzellini 2010b, p. 279.
16   Banko 2008; García-Guadilla 2008; Lovera 2008.
17   AN-DGIDL 2007.
18   Capital is based on this separation and reproduces it constantly, while the state regulates the separations. Holloway 2004, p. 94.
19   *Aló Presidente* 290, 19 August 2007, in Chávez 2008, p. 67.
20   Massey 2009.

relations in Venezuela, are highly unequal and antidemocratic; it is thus necessary to reorganise the territorial dimensions of politics in the country.[21] CCs
provide a stronger voice to the territories with a long history of marginalisation, such as impoverished rural communities, or poor urban barrios. The form
of political participation has likewise changed in this context, from passive
and individual to active and collective: 'Needs that until recently were solved
in the domestic sphere, within each home, now assume a collective character
and are considered problems of the whole community which must participate
actively to solve them, valuing therefore the *space of the collective*'.[22]

By 2011, the overall number of CCs in Venezuela reached 40,000. To establish
the initiative of the CC at the community level proved to be the right step to
promote participation. The dimension of the community corresponds to an
existing self-identification with a neighbourhood, a sector, and in its smallest
dimension, with a community, which usually is the centre of the construction of social relations and the centre of life. As already noted, the identification with the community usually is stronger than a professional or workplace
identification.

While the state initiative has been fundamental for the rapid proliferation
of the CCs and made it possible to reach out to many communities which otherwise lack the experience necessary to start a process of self-organisation
towards self-administration, in the concrete experience of day-to-day activities, state institutions often continue to constrain the initiatives of communities. The relationships between the communities and the state are riddled with
tensions. Every CC and commune that I visited during my fieldwork reported
bad experiences with state institutions. The most frequent complaints concern the length of proceedings, delays because of incomplete information,
bad accessibility, unfulfilled promises, lack of coordination and competition between different institutions, insufficient support, and attempts at co-
optation. Institutional inefficiency has led to frustration and disappointment,
even demoralisation. Similar, or even identical, projects presented to the same
institution by different communities can take between three and 18 months
to be financed, which makes it difficult for communities to plan, obstructing
their development as self-administered units. Paradoxically, there are also
cases where finances from the state were made available too quickly, without
sufficient preparation or planning. There is significant unevenness of capacity across existing CCs, depending on the local historical experience of organisation, pre-existing activism, education, access to information, and political

---

21   Di Giminiani 2007.
22   Lacabana and Cariola 2005, p. 37.

orientation. While communities usually have relatively clear ideas about their needs and desires, they often lack the necessary finances, know-how, and resources for planning. Communities therefore request institutional support from the state, but want the institutions to submit to the will and needs of the autonomous entities of the ccs. The communities, in other words, see access to benefits as their right, but in dealing with state institutions they frequently run into attitudes of contempt, and the expectation from officials that they be subordinate and grateful.

Almost all the cc activists interviewed during my field work pointed out in different ways the basic contradiction between constituent and constituted power: 'These nice people who already made themselves comfortable in their offices are not willing to renounce their benefits, they live on the needs of the people. It is like a little enterprise, you understand?'[23] So the solution is not to simply hire better employees, but to create a new institutionality, which gradually abolishes the separation between institution and 'object' of the programmes. However, mere intention does not mean that it will take place. Since institutions tend to try and stay in control of social processes and reproduce their power, it is necessary to subordinate the old institutions to popular power. And at the same time the new institutionality, created from below – this could be the ccs, communes, etc. – have to take over collectively and self-administer the tasks and services that the old institutionality offered and fulfilled.

The struggle to build local structures of self-administration and direct democracy, to overcome the bourgeois model of autonomous spheres (political, social, and economic) which underlies capitalism, is a struggle between two different systemic visions, and is potentially a struggle for the dismantlement of the bourgeois state necessary for capitalist production and reproduction. It is also a struggle about who decides, and how decisions are made, with regard to how to use a relevant part of the social wealth. It is, furthermore, a struggle over different criteria, particularly regarding the ordering and character of the priorities of society. All of this taken together is a struggle between capital and labour; it is class struggle.

Ownership and Management of Means of Production

The approaches from below and above present in the Bolivarian process and within the government maintain a constant and unresolved tension with

---

23 Thamara Esis, personal interview, 31 March 2008. Thamara Esis is spokesperson of a cc in the district of Santa Rosalía, Caracas.

regard to the economy as well. Between 2001 and 2006 the Venezuela government – in addition to asserting state control over the core of the oil industry – focused on promoting cooperatives for any type of company, including models of mixed property, co-administrated cooperatives with the state or private entrepreneurs. In the pre-Chávez era, Venezuela was one of the Latin American countries with the fewest cooperatives.[24] The 1999 constitution assigned the cooperatives a special weight. They were conceived of as contributing to a new social and economic balance, and, thus, received massive state assistance. The favourable conditions led to a boom in the number of cooperatives founded. In mid-2010, according to the national cooperative supervisory institute (Superintendencia Nacional de Cooperativas, SUNACOOP), 73,968 cooperatives were certified as operative, bringing the national cooperative membership to an estimated total of two million, although some people participated in more than one cooperative and also have another job.[25]

But the rapid growth of cooperatives made it difficult to create effective mechanisms to control the use of governmental aid.[26] The initial idea that cooperatives would automatically produce for the satisfaction of social needs, and that their internal solidarity based on collective property would spontaneously extend to their local communities, proved an error. Most cooperatives still followed the logic of capital; concentrating on the maximisation of net revenue without supporting the surrounding communities, many failed to integrate new members.[27] Many were also ridden with internal conflicts, a consequence mainly of inexperience in both social relations with the wider community and basic administrative tasks. These problems were magnified in the absence of collective supervision mechanisms.[28] Given these experiences SUNACOOP started to cooperate closely with the Communal Councils while promoting cooperatives.

In 2005, a new enterprise model was created to push a new orientation among companies. The *Empresas de Producción Social* (social production companies, EPS) received aid from the state and were prioritised in the distribution of state contracts. In exchange, they had to invest a part of their profits into the communities and introduce some sort of co-management in accordance with the

---

24   At the beginning of the Chávez government in 1998, there were only about eight hundred officially registered cooperatives with about twenty thousand members in total. For details about cooperatives in Venezuela, see Azzellini 2011a.

25   Baute 2009.

26   Ellner 2008b.

27   Piñeiro Harnecker 2010.

28   Ibid.

workers, and support the creation of cooperatives forming production chains.[29] The form of property, state, private, or collectively owned, was not considered important. No strict criteria were established. Private companies favoured models where workers would enjoy minority participation in ownership, with little or no participation in decision-making. Many companies not even fulfilling any of the different EPS criteria also registered as EPS to take advantage of the government aid. Some state-owned companies started creating chains of suppliers and processors with cooperatives, but no general reorientation could be forced. From the second half of 2007, no more EPS were created, although the term continues to be used ambiguously to refer both to socialist production companies and companies of social property.[30] Even if no clear distinction between both is made, the first refers more to the production mode while the second refers more to the property model. But all socialist production companies are also supposed to be companies of social property and vice versa.

Beginning in 2002–3 workers in larger and more coordinated numbers began the process of taking back workplaces. This was at first in response to, and in the aftermath of, the employers' lockout of 2002–3, which the employers referred to as a 'strike', with the stated intention of toppling the Chávez government. They then refused to pay the workers, arguing that they were 'on strike'. And after a number of months, several employers then argued the financial loss made it impossible to re-open the factories. In the meantime the workers had not been paid, and in response took over several small- and medium-sized factories. At first, the government relegated the cases to the labour courts, and then in January 2005 began expropriations.[31] Beginning in July 2005, the government began to pay special attention to the situation of closed businesses, and since then hundreds of such companies have been expropriated. While coming two years after the occupations and entrepreneurs' strike of 2002–3, the government response was a result of the pressure exerted by the workers together with the urgent need to boost national production.

---

29   It refers to the process beginning with the raw product, through the various stages of production and then to distribution, with as many instances as possible being taken over by cooperatives. For example, the Cooperativa Agroindustrial de Cacao in Sucre, which produces chocolate and chocolate-based sweets, formed a larger umbrella cooperative together with the cooperatives of the cocoa producers. The coop gets the sugar it needs from a regional sugar producing company. It also helped the peasants living in the communities near the factory to set up cooperatives for milk production, and now buys the milk it needs from them.

30   Álvarez and Rodríguez 2007.

31   Ellner 2006, p. 85.

At the time this occurred, in 2005, the workers' movement was not sufficiently organised to respond to the call by the government to take over and restart production in previously unproductive factories. The government offered support for those wanting to take over factories, and Chávez read a list of approximately 1,000 unproductive workplaces on TV. In addition, the Bolivarian trade union umbrella organisation, Unión Nacional de Trabajadores y Trabajadoras (National Worker's Union, UNT), put out the call to take over 800 closed-down businesses, but in the end only a small number of the companies listed were actually occupied.[32] But also the government institutions did not show serious engagement in supporting workers' occupations.

Most of the factories taken over by workers have faced massive challenges. The previous owners made these factories unproductive. They were equipped with obsolete machinery and were generally not producing. Most of the recuperated or expropriated production sites need huge investments to restart efficient production. Apart from the private sector, it is only the state that is in a position to dispense such large amounts of money, so state support is crucial. And even if the factories are in a condition to restart production, without state support the factories have to compete entirely in the capitalist market and adopt its rules, a situation which raises another host of challenges.

A systematic policy for expropriations in the productive sector did not exist until 2007. Between 2002 and 2005 the occupations of production sites were born out of defensive situations, mainly motivated by the will to maintain the workplace in the face of a company's closure. The radicalisation of practices, and a profound political reflection, usually followed the takeovers. Expropriations have been mainly the result of the pressure placed on state institutions by occupations and mobilisations. The best-known example of workers' struggle for nationalisation, and also the biggest production site that has been nationalised, is the Siderúrgica de Orinoco (Sidor) steel plant in the southeastern region of Bolívar. The steelworkers of Sidor – which at the time

---

32 See Azzellini 2009, p. 174. The UNT was formed in 2004 as an umbrella organisation for most of the leftist union currents. The biggest and most active currents are Marea Socialista (Red Tide), which also forms a current in the governing Partido Socialista Unido de Venezuela (United Socialist Party of Venezuela, PSUV) and the Colectivo Trabajadores en Revolución (Collective of Workers in Revolution, CTR), who both have been supporting takeovers and a strong autonomous stand as unions while also supporting critically the government. The third big current is the former Frente Bolivariano de Trabajadores y Trabajadoras (Bolivarian Workers' Front, FBT, later renamed FSBT, S for Socialist). The FBT is the most moderate and is allied to the more centrist factions of the government; it did not support takeovers of enterprises. Some smaller unions that are very active in struggles are also part of the UNT.

was owned by an Argentinean transnational company – led a struggle in 2007–8, together with subcontracted workers, to achieve nationalisation of the plant. Workers of some state-owned basic industries, as well as the communities in the region, also supported the struggle. Despite the negative attitude of the Bolivarian governor of the Bolívar region, Francisco Rangel Gómez, the movement mobilised until Chávez ordered the nationalisation.

In the context of an overarching strategy of industrialisation, the government initiated a plan in 2007 to build 200 new 'socialist factories'.[33] Local communal councils select the workers and the required professionals are drawn from state and government institutions. The aim of the plan is to gradually transfer the administration of the factories into the hands of organised workers and communities. But most state institutions involved do little to organise this process, or prepare the employees, which generates growing conflicts between workers and institutions. The same is happening more and more in expropriated enterprises where workers have begun to realise that the fact of being a state employee might have saved their job and gives them more guarantees of keeping it, but that it did not fundamentally change their working conditions or automatically accomplish co-management or workers' control.

One of the main motivations of workers to push for workers' control relates to production efficiency. Apart from better working conditions and a greater sense of dignity in their jobs, workers mainly demand workers' control because they see it as the only guaranteed way of lowering production costs and of producing in order to satisfy the needs of the majority of the population. Their experience with the state bureaucracy has shown them that most of the representatives of the state apparatus are not qualified for their jobs, or, for various reasons including corruption or internal power struggles, are not interested in efficient national production with worker participation in management, or in changing the relations of production.

Such was the experience in La Gaviota located in Cumaná, in the eastern state of Sucre, a plant producing canned sardines and *pepitonas* (a Venezuelan clam) and fish flour. The workers, together with surrounding communities, occupied the enterprise in early 2009 after the owner downsized production, stopped delivering products, and disrespected workers' rights. In May 2009 the national government ordered a temporary seizure of the plant, and at the

---

33   88 food industries, 12 chemical plants, 48 for machines and tools, 8 for electronic devices
      (computer, cell phones), 10 for plastics, tires, and glass, 8 for transport facilities, 4 con-
      struction companies, and 3 recycling industries. These socialist factories included in
      the plan are all newly built, mostly with the transfer of machines and know-how from
      Argentina, China, Iran, Russia, and Belarus. Azzellini 2009, p. 188.

end of November 2009 declared the nationalisation of La Gaviota. In this process, La Gaviota was subsumed into the newly constituted Venezuelan-Cuban mixed socialist enterprise, Pesquera Industrial del Alba (Industrial Fishing of the ALBA, Pescalba). Under state control the nearly 300 workers of La Gaviota enjoyed job stability, better wages, food coupons, and other basic rights.[34] After the plant began producing again, and the national government financed a partial modernisation of the machinery, La Gaviota increased production levels. Nevertheless, workers and communities did not have control of the plant. It was under the authority of Pescalba.

In 2010, production once again declined without any reasonable explanation. The workers of La Gaviota and the surrounding communities strengthened their struggle for workers' control. Intense protests in the plant at the beginning of October 2010 forced Pescalba to accept the participation of workers and community delegates on the directors' board of the enterprise. After elections in the plant and the surrounding community had been held, a new directors' board made up of three delegates each from the state, the workers, and the community, was constituted in January 2011.[35]

In April 2011, workers of La Gaviota and Pescalba, supported by other workers and nearby communities, organised protests because production in both enterprises was paralysed, and large amounts of production output was being held back in stock, instead of being distributed. Protesters accused the administration of the two enterprises of responsibility for these problems. Finally, Juan Carlos Loyo, Minister for Agriculture and Land, came to Sucre – following a direct order from Chávez – to talk with the protesters. Following the ministers' workers-guided visit to the La Gaviota plant, a general assembly with all workers of La Gaviota was held. Loyo announced that all members of the directors board of Pescalba corresponding to Venezuela were to be replaced, the whole financial administration of La Gaviota was to be handed over to the mixed board of directors of La Gaviota, and the workers and communities would soon start participating in the distribution of products as well as in every other part of the production process. Loyo also announced the opening of an investigation into the irregularities in La Gaviota and Pescalba. This was to be carried out by a commission in which he would personally participate alongside elected workers' delegates. A few days later, direct workers' participation was extended to Pescalba as the new president of Pescalba announced that workers, 'can have access to all enterprise information including sales,

---

34   *Prensa UNETE* 2011b.
35   *Prensa UNETE* 2011a.

acquisitions, inventory, finances, distribution and labour relations, and take decisions for all these areas together with the state and the Cuban partners'.[36]

Conflicts about working conditions, workers' rights, participation, co-management, and workers' control also arose in numerous other nationalised and state-owned factories, such as Café Venezuela, Fama de América, the energy supplier FETRAELEC, and the cement enterprises, among many more. Class struggle has been strengthened, or is bubbling up, where it was previously weak or absent. The day-to-day experiences in enterprise-management and the political training workers often received through the same institutions, which paradoxically later prevented effective workers' participation, ultimately contributed to the formation of a movement for workers' control, as demonstrated in the case of CVG-Alcasa.

The production costs of aluminium in CVG-Alcasa are above the world market price. CVG-Alcasa workers involved in the process of workers' control estimate that up to 40 percent of the aluminium production cost in CVG-Alcasa is actually caused by corruption.[37] This development is not recent, but rather a longstanding deformation created by the Venezuelan rentier economy in combination with the specific Venezuelan political and societal model. As Blankenburg writes:

> For decades the mining and basic industries in Venezuela have been infested by clientelistic networks. Foreign capitals, regional clans of rentiers and an elite of privileged workers operated in some kind of paradise of 'free robbery'. Before 1998 the oligarchic state showed little interest in intervening in this situation. After 1998 the arm of the state has not been strong enough to turn around the clientelistic control of the sector.[38]

The need to restructure the sector is an old one, but it has taken on novel characteristics in the most recent period of Venezuelan history. The different 'factions' in CVG-Alcasa, as well as in workers' organisations and government institutions generally, are an expression of antagonistic economic, social, and political models. The model from below is the only one with the capacity to transform the basic industries into productive industries within a framework of new labour relations, oriented towards overcoming capitalist relations. Therefore it is impossible to analyse the 'material potentiality of forms of

---

36   *Prensa UNETE* 2011c.

37   *Aporrea* 2011.

38   Blankenburg 2008, pp. 20–1.

"socialist" production at CVG-Alcasa' (Purcell, this volume) if the contradictions in the transformation process and the different interests among the actors, and finally the struggle itself, are not taken into account.

When the Marxist sociologist and former guerrilla Carlos Lanz was appointed director of CVG-Alcasa in mid-February 2005 with a government mandate to introduce a co-management model, just a small group of CVG-Alcasa workers were in favour of *cogestión* (co-management). Most workers did not have much of an idea of *cogestión* or workers' control. The factory assembly was established as the highest authority inside the factory, followed by roundtables of the department speakers elected in the departments, and then by the heads of department. All positions were elected in assemblies and could be revoked by these same bodies. The departments decided collectively from below about work organisation and investments. The workers brought various training missions into the factory, including political education seminars. The newly founded department for cooperatives supported the organisation of the cooperatives working in CVG-Alcasa and the inclusion of contract workers and cooperative workers as part of the staff of the CVG-Alcasa.[39]

CVG-Alcasa managed to pay in 2005 and 2006 all accumulated debts in salaries and pensions to workers and former workers. The higher gains of CVG-Alcasa in 2005–6 were due partly to the rise in world market aluminium prices, but production levels also rose 11 percent and the collective decisions and control of the different departments and processes of the plant reduced corruption and therefore financial losses.[40]

When Carlos Lanz left CVG-Alcasa in May 2007, the whole process of co-management suffered a severe setback. The new director did not respect the collective decisions of the departments, so workers' participation dropped, and in 2008 only four (all in production) out of the seventeen departments of the factory still had roundtables. The plans that had been initiated for the construction of workers' councils fell apart. Productivity dropped and CVG-Alcasa began to produce enormous losses once again (about US$180 million in 2007). The staff of CVG-Alcasa grew from 2,700 to 3,300, but just 60 were former cooperative members. The rest were mainly relatives, friends, or clients of the clientelistic networks in and around CVG-Alcasa. Trucks loaded with tons of precious aluminium leftovers from the production process were sold illegally.

---

39 *Prensa CVG-Alcasa* 2007. For further information about the transformation efforts in Alcasa under Carlos Lanz see Azzellini 2011b and Azzellini and Ressler 2006.

40 Bruce 2005.

When Carlos Aguilar took over as CVG-Alcasa director in April 2008 the situation deteriorated rapidly. Aluminium was sold below world market prices for immediate cash flow, and future sales were committed with the transnational Glencore. CVG-Alcasa production equipment was dismantled and sold to fake enterprises, contributing to the reduction of productive capacity and rising debts. Aguilar also forced the cooperatives to compete again for the contracts, and tried to turn down the social projects elaborated by CVG-Alcasa workers in four communities (for example, school repairs), which are financed by the social fund of CVG-Alcasa. The CVG-Alcasa union Sintralcasa, which was dominated by a group of workers hostile to worker control initiatives known as M21, remained silent. Sintralcasa was a strategic ally of Aguilar, most likely because some members participated in lucrative business contracts.[41]

But the experiences of the CVG-Alcasa workers with co-management were not in vain and the movement for workers' control in the plant, and among workers of the other CVG enterprises and communities, continued to expand:

> *Cogestión* represented huge gains in consciousness. Just the fact that hundreds of workers participated actively in the process of transformation of Alcasa is very important. The fact that they spoke out in assemblies and discussed directly with the company's management – something that had never happened before in this plant – is also an important lesson. The roundtables did not work out and the dense bureaucracy led to the current situation of *cogestión*, one that is close to being paralysed ... but still with great experiences and progress. The workers learned that it is possible to manage and control the whole production process by themselves. A great lesson! We had always been told that that was impossible.[42]

The fact that the basic industries in Venezuela need modernisation is clear. The best option for maximising both democracy and the viability of firms is an efficient and transparent network of basic industries in transition to models of workers' control. In spite of these clear necessities, the transformation of the sector had not advanced at all. As a consequence, Chávez himself participated in May 2009 in a weekend workshop with more than three hundred workers from the iron, steel, and aluminium plants of the CVG, including the workers from Alcasa. They discussed possible solutions to the problems of the respective sectors and drew up nine strategic guidelines for the restructuring and

41   PFST 2011.

42   Osvaldo León, Alcasa worker, personal interview, 21 April 2008, Alcasa, Ciudad Guayana.

transformation of the CVG. Production control by the workers was at the top of the list. Chávez authorised a ministerial commission to develop a plan based on the guidelines drafted during the workshop.

The 'Plan Socialist Guayana 2009–2019' was born and approved by Chávez in August 2009. He bypassed the regional governor, Rangel, and Rodolfo Sanz, at that time head of the ministry of Venezuela's mining and basic industries (Ministerio de Indústrias Básicas y Minería, Mibam) and director of the CVG, as both showed little enthusiasm for the plan. As the title indicates, the restructuring is a long-term plan. Factory councils were not decreed by Chávez, a fact appreciated by the workers since councils need to be created by the workers' own efforts; otherwise they have little or no chance of success.[43] After months of inaction, José Khan, an economist and former union leader who had been Mibam minister before Sanz, replaced Sanz in April 2010. In May 2010, Chávez nominated for each of the nine CVG iron, steel and aluminium plants' (Alcasa, Venalum, Bauxilum, Sidor, Carbonorca, Cabelum, Alucasa, Alunasa-Costa Rica, and Ferrominera Orinoco-FMO) workers who had participated in the workshops and discussions to serve as their respective directors. Elio Sayago, an environmental engineer and activist for workers' control, was named director of CVG-Alcasa. Immediately conflicts arose in Alcasa and other CVG plants, with the corrupt unions striking in an effort to sabotage the whole process of transformation and construction of workers' control.

The Plan Socialist Guayana 2009–2019 defines as one of its goals the creation of two huge iron and aluminium companies. This proposal originally comes from the workers' control collectives of the CVG plants. Alcasa cancelled the contracts for future sales to transnational companies, mainly Glencore, since the price of the aluminium being sold to Glencore was lower than Alcasa production costs. Alcasa plans to intensify further processing of aluminium, since this is where most value-added is realised. Alcasa also started importing aluminium for further processing to improve its cash flow, since the earnings realised through further processing are bigger than with the still loss-making aluminium production. In addition, workers' control should help to reduce and eliminate corruption. President Chávez officially supports this plan. M21 also opposed this decision and is in favour of selling the raw aluminium exclusively to Glencore.

Lined up against the Plan Socialist Guayana 2009–2019 – according to the workers from Guayana – are certain power and interest groups including the governor of Bolívar, Rangel, and the moderate Bolivarian union Fuerza Socialista Bolivariana de Trabajadores y Trabajadoras (Socialist Bolivarian

---

43   Trabajadores de CVG-Alcasa 2009.

Workers' Force, FSBT, named FBT until 2008), important sectors of the Ministry of Labour, the former Minister of Labour and now member of the National Assembly José Ramón Rivero,[44] mayor José Ramón López of the municipality of Caroní (to which Alcasa and other CVG plants belong), some members of the National Assembly, and other sectors of the government and state institutions. They want at any cost to avoid the success of workers' control.[45] Inside Alcasa the union list M21, which is headed by José Gil, is the vehicle for their interests. The list won the leadership of the Alcasa factory union Sintralcasa in August 2008. But the union leadership is not legally in charge any more. Its election took place in August 2008 and it has to be re-elected every two years.[46] The union does not enjoy the support of the workers. Rather, it is clear that Elio Sayago and the plan for restructuring Alcasa and implementing workers' control have the support of the vast majority of workers. Early on the morning of 9 November 2010, a scant two dozen corrupt union leaders entered the factory before the first shift, chained the gates, and attempted to "take over" the presidency of the factory as in a coup d'état – but an estimated 600 workers from the first shift accompanied Sayago into the factory to make it perfectly evident who has their support.[47]

The activism of the opponents to workers' control is based on a network of F(S)BT militants who are paid without working in the plant. Their role is to respond to the political and economic interests of the governor inside the plant. In Alcasa there are 120 militants on the Alcasa payroll named the M21 group. The situation is similar in the other CVG enterprises: 80 FBT militants receive a salary without working in Venalum, 150 in Ferrominera Orinoco, and 150 in Edelca.[48] Some of them are even armed and are threatening their opponents.[49] Neither the ruling Partido Socialista Unido de Venezuela (United Socialist Party of Venezuela, PSUV) nor the government take a clear stand or

---

44   Rivero, also coming from the FBT, was the Minister of Work and Social Security from January 2007 to April 2008. Together with governor Rangel he was responsible for the repression against the Sidor workers during their struggle for nationalisation and also publicly backed plans by the FSBT to form a rival union confederation to the UNT. Chávez dismissed him because of his handling of the Sidor case.

45   *Aporrea* 2011; Estévez 2011.

46   Figuera 2011.

47   Marea Socialista 2010.

48   *Aporrea* 2011.

49   Ligia Duerto, Alcasa worker, personal interview, 25 February 2011, Alcasa, Ciudad Guayana. In February 2011 a group of 'unionists' led by José Gil attacked the spokespeople of the cooperatives working for Alcasa because they had signed an agreement with the Alcasa director about the payment of accumulated debts. One unionist pulled out a gun and

intervene in support of the workers, since the conflict is among different currents of the Bolivarian process, and no mechanisms of democratic or collective decision making exist.

In January and February 2011, M21 went on a 34–day 'strike' in Alcasa. The 'strike' meant that less than 100 workers, mostly union officials who are on the payroll but do not work, blocked the access of the other workers to the plant. The justification for the 'strike' was that Alcasa owed the workers a certain amount of benefits, and the M21 demanded that Elio Sayago had to resign. But the so-called strike was organised by M21 after workers and community assemblies had approved a plan presented by Sayago and his staff on how to gradually pay all debts owed to the workers, social security, and enterprises delivering prime materials and services. These assembly-based decisions were not recognised by the M21, which also refused to participate in the assemblies. The strike declared by the M21 was not defending workers' interests but rather aimed at blocking initiatives to give workers control over the aluminium company's finances. This position becomes even clearer when we consider M21's positions before Sayago took over the Alcasa presidency. The current debts were mainly accumulated when Cesar Aguilar was president. Aguilar even refused to recognise the workers' benefits, but since he and Gil are strategic allies, Gil and the M21 did not criticise Aguilar. Nor did they call for a strike.[50]

As a result of the 34-day 'strike', the number of still functioning cells of lines III and IV of the reduction plant dropped to 172 (out of a total of 396). Moreover half of the ones still in use had already passed their expected lifetime, and were overheating and producing lower quality aluminium.[51] The 'strike' coincided with the government's approval of US$403 million for Alcasa out of the Chinese investment fund to modernise the different plants and departments and to build a new extruder plant.[52] The workers' control collective estimates that with the investment Alcasa could boost production, develop the manufacturing sector for further processing, and pay off creditors and the accumulated debts the company holds with the workers in about 10–12 months.[53] Once the modernisation starts it will take about three years to finish the operations and reach an annual production of 170,000 tons of aluminium

---

shot. Fortunately nobody was hurt. The man was arrested and is now facing charges (*Agencias* 2011).

50   PFST 2011.

51   CVG-Alcasa 2011.

52   Ibid.

53   Sierra Corrales 2011.

in the reduction areas.[54] The different projects are to be assumed by the technical tables established by workers. Many workers suspect that some people within the government want workers' control initiatives to fail, to shut down the plant, and to reopen it under the bureaucratic control of state institutions and the political control of the union faction of José Gil. With a US$403 million dollar investment involved the stakes were high indeed.[55] This explains why this interest group is opposed to workers' control and also to the constitution of an aluminium corporation made up by the three aluminium smelters of the CVG.

The severe crisis in Alcasa contributed to advances in efforts to coordinate among the aluminium enterprises. Alcasa's director Elio Sayago set up emergency and maintenance commissions formed with workers of all three CVG aluminium smelters (Alcasa, Venalum, and Baxilum) and with the coal enterprise CVG-Carbonorca (for unification of the reduction process), an exercise of integration and a first step towards the planned aluminium corporation. In Alcasa a 'council of coordination of processes' was created, which is in effect already taking the place of the actual directors' board.[56] Even if the future of Alcasa and the CVG industries is uncertain, there is now at least a strong and determined movement for workers' control supported by the majority of workers, and there is class struggle where there was none before. As expressed by Ligia Duerto of the cooperatives department, 'we have the highest level of internal conflict we ever had, but it is also the highest level of class struggle ever'.[57] It is 'a hard battle between the ones who like us do strongly believe in abolishing the hierarchy and division of labour, market relations, and transforming this corporation into property of the people, and the ones who want to keep the social relations of capital and power untouched'.[58]

The workers' protagonism is showing positive results in various CVG plants: not only have the first steps towards the constitution of bigger joint corporations been made, but also new initiatives not considered before have emerged. In May 2011, a commission of workers proposed that Mibam Minister José Khan build a state-owned and worker-controlled shipping enterprise on the Orinoco River. This enterprise would coordinate all ports, piers, and ships owned by state enterprises along the Orinoco and so improve their efficiency.

---

54   *Prensa CVG-Alcasa* 2011.

55   Ligia Duerto, Alcasa worker, personal interview, 25 February 2011, Alcasa, Ciudad Guyana.

56   PFST 2011; Ligia Duerto, Alcasa worker, personal interview, 1 May 2011, Alcasa, Ciudad Guyana.

57   Ligia Duerto, Alcasa worker, personal interview, 25 February 2011, Alcasa, Ciudad Guyana.

58   Osvaldo León, Alcasa worker, Prensa Marea Socialista 2011.

The new enterprise would also address environmental questions, as well as the labour situation of the more than 2000 workers involved who are mainly subcontracted. The minister approved the initiative and immediately built a mixed commission (ministry and workers) to push the project further.[59] The project, however, did not advance. In March 2012 the pier and ship workers of the CVG protested, demanding further advances in the workers-led construction of the shipping enterprise.

At the beginning of 2012 the government made some decisions intending to clarify the situation and move forward with the restructuring of the CVG, but ultimately the decisions were controversial and did not create a clearer picture as to where the CVG is moving. On the one hand the decision to create a new ministry for small, middle, and basic industries, and to move it from Caracas to the region of Guayana where the basic industries are located, was well received by the workers involved in the Plan Socialist Guayana 2009–2019. Ricardo Menéndez, appointed by Chávez as head of the new ministry, is considered a militant of the Bolivarian cause and not belonging to any of the interest groups inside the government structures. And the goal of introducing workers' control in the basic industries and other government enterprises was even included in the founding statutes of the new ministry. Nevertheless the replacement of the Alcasa president Elio Sayago in February 2012 by Chávez (in a manoeuvre that was not very transparent) is considered a huge set back by the revolutionary workers and movements of the region of Guyana. Sayago was replaced with former Alcasa worker Ángel Marcano, who twice served as a PSUV National Assembly member. Marcano, close to the regional governor and the M21 union leaders, is accused of being a part of the same group that had previously tried to sabotage Alcasa. Workers' control collectives from the different CVG plants, Alcasa workers, communal councils, grassroots organisations, various union currents, the Communist Party, and even the workers' spokespeople of the Plan Socialist Guayana 2009–2019 declared publicly their disagreement with the decision to name Marcano Alcasa's new president.[60]

Conclusion

Without a doubt class struggle has grown in Venezuela during recent years. Even if the normative orientation of the transformation process emphasises that the state cannot be the central agent of change, the specificity of

---

59   *Prensa Sidor* 2011.

60   *Aporrea* 2012.

the Venezuelan context nourished this illusion among the Venezuelan working class during the first decade of the Chavista government. Meanwhile, the
working class constituted in barrios and workplaces recognised more and
more that it has to struggle for strategic achievements and structural changes,
which transcend mere improvement in social conditions.

The private appropriation of public finances and resources by clientelistic
networks makes internal industrial development in the country much more
difficult. The most reliable instrument against corruption is workers' control.
This is also the reason for its many enemies. Transforming the state-owned
companies into direct social property is moving class struggle into the centre
of production.

After the difficulties with the described company models, the property
model preferred by the workers and also officially supported by the government is the 'direct social property' model. This represents social property managed directly by factory councils, communal councils, and communes.[61] Since
2008 the constitution of enterprises of social property has been promoted in
the communities. They are meant to take over local services, like the distribution of cooking gas[62] and local transport, and also set up local production. The
core of this process is the re-communalisation of formerly privatised public
services under direct and collective community control. The decision about
the form and administration of the companies lies in the hands of the communities via the communal councils, who also decide who is to work in the
community-managed companies.

Although many expropriations have taken place, overall the state owned
sector has become smaller as private business has grown faster in recent years.
In 1998 state property made up 34.8 percent of the GDP, in 2008 it dropped to
29.1 percent.[63] But this growth in private property should not be surprising
since the margins of gain are smaller in production for local trade, which is the
focus of state owned enterprises and the solidarity economy, than they are in
production for external trade, which is the focus of the private sector. The transformation and democratisation of the economy have proved to be the most
difficult tasks of the transformation process. The different models of property
and administration led to the democratisation of the means of production in a
limited way, but could not overcome capitalist rationality. Until now, capitalist
relations in Venezuela are mostly intact in most sectors of production, distri-

61   In contrast to indirect social property – i.e. strategic national industries – which is man-
      aged by the state.
62   Community-controlled vendors' network for liquid gas.
63   Álvarez 2009b.

bution, exchange, and consumption. The administration of most companies is not under the control of workers or communities. It is doubtful that the state or solidarity-based economic sectors are already a socialist alternative that will slowly expand over time and displace the private sector in a linear development. Such a transformation will require more radical steps to shift the relationship in favour of a public and collective sector.

For the construction of an economy that does not obey the rationality of capital it will be fundamental to connect the various new company models and create conditions for their functioning without state support. The central question, as Immanuel Wallerstein has argued, does not concern ownership or control of economic resources but the decommodification of economic processes:

> Decommodification, it should be underlined, does not mean demonetization, but the elimination of the category of profit. Capitalism has been a program for the commodification of everything... Socialism ought to be a program for the decommodification of everything.[64]

A serious attempt at this will only be possible if the economy and society are controlled directly by workers and communities, if the working class dominates over capital. Thus, the questions of whether a radical endogenous development will be achieved, as a base for the development toward socialism, or whether there will rather be merely a reconstitution of import substitution policy under state bureaucratic administration, or even a continuation of the rentier model based on the export of oil, are entirely questions of class struggle and not of 'correct' political or economic decisions.

Post script: After Chávez

In his government plan for 2013–19, presented during the electoral campaign of 2012, Chávez stated clearly '[w]e should not betray ourselves: the still dominant socio-economic formation in Venezuela is of a capitalist and rentist character'.[65] In order to move further towards socialism, Chávez underlined the necessity to advance further the construction of communal councils, communes, and communal cities and the 'development of social property on the basic and strategic factors and means of production'.[66]

---

64   Wallerstein 2000, p. 157.
65   Chávez 2012, p. 2.
66   Ibid., p. 7.

On 5 March 2013, Chávez died of cancer. Nicolás Maduro, former foreign minister and the preferred successor designated by Chávez, won the presidential elections on 14 April 2013 with a margin of about two percent over his right-wing opponent Henrique Capriles – half a million fewer votes than Chávez obtained a few months earlier. Nevertheless, Maduro's victory has proven that the Bolivarian Revolution is a solid project of transformation and not a one man show based on populism. The elections were once again confirmed as free, fair, and democratic by hundreds of international observers. Despite the internationally acclaimed democratic qualities of the Venezuelan elections, the opposition refused to recognise Maduro's victory and promoted violent demonstrations which left nine Chávez supporters dead.

Maduro committed himself publicly to Chávez's programme and declared several times that the construction of communes is central to Venezuela's own path towards socialism. During his electoral campaign he promised not to negotiate with the bourgeoisie and to put popular power at the centre of his politics.

Under attack by the opposition and with Maduro as the new president, unity among Venezuela's broad left has turned out to be even more important than before. Nevertheless political differences in the Bolivarian movement have become increasingly visible. Movements, rank-and-file Chavistas, and more leftist leaders advocate a radicalisation of the process and a decisive turn in revolutionary politics (a 'golpe de timón', as Chávez also titled one of his last written political interventions before his death).

Chávez's death has meant not only the loss of the Venezuelan president but also the loss of the movement's most important interlocutor in government. The movements are very aware of this. While they maintained an extraordinary discipline and did not react deliberately to the opposition's violent attacks, initiatives for a better coordination of movement forces are proliferating, as are concrete struggles like land occupations and struggles in work places.

The political orientation of the government has been openly criticised, and the bureaucratic apparatus has reacted by cancelling TV and radio programmes of some of the most critical voices of the process (some of them more dogmatic leftists, others more rank and file oriented). For some observers this was considered a concession to the opposition after the most aggressive opposition TV channel Globovisión (which participated in the organisation of the *coup d'état* in 2002) was sold and reduced its constant anti-government propaganda. But the government's move against these critical leftist media outlets provoked massive critiques from popular forces of the Bolivarian process. While calls for the construction of a collective leadership of the revolution are becoming more frequent, it is also clear that class struggle inside the Bolivarian process will continue to intensify in the future.

CHAPTER 8

Socialist Management and Natural Resource Based Industrial Production: A Critique of *Cogestión* in Venezuela

Thomas F. Purcell

Over the past ten years the Chávez government has been at the forefront of anti-neoliberal development initiatives that have emerged across Latin America, especially in states endowed with a significant source of natural resource wealth. Chávez's second presidential term ushered in the 'Simón Bolívar First Socialist Plan 2007–2013' (PPS – *Proyecto Nacional Simón Bolívar, Primer Plan Socialista*). This development vision calls for the 'establishment of a socialist productive model with new forms for the generation, appropriation, and distribution of economic wealth and a new form of distribution of the oil rent that reflects the substantial advance in collective values'.[1] Central to this vision is how to deal with a perennial feature of Venezuelan political economy – oil rent. Long considered a 'curse' or 'disease' by mainstream accounts, the presence of abundant oil wealth apparently arrests industrial, agricultural, and political development. This simple casual link, however, overlooks the role of natural resources in the global dynamics of capital accumulation and as such reifies the national as the cause and outcome of resource-based development. In contrast, this chapter will explore twenty-first century socialism in Venezuela as a reaction to, and consequence of, a landlord state within the dynamics of global capital accumulation.

The contemporary project of overcoming 'rentier-capitalism', a term used to capture Venezuela's appropriation rather than production of wealth,[2] promotes a mixture of numerous, small-scale interventions into the so-called social economy, largely through state-funded cooperatives, in addition to a number of re-nationalisations of heavy basic industries and utilities.[3] The feature that unites these development experiments is the attempt by the Chávez government

---

1   MPD 2007, p. 20.
2   Baptista and Mommer 1987, p. VII; Baptista 1997.
3   The 'social economy' is conceptualised by the government as an arena for the organisation of production and the provision of services, both public and private, geared primarily towards overcoming widespread social marginalisation and poverty. See MINCI 1999, p. 78.

to institute 'socialist' forms of management that, through a burgeoning parallel state of new development institutions, target workers' consciousness as the basis of changing production relations. In 2005, the state-owned aluminium plant GVC-Alcasa became the most high profile testing ground for the industrial form of one such strategy known as *cogestión* or co-management. At the time *cogestión* embodied the principles of endogenous and Bolivarian socialist development, designed to democratically reorganise the structure and management of state-owned industrial plants.[4] It is distinct from other initiatives such as cooperatives and social production companies (*Empresas de Producción Social* – EPS),[5] insofar as it involves an already established large-scale industrial project, with huge sunk capital costs, pre-existing bureaucratic and labour organisations, and, therefore, much larger financial and organisational challenges. Part of the motivation for *cogestión* was to make state-owned primary industries productive, profitable, and efficient under a non-capitalist logic. Following a reported period of successful worker mobilisation and raised productivity (2005–6), in 2007 the initiative fell by the wayside and as of 2011 the CVG-Alcasa rests on the brink of closure. The argument of the chapter is that the state-led initiative of *cogestión* was a last ditch attempt to make a deteriorating, relatively backward capital profitable without significant financial outlay; in effect, to improve efficiency through workers' control. The argument will demonstrate how despite its progressive political form, *cogestión* lacked the scale of intervention necessary to address the material root conditions of declining productivity.

Accounts dealing specifically with *cogestión* have focused upon its progressive ideology and practice of human-centred development;[6] its juridical innovations and limits;[7] and the contested role of trade unions.[8] But they have largely eschewed the specific political economy and material challenges posed by the *cogestión* model of industrial renewal. A recent book length study by Víctor Álvarez has identified the emergence of a 'New Productive Model' (NPM) that presages the overcoming of Venezuela's rentier economy.[9] The basis of this NPM is the transformation of the relations of production through a contemporary form of Import Substitution Industrialisation (ISI) whose macroeconomic design (price controls, access to cheap foreign exchange, and various subsi-

4 *Cogestión* translates as co-management; the Spanish term is used in what follows.
5 See Piñiero-Harnecker 2009; Purcell 2011.
6 Harnecker 2005; Lebowitz 2006b.
7 Abreu and Espot 2006.
8 Lucena 2007.
9 Alvarez 2009b.

dies) would favour the social economy based on new forms of collective property, non-exploitative labour relations, and the socialisation of profits.[10] The
problem, however, is that conceptual claims about the explicit political will
of the Chávez government to pursue these measures are all too often treated
in isolation from the material bases for an alternative mode of production.
Instead, focus is placed exclusively on the social character of institutions.[11]

Thus it is somewhat curious that, despite 'revolutionary' proclamations
from the Chávez government and an enthusiastic reception among the international left, there has been little Marxian analysis of the Chávez project.[12] In
contrast to much of the literature that concentrates on the novelty of *chavismo*
to explain recent events, this chapter is organised historically to capture the
structural continuities in the accumulation of capital that form the material
basis for political struggle in Venezuela. From this perspective, class is not
an empiricist category that can be fleshed out according to the immediately
observable power of political agents.[13] Rather, class struggle is the most general form taken by the organisation of (alienated) social labour through the
private and independent production of commodities.[14] As such, the working
class cannot obtain any historically specific revolutionary powers other than

---

10   Ibid., p. 232. It is noted that such policies will not exclude private capital only on the basis
     that they adhere to the transformation of the productive model.

11   See Azzellini, this volume.

12   See, however, Hellinger 2008, for whom natural resource wealth, when controlled by land-
     lord states in Venezuela and the region at large, is a potential source of power to regulate
     the pressures of globalisation. See also the framework offered by Fernando Coronil 1997,
     pp. 58–61, whose category of the 'magical state' offers an original synthesis of Marx's the-
     ory of ground rent and heterodox theories of the state to account for Venezuela's appro-
     priation of wealth from nature rather than labour. The argument developed here differs
     from Coronil in the key respect that I do not jettison the labour theory of value in order
     to place 'land' at the centre of analysis. Instead, this chapter maintains that the only basis
     of surplus value for the critique of political economy is human labour – 'all ground rent
     is surplus value, the product of surplus labour' (Marx 1991, p. 773). Therefore, the critical
     project undertaken here is not to elevate land to the same theoretical level as labour,
     but to dissolve the mystification of land as a category endowed with independent mate-
     rial power expressed in the agency of the state. Other 'Marxists' take a radical-voluntarist
     approach, such as the Trotskyist Woods (2006) and the popular educational work dissem-
     inated by Lebowitz, Harnecker, Álvarez, and Troudi and Molina through the state-funded
     think tank Centro Internacional Miranda (CIM), which seeks to re-interpret Marx in line
     with the 'human-centred' ideology of twenty-first century socialism.

13   Azzellini, this volume.

14   Kicillof and Starosta 2007.

those it gets from its general social relation, that is, the nationally-processed but globally-determined production of surplus value.[15]

This differs markedly from what I term the 'radical-voluntarist' approach, according to which the very political form of the Bolivarian Revolution encapsulates the revolution's dynamism and potential. From the radical-voluntarist perspective, initiatives such as cooperatives and co-management initiatives can be said to represent the emergence of an alternate economic model, linked to a new vision of production for collective needs that can challenge the logic of capitalism.[16] For Lebowitz, the democratic and emancipatory potential is immanent in the very process of struggle, which can realise its potential in new revolutionary forms of political and economic organisation.[17] Important in this process is the new body of parallel Bolivarian institutions, which are seen as essential vehicles to facilitate 'autonomous popular power', direct democratic participation, and nurture the self-development of the working class.[18] When the capital relation is conceived of as a direct relation of power and subordination, its transcendence becomes consequently represented as the abolition of its institutional forms – a question of radical democracy – realisable through direct political action.

In contrast, the materialist point of departure adopted in this chapter precludes the analysis of certain leaders, political parties, state institutions, policy objectives, or social movements before the analysis of the relations of production. According to this approach, the potential of alternative forms of socioeconomic development cannot be deduced from abstract ideal types, such as the much-vaunted revolutionary 'dialectic' between Chávez and the masses,[19] or the struggle between *constituent* power (the abstract power of human agency)

---

15   Iñigo Carrera 2002.

16   Harnecker 2005; Raby 2006; Piñeiro Harnecker 2009; Wilpert 2007; Lebowitz 2007; McKenna 2009.

17   It is noteworthy that Lebowitz's recent book on Venezuela *Build It Now: Socialism for the Twenty-First Century* (2006), can be read as a real-life practical extension of his major work in Marxist theory *Beyond Capital* ([1992] 2004). In the latter work, it was argued that because Marx was concerned with the movement of capital he analytically froze the workers' side of class struggle. Therefore, *Capital* did not adequately focus upon workers as human beings in their struggle for self-development. The upshot of this argument is that an ontologically separate logic is found in wage-labour struggles that form the basis of the capital relation, and as a result, analytically the state is an instrument than can be separated politically from capital.

18   Harnecker 2006; Troudi and Monedero 2006; Lebowitz 2006a; Achkar 2007; Acosta 2007; Monedero 2007.

19   Lebowitz 2006a; Raby 2006; McKenna 2009.

and *constituted* power (power invested in the state and its institutions),[20] but is best analysed through the prism of value-production within the social relations of rentier-capitalism. This methodological starting point does not downgrade politics; on the contrary, it allows for the materialist conceptualisation of politics and the state as a social form of class struggle.[21] The task, therefore, is to develop an understanding of the state-sponsored project through analysis of the production of value. This chapter takes up this challenge with a particular focus upon the state-sponsored strategy of *cogestión* or co-management.

The argument is developed in three sections. Section one outlines a theoretical approach based upon the analysis of capital accumulation through the accumulation of ground rent. Drawing upon the work of Juan Iñigo Carrera and those who subsequently developed this approach,[22] I develop the category of the landlord state and theorise its relationship with spaces of capital accumulation at the global and national scale.[23] This work provides insights into the politico-economic effects of the accumulation of capital through the appropriation of a portion of the ground rent. This approach can first explain the social role of the Venezuelan state in the world energy market *vis-à-vis* its monopoly ownership of a non-reproducible natural resource (crude oil, the fuel of industrial capitalism). And second, how this insertion into the world market forms the source of and limit to national industrialisation. Approaching the global and national dialectically as content and form respectively, it will be possible to lay the basis for a materialist analysis of the developmental capacity of the Venezuelan state and, subsequently, a Marxian critique of Chávez's brand of populism. Section two presents an historical analysis of CVG-Alcasa in the context of Venezuela's ambitious heavy industrialisation following the impact of the 1970s oil boom. The purpose of this section is to account for the initial successful period of heavy ISI during a time in which the magnitude of ground rent, both from inter-sectoral transfers of oil wealth and the global aluminium industry, was sufficient to buttress productivity – under the

---

20 Azzellini, this volume.

21 Clarke 1991.

22 Grinberg 2008; Grinberg and Starosta 2009.

23 For the original discovery see Iñigo Carrera 2007a. With reference to Argentina, this work pioneered the analysis of the effects of key policies upon the appropriation of ground rent. Grinberg 2008 has subsequently used this approach in the analysis of the Brazilian economy to assess the flows of extraordinary wealth (ground rent) in sustaining the process of accumulation of industrial capital. While these studies are largely quantitatively led, the present investigation is orientated around a more qualitative investigation of how the general dynamics of ground rent (as a social relation) inform and give shape to the developmental initiatives of the Chávez government.

political form of Carlos Andres Pérez's developmental populism. Whilst I will focus mainly upon the plight of CVG-Alcasa, it is instructive to place this case study within the broader context of the development of rentier capitalism in Venezuela. And, following the theoretical approach established in section one, rather than stopping short at the level of the nation state (form), this account will be necessarily grounded in the dynamics of the last thirty years of capital accumulation (content), more commonly referred to as globalisation. This analytical move will allow me to generate insights into the specific origins and unfolding of the *cogestión* experiment at CVG-Alcasa, the subject of section three. Drawing on primary interviews and secondary sources, I argue that we can reveal the state's turn to socialist production as an *ad hoc* project to raise efficiency without significant capital outlay.

The Landlord State and the Development of Rentier Capitalism

The capricious presence of favourable natural conditions can significantly increase the productivity of labour, whether in mining or agriculture, thereby reducing the price of the raw material and, in world market terms, the costs of reproducing the global labour force.[24] The combined and uneven process of global capital accumulation has,[25] following the exhaustion of easily accessible raw materials in the core, historically determined those countries where favourable natural conditions abound as suppliers of raw materials. As a result of this historical-geographical development process, within national spaces of nature-dependent capital accumulation, a large portion of social wealth exists under the form of ground rent, the centre of gravity of which lies firmly in the dynamics of global capital accumulation. This form of capital accumulation lies in contrast to the exploitation of different branches of the global collective labourer.

Ground rent has as its source the surplus value generated by workers and capital of the importing countries where primary commodities reach individual and industrial consumption.[26] Landlord access to this source of surplus value is based upon the appropriation of surplus profits which, unlike in industrial conditions of production, do not dissipate in the course of competition but endure over time as a social function of the landlord's monopoly. This source of surplus value can take the form of differential or absolute ground rent. The

---

24   Iñigo Carrera 2002.
25   Harvey 1982.
26   Iñigo Carrera 2008a, p. 10.

former is determined within a sector in two ways: differences in the quality of natural conditions (DRI) and differences in the magnitude of capital invested in the land or mine (DRII). The more fertile the land and the more productive the mine (DRI), the lower the production costs and the higher the profit to the capital in question (DRII).[27] This surplus profit is capitalised as differential rents by the landowner in the form of the price or royalty they can charge for access to a particularly desirable natural resource. The latter – absolute rent (AR) – is a product of the social power of private ownership, whereby capital must pay a fee to access a non-renewable natural resource. Again, unlike industry, when nature is the basic input, prices of production are set by the marginal, not by the most productive or weighty, product in the sector. Thus a rent is paid even on the worst land or mine for which there is solvent demand.[28]

The *differentia specifica* of the oil landlord states derive from the materiality of mineral *vis-à-vis* agricultural production. As Iñigo Carrera has pointed out, in general the materiality of mineral resource production has a determinate effect on the magnitude of rent appropriated by the landlord.[29] As opposed to individual agrarian landowners, whose resource is reproducible and temporally dependent upon each production cycle, mining landowners 'can sit on their natural resources' until the conditions to appropriate a larger mass of ground rent are more favourable.[30] Drawing upon Marx's original insights,

---

27   Most of Venezuela's production is 'infra-marginal', meaning that production costs are below the marginal producer, therefore extra surplus, or differential rent, accrues to the state relative to world market norms. Manzano and Monaldi 2008.

28   Marx 1991, pp. 882–907. Ground rent can take the social form of Differential Rent (DR) and Absolute Rent (AR). DR springs from the monopoly over portions of the planet with differentially favourable natural conditions allowing lower production costs than those prevailing in the world's marginal lands for which there is solvent demand (pp. 779–87). AR derives from the simple monopoly over land and is paid even for the use of marginal lands (pp. 882–907). Therefore, ground rent is paid by industrial capital at world-scale either directly through its purchase of raw materials or indirectly through the value of wages. In the presence of elevated prices of raw material the working class may require higher wages to consume the quantity of use-values necessary to reproduce their labour-power, thereby entailing a potential deduction of surplus value available for further rounds of accumulation and (or) a deduction of workers' income. The latter point attests to the political significance of (Venezuelan) nationalists' demands for higher oil prices and the origin of ground rent being dialectically related to the value of labour-power (wages) in the importing countries.

29   Iñigo Carrera 2007a, pp. 13–14.

30   If the agrarian landowner were to remove lands from production the absolute ground rent would not return to them, but to those landowners who remain in production, see Iñigo Carrera 2007a, p. 13.

Iñigo Carrera has termed this 'simple absolute monopoly rent', which derives from landowners collectively charging commercial prices for their commodity above prices of production, but not acting as a barrier to the formation of the general rate of profit.[31] Outside of the mining sector a large portion of the absolute rent can come from the lower organic composition capital (OCC) of agriculture relative to industry. However, because the oil sector has developed with a high and increasing OCC, with expensive and sophisticated technology, this form of rent is not available,[32] placing much more political emphasis on the appropriation of 'simple absolute monopoly rent'. And unlike the differential portion of the rent, this portion varies not only according to fertility and productivity within the sector, but according to monopoly ownership of landowners relative to the size of the demand from the global economy in general.[33] Therefore, mining landowners, when organised as a class at the world market level in organisations such as the Organisation of Petroleum Exporting Countries (OPEC), will have more bargaining power vis-à-vis industrial capital than agrarian ones, making the absolute rent of oil landlord states much larger.[34] However, as the vicissitudes of global oil prices demonstrate (see Figure 8.1), the conditions for the appropriation of this form of rent are volatile and ultimately circumscribed by wider demand conditions in the global economy.

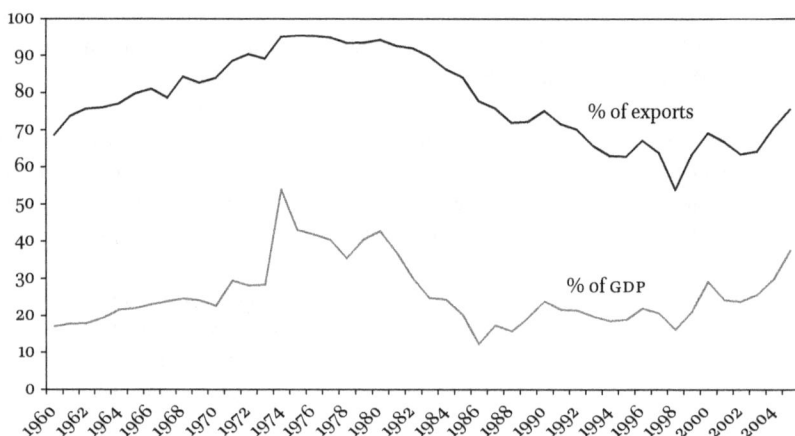

FIGURE 8.1   OPEC dependency on oil.[35]

---

31   Ibid.
32   Bina 2006, p. 335.
33   Ibid.
34   Grinberg 2010.
35   Ramírez 2006.

For developing nations whose predominant insertion into the world market is based upon the export of oil (for OPEC nations, on average oil accounts for 38 percent of GDP and 76 percent of exports; as of 2008 oil represented a third of Venezuela's GDP and 93 percent of exports), processes of national industrialisation, production, and capital accumulation are dependent upon the state transfer of rent.[36] This 'transference of rent to the "rest of society" (that is, industrial and commercial capital) has to involve the public budget giving place to inherently more "interventionist" policies and political institutions'.[37] The central mechanism for a direct or automatic rent transfer – that is, without some form of visible state intervention – is an overvaluation of the national currency.[38] Through this mechanism, national and foreign capital orientated to the domestic market can appropriate a portion of the ground rent when importing machinery and raw materials with cheap foreign exchange. Indeed, the selling of foreign exchange (US dollars) cheaply has been one of the central mechanisms by which the landlord state has distributed ground rent. This mechanism can be sustained as long as the administrator of foreign exchange, the central bank, possesses a permanent flow of additional social wealth to sell foreign currency below its value.[39] Private industrial capital also benefits from state policies that sustain internationally low levels of taxation, cheap energy inputs, and market protection for capital goods sold domestically. Furthermore, the state can act as a source of demand in the national economy through the provision of cheap money (public credit at negative real interest rates), an over-expanded public workforce, and the purchase of final goods at inflated prices.[40]

The implications for those developing societies where a large mass of social wealth has taken the form of ground rent, particularly from mining, is that both national and international 'industrial capital has not maximised its valorisation by producing for the world market on the basis of advanced methods of production. Instead, capital has accumulated by producing on a small scale for limited domestic markets (according to world market norms)'.[41] The inability

---

36   Ramírez 2006; Weisbrot et al. 2009. Even though states such as the US, Canada, UK, and
     Norway have high levels of oil exports, their level of diversification does not restrict the
     accumulation of capital to the appropriation of ground rent. For this reason the taxon-
     omy of oil state, rentier state, and landlord state are reserved for developing states whose
     capitalist development was predicated upon the export of primary resources.
37   Grinberg 2010, p. 194.
38   Iñigo Carrera 2007a.
39   Ibid., pp. 18–21.
40   Ibid.
41   Ibid.; Grinberg and Starosta 2009, p. 769.

of individual nationally-orientated capitals to reach the scale needed for profitability utilising advanced technological conditions has been periodically compensated by the appropriation of a portion of ground rent. This means the scale of these processes of capital accumulation have, since their origins, been structurally dependent on the evolution of the magnitude of ground rent available for appropriation.[42] Thus, despite the higher production costs of nationally-located capitals, because of their limited magnitude and older technologies, ground rent, along with limited surplus value extracted from the domestic labour force, has allowed them to valorise at the average rate of profit. This process of ground rent dependent industrialisation in developing states illustrates the structural relation between the landlord state, the specificity of processes of national capital accumulation, and the availability of ground rent at the global scale.

The high degree of dependence on the world market, the relatively small internal market, and the role of state subsidies in the accumulation process imply a twofold distortion in the operation of the law of value.[43] First, as mentioned above, in relation to other primary products and manufactured goods, the oil sector is extremely capital-intensive and highly productive. The productivity of this labour-power, however, cannot be generalised to the rest of the economy as it can be with industry, because it is nature, and not technology or machinery, which determines labour's productivity.[44] This is the basis of oil's enclave character, the growth of a small and relatively well-paid workforce, and the limited forward and backward linkages. Second, as a proportion of GDP, processes of national reproduction occur with a close dependence upon oil fiscal revenue and not surplus value from economic activity in the wider economy. As a result, industrialisation, technological development, and national development have not historically been based on increasing levels of national social productivity or competition among individual national or international capitals. The social power of capital, therefore, is not embodied in the capitalist class, but in the power of oil-money concentrated in the form of the landlord state. This is expressed in the growth of state ownership in the economy, the size of the bureaucracy, the magnitude and orientation of public expenditure, the concentration of economic activity in the non-tradable sectors (services, utilities, and construction), and the subsidisation of national industries.[45] These state-led developmental initiatives, 'like any other kind of

---

42   Iñigo Carrera 2007a.
43   Hein 1980, p. 236.
44   Massaraat 1980, p. 27.
45   Pérez Sainz and Zarembka 1979.

state policy', can be understood as the 'concrete political form taken by the specific contradictions immanent in the accumulation process'.[46] The relationship between the social power of money and the political power of the state,[47] therefore, takes on added significance in societies where the majority of social wealth accumulates in the hands of the state. This holds particular salience for the chapter's investigation into the state's management of this extraordinary pool of social wealth that determines its intervention into social life and ultimately the forms of institutionalising class struggle.[48]

This theoretical approach provides the point of departure for the analysis of Venezuelan industrialisation, *cogestión* specifically, and Chávez's presidency more broadly. It will be shown how control of the landlord state confers a considerable amount of discretionary power upon the president, who can respond politically to conditions of rentier-capitalism, but not abolish it. It is the dynamic of global capital accumulation and the form taken by the international division of labour that is the real 'curse' of natural resources. First, however, we turn to the historical development of rentier-capitalism, and the founding of CVG-Alcasa.

Alcasa and Venezuelan Industrialisation

By 1960, forty years into intensive oil exploitation, Venezuela had been through a sustained period of 'exceptionally high levels of consumption and investment, and its capital absorptive capacity was approaching exhaustion'; 'dependency on oil had not diminished but increased'.[49] As a response Venezuelan planners sought to deconcentrate economic activity from the capital Caracas and integrate remote resource rich territories of the country, by channelling oil revenue to set up new mineral extraction and processing ventures within the industrial mega-project of Ciudad Guayana.[50] A centrepiece of Venezuelan efforts to 'sow the oil', 'Ciudad Guayana is a uniquely Venezuelan phenomenon, bolstered by a state ideology that privileged domestically controlled industrialisation' coupled with the oil revenues to pursue inflated goals.[51] Led by the state-owned regional development agency *Corporación Venezolana de*

---

46   Grinberg and Starosta 2009, p. 762.
47   Clarke 1988.
48   Hein 1980, p. 227.
49   Mommer 1998, p. 17.
50   Hite 2004.
51   Ibid., p. 53.

Guayana (CVG), which owns half a dozen enterprises producing steel and aluminium products for domestic and foreign markets, the region benefits from a direct shipping route to the Atlantic, low energy costs from huge hydroelectric operations, and abundant, easily accessible raw materials. These geological, geographical, and above all political conditions make it a potentially abundant source of differential rent and competitive advantage in the world market.

Ciudad Guayana houses the world's fifth largest aluminium complex, one capable of producing complete commodity chains from mining bauxite (the raw material of the industry), transforming it into alumina, and then producing a full range of aluminium products for both domestic and foreign markets.[52] The plan was to use natural resource endowments as the basis for further downstream integration into semi-finished and finished goods for import substitution and export to regional markets. Initially in a joint venture with US-American firm Reynolds, CVG-Alcasa began production in 1967 with a yearly capacity of 11,250 Tonnes Per Year (TPY). This was increased to 22,500 in 1969, 54,000 in 1973, and 120,000 in 1979, reaching 220,000 by 1999. By 1974, the import substitution savings for Venezuela derived from Alcasa were US$22 million per year, exports earnings were US$14.9 million, over 1,000 jobs were created, and the profits to Alcasa in 1974 alone were almost equal to 100 percent of the total government investment in the aluminium industry.[53] In fact, aluminium became Venezuela's second most valuable export (after oil), since the late 1970s. Alcasa's financial results between 1975 and 1990 were positive in all but four years, during which very large investments were being made to expand the plant.[54]

This relatively successful period, however, concealed serious imbalances. The political character and scale of this period of heavy industrial development was transformed by a massive global rise in the magnitude of ground rent. The goals of the initial phase of resource-based development joint ventures, export promotion, and medium-scale production were inflated when Carlos Andrés Pérez (CAP) was elected under the banner *'Democracia con Energía'* (Democracy with Energy). In a mere five years, the Pérez administration would receive more fiscal revenues than did all other (combined) Venezuelan governments since 1917.[55] Indeed, during his first presidential term, congress bestowed CAP with extraordinary powers to channel US$13.6 billion towards

52   Ciccantell 1994.
53   Ciccantell 2000, p. 9.
54   Ibid., p. 17.
55   Karl 1997, p. 116. The subtotal of government revenue (in millions of Bolivars, Bs.) 1917–73 was Bs. 100,356, whereas from 1974–8 Carlos Andrés Pérez received Bs. 148,640.

national development.[56] With this unprecedented influx, CAP set about building *La Gran Venezuela* (The Great Venezuela) under an expansive state project
known as the Fifth National Plan (1974–9). The basic elements of the plan –
i.e. the mechanisms of ground rent transfer to society and industry – were
the deepening of import substitution and state expansion in the economy in
an attempt to diversify the country's export structure, while at the same time
fighting poverty through a combination of price controls, income increases,
and increased social expenditure.[57] Evoking the Special Power Act that permitted the president to rule by decree, CAP nationalised the oil industry in 1976,
creating Petroleum of Venezuela Joint Stock Company (PDVSA) with the state
as its sole shareholder, and proceeded to invest heavily in capital-intensive
industry. The emphasis was on large-scale and fast industrial development and
export promotion. Agricultural production was neglected and suggestions to
create a domestic tax base were ridiculed. The landlord state pushed ahead
with an ambitious resource-based public industrialisation programme, especially in petrochemicals, steel, and aluminium.[58]

   This process was internally related to the transformations taking place in the
global oil industry during 'the era of post-cartelisation and globalisation since
1974' and an unprecedented growth in the magnitude of ground rent appropriated by landlord states.[59] The 1973–4 oil crisis, during the Arab-Israeli war,
and the subsequent Arab oil boycott (in which Venezuela incidentally refused
to participate) can be understood as parts of 'much larger manifold transformations'. These transformations derive from the unification of the global oil
industry: the de facto nationalisation and concurrent transnationalisation of
oil against the International Petroleum Cartel (IPC) by OPEC under the one
pricing rule; the universal valorisation of landed property and competitive formation of global differential oil rents; and the proliferation of global oil markets
which involved the complete transition from posted prices (monopoly pricing
dictated by the IPC) to global spot prices (based upon immediate conditions
of productivity, supply, and demand).[60] These transformations turned OPEC
from a rudimentary rent-setter, formerly based upon arbitrary and devalued
posted prices dictated by the IPC, to a fully-fledged differential rent collector

---

56   Mommer 1998.
57   Hein 1980.
58   Mommer 1998.
59   Bina 1989; 2006.
60   Bina 2006, p. 16. Also related to these factors are the decartelisation of US oil and ratio-
     nalisation of the US oil industry and the redundancy of the unmediated (physical) access,
     utopian self-sufficiency, and dependency of a particular oil region.

at full market (spot) prices. At this juncture OPEC was able to raise prices, and therefore rents, because the entire oil industry was at the threshold of a social transformation that practically revolutionised its institutional structure – and not the other way around.[61]

As a result of Venezuela's emergence as a fully-fledged landlord state, development in the Guayana region assumed an intensified rentier character. The state's capacity to import capital and skilled labour (made possible by the overvalued Bolivar) without ceding control to transnational corporations (TNCs) was evident in the fact that although most engineering projects, the import of new technologies, and plant construction were contracted to foreign firms, substantive foreign TNC ownership was in fact quite limited.[62] This strategy to prioritise national ownership of production amidst an abundant flow of foreign exchange facilitated the adoption of capital-intensive techniques and permitted the financing of manufacturing plants whose minimum efficient sizes were to exceed the size of the domestic market.[63] This expanded scale of production included the targeting of CVG-Alcasa as a primary export platform – exposing production to highly competitive world markets. Expansion started in the mid-1980s, which included its rolling mill plant in Guayana as well as the construction of plant lines IV and V for increasing its capacity up to 420,000 TPY. CVG-Alcasa installed the service areas required for supporting the capacity of all five plant lines; however, they only managed to build line IV for a total production of 210,000 TPY. Large resource-based industrialisation strategies that use sophisticated technology are characterised by long lead times and, therefore, require the careful synchronisation of technical, financial, and marketing negotiations.[64] Ultimately, this big push strategy created a structural deficit because of large sunk costs and the expansion of operating capacity, leading to the inability to valorise large amounts of fixed capital. This ambitious and, in part, politically motivated project doubled capital costs and eroded the competitiveness of the entire aluminium sector.[65]

To compound matters, during this period the aluminium industry was experiencing a global transformation: the decline of old monopolies, new technological developments pushing performance benchmarks upwards, and a growth of joint ventures all increased the economies of scale needed to be

---

61   Bina 1985.

62   TNC participation was kept below 20 percent in operating contracts so as to maintain full national control over all production and investment decisions.

63   Parot 1998, p. 225.

64   Auty 1986, p. 326.

65   Ibid.

competitive. This created excess capacity in the industry as a whole and drove down prices.[66] In the face of intensified global competition and national over-capacity the Venezuelan aluminium sector became chronically dependent upon state support. As Hite comments, this produced a paradoxical situation where, to remain in production, the Venezuelan state actually subsidises the value of aluminium for advanced capitalist economies:

> The control over global production chains for metal markets exerted by TNCs, as well as declining terms of trade for these commodities, meant that Venezuela's model for developing extractive and related industries ultimately produced surplus/or subsidies to core economies in which TNCs and their primary consumers are located.[67]

The Fifth National Plan (1974–9) had anticipated a sustained rise in oil revenues to cover vast expenditures being laid out on imported expert labour and cheap capital inputs.[68] As a result Carlos Andrés Pérez (CAP) presided over a development strategy that intensified the structural tension between the rate of growth of ground rent and its requirement by industrial capital, in particular, and the rest of the economy in general. In fact, during the major boom period 1974–8 annual growth rates of seven percent were only high in absolute terms but low compared with the enormous amount of state spending.[69] Therefore, we can see that it was the changed status of landlord states on the world market and the oil euphoria that underpinned CVG-Alcasa's expansion. Abundant raw materials, cheap energy supplies, and multiple mechanisms of rent circulation lowered CVG-Alcasa's production costs and buttressed its first 15 years of productivity.

An indication of the inherent limits of this industrialisation strategy was the periodic recourse to credit capital and a growing dependence upon contingent spikes in the level of ground rent in order to ward off harsh structural reform. In fact, under the CAP government a Bs. 63 billion (US$14.734 billion) loan was not adequately tied to projected returns from domestic development. It is for this reason that the incumbent president Luis Herrera Campíns (1979–84) is said to have inherited a mortgaged country.[70] Along with Campíns, the following President Jaime Lusinchi (1984–9) continued with huge spending,

---

66   Ciccantell 2000.
67   Hite 2004, p. 67.
68   Coronil 1997; Karl 1997.
69   Mommer 1998.
70   Coronil 1997.

attempting to maintain the inherited myth of progress. Given a certain amount of leeway created by the global shock of the Iranian Revolution in 1979 and the subsequent war with Iraq in 1980, the oil spending and foreign borrowing that underwrote this development model in Venezuela continued unabated. However, conditions came to a head on the 'Black Friday' of 1983. Unable to obtain finance to consolidate foreign debts, which had increased from US$9 billion to US$24 billion, and faced with massive capital flight, Campíns devalued the Bolivar in order to reactivate the economy. As Mommer remarks,

> The importance of this event is difficult to exaggerate. Until then the Bolivar had been an extraordinarily stable currency, more comparable to the Swiss Franc than to the US Dollar. It was the symbol of Venezuelan prosperity. However, it was also one of the two most important devices for transferring the international ground rent in oil from the government to Venezuelan consumers.[71]

The once perennially cheap foreign currency was now controlled through the Regime of Differential Exchange Rates (*Régimen de Cambios Diferenciales*, RECADI), a multi-tier exchange system according to which foreign currency was sold at preferential rates for select purposes, such as the import of basic consumer goods, raw materials, and the payment of foreign debt. However this tactic failed to stimulate the economy or redirect state policy. In fact, the presidency of Lusinchi took the form of increased macroeconomic populism,[72] spending extravagantly to appease social unrest in the context of declining real wages. Further borrowing to sustain spending levels saw foreign debt reach the fourth highest level (in absolute terms) in Latin America (US$36 billion), while historically single-figured inflation neared 30 percent.[73] Despite the collapse of oil prices by 50 percent in 1986, Venezuela's unsustainable version of import substitution industrialisation continued. Vested interests were given preferential access to cheap foreign exchange and the remaining government funds were directed to loan interest repayments.[74] As a result the dramatic 'fall in rent was thus combined with the obligations associated with an enormous external debt that accumulated during the years of rentier euphoria'.[75]

---

71   Mommer 1998, p. 20.
72   Dornbusch and Edwards 1991.
73   Lander 1996; John 2005.
74   John 2005.
75   Baptista 1993, cited in Lander 1996, p. 51.

This was the macroeconomic context in which Alcasa went from one of the world's leading aluminium plants to the so-called black sheep of the region, with the highest production costs for aluminium in the world.[76] Venezuela's industrial decline was the national expression of interrelated changes taking place in the global economy since the mid-to-late 1970s that included: a burgeoning new international division of labour (NIDL) based upon the mechanisation of large-scale industry and increased labour productivity;[77] the overproduction of capital and slower economic growth;[78] and the related decline in global commodity prices in the light of falling demand.[79] The economic outcome for Venezuela was a decline in the mass of ground rent available for the transfer to industrial capital. Unable to sustain the state policies that transferred a portion of the ground rent to industrial capital, the scale of production at Alcasa quickly contracted and Venezuelan aluminium became uncompetitive on the world market. The fortunes of Venezuelan industrialisation deteriorated further when the protection for all CVG companies was removed during the period of neoliberal reforms (1989–91, 1996). In fact, the dire condition of the aluminium industry was reflected in the reluctance of international capital to purchase state-owned facilities even when solicited by producer nations. One such example came in the late 1980s when Venezuela sought to attract foreign capital into new ventures in a restructured aluminium industry and to privatise two aluminium smelters, an alumina refinery, and a bauxite mine. Despite having one of the world's lowest-cost sources of hydro-electricity power, in what was once one of the most promising sites for TNC investment in aluminium smelting, Venezuela had become the site of decaying smelters starved of investment capital. The government's privatisation strategies collapsed in the face of wavering TNC interest.[80] Therefore, within the new international division of labour, Venezuela has been consolidated as an oil exporter, but this has been accompanied by an increase in the surplus population due to the contraction of industrialisation and the diminished requirements of capital for labour-power.

The dissipation of ground rent, the shrinking of international markets, and the decline in investment meant that basic industries could not obtain sufficient capital even to maintain existing facilities. By 1998 state-owned enterprises were losing US$300 for each metric tonne of primary aluminium they

---

76   Hite 2002.
77   Alcorta 1999.
78   Kettell 2006.
79   Ciccantell 2000.
80   Ibid., p. 303.

produced. The industries bore a combined debt of approximately US$1.5 bil-
lion; 1998 losses alone were about US$350 million.[81] CVG-Alcasa was forced
to shut down 40 percent of its operating capacity, as the state was unable to
attract foreign capital or meet basic operating costs. When Chávez assumed
power, oil prices were at first languishing at around US$8 dollars a barrel, and
his government initially pursued a policy of offloading CVG-Alcasa from the
state's books, which signally failed. What this heavy industrialisation strategy
reveals empirically is that processes of national development pursued by the
Venezuelan landlord state were tied structurally and politically to the magnitude of oil rents. In Venezuela, this took the form of an ambitious industrialisation strategy that exceeded the scale of the domestic market, but was
also unable to compete internationally, thus becoming chronically dependent
upon state support. As Coronil puts it, 'national development in Venezuela has
been premised on the local expansion of industrial capitalism, but industrialisation has expanded only within the limits of the national social structure
whose internal organisation and links to the world market have been built on
the extraction and circulation of oil rents'.[82] Therefore the point of departure
for the following section is to unpack the implications of an industrial capital
in chronic decline, CVG-Alcasa, becoming the testing ground for *cogestión*.

The Nature and Limits of 'Socialist' Management: The Case of *Cogestión*

This section draws upon primary research carried out at the CVG-Alcasa plant
with workers, union leaders, and cooperative members with direct experience of the *cogestión* experiment under Chávez. The analysis is supported and
updated by secondary research from Venezuelan newspapers, websites, economic data, and literature from the union movement at CVG-Alcasa. As noted
in the introduction, the story of *cogestión* unfolded in a tumultuous fashion:
from the first state sponsored example of twenty-first century socialism to
growing labour unrest and possible bankruptcy. There are two principal contradictions that the prospect of *cogestión* engenders at CVG-Alcasa. The first
derives from the material conditions of rentier capitalism. As highlighted in
the foregoing section, the deterioration of industrial production in Venezuela
was an expression of the state's inability to buttress productivity following the
fall in the magnitude of ground rent. The upshot of this scenario is the growing

---

81   Hite 2002.
82   Coronil 1997, p. 284.

breach in the scale of production needed to be competitive on the world market. Following on from this, the second contradiction is inherent to the concept of *cogestión* itself. By assuming control of the production process, workers
also bear the greater responsibility for productivity and performance. In this
light, workers' efficiency and collective responsibility can be used to temper
wage demands and become pseudonyms for the valorisation of capital. The
following explores these contradictions in empirical context.

The ambition of *cogestión* was to facilitate worker-led decision-making on
questions of production, technology, commercialisation, and investment in
co-responsibility with the state. In line with previous examples of industrial
democracy this required the eradication of the meritocratic and bureaucratic
management structures and the division between manual and intellectual
labour. Thus existing heads of departments and managers were removed in
order to elect new ones through a democratic workers' assembly. All elected
leaders are to receive the same wages as the workers, and their positions can be
revoked through the same democratic process.[83] The idea is to break down old
hierarchies through the 'democratisation of knowledge', as workers are encouraged to participate in the integral, productive restructuring of the company.[84]
Consistent with articles 62, 70, and 184 of the Bolivarian Constitution,[85] which
stipulate that the state should promote citizens' participation in public matters, an extra onus is placed on state companies to be responsive to their
respective local communities and the Venezuelan people.[86] This has taken
the form of the inclusion of local unemployed people through service cooperatives in transport, maintenance, and catering which large firms demand.
Indeed, each state company of primary industry has the mission of creating
Nuclei of Endogenous Development (NDE) and Social Production Companies
(EPS) as new points of employment and economic activity to stimulate feelings of community ownership.[87] The hope was that *cogestión* could be the
motor for a qualitatively new relationship between the state, the workers, and
the surrounding community whose cooperation and solidarity would combine

---

83 Personal interview, 8 April 2008, Bolivar.

84 MIBAM 2006.

85 Respectively, these articles of the Constitution delineate: 'the participation of the people
     in forming, carrying out, and controlling the management of public affairs' (62) 'citizen
     services organs, self-management, co-management, cooperatives in all forms' (70), 'par-
     ticipation by workers and communities in the running of public sector business enter-
     prises, through self management and joint management methods' (184).

86 Ibid.

87 CVG-Alcasa 2005.

as a practical vehicle to build the 'socialism of the twenty-first century' on the move.[88] Such initiatives included the purchasing of company uniforms from textile cooperatives and donations made by workers to community groups.

In 2005, the newly created head of the Basic Industry and Mines (Ministerio del Poder Popular para las Industrial Básicas y la Mineria – MIBAM), Victor Álvarez, placed Carlos Lanz as president of the company.[89] Lanz was deployed to provide 'revolutionary' leadership, and initiated the democratic reorganisation of the plant's decision-making structure and the introduction of workers' councils. Giving the workers' power over all aspects of the production and distribution process would be accompanied by a diversification of production, increased downstream activities, and securing new clients internationally with a superior and more abundant product.[90] Concomitantly, this was designed to lead to the development of a bigger internal market, where aluminium could be made available for cheap, high-quality housing, which has a multiplier effect on the social economy and generates jobs in the production of use-values (housing, clinics, and schools) that communities demand.[91] However, a large part of the underlying rationale for the implementation of *cogestión* was to make the plant (which, as shown above, has historically survived on state subsidies) productive and profitable. As Rodolfo Sanz, Minister of MIBAM explains, '[t]he big challenge is to combine a company that can be efficient from the point of view of production and humanistic from the social point of view ... because socialism is not contradictory with efficiency'.[92]

This tension between the principles of workers' control and the mechanisms needed to make the plant productive has been compounded by a divided and, some say, contradictory workers' movement.[93] However, it is not the purpose of this section to analyse the factional struggle among workers or the role of the trade union movement,[94] but, as above, to reflect upon the political economy, and therefore material potential, of forms of 'socialist' production at CVG-Alcasa.

---

88   Rodríguez et al. 2009.
89   Carlos Lanz is a Marxist sociologist and ex-guerrilla fighter.
90   Personal interview, 8 April 2008, Bolivar. The interview took place during a roundtable of semi-structured interviews with workers at the on-site socio-political training school Negro-Primero at the Alcasa aluminium factory.
91   MIBAM 2006.
92   *El Universal* 2009.
93   Albrecht 2006.
94   See Lucena 2007; Azzellini 2009; this volume.

Workers' Efficiency?

The first stage of cogestión (2005–6) was said to have ushered in an unprecedented 11 percent boom in productivity, as can be read in Figure 8.2, through the narrowing of the historical deficit between the cost of production and world market prices. Given the deteriorating conditions of production at the plant and, as shown above, CVG-Alcasa's infamous position as the 'black sheep' of Guayana's industrial region, the significance of this achievement for the workers involved (confirmed by on-site interviews) in the process of cogestión cannot be overstated.[95] However reports of CVG-Alcasa's apparent success, from the workers themselves, media, and academic commentaries, often elided mention of how productivity was being measured or achieved. It was assumed that workers' democratic control was naturally superior in reducing bureaucratic costs, raising productivity, improving efficiency, and stamping out corruption (particularly of the so-called aluminium mafias who controlled prices and production quotas with international companies). Initial commentary from Lanz reported a direct link between workers' control and productivity gains.[96]

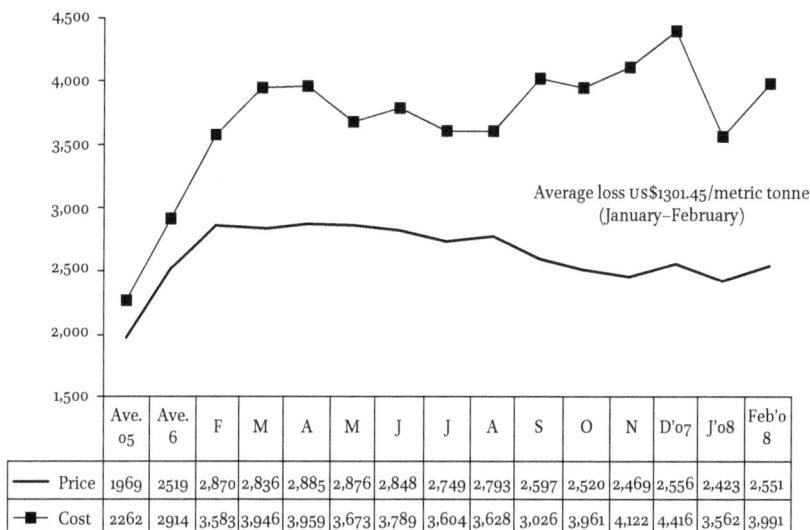

	Ave. 05	Ave. 6	F	M	A	M	J	J	A	S	O	N	D'07	J'08	Feb'08
—— Price	1969	2519	2,870	2,836	2,885	2,876	2,848	2,749	2,793	2,597	2,520	2,469	2,556	2,423	2,551
—■— Cost	2262	2914	3,583	3,946	3,959	3,673	3,789	3,604	3,628	3,026	3,961	4,122	4,416	3,562	3,991

(*) Cost of Sales + Administrative Expenses

FIGURE 8.2 Alcasa cost of production and world market price.
Source: Document obtained directly from the CVG-Alcasa plant during fieldwork, 8 April 2008, Bolivar.

Average loss US$1301.45/metric tonne (January–February)

95   Personal interview, 9 April 2008, Bolivar.
96   BBC News 2005.

This is not to deny that worker-controlled enterprises have indeed proved to be
superior to hierarchical models of management,[97] nor to assert that the workers committed to the project at CVG-Alcasa thought otherwise. Nevertheless,
such a causal justification reduces the complexity of primary resource based
capital accumulation to the moral and ideological character of worker-based
management strategies.

If we look more closely at the source of the apparent rise in productivity, it
becomes clear that there was a significant rise in world market prices of aluminium from an average of US$1,969 a tonne in 2005 to US$2,519 in 2006, a
28 percent rise. In fact, conditions of production (technological capacity and
investment levels), both during and following the *cogestión* experiment, have
continued to deteriorate. Levels of recorded output for the same period show
a decline of around 9000 tonnes between 2005 and 2006 (see table 8.1). Thus,
in the first instance, so-called productivity gains are not productivity gains at
all. Reduced costs do not have their source in either new capital or labour, but
in the magnitude of ground rent in the aluminium sector. As the demand for
a non-reproducible raw material grow, the location of the sector's marginal

TABLE 8.1   *Aluminium production 1997–2007 [metric tonnes (thousands)]*

Year	Production	Export	National Consumption
1997	213.44	129.35	72.87
1998	204.62	126.98	72.16
1999	159.80	106.39	55.60
2000	159.04	97.29	58.98
2001	159.09	101.96	55.54
2002	170.48	108.57	60.45
2003	167.95	120.54	53.08
2004	184.87	119.61	63.33
2005	179.04	109.61	59.26
2006	168.76	110.57	66.28
2007	175.90	65.30	110.40

Source: http://www.veneconomia.com/site/files/indicadores/indicador96_3552.pdf

97   Bradley and Gleb 1983.

producer changes (those with the highest costs such as Alcasa), increasing the average price of production, thus bringing in either new sources of supply or increased quantities of the marginal product. However, due to the volatility of world aluminium prices, as prices fell and Venezuelan aluminium became uncompetitive new political emphasis was placed on the future direction of *cogestión* and the role of the state (as can be seen in the slowing of demand taken up by internal consumption, see figures in table 8.1 for 2007).

To stimulate downstream production and internal consumption MIBAM tripled the number of firms authorised to buy aluminium at the official (over-valued) exchange rate (Bs. 2.15) from 172 to 632. The preferential sale of aluminium in the national market is regulated by the decree that this material must be processed nationally to strengthen the development of value added products in downstream aluminium industries. Under the same directive, it is stipulated that these companies should have favourable links with coop-eratives in the social economy. However, few of these companies presented as processors actually have the capacity to transform the primary material.[98] Rather, aluminium bought for the purpose of internal development is being sold to international buyers as a means of generating lucrative foreign exchange (dollars), which can be converted through the parallel market rate averaging between Bs. 4 and Bs. 7 per US dollar between 2004 and 2008. This mercantilist practice allows these groups to double or triple the value of subsi-dised aluminium, thereby directly appropriating the ground rent embodied in its sale – giving rise to what have been referred to as 'aluminium mafias'.[99] The provision of subsidised inputs coupled with a normative imperative to create links with cooperatives in the social economy, illustrates how socialist man-agement is an *a priori* moral command without any integrated mechanisms through which new value-added goods will be produced and distributed. This puts into perspective the structural role of corruption in the aluminium sector, which emanates as much from the lack of integrated worker-controlled net-works of aluminium processing as it does from the simple moral misdemean-ours of groups opposed to workers' control.

In fact, the attempted reorganisation of the plant and the political economy of the *cogestión* points to an interesting process of a self-disciplining work-force. In 2004, there were 266 hours of strikes; this labour strife had a significant impact in reducing operating output for that year.[100] In contrast, in 2005–6,

---

98   Cova 2009.

99   Ibid. This article in the national newspaper *El Nacional* identified that a Panamanian pro-cessor had purchased 2,000 tonnes of aluminium through this illegal line of exports.

100   MIBAM 2005.

during the height of the *cogestión* experiment, only four hours of operating activity were lost to strikes – an unprecedented level of labour acquiescence in CVG-Alcasa's conflict-prone history of organised labour militancy.[101] In part, therefore, increased productivity derives from more working hours, of greater intensity, due to the workers' enthusiasm for the project. This issue points toward the limits of a project that reduces socialism to job control, especially in the absence of significantly renewed state investment. Indeed, the issue of tempering wage demands (which in essence is a levelling down in the context of stagnant real wages and growing inflation) became the dominant organisational issue for workers aligned with the socialist reorientation of the plant. This problem raises one of the 'thorniest' issues of all in worker-controlled ventures – the role of trade unions.[102] Debate within the self-management literature long ago recognised a tension between unions as obstacles to workers' control, thus requiring a transformation of their attitudes and practices, to a justification of unions becoming integrated into new worker-controlled management structures.[103] This tendency is even more complex in the Venezuelan context because of the politically, and therefore ideologically, divided nature of the trade union movement. For instance, the leader of the union current Causa R, Henry Arias, has espoused a model based upon share ownership by the worker; here the 'democratisation of capital' is seen as a means to achieve commercial efficiency and social justice.[104] This contrasts with the more radical and idealistic Chavista union currents that see *cogestión* not as worker ownership, but as a pre-figurative form of socialist society and the only meaningful way to overcome their domination by capital.

This divide came to the fore during internal union elections in 2008 as left-wing currents won power in production departments, while right-wing representatives won elections within technical and administrative departments.[105] This division has deeply affected the running of the plant on a day-to-day basis and some claim led to the sabotage of *cogestión*. Internal opposition was identified as the primary force aiming to undermine early gains made during workers' control, as this reflected badly on the roles of technical support staff that

---

101   Ibid.

102   Clarke 1984.

103   See Egan 1990; Rubinstein 2001.

104   Henry Arias has claimed that the plant's financial and operational condition indicates the failure of Alcasa's Socialist Plan, stating that it needs US$2.5 million to stay in production, and upwards of US$3 billion to modernise the sector.

105   Azzellini 2009.

had previously acted autonomously from workers.[106] In addition there were reported conspiracies against workers' control from vested interests linked to the sale of the aluminium, leading to strong opposition from the company's bureaucracy. The main obstacles for the project remained the need for a new investment to update technological and productive capacity.[107] Reportedly, Chávez had recently signed off on a US$104 million investment at the time of the workers' experiment. The plant's management withheld this money, and pursued instead a contract with the aluminium company Glencore to finalise the expansion of productive capacity.[108]

Notwithstanding the plant-level struggles that have clearly acted as a fetter on any new development drive, the underlying obstacle that persists is the chronic deficit in productivity. Minister Sanz reported that the labour cost per tonne is 53 percent, while in Australia and the US it is at 16 and 17 percent.[109] The upshot has been that it costs US$4,000 to produce what they can only sell for US$1,300.[110] Electricity shortages, a lack of basic inputs, and spare parts have dramatically reduced productivity. By the end of 2010 the conditions at CVG-Alcasa had deteriorated to such an extent that the plant teetered upon the brink of closure and the government pursued partial divestment. As part of a national energy saving drive in 2009, along with a lack of operating capital, plant lines I and II have been dismantled. This led to the temporary unemployment, and/or relocation of some of the workforce to lines III and IV. The income and social security of these workers were to be guaranteed. However, non-payment of salaries has intensified labour unrest, as accrued interest on severance payments and benefits were withheld to meet the company's capital shortfalls. The plant was reported to require US$800 million to meet immediate operating costs and US$3 billion to fully recover the plant.[111]

The combined crises of politics (the failure of *cogestión*) and production (spiralling costs and falling productivity) have been met with what is perhaps the default position of the landlord state – to subsidise production for the domestic market whilst ideologically presenting this strategy as interim steps towards its developmental summit, in this case the Socialist Plan of Guayana 2009–2019. As part of this plan, on 21 May 2009 Chávez became the major instigator of renewed workers' control in the Guayana region and CVG-Alcasa,

---

106   Personal interview, 9 April 2008, Bolivar.
107   Personal interview, 8 April 2008, Bolivar.
108   Rivero 2009.
109   *El Universal* 2009.
110   Personal interview, 9 April 2008, Bolivar.
111   *El Universal* 2009.

stating that he 'no longer wants to play around with the workers' ('*ya no me juego con los trabajadores*'). Under the new plan, *Corporación Venezolana de Guayana*

> will reduce the high levels of exportation of primary materials like steel and aluminium, and divert them instead towards local and national proj-ects ... The primary material companies in Venezuela were designed just to produce and hand it over to the international and national private sec-tor so that they could process it and add value, at each stage of the pro-ductive chain they were exploiting the workers and speculating with prices.[112]

Thus the political response has been to increase (Chavista) workers' control by reverting to a scale limited to the domestic market, where aluminium that is uncompetitive on the world market will be subsidised by the state for national consumption. Indeed, for 2009 alone the aluminium sector as a whole reported a deficit of US$1.3 billion; in normal conditions these capitals would be forced out of the sector due to their inability to valorise at the normal rate of profit. However, the ability of the state to carry the debt is, for the time being, sustain-ing the industry.

Therefore, the resources (ground rent) required to concentrate industrial capital, update machinery, and expand the scale of production to compete internationally are of such a magnitude that the project cannot be localised to, or determined by, events at CVG-Alcasa alone. In the initial period of 2005–6 *cogestión* was able to successfully project the correct ideological vision for the revolutionary process that included the workers' efficiency, and the progressive inclusion of cooperative-based labour. However, this was based upon reducing costs and was sustained by a rise in global aluminium prices.

Conclusion

This chapter has tracked the historical development of CVG-Alcasa and the recent plight of *cogestión* as a means by which to unpack the dialectic of ground rent dependent industrialisation and the political economy of inter-vention under the Chávez government. The development impasse was located in the link between the scale of industrialisation and the magnitude of ground rent that can be transferred through the landlord state. This chapter has shown

---

112   Chávez, cited in *El Universal* 2010.

that for the period of *cogestión* the Chávez government did not substantially alter the material scale of intervention at CVG-Alcasa, but repackaged its political mode of operation. This process relied upon greater labour acquiescence; efficiency drives through the use of cooperative labour, and stopgap subsidies in light of no new investment. In addition, when the landlord state continues to infuse loss-making basic industries with subsidies, in order to keep these key sectors in operation, any exports also represent effective subsidies to global market prices.[113] Therefore, reflecting upon the example of *cogestión*, there is a tension between the objective capacity of workers dependent upon globally determined prices of primary materials – barriers that the Chávez government cannot abolish through an idealised organisational restructuring – and Chávez's voluntarist and normative injunction for 'socialist' action.

The most pressing issue facing transformations of production relations in Venezuela is the form in which ground rent can be transferred into capital able to actively participate in the transformation and development of society's productive forces – by acting as a normal productive capital. This would require its concentration on a scale necessary to compete in the world market. Chavista unions in the Guayana region have recently called for such a strategy, by consolidating all aluminium companies (Bauxilum and Venalum) in a unified worker-controlled enterprise on the grounds that socialist production can compete internationally. Such a transformation, however, could only take concrete political form in the progressive abolition of the private ownership of capital, as the working class becomes the collective owner of this capital under the political form of state capital. Whether 'twenty-first century socialism' points in this direction is not a question of the political will of *chavismo* but rather of working class action.

---

113   Hite 2002, p. 16.

PART 2

State and Market in Late Capitalist Development

••

Conspicuous Silences: State and Class in Structuralist and Neostructuralist Thought[1]

Juan Grigera

More than a decade of successful social resistance and a series of financial and economic crises (that started in the mid-1990s in the periphery and finished with the 2008 'credit crunch' in the US and Europe) have severely damaged the prestige of neoclassical economics and its political proposals in the global South. As a result, many critical responses to the neoliberal prescription for limited state intervention have emerged. In this competition for the hearts and minds of economists in Latin America, the neostructuralist tradition – an updated version of the structuralist thought put forward by the United Nation's Economic Commission for Latin America and the Caribbean (ECLAC) in the 1940s and 1950s – has come to the fore. Neostructuralism owes its prominence to the long-term intellectual influence of ECLAC in the region, which is evident in the widespread current use of some of their earliest ideas such as the terms 'centre' and 'periphery' and the strong association of development with industrialisation. Furthermore, the originality and the autochthonous character of this Latin American school of economic thought have also granted them some esteem in the subcontinent and beyond.

The purpose of this chapter is to unveil the hidden class politics of structuralism and neostructuralism. It argues that while neostructuralism is currently presented as the main challenger to neoliberalism, like its predecessor, it rests on neoclassical intellectual foundations that present a binary conception of state and market, representing the state as an institution that serves the 'general interest' of the population at large. It further argues that the undertheorisation of the capitalist state and accumulation within the structuralist and neostructuralist schools of thought results from systematic choices, rather than merely the unconscious underdevelopment of these concepts within the theoretical framework. Lacunae in these two cornerstone areas constitute 'conspicuous silences' which obscure the contradictions of the process of capital accumulation and the class nature of the capitalist state.

---

1 Thanks to Pablo Miguez, Rodrigo Pascual, Alberto Bonnet, and especially to the editors of this volume for insights and debate.

The first section of the chapter summarises structuralist proposals, identifying their main contributions and contextualising the criticism that follows. The second section establishes that ECLAC's structuralism is underpinned by an (implicit) instrumentalist conception of the state. The third section compares neostructuralism to structuralism, arguing that they both put forward a similar concept of the 'strong state', which reinforces rather than criticises the neoliberal view. The fourth section deals with the assessment of the structuralists' (more explicit) theorising of capital accumulation, which can be traced to the school's model of development. Finally, the last section deals with the neostructuralists' renewal of the idea of capital accumulation under the concept of 'productive transformations with equity'.

Key Tenets of Structuralism

Most Latin American countries, alongside many other regions of the global South, went through a transition from primary export-led growth to import-substituting industrialisation (ISI) in the aftermath of the First World War that lasted until the late 1970s. Just as it is commonplace to note the correspondence between the rise of Keynesianism and the crisis of the 1930s, we can equally correlate the emergence of the first original contribution to political economy from Latin America to the dynamics of industrialisation during these years.

Structuralism (also known as *cepalismo* after CEPAL, the Spanish acronym for the *Comisión Económica para América Latina y el Caribe*, or ECLAC in English) provided the theoretical framework necessary to bolster a development strategy that sought to replace imports with the production of value-added goods domestically, which would entail a long-term widening and horizontal integration of the manufacturing industry.[2] Their 'manifesto'[3] proposed an innovative view attributing the ongoing changes to a response to the new international situation, in sharp contrast with the dominant neoclassical interpretation that assumed there were no alternatives to primary export-led development, and understood the moment as a long catastrophic conjuncture for economic growth.[4] Structuralists interpreted this as a positive

---

2   Saad-Filho 2005.
3   Prebisch 1949.
4   Neoclassical discourse insisted on relying blindly on the benefits of comparative advantages; in practice, this meant a policy orientation toward the further development of agriculture, combined with birth control measures (Dosman 2001). Furthermore, Latin American coun-

transition towards internally-oriented urban-industrial development (*desarrollo hacia adentro*) and took the opportunity to criticise the limits and social drawbacks of export-led development (*desarrollo hacia afuera*). Their proposal was to further support the transformation of the state and economy in order to overcome backwardness and income inequalities by sponsoring a project of industrialisation.

But if this was the context that these theories originally attempted to explain, their enduring influence goes well beyond these initial parameters. Structuralism can be characterised by three central ideas and policy prescriptions. First, it introduced the idea of dualism, which posits that the world can be divided into a 'centre' and 'periphery'. As Saad-Filho notes, the fact that these terms require no explanation is a clear gauge of structuralism's widespread influence.[5] Second, structuralists theorised the deterioration of terms of trade for Latin American (or more broadly primary exporter) countries. Third, structuralists developed a framework to advance late industrialisation in order to overcome underdevelopment.

Dualism is at the core of structuralism on two different scales. At one level, structuralists argue that the centre and periphery have different production structures arising from a certain historically constructed international division of labour. The periphery has 'another economy', in the sense that is supposedly governed by a different set of rules.[6] At the same time, the productive structure of the centre is assumed to be homogeneous, whereas the periphery suffers from structural heterogeneity; that is to say, dualism on an international scale is replicated *within* the peripheral countries. Structural heterogeneity is defined mainly in terms of productivity: homogeneous countries have highly productive sectors all across the economy, whereas in peripheral countries a 'modern pole' coexists alongside 'primitive sectors whose productivity and income per capita are probably comparable to those that prevailed in the colonial economy or even in the pre-Columbian era'.[7] High productivity is usually restricted to a small enclave dedicated to primary exports, generally owned by foreign capital, and to a large extent isolated from the rest of the economy. Thus, there are few potential spillovers from 'progress' within the

---

tries sometimes expected international trade to return to 'normality', i.e. *belle époque* levels, and even made numerous attempts to return to the gold standard (for instance, Argentina suspended it 'for 20 days' in 1914, and went on extending this temporary measure until 1943).

5 Saad-Filho 2005.

6 Love 1984.

7 Pinto 1970.

'modern pole' – for instance, profits are expatriated via imported luxury goods or remittances. Structuralist ontology thus begins by dividing the world system into centre and periphery, and then further applies this dualism to the internal dimensions of peripheral countries.

Dualism on a world-scale gives rise to another distinctive feature of structuralism: against the neoclassical narrative of comparative advantage, structuralism has advanced the hypothesis of the deterioration of the periphery's terms of trade (the Prebisch/Singer hypothesis).[8] Defined as the ratio between the unit prices of exports and imports, the terms of trade decline when the relative price of the country's imports increases. Besides highlighting the obvious pressures that this situation places on the current account (exacerbating a trade deficit), structuralists also attempted to verify the empirical validity of the hypothesis that relative prices have been constantly moving against primary production since 1870. It is regrettable that relative prices do not reflect quality changes of the final products.[9] Furthermore, structuralists offered two alternative sets of explanations for this phenomenon, from both supply and demand sides respectively.[10] In the former, a situation characterised by high rates of long-term rural (and urban) unemployment, in which many producers subsist on small-scale food production, exerts a pressure on wages that ultimately prevents redistribution of productivity improvements in the peripheral modern sector, and thus unit costs fall, allowing a transfer of productivity gains to the buyers, i.e. to the centre. From the demand side the story is better known: a disparity in income elasticities of imports in central and peripheral economies favours the increase in prices of products produced by the centre. As the periphery exports food and other primary products while importing luxury goods, any rise in the income of the periphery leads to an increase of the demand of imported goods and a further deepening of its imbalances. At the same time, the centre improves its balance of payments, even as its income rises.

Having identified the key structural constraints to development in the periphery, structuralists then advance a series of policy prescriptions to overcome these constraints. Structuralists envisioned industrialisation as the process that would allow peripheral countries to escape the traps of underdevelopment. Domestic production of manufactured goods would counteract the tendency towards declining terms of trade and contribute to rapid productivity growth. At the same time, industrialisation would raise wages and liv-

---

8   Named after Prebisch 1949 and Singer 1950.

9   Pinto 1970, p. 97.

10   Saad-Filho 2005.

ing standards, and more broadly propel a movement towards 'modernisation' (through the introduction of new technologies, as well as urban/democratic values). Structuralists identified ISI as the only possible strategy of industriali-sation in a peripheral country, in a context of highly protectionist centre econ-omies and the difficulties of competition. Since these international constraints place serious limits on 'spontaneous' industrialisation in the periphery, the only way to overcome them was to offer state support to infant industries. They strongly advocated that the state should coordinate investment decisions (e.g. force the transfer of surplus from the primary sector to manufacturing), create the needed infrastructure, provide soft credits and subsidies to domestic firms, and attract foreign capital and technology.[11]

As with any other major school of economic thought, substantial critiques have been formulated. Neoclassical economists have usually assimilated struc-turalism to ISI and blamed the failures of the latter on the theoretical weak-nesses of the former.[12] Rent-seeking behaviour due to blanket protection, small market size, and misallocation of resources are frequently cited as negative by-products of policies inspired by structuralism. ECLAC addressed some of these criticisms by putting forward ad hoc proposals, such as the proposal to create a common market of the world's periphery.

Regarding terms of trade, Viner advanced another strand of critique against structuralism.[13] Viner argued that because of an economic law – ignored by structuralists – that technology would advance most rapidly in the manufac-turing sector relative to agriculture, terms of trade should, *pace* the structur-alists, actually favour agriculture in the long-term. Viner's line of argument would later be quite closely replicated by Baumol, regarding the relative prices of manufacturing and services, a process that came to be known as Baumol's disease.[14] The reformulation of international trade theory spawned a large number of debates, both empirical/statistical (such as the choice of base years and countries of reference) and theoretical.[15] Criticism of structuralism stemming from Marxism and dependency theory, on the other hand, often pointed out the ambiguities in the structuralist definition of 'sector' (primary vs. manufacturing), the obscure account of labour differences, and the depen-dent nature of the local bourgeoisie.[16] Despite this wide range of criticism,

---

11   Hirschman 1968.
12   Bruton 1998.
13   Viner 1951.
14   Baumol 1969.
15   Viner 1951; Spraos 1980.
16   Cardoso y Faletto 1969; Saad-Filho 2005.

a detailed analysis of the theory of the state within structuralist thought has received surprisingly little attention.

The Role of the State in Structuralist Thought

No matter how brief our previous review of the main insights and presumptions of structuralism might look, it suffices to point out the emphasis this school has given to the role of the state in overcoming underdevelopment. Several analysts have also pointed to the supposed originality of structuralist thinking about the relationship between state and market.[17] It must be stressed, however, that while structuralists never presented a coherent theory of the state, there are two ways in which their insights on the state may be gleaned from their analyses: from their polemics against neoclassical conceptions on this issue, and from random and sporadic remarks on various policy areas.

The structuralist argument against the liberal prescription of minimising state functions is in line with other heterodox (non-Marxist) currents. Advocacy for a 'bigger' and 'stronger' state is seen as a crusade against the non-interventionist agenda of neoclassical economists. Prebisch lists the functions that the state should handle better than the market (for instance, solutions to 'market failures'), while always being careful to state that it is necessary to keep an eye on building technocratic knowledge to prevent state hypertrophy and guarantee efficiency.[18] The advocacy of state intervention to correct market-failures certainly sets the structuralists apart from mainstream neoclassical economists, who are reluctant to recognise their very existence, or, if they do, incorporate them into their analyses in a highly ad hoc fashion. However, it is important not to overstate these differences, since both neoclassical economics and structuralism are built on a large number of shared assumptions. First, they agree on a list of common areas of state intervention: they affirm that the state should defend property rights and provide basic infrastructure (different types of 'public goods'), maintain macroeconomic stability, and several market institutions, including, for example, currency. Second, it is no longer true that recognition of market failures is a monopoly of 'heterodox' economists. Rather, as Wade has noted, debates between neoclassical economists and heterodox economists turn on the types of remedies put forward to 'fix' market failure: neoclassical theorists stick to 'horizontal' measures, such as enforcing intellectual property rights, investing in 'human capital', or facilitating access to

---

17   Dosman 2001, p. 89.
18   Prebisch 1981; on a similar line see the neo-Listians Evans and Wolfson 1996.

credits or other financial assets; structuralists and other heterodox economists, on the other hand, agree with some of these proposed remedies, but
also endorse vertical or sectoral measures, such as industrial policies, protec-
tionism, or income distribution.[19]

Structuralists put forward the key concept of a 'hard' state that leads industrialisation or systemic competitiveness. The 'regulatory capacity' of the state
should be strengthened to let it become the 'stimulus' of industrialisation.[20]
State regulation can be more effective or rational than market distribution
of productive resources because the market reproduces inequalities in initial
assets, lacks a 'social horizon' and is short-term in orientation, and thus unable
to plan long-term investments or pay attention to ecological damage.[21] The
'economic efficiency' of the market is to be contrasted with a different product
to be achieved through state intervention, that of 'social efficiency'. However,
at the same time, structuralists warn that the state should let the economy
be driven ultimately by the private sector.[22] This rhetorical idea of equilibrium between state and market is captured by Prebisch's term 'Estado sagaz'
('shrewd State'): a state that should not 'suffocate private initiative and entre-
preneurship, which inevitably require the incentive of profit',[23] and should not
protect inefficient industries only because they are national. The state should
avoid becoming hypertrophied by following the logic of bureaucratic and/
or military power.[24] In sum, a 'shrewd State' is the administratively coherent
entity that overcomes both market and state failures.

While the structuralists managed to overcome the neoclassical conception
of a zero-sum relationship between state and market, their conception of the
state-market relationship is equally dichotomous, in another respect. The market is presented as the place of unconstrained private free trade between individuals, underestimating or denying the role of primitive accumulation and the
state in its production and reproduction. Correspondingly, the latter (state or
institutions) are framed as completely free of constraints from social relationships or the sole product of will or social contract. In the structuralist world,
however, the growth of the market is not accomplished at the expense of the
state, or vice versa. For instance, structuralists call for an explicit set of policies
that will nurture the private sector, increase market size, and strengthen the

---

19   Wade 2003, pp. 11–13.
20   Gurrieri 1983.
21   Prebisch 1981, pp. 16–7.
22   Dosman 2001.
23   Ibid., p. 93.
24   Prebisch 1981, p. 42.

state (for example, in the 1960s, *cepalistas* advocated for a common market for the periphery in order to overcome market size constraints).[25] The particular conceptualisation within structuralism of this pair of concepts – the state and the market – is therefore an original contribution and valid criticism of the neoclassical view. Yet while structuralists (correctly) criticise neoclassical economics for failing to understand market failures, they commit an error on the other side of the spectrum in their idealisation of an almighty state, a 'visible hand' that is always capable of achieving equilibrium. That is to say, the inefficiencies of the market, for structuralists, can always be overcome with correct state intervention.

Digging further into the logic of the structuralist view of state-market relations, one finds that it systematically gives precedence to the state, or institutional power, over that of the market. The state is always assumed to be more powerful than market forces. The explanation of inflation is one example: the structuralist account conceives of inflation as a consequence of state redistributive activity: a profit-squeeze results from taxes placed on wages or profits, which raises the cost of production, which in turn puts upward pressure on prices.[26] Moreover, the supremacy of the state is extended to many other institutions. This is at the core of the causal explanation of the deterioration of the terms of trade. For structuralists, trade union pressures in industrialised countries create a price distortion mechanism. This dynamic, together with the oligopolistic protection of the rate of profit, prevents a decline of manufactured products' price proportional to the constant rises in their productivity. Cardoso's correct inference from this statement, namely that in ECLAC's view agents of production 'manage, by virtue of their *politico-organisational* strength, to obstruct the operation of the [international] market', helps us further ascertain the causal hierarchy within Structuralist theory.[27] In sum, at the core of structuralist thought, institutions are conceived in a normative fashion as separate from (and above) social relationships of production and exchange.

Furthermore, alongside this positioning of the state above market forces, structuralism repeatedly highlights the need to constrain state dynamics in order to avoid hypertrophy. Structuralists only offer scarce or puerile remarks, however, as to which social subjects are capable of disciplining the state.[28]

---

25   Cardoso 1977.

26   CEPAL 1969; Prebisch 1981.

27   Cardoso 1977, p. 13.

28   This is one of the most important differences with dependency theorists, who did have discussions about which political subject was potentially capable of leading transformations of the state.

Trade unions and the middle classes are responsible for overburdening the state with spurious jobs or services, bureaucratic and military power have their own interests 'within the state', and elites are also self-interested in other ways.[29] Thus, '[i]ndividual decisions in the market must be combined with collective decisions outside the market that override the interest of dominant groups. But in all this a great vision is needed, a transforming vision ... inspired in ethical designs of the long term where economical, social, and political considerations are conjugated'.[30]

Strangely, despite the litany of statements stressing the centrality of dualism in ECLAC's tradition, the concept of dualism is not applied to the state. Dualism is a feature of the productive structure and of (exploitative) market relationships that have no impact on the state. Again, the state is above (or outside) the social structure, in this case outside the 'centre–periphery system', and thus there are no references to any thinking in terms of peripheral (and central) states. Rodríguez's considerations of the 'geopolitical aspects of the state' under globalisation are restricted to the rather obvious verification of the existence of 'foreign interests' within Latin American countries.[31] Nor is the sovereignty of the peripheral state interrogated. This is evident, for example, when structuralist thinkers offer 'prescriptions' for better capital accumulation. In an argument representative of broad trends in structuralism, Prebisch states that foreign investment should be 'well-directed', and that it should be constrained by the state in order to best transfer technology and know-how.[32] Thus, the disciplining of foreign capital by a (peripheral) state raises no problems in this structure, where (imperialist) relationships of expropriation and/ or exploitation take place in the market.[33] Structuralists state that 'decision-making' should be moved to the periphery, but they do not provide insight as to how this might occur in practice. How is decision-making power to be 'moved' in that direction? Who is to be the subject of this transformation in power relations?

---

29   Prebisch 1981, pp. 16–18, 41, 42, 76.

30   Ibid., p. 38.

31   Rodriguez 2001.

32   Prebisch 1951.

33   Just to stress our point, we do not imply here that any type of disciplining is in every case impossible, but rather that it should be understood alongside the multiple social conditions that make it possible. As Selwyn (2009, p. 177) notes with reference to the Neo-Listian description of historical cases where state disciplining of capitalist power does seem to have happened, 'the question arises of why foreign capital allowed itself to be disciplined to such an unusual extent'.

Overall, the crude instrumentalist character of the underlying theory of the state in structuralism is undeniable. Instrumentalist theories of the state advocate action based on moral or logical principles, assuming the universality of benefits.[34] As we have seen, the state is always placed above social relationships, in a mechanistic fashion, as if the state were an 'organ' whose direction can be determined by mere 'decision-making'. However, the assumption of state neutrality in social conflict is far from neutral.

The Rise of Neostructuralism and the 'Strong' (Neoliberal) State

The ascendance of neoliberalism in the 1980s and 1990s constituted a massive shock to the erstwhile hegemony enjoyed by structuralism within Latin American economic thought and policy.[35] The ultimate cause of structuralism's declining influence lay in its gargantuan failure to understand the new shape of international capitalism after the crisis of 1973. While structuralism emerged due to its appreciation of the 1930s, it faded away due to its inability to come to grips with the multiple transformations that marked the end of Golden Age capitalism, such as the changes in world financial and trade regimes. As the secretary general of ECLAC recalls: in the 1980s 'the institution was frankly on the defensive, both in terms of the collective imaginary as well as in the academic world'.[36]

A renewal of ECLAC's thought in the neoliberal era is usually said to have begun with the contributions of Fajnzylber.[37] He concluded that, on balance, Latin American ISI had been merely 'frivolous interventionism', drawing on the influential work of political economist Alice Amsden, who celebrated the developmental processes of the East Asian 'miracles', advancing a reading of these quite distinct from the neoliberal narration. The influence of other heterodox economists such as the neo-Listians (for instance, in their refutation of the World Bank's report of East Asian 'miracles', and the reassessment of industrial policies and their defence of national 'policy spaces' even under globalisation)[38] and neo-evolutionists (for the idea that economic growth should be understood mainly from studying firms' behaviour, particularly their ability to compete in a Darwinian context by introducing technological inno-

---

34   Barrow 2007; Clarke 1991.
35   Webber 2010b.
36   Rosenthal, quoted by Leiva 2008a.
37   Fajnzylber 1983; 1990.
38   Such as Wade 2003; Evans 1995; Amsden 1989; Chang 1993.

vation and progress)[39] were also decisive in the formulation of neostructuralism in the following decades,[40] deepening the common features that were shared with List and were already implicit in structuralism.[41]

The areas of conceptual innovation of neostructuralism in the 1990s and 2000s were forged around systemic competitiveness, technical progress, proactive labour flexibility, and virtuous circles.[42] Neostructuralist thinkers also attempted to make globalisation politically and socio-economically viable, stressing the benefits of globalisation, and seeking changes in the export profiles of Latin American countries.[43] Neostructuralism insisted on the importance of social compromises between classes, adding subjectivity, symbolic politics, and a cultural dimension to their policies.[44] Thus, we share Leiva's characterisation of neostructuralism as a current that gained ideological power in the late 1990s by proposing itself as an alternative to neoliberal reforms, while in fact it was inclined to deepen and extend them. Nowhere is this continuity more obvious than in the role of the state.

Neostructuralists display an astonishing continuity with neoliberals with regard to their understanding of the role of the state and their implicit conceptualisation of it. While the classical structuralists argued that the state was the crucial actor required to steer industrialisation, neostructuralists insist that the competitiveness of the entire social system depends on effective state intervention. Effective state intervention, in the neostructuralist view, generates political consensus, increases competitiveness of exports, and helps the upgrading and adaptation of the labour force.[45]

Despite these important elements of difference, however, neostructuralists reproduce many of their predecessor's underlying conceptions, particularly in their definition of what constitutes a 'strong' versus a 'weak' state. Evans and Wolfson define the strength of the state based on its links to 'civil society' and its embeddedness in business networks.[46] The call of structuralists and neostructuralists to strengthen the state by tying it to a strong civil society-state alliance, presents what Leiva has named the 'heterodox paradox': the set of

---

39 Nelson and Winter 1982; Nelson 1998.
40 Bielschowsky 2010.
41 For a very insightful analysis of the neo-Listian conceptualisation of the state, which has many parallels with structuralism, see Selwyn 2009.
42 Leiva 2008a, pp. 3–6.
43 Leiva 2008b.
44 Bielschowsky 2010.
45 Leiva 2008b, p. 4.
46 Evans and Wolfson 1996.

economic and political policies that are supposedly aimed at expanding the role of participatory governance end up reinforcing the subordination of the political sphere to capital.[47] The issue is not so paradoxical, however, once we restore proper class terms to the distinction between weak and strong states. As Bonnet has argued, the strength or weakness of a state is not a function of the extent of intervention in the economy, nor its regulatory power; rather, from the viewpoint of class, the strength or weakness of a state is measured against its capacity to reproduce accumulation, that is, against the extent of its command over the working class.[48] The neoliberal state, in this sense, was a strong state, expressed not least in the increases to the power of the executive branch under neoliberalism. Structuralist and neostructuralist proposals generally end up 'in a constant fluid state, given that [they] must constantly negotiate to overcome the gaps between ... rhetoric and socioeconomic reality'.[49] Indeed, if there is a 'paradox' inherent in neostructuralist analysis, the proposed state form is usually a *weaker* state insofar as it is constantly mediating between different interests instead of disciplining them.[50] The paradox arises as a result of their ultimate aim for a stronger state in terms of rule over the working class.

Industrialisation: Development and Capital Accumulation

As we have seen, industrialisation has been one of the central concerns of structuralism since the very beginning. Structuralism contends that the state should support 'deliberate' or forced industrialisation, either through facilitative policy making, or by becoming directly involved in production (the latter particularly where large amounts of investment are needed, such as infrastructure projects, and essential goods or services). In this section, we will unpack the arguments of structuralism regarding industrialisation, particularly its principal role in development as conceived by structuralists, before offering a sustained critique.

First of all, we should note the displacement introduced by industrialisation. In a similar vein to the decision of the Sixth Congress of the Communist International (Comintern) in 1928 to introduce industrialisation as a goal

---

47   Leiva 2008a, pp. 147–9.
48   Bonnet 2008.
49   Leiva 2008b, p. 18.
50   For a detailed description of the state-form in the post-2011 era in Argentina, see Bonnet and Piva 2011; and Leiva 2008a, Chapter 10 for the Chilean case.

against the 'feudal–imperialist alliance',[51] ECLAC substituted development with industrialisation, despite occasional remarks over the decades warning that the two concepts should not be misunderstood as synonymous.[52] Development as synonym for industrialisation was also inherited by dependency theory, despite the latter's sophistication in differentiating between development and growth (growth, for dependency theorists, should come with equality, social welfare, employment, and the national control of economic and political life in order for it to be reasonably called development).[53] If the main aim was industrialisation, then structuralists could call for the state to make the 'correct' intervention, whereas dependency theorists could say that only socialism would bring industrialisation to the periphery. Thus, the strong association of development with industrialisation was a widely shared ideal of the 'progressive' and 'left agenda'.

Structuralists argued that industrialisation through capitalist development was a major goal to be embraced universally because of the 'good' externalities it carried with it. The first argument has already been mentioned: producing manufactured goods would allow the periphery to escape the trap of declining terms of trade. Also, real wages would rise and thus income distribution would become more equitable, unemployment less acute, and other positive spill-over effects would then take place. One of the latter would be the introduction of new technologies to agriculture, because the primary sector was identified with poor peasant production and an ossified, dormant oligarchy; agricultural products were assumed, furthermore, to have deteriorating relative prices, and little potential for productive growth. If this was the general (prejudiced) conceptualisation of agriculture, it must be said that ECLAC had no explicit argument against agricultural production per se. Even Prebisch argued, for example, that higher agricultural productivity was a useful tool for raising standards of living,[54] though it was not an instrument that would lead a nationwide process of change as urban industry could. Another by-product of industrialisation, according to structuralist theory, would be the democratisation of society, with the growth of 'clear rules' for all, and a more Weberian, rational state.[55]

Another interesting confusion introduced by structuralism regards the defence of a nationalist or regionalist view of industrial development. In

---

51   Palma 1978, p. 897.
52   Lewis 1999.
53   Palma 1978, p. 908.
54   Cardoso 1977, p. 19.
55   Hirschman 1968.

their discourse of national economic independence and autonomy, in and through industrialisation, ISI was a strategy that fit perfectly with the international conditions of post-war capitalism. In other words, 'the struggle for industrialisation which was previously seen as an anti-imperialist struggle had increasingly become the *goal* of foreign capital'.[56] Thus, two important conclusions follow. First, the widely assumed anti-imperialist nature of ECLAC is not rooted in ISI *per se*, but most probably in US opposition to the institution itself, given US fears of ECLAC's promotion of state subsidies, and state-owned enterprises.[57] ISI was *a common goal* of national and international capitals to build protected plants under tariff-walls oriented towards domestic markets. Dependent development thus was not precluded by ISI. Second, ISI as a policy was not the result of ECLAC's policy proposals and the dissemination of its ideological perspective throughout the region nor the rational expression of a 'general interest' of capital, but rather 'the result of a particular resolution of the conflicts between particular capitals and of the contradiction between capital and the working class'.[58] This seems to be forgotten both by structuralists, when assuming that ISI was the result of (surprisingly similar) sovereign decisions by different nations in the periphery, and by the neoclassicals, when they criticise ECLAC's emphasis on the importance of self-sufficiency.[59]

The structuralist school of thought exhibits a further crucial silence regarding industrialisation. Structuralists disregard the centrality of primitive accumulation when assuming, for instance, that labour can freely move from agriculture to manufacturing. This silence is a particularly delicate topic in the context of the contemporary developing world, along with the theoretical consequences it carries. First, this is because assuming that labour-power *can* and *will* be transferred from rural agriculture to urban manufacturing also assumes that agricultural productivity is sufficient to sustain the urban population. The assumption similarly implies the 'freedom' of direct producers, that is, that there are no restrictions regarding the mobility of labour-power and that direct producers have been dispossessed of the means of production.[60] The single prescription of industrialisation for all states on the grounds that manufac-

56   Palma 1978.
57   Webber 2010b, p. 213.
58   Clarke 1991, p. 186.
59   For instance, analysing Argentina's ISI, Llach regrets Peronism's 'fatal decision in favour of autarchy': Llach 2010, p. 96.
60   Brenner 1977, p. 34.

turing could 'absorb excess labour'[61] can better be thought, along with their perception of the Latin American reality of the 1950s and 1960s as 'structurally heterogeneous', as a battle cry promoting primitive accumulation.

In this regard, we should note a striking similarity between classical and structuralist economic thought. While the former denies dualism theoretically, it has historically exercised it in practice, as Perelman has shown.[62] Classical economists, while theoretically teaching the self-correcting nature of capitalism without government intervention, advocated policies to coerce small peasants and force them into the factories. The contradiction of these thinkers with *laissez-faire* principles was not repeated in the case of structuralists, who took this 'dualism in practice' to the level of theory, thus fostering primitive accumulation both in principles and in policies.

Finally, in parallel with their tactical erasure of any explicit reference to processes of primitive accumulation, structuralists also view production as a neutral process, the gains of which can simply be distributed post facto. Prebisch warned that the aim to use planning as a means of redistributing income should come *after* income has increased.[63] This contrasts dramatically with what we can ascertain of the realities of the capitalist labour process and how accumulation undermines distribution.[64]

Underneath the promises of widespread profit through the 'gains of productivity' stemming from industrialisation, we can find structuralists' concerns about how to ensure a process of internal division of labour favourable to capital accumulation[65] or the proposals of a pattern of accumulation that would facilitate capital formation.[66] The ultimate aim of structuralism, of favouring and accelerating capital accumulation in the periphery (again a theme that resonates from classic economics) is present again in the idea of 'structural heterogeneity'. One of the key worries raised is that a country with heterogeneous levels of productivity has less capacity for capital accumulation.[67] In sum, as much as Smith prescribed measures to favour capital in order to speed growth, structuralists were driven by a similar concern, though applied to the particular conditions of the peripheral economy.

---

61   Prebisch 1951; Ocampo 2001. The metaphor of 'absorption' is another sign of the extremely conservative concerns of Prebisch and his followers.

62   Perelman 2000.

63   Prebisch 1961.

64   See Braverman 1974.

65   Prebisch 1951.

66   Cardoso 1977, p. 27.

67   Pinto 1970.

'Productive Transformation with Equity' or Another Turn of the Screw of Neoliberalism

With the uprising of neostructuralism within the ECLAC, the idea of industrialisation gave way to the new core concept of 'productive transformation with equity'. More than concentrating on fostering the manufacturing sector, neostructuralists concluded (after the successful experiences of East Asia) that the main task was to choose a form of integration with the world market based on competitive advantages arising from industrial policies in the wide sense of the term (in other words, state support of export-oriented activities).[68] Economic development could be achieved by acquiring systemic competitiveness, a function of the physical infrastructure, human resources, and a country's capacity to innovate.[69] Also, key to better competitiveness is improving productivity by means of 'genuine' productivity increases (enhancing technical processes) rather than spurious ones (reduction of wages, exchange rates advantages, exploitation of natural resources).[70]

Industrialisation, and especially ISI, has been removed from the current concerns of neostructuralism, besides remarks to the effect that the manufacturing sector is a privileged player in the arena of technical innovation. The current agenda is built on top of the neoliberal structural reforms, that is to say it proposes how to move further from an unavoidable reality.[71] It takes for granted that development can only occur in a 'sane macroeconomic context' with efficient state expenditure (under strict monetarist fiscal discipline).[72] In this sense, neostructuralists become *complementary* to neoliberal structural transformations, by 'adding' equity at the microeconomic and 'meso-economic' levels, thus discarding any remains of the narratives of profound transformations as preconditions for development.[73] Let us just point out that the idea that you can 'correct' neoliberal reforms by 'adding' social concerns is consummately absurd.

The neostructuralist project is targeted towards fostering a successful microeconomic environment (capable of introducing innovations and building know-how) that will help peripheral countries 'enter globalisation'.[74]

---

68   Kay 1998, p. 114.
69   Ocampo 1998.
70   Bielschowsky 2009, p. 179.
71   Leiva 2008a.
72   Ocampo 1998.
73   Sztulwark 2006, p. 73.
74   Bielschowsky 2010, p. 179.

'Convergence' of mean income levels will come once 'technical progress is introduced and disseminated in the productive structures of the region'.[75] Thus, what were silences in structuralism regarding the hidden processes of industrialisation became now a supposedly neutral discourse of 'technical progress'. Behind the introduction of technical transformations of the labour process there is a renewed attempt to subsume labour.[76] Frequently, this would mean, in the context of the global South, the introduction of techniques that were developed under different social relations, for instance, class struggle. In sum, the neostructuralists' call to make productive sectors 'internationally competitive' is simply a synonym for the call to introduce international market discipline in national contexts of accumulation.

Conclusions

Members of ECLAC have never been 'ivory tower' academics: they trained and indoctrinated middle-ranking personnel in central banks, development and finance ministries, and university faculties.[77] They helped to legitimise the ideology of autonomous national development, providing research, analysis, and a theoretical framework for pushing the model further.

By briefly summarising structuralism's main tenets we have shown how the state was at the core of its political proposals. Yet, we could identify an important silence regarding its theorising. In an attempt to explain this silence, structuralists or neostructuralists might say that *the state is the state*; there has never been a need to define or discuss its nature. Or, they might equally argue that the silence is only an oversight, one that further analysis within this framework should be able to overcome. For his part, Cardoso suggests that the question of expanding state participation was hidden in most texts 'for obvious reasons in the case of a UN agency often dependent upon somewhat unprogressive governments'.[78] On the contrary, this chapter has argued that the silence is not a 'gap' or a product of (self)censorship that can be corrected by simply extending ECLAC's theorising to include the state. Rather, the silence on the topic of the state is a structural silence, symptomatic of underlying implicit assumptions within structuralism regarding both the state and the market. First, we have shown that structuralists have a dichotomous idea of state and market,

---

75   Ibid., p. 187.
76   Braverman 1974.
77   Faria 1978, p. 11.
78   Cardoso 1977, p. 27.

like the one in neoclassical economics but with opposite appraisements. Then, we have seen how structuralists place the state above everything, free of any constraints. The precedence of state power over any other social relationship goes as far as to ignore dualism, one of the key tenets of this tradition, failing to explore the differences between 'central' and 'peripheral' states. Overall, we have shown how structuralist thought on the state is a crude form of instrumentalism.

Then we have characterised the rise of neostructuralism as a continuity of neoliberal reforms under different premises. The demise of structuralism after changes in international political economy in the 1970s gave rise to a readjustment and adaptation of the tradition. Neostructuralist thinking on the state showed a continuity with structuralist instrumentalism and conspicuous silence. While the neostructuralists opposed neoclassicals on the issue of state intervention they were aiming for a common goal a strong state.

Finally, we have turned towards the structuralist and neostructuralist defense of capital accumulation. We have seen that behind structuralist proposals for rapid late industrialisation, it is possible to identify particular interests, as well as the goal of deepening primitive accumulation and speeding capital accumulation. The neostructuralist shift towards increasing productivity and 'structural competitiveness', in turn, was shown to be an undisguised attempt to complement neoliberal reforms and further introduce international market discipline in the global South.

In the context of the current crisis, a thorough critique of structuralism and neostructuralism is a critical endeavour insofar as it is necessary to prevent their narratives of both the crisis and its possible exits from becoming the dominant narrative. This paper has shown that far beyond any kind of nostalgia for these lines of thought, a restatement of class-based theorising is the only starting point for genuine working-class alternatives to neoliberalism.

CHAPTER 10

Sugarcane Ethanol: The Hen of the Golden Eggs? Agribusiness and the State in Lula's Brazil

Leandro Vergara-Camus

In a discourse eerily reminiscent of the 1970s 'Brazilian Miracle' the international corporate media today is fixated on the notion that Brazil's recent economic performance is 'lifting the country out of poverty'. Any available 'evidence', such as the fact that star football players like Ronaldinho are leaving Europe to come back to play for Brazilian clubs for multi-million dollar contracts, is presented as another sign that Brazil is on its way to 'economic superpower' status. In a less trivial sense, we are told that high world prices for natural resources and agricultural commodities are probably driving this growth. Among the several sectors that are based on the exploitation of natural resources, the sugarcane ethanol industry has been given prime time in the corporate media because it represents one of 'the industries of the future'. It is indeed among the most dynamic, capital intensive, and 'national' of the different sectors of the Brazilian economy. Within Brazil, it is portrayed as the next 'engine of growth' and the state has decided to put its weight behind it. Brazilian agrarian capital and the state in fact want to cash in on a favourable global context, which combines the recognised urgent need to tackle global warming, the foreseeable end of the oil era, and the coming of the biofuel epoch. In his speech at the UN General Assembly in New York on 23 September 2008, Brazilian President Luiz Inácio Lula da Silva said:

> Attempts to tie high food prices to the dissemination of biofuels do not stand up against an objective analysis of reality...Brazil's experience demonstrates – and this could be the case for countries similar to ours – that sugarcane ethanol and biodiesel production reduces our dependency on fossil fuels, creates jobs, regenerates degraded land and is fully compatible with expanding food production.[1]

A year later, in 2009, at the same podium, President Lula was trying once again to sell sugarcane ethanol to the world in the midst of the global financial

---

1 Silva 2008b.

crisis that was drying up investment in the sugarcane sector in Brazil. He thus addressed in his speech several of the contentious issues, such as deforestation and poor labour conditions, for which the Brazilian agricultural sector is infamous abroad:

> Brazil's ethanol and other biofuels are produced in ever-improving conditions, under the aegis of the agricultural zoning plan we have just implemented nationwide. We have banned sugarcane plantations and alcohol plants in areas with native vegetation. This decision applies to the entire Amazon region as well as to Brazil's other major biomes. Sugar cane production covers no more than two percent of our tillable land. In contrast to other biofuels, it does not affect food security, much less compromise the environment. Companies, workers and the government have signed an important commitment to assure decent working conditions on Brazil's sugarcane plantations.[2]

In other words, like the famous children's tale, it is as if ethanol from sugarcane will be the hen that lays the golden egg from which the entire Brazilian nation will benefit, while contributing to solving the problem of global warming. How much of this miracle story is true and what is the basis upon which the recent economic growth of Brazil stands? What strategies are Brazilian capital and state mobilising to produce the conditions for this promising future to materialise? Why does the Brazilian state, in the words of its highest representative, need to defend and promote sugarcane ethanol in every possible international forum?

This chapter will examine the role of the Brazilian state in the recent rise of the sugarcane ethanol industry. It will explore the strategies that the Brazilian state is using in order to present the sugar/ethanol sector as a 'responsible' and 'green' industry with a view to accelerating capital accumulation and internationalising its activities.[3]

I will argue that recent shifts in the ideological framing of global environmental debates are generating a new alliance within Brazil, between the state, agribusiness, and traditional landlords, which is, in turn, reconfiguring rural class conflicts in the country. Processes of 'accumulation by dispossession' have been occurring in Brazil for the past 40 years (and are still ongoing in

---

2   Silva 2009.
3   Important companies within the ethanol industry itself are leading an international campaign to convince global investors and public opinion of the sustainable character of sugarcane ethanol, but for lack of space I will not explore this facet of the issue in this chapter.

several regions of the country) and have been essential to the capitalist development of agriculture and the rise of sugarcane ethanol.[4] However, recent transformations in the country's political economy, typical of the uneven and combined development of capitalism, suggest that in certain sectors – in this case, the production of ethanol – we are also witnessing strategies geared to the expanded reproduction of capitalism – that is, an accumulation strategy that combines the extraction of absolute surplus value and relative surplus value, with the strong support of the Brazilian state.[5]

The chapter begins by highlighting some theoretical discussions around the role of the state in capital accumulation, particularly its relation to the national bourgeoisie, and the importance of state discourse for the process of capital accumulation. The following section traces the origin of the sugarcane industry by offering a summary of the conservative modernisation of the countryside that began in the 1960s under the military dictatorship, and that created the conditions for the rise and consolidation of an agrarian capitalist sector fully integrated with transnational agribusiness. In the following sections, the chapter examines how the Brazilian state, under the Lula administration, mobilised several of its institutions to support and accelerate capital accumulation within the ethanol industry in Brazil and abroad. Simultaneously, the state developed social policies that contributed to maintaining low rural labour costs, and more specific targeted policies that allowed family producers to integrate into the ethanol commodity chain, without requiring any significant concession from agrarian capital. The chapter will end with a short illustration of the importance that the state discourse has had in the rise and consolidation of the sugarcane ethanol industry.

The study of this sector is important because it is mainly in the hands of Brazilian nationals. Many of its enterprises are still family-owned and not publicly traded and the current source of financing and growth of the industry is the domestic market. This makes it an interesting representative of what we could still call 'the national bourgeoisie', without implying by this that it is in opposition to foreign capital. Indeed, although not yet predominant, transnational agribusiness groups of all types have been gradually gaining ground, either by buying up sugar/ethanol mills, setting up their own plants, or associating themselves with local capital.[6] Sugarcane ethanol also represents one

---

4 Harvey 2003.

5 Brenner 2006a, pp. 100–1.

6 Corporations like Abengoa from Spain, Cargill and Bunge from the United States, Infinity Bioenergy and British Petroleum from the United Kingdom, Louis Dreyfus and Tereos from France, and Sojitz Corporation from Japan have recently invested in the ethanol sector.

of the most dynamic sectors of agrarian capital, requiring large capital investment in the mechanisation of agricultural production, and in its transportation and distribution infrastructure. This sector is also responsible for pushing
several other sectors of the rural economy into modernising their production
methods.

An important distinction between the Brazilian case and other Latin
American cases, like Mexico for instance, has to do with the role of the state in
the economy. Contrary to what has happened in other countries of the region,
the state in Brazil did not do away with all the institutions that allowed it to
intervene and orient economic sectors. Although privatisation was widespread,
the Brazilian state has kept the Banco do Brasil, the second largest bank in
Latin America, Petrobras, the largest company in Latin America and the fourth
largest in the world by market capitalisation, and the Brazilian Development
Bank (Banco Nacional de Desenvolvimento Econômico e Social, BNDES), the
most important source of long-term credit for Brazilian enterprises, which is
now the largest development bank in the world.[7] These three state institutions
have been mobilised to support the sugarcane ethanol industry.

The Role of the State in Capital Accumulation

The study of the role of the state in developing countries in non-Marxist academia was carried out through the Weberian concepts of the developmental
state and state capacity. A developmental state can be said to include the six
following characteristics: (1) a developmental elite, (2) relative autonomy from
civil society, (3) an insulated professional bureaucracy, (4) a weak subordinated civil society, (5) effective management of non-state economic interests,
and (6) a combination of the use of repression, legitimacy, and performance.[8]
Advocates of the concept of the developmental state believe that state action
was responsible for the economic development of newly industrialised countries in the 1970s. Peter Evans applied the idea to the Brazilian case, as part of
a comparative study including India, Japan, South Korea, Taiwan, and Zaire
in which he elaborated the concept of 'embedded autonomy'.[9] Embedded
autonomy combines bureaucratic insulation with intense connection to surrounding social structures. Central to Evans's embedded autonomy is the idea
that the state has to be autonomous from the interests within society in order

---

7   Morais and Saad-Filho 2011, p. 34.
8   Perraton 2005.
9   Evans 1995.

to have the ability to establish goals. However, state officials also need to be embedded in society, that is, connected with business circles, in order to be able to know if policies have a chance of succeeding. According to Evans, developmental states have the capacity to impose goals on the private sector through a pilot public agency that coordinates industrial policy. On this score, Evans argues that the state in Brazil from the 1970s to 1990s was not developmental because the state had only limited autonomy as it was captured by the traditional elite, who used state resources as a source of power and wealth. This meant that its bureaucracy was not professional and permanency within it depended strongly on political battles. Brazil was for him an 'intermediary state' (between a developmental and a predatory state) because it included 'pockets of efficiency', such as the BNDES.[10]

Proponents of the concepts of developmental state, state capacity, or embedded autonomy fall into several theoretical difficulties because they conceptualise the state as a neutral arbiter separated from civil society, believe that the state can actually impose certain economic goals on capital, and that state agencies are the rational agent of economic activity. Central to these claims is a view that the state has the ability to discipline the national bourgeoisie by using subsidies but also coercive policies. Several Marxist scholars have questioned this idea that the state had the upper hand over capital. Vivek Chibber for instance has argued that during the period of import substitution industrialisation (ISI), national capital was never clearly differentiated from the comprador sector, was never subordinated to the state, and actively worked at going around the dictates of the state. What actually happened during that era is that the national bourgeoisie accepted the subsidies and avoided the planning that would have meant sacrificing short-term profits. National bourgeoisies preferred to establish national monopolies and used the state to socialise the risks of industrial development. The obvious conclusion from Chibber's historical analysis is that the idea of a 'national bourgeoisie' opposed to foreign capital and with a clear commitment to national planning that the developmental state could steer is simply a myth. This type of bourgeoisie never existed and the analysis of the re-emergence of developmentalism should not reproduce this myth.[11] Following Chibber's insights, this study of the sugarcane ethanol industry will explore how certain sectors of the national bourgeoisie can use the state to position themselves in the global

---

10   In Evans's typology, the predatory state is the opposite of the developmental state, because its bureaucracy is not independent and uses the state as a source of wealth accumulation against civil society. Evans 1995, p. 61.

11   Chibber 2004.

arena, without necessarily demanding protection from transnational capital or accepting concessions to the state.

The Importance of State Discourse for Capital Accumulation

An element that is often missing in many accounts of state development policies, whether Weberian or Marxist, is the importance of state discourse. Discourse is often presented as an additional dimension to policy, that comes to cover up or justify policy choices, but more rarely is it presented as a crucial element of capital accumulation. The case of sugarcane ethanol suggests that state discourse is much more than a simple justification or cover up mechanism. It is constitutive of the reproduction of capital.

At the very beginning of the first volume of *Capital*, Karl Marx uncovered the powerful force of the capitalist commodity by referring to the idea of fetishism. He wanted to point out the social process peculiar to the capitalist commodity form in which relations between human beings are hidden and transformed by human beings themselves into relations between things with a life of their own.[12] It is by this process of fetishism, rendered possible by the *common expression of all commodities in money*, that value becomes attached to the commodity, in abstraction from the social relations that produce that value.[13] This idea of the fetish character of the capitalist commodity must be taken into consideration when one aims at understanding the social practices of social subjects with respect to capitalist accumulation in any given sector.

In a recent work on the centrality of capitalist oil production for state formation and discourse in a dependent capitalist formation, Fernando Coronil applied Marx's understanding of fetishism to land and oil, conceived by the majority of Venezuelans as the direct and exclusive sources of wealth in their country. Coronil's theoretical objective was to bring together the sphere of social representation of reality with a materialist explanation of social phenomena that does not give predominance to one or the other. Coronil begins his theoretical construction with a critique of a certain interpretation of Marx's labour theory of value that simply focuses on labour and capital, and proposes instead to retrieve Marx's identification of the three sources of wealth under the capitalist mode of production: capital, land-ground rent, and labour: 'A focus on the commodification of land, labour, and capital – Marx's trinity formula – embraces within social analysis, as Lefebvre proposes, a wider range

---

12   Marx 1990, p. 165.
13   Ibid., p. 168.

of social actors and social formations, unifies temporal and spatial dimensions, and brings out more forcefully the play of structure and contingency in history'.[14]

This approach not only recognises the importance of land for capital accumulation and power in underdeveloped countries, but also opens up the dynamic of capitalist development and allows us to consider a multiplicity of agents that a merely dual dialectical perspective prohibits. State formation is also analysed through the state discourse created by politicians and state officials that have their own objectives. State discourse or ideology is thus not simply a super structural reflection of the structural development of the mode of production, but is rather understood as a fundamental device necessary for the state's concrete power, policies, and actions, which in turn allows for the construction and development of this discourse.

Overall, the major strength of Coronil's perspective is that it emphasises the dialectical relationship between agents and structures in a way that some other versions of Marxism have been unable to achieve. His perspective gives importance to the social representation of structures without losing sight of the real determining character of structures. Within this perspective, ideology can neither simply be false consciousness, nor can discourse be the unique foundation of social reality. Therefore, discourse becomes important not by itself, but because it is produced by social subjects (state elites, dominant classes, subaltern classes, etc.) in a specific position of power, materially and symbolically, and is central to their social reproduction. This approach to the state is of fundamental importance in this study of the sugarcane ethanol industry in Brazil, because, as it will be shown, not only the Brazilian state's action but also its discourse has been fundamental for the expansion of the industry.

Primitive Accumulation and the Conservative Modernisation of the Countryside: Going Back to Nature

Brazil's original insertion into the world economy was through the production of sugar. It was through the constitution of large slave sugar plantations, which 'imported' approximately three to four million slaves from Africa from the sixteenth to seventeenth centuries, that the landed class amassed huge fortunes and became the ruling elite. Ever since, the Brazilian countryside has been the principal source of wealth for the nation. It has also been characterised by a diversity of labour regimes, ranging from slavery to free wage-work and from

---

14   Coronil 1997, p. 62.

debt-bondage to small peasant farming. One of the limitations to the generalisation of wage labour in the countryside was the type of property regime that
only began to favour private property in 1850. For many years after the abolition
of slavery in 1888, indeed well into the mid-twentieth century, the subordination of rural workers and peasants to a landlord in order to gain access to land
was a common phenomenon across Brazil. Throughout this period, traditional
landlords, that is, those whose wealth and power depended on the control of
land and access to land through non-capitalist means, were able to remain
within the power bloc because they sat on extensive properties from which
they extracted ground rent from peasants. This said, at least since the 1930s
the historical tendency has been toward the increased use of wage labour and
hence the proletarianisation of rural producers, albeit with constant resistance
from peasant movements demanding land reform. An important turning point
that established the conditions for the capitalist expansion of sugarcane ethanol was the 'conservative modernisation of the countryside' implemented by
the military dictatorship in the 1960s.[15]

The appearance of the conditions for the emergence of capitalist social relations in the countryside is not part of a logical culmination of previous historical patterns. It is made possible through what Marx referred to as 'so-called
primitive accumulation', where land is expropriated from labourers (peasants)
through a series of political measures and laws that allow for the commoditisa-
tion of land and force market discipline upon labourers.[16] Wood, referring to
Robert Brenner, characterises the form of property relations that corresponds
to the non-capitalist contexts as 'politically constituted property', because it is
political power (or the control of the state) that gives access to property and
the appropriation of surplus labour.[17] In contrast, capitalist social relations are
enforced through 'absolute private property', which relies mainly on economic
means to appropriate surplus labour.[18] When the process of full commodification of land is unleashed, the social reproduction of the different social subjects of the countryside gradually becomes dependent on the market, either as
a place to sell produce or to sell one's labour. This movement toward the establishment of absolute private property, and corresponding generalisation of
capitalist relations, was crucial for the rise of the sugarcane ethanol industry.

In 1963, within a context of growing peasant mobilisation, and in an attempt
to incorporate rural workers and peasants within a populist political pact,

---

15   Vergara-Camus 2012.
16   Marx 1990, pp. 873–940.
17   Brenner 1985, p. 209; Wood 1999, pp. 49–50.
18   Wood 1995, pp. 29–31, 37–9.

President João Goulart codified rural labour rights through the *Estatuto do Trabalhador Rural* (Rural Worker Statute), and then followed this with a mild agrarian reform. These moves were unacceptable for the São Paulo landed oligarchy, because their properties would be affected, and together with other sectors of the Brazilian ruling class, they immediately sponsored a military coup in 1964. After the coup, the military decided to support the agrarian bourgeoisie (the most capitalist sectors of the rural ruling class) instead of the landed oligarchy, and favoured a project of modernisation of the countryside. The 'new' strategy led to the encouragement of mono-crop export, the development of agribusiness, the concentration of agricultural production, and the generalisation of capitalist relations. The modernisation of agriculture really took off after 1968 with heavily subsidised credit schemes, as well as fiscal incentives to any company that invested in land.[19] As an indication of the importance of the increase in public credits for agriculture, Coletti estimates that rural credits were multiplied by 504 percent between 1969 and 1979.[20]

These monetary incentives raised the value of land and eroded the mechanisms through which peasants and certain rural workers had become accustomed to having access to land. The inflow of credit and the obligation to pay back these loans introduced the market imperative of competition among capitalist farmers. As Marx theorised in his section on the tendency of the rate of profit to fall, the possibility of losing their land if they did not reach average levels of profitability compelled rural landowners to cultivate land with modern technology or move to seeking cash rents instead of maintaining paternalistic arrangements with sharecroppers.[21] Simultaneously, the modernisation of agriculture, the increased mechanisation of most sectors, and the growth of cattle ranching drastically diminished the need for labour. As a consequence, between 1960 and 1980, 28 million rural workers and peasants were expelled from the countryside to cities that were unable to provide employment for these newcomers.[22] Throughout this process, Brazil was under military dictatorship. It was hence difficult for rural workers and peasants to collectively respond to the modernisation, which was accompanied by a witch hunt against communists inside rural unions and with the establishment of neocorporatist links between unions and the state, in which rural workers, through the Confederação Nacional dos Trabalhadores Agrícola (National Confederation

---

19   Goodman and Redclift 1981, p. 144; Houtzager 1998, p. 124.
20   Coletti 2006, p. 134.
21   Marx 1991, pp. 273–306.
22   Sparovek 2003, p. 24.

of Rural Workers, CONTAG), were provided with access to state services and pensions.

The modernisation policy of the 1960s and 1970s is thus the turning point that almost eliminated non-capitalist social relations and triggered another round of land concentration allowing for the fully capitalist development of agriculture, in which accumulation became much more capital-intensive than before.[23] Property in land and access to surplus labour became less based on 'politically constituted property' and extra-economic forms of extraction and more on 'absolute private property' and economic means of extraction.

It was only in the early 1980s, with the retreat of the military from power, that rural workers and peasants were able to begin to mount an opposition to their loss of jobs and access to land. The struggle for land resumed in the south and southeast of Brazil, led to the formation of the Movimento dos Trabalhadores Rurais Sem Terra (Landless Rural Workers' Movement, MST) in 1984, and pitted land-poor peasants and landless rural workers against the state, as many of the land occupations first targeted public land. In the 1990s, the target of the struggle turned to the 'weakest' link of the traditional landlord class: landlords who had been incapable of modernising their estates, who had lived off extensive cattle ranching, and whose political control or connections were limited to the local arena. Simultaneously, as the new unionism movement led by a young metalworker named Luiz Inácio Lula da Silva was winning its first battles in the industrial outskirts of the city of São Paulo, a new generation of the rural workers also began to mount an attack on the old corporatist leadership of their unions. The sugarcane regions of the state of São Paulo were particularly vibrant during this process of radicalisation of rural unions. This new generation of leaders preferred to avoid the CONTAG and created instead new unions (*sindicatos de empregados rurais*, unions of rural employees, SERs), affiliated to the newly created Central Unica dos Trabalhadores (Unitary Workers Union, CUT). The mid-1980s were marked by important affiliation drives, strikes, and labour actions that managed to improve some of the working conditions of rural workers, but were never strong enough to extract serious concessions from agrarian capital.

Neoliberal restructuring of the countryside happened within this historical background. Agricultural credits were cut fivefold during the 1980s, but the state continued to intervene in the market throughout the 1980s and the early 1990s by purchasing and stockpiling food crops and maintaining guaranteed

---

23   Non-capitalist relations of production, reproduced through family labour and production for self-consumption, are still important in the peasant sector.

prices.[24] As a result, large Brazilian capitalist farmers who were protected during several decades are now fully integrated with the transnational agribusiness sector.[25] On the other side of the spectrum, rural workers and peasants have paid the price of this restructuring. Between 1985 and 1995, 10 million of them lost their jobs in the agricultural sector and it is estimated that another four million people abandoned agriculture between 1995 and 1999.[26] With the affiliation of the CONTAG to the CUT in 1995, the former rural branch of the CUT ended up choosing the path of institutional integration over frontal confrontation with capital. Rural unions now also favoured participation within the *conselhos de desenvolvimento rural* (Rural Development Councils), neocorporatist regional consultative councils inscribed in the Constitution of 1988.

Rural unions, although they won several victories, were not able to resist this process of modernisation. In the sugarcane sector, the use of manual labour, principally for cutting sugarcane, has traditionally represented an important element of the production process. However, with growing competition and the concomitant necessity of increasing productivity, manual labour has been gradually phased out, while the rate of exploitation of the remaining labour force has increased. A decade and a half ago, there were approximately one million sugarcane cutters in Brazil, whereas today only 400,000 to 450,000 remain; a large portion of them are temporary migrant workers from the impoverished northeast. According to industry representatives, the average salary of a sugarcane cutter is around two minimum salaries (1000 reals per month) – the second best wage in agriculture – and is paid based on a daily rate which requires that the worker cut at least five tonnes per day.[27] However, these figures are challenged by Antonio Thomaz Junior, a specialist of labour relations in agriculture, who found that sugarcane cutters earn on average only 600 to 750 reais per month. He also found that with mechanisation, the amount of sugarcane that a worker needs to cut has increased constantly. In 1969, a sugarcane worker needed to cut on average three tonnes of cane per day. In 2007, the average was 12 tonnes or a minimum of nine tonnes, if he/she wanted to stand a chance of keeping his/her employment in a context of a highly depressed rural labour market, and abundance of unemployed and underemployed workers. According to Thomaz Junior's estimates, a sugarcane cutter averaging 12 to 15

---

24   Belik and Paulillo 2001, p. 96.
25   Ibid., p. 98.
26   Filho 2001, p. 196; Petras and Veltmeyer 2003, p. 75.
27   Altieri Adhemar, corporate communication director of the União da Indústria da Cana-de-açucar (UNICA), personal interview, São Paulo, July 2009.

tonnes of cane per day has a productive lifetime of 12 years or fewer.[28] The exhausting working conditions that these figures imply have been confirmed in numerous interviews conducted with former sugarcane cutters, suggesting that the industry is still partly based on the super-exploitation of labour, even though it is rapidly moving to complete mechanisation.

The sugarcane ethanol industry is thus part and parcel of this conservative modernisation. It was indeed the military regime that created the ethanol industry when in 1975 it created the *Programa Nacional do Alcool* (Alcohol National Programme, Proálcool). This programme was intended to diminish the effects of the first oil shock by mixing a certain amount of locally produced alcohol to imported oil and to provide an alternative to sugar producers and sugarcane mill owners. In 1979, with the second oil shock, the programme was expanded and included the production of cars running entirely on alcohol. The programme provided sugar mill owners with subsidies and incentives to invest in the modernisation of their plants and further mechanise sugar production. With the oil prices coming down in the 1980s and 1990s, and subsidies being reduced, the number of alcohol-powered vehicles in Brazil constantly decreased. They only began to grow again in the 2000s when the oil prices reached new highs as a consequence of the Iraq invasion. The ethanol industry received a major boost in 2003 when the car industry introduced the 'flex-fuel' engine that can run on gasoline or ethanol. Ever since, the sale of 'flex-cars' has not ceased to increase; it is estimated to currently represent 90 percent of all new car sales in Brazil, which means that by 2017, 75 percent of all cars will be able to use ethanol.[29]

The sugarcane industry likes to present this recent rebirth as being market-driven. It is true that the flex-car was developed and commercialised by the private sector and that an important part of the capital investment in the expansion of the ethanol producing capacity of traditional sugar mills has come from the savings and business decisions of the sector itself, such as mergers or strategic alliances with transnational groups from Japan, England, and the US, among others. However, this is only part of the truth, because the Brazilian state, like it was for the emergence of the sector, has also been instrumental in setting the conditions for this latest phase of growth. For instance, the Brazilian state has set the amount of anhydrous ethanol that needs to be mixed to gasoline to 25 percent, providing a lucrative market for mill owners. It has also provided the industry with all kinds of credit and incentives to expand production. This time, however, all this has happened in the context

---

28   Thomaz Junior 2007, p. 22.
29   Milanez, de Sa et al. 2008, pp. 25–6.

of international negotiations to mitigate climate change that require Brazil to reach its commitments of further reducing greenhouse gas emissions.

Times have indeed changed in some important respects. In less than a decade, the world has moved from a global environmental debate that pitted environmental whistle blowers against corporate sceptics, to a broad planetary consensus (that is, new though instable hegemony) that recognises the reality of climate change and global warming, basically agreeing on the sources of this situation and the need to tackle it as fast as possible.[30] As a consequence, the green energy sector is growing very rapidly and, for some, has become an integral part of a reconstituted historical bloc.[31] For others, the green energy sector represents new competing interests to the fossil fuel fractions, signalling the rise of intra-capital struggle.[32] What is clear is that this shift in global environmental hegemony opens the door for the rise of new capitalist enterprises, which, as in the case of any emerging industry, need the support of the state to facilitate the process of capital accumulation, as well as the mobilisation by the private sector of corporate marketing and branding strategies in order to attract venture capital. Therefore, rather than understanding the Brazilian state's position within the climate change discussion as one simply responding to an environmental threat, we should understanding it, as Matthews and Paterson propose, as a case in which the state is stimulating an existing but small market, accelerating its development, and creating new sites of accumulation.[33]

The Brazilian State under Neoliberalism: Promoting Internationalisation

From a Marxist perspective, we could characterise President Luiz Inácio Lula da Silva's (2003–10) policies as 'neodevelopmentalist' because they favoured the sectors of the national bourgeoisie whose activities are centred on the domestic market.[34] However, it is also important to recognise the 'neopopulist' character of his social policies because they allocated poverty-alleviating funds to popular classes along clientelistic lines. Lecio Morais and Alfredo Saad-Filho argue Lula's first government represented a 'losers' alliance' composed of

---

30   Newell and Paterson 1998; Levy and Egan 2003.
31   Levy and Egan 2003, p. 823.
32   Newell and Paterson 1998, p. 696.
33   Matthews and Paterson 2005, pp. 62, 69–71.
34   Morais and Saad-Filho 2011.

several sectors that had not benefited from the policies of President Fernando
Henrique Cardoso (1994–2002).[35] Among these losers figured the traditional
manufacturing elite of the southeast, who favoured nationalist and expansionary policies, and several 'notorious right-wing oligarchs, landowners, and influential local politicians from the poorest regions of Brazil'.[36] What Morais and
Saad-Filho could not foresee, however, was that some class fractions of this
'losers' alliance' would manage to use the state to relocate themselves within
the 'historical bloc' by linking themselves to a booming and promising economic sector. Indeed many traditional landlords from the states of São Paulo,
Mato Grosso do Sul, Mato Grosso, and Goiais, whose power had been diminishing in the preceding years, linked themselves to the sugarcane sector during Lula's presidency. By doing this, traditional landlords fixed themselves to a
more modernised sector of the agrarian bourgeoisie, such as mill owners and
agribusiness companies, but also to several upstream interests in the auto and
transportation industries.

In 2005, in their analysis of the transformations of the Brazilian state
since the demise of the ISI model, Morais and Saad-Filho rightly argued that
'the state has deliberately dismantled its institutional capacity for macroeconomic planning and micro-economic intervention through mass privatisations, downsizing, SOE and agency closures and large-scale subcontracting
at the ministerial level'.[37] In regard to public banks that continue to exist, like
the Banco do Brasil, the Caixa Econômica Federal and the BNDES, Morais and
Saad-Filho argued that they essentially operated under market rule and had
'been neutralised from the point of view of industrial and financial policy
objectives'.[38] In an article in 2011, the same authors signalled a shift in Lula's
economic policies that took place in 2007 in which these same state-owned
banks began to be mobilised to support national industries.[39] Because of the
very peculiar context of the race to find a substitute for fossil fuel energy, the
sugarcane industry benefited from the support of the state even before this
policy shift.

Since Lula took office, the Brazilian state has been instrumental in the development of the ethanol industry, a pattern that has continued under Dilma
Rousseff, Lula's presidential successor in 2010. The state, through Petrobras, is
even participating directly in the production of sugarcane ethanol, and it is

35   Morais and Saad-Filho 2005, pp. 4–6.
36   Ibid., p. 6.
37   Ibid., p. 13.
38   Ibid., p. 14.
39   Morais and Saad-Filho 2011, pp. 34–7.

estimated that it could increase its participation to up to fifteen percent. However, the BNDES has been, to date, the main instrument of the state to support the sector. Since January 2003, the BNDES budget increased from 35.1 billion reals[40] to 168.4 billion reals[41] in 2010, of which 24.7 billion reals went to Petrobras. In comparison, Cardoso's best year in terms of BNDES funding was 2002 with 38.2 billion reals.[42] In five years, the BNDES increased its funding to ethanol producers by 11 times, passing from 600 million reals in 2004, to 6.4 billion reals in 2009, which represents five percent of the loans of the development bank.[43] According to the BNDES, its financial assistance contributed to increase ethanol production by 54 percent between 2004 and 2010.[44]

To coordinate the government's policy toward the sector, a special department, the Departamento dos biocombustiveis (Department of Biofuels) was created within the industrial branch of the bank in 2007. The Department of Biofuels began functioning with a budget of 19.7 billion reals (approximately 10 billion dollars), 15.4 billion to finance projects for the production of sugar and ethanol, 2.3 billion for co-generation of energy for the grid, 1.8 billion to support the harvest of sugarcane, and 142 million reals to support research and development.[45] In addition to providing funding, it has organised seminars bringing together industry representatives with state officials and academics, participated in the organisation of world conferences on biofuels, been present in different international forums, published a number of studies, and offered policy recommendations. To some extent, it could be said that this department is the sounding board of the industry within the state apparatus.

The barons of the ethanol sector have indeed benefited from all kinds of state policies that have contributed to the recent growth and modernisation of their sector. First, the Brazilian state has facilitated capital accumulation by extending public credit under favourable conditions or by presenting itself as guarantor for private loans for ethanol production. Due to the very high interest rates that have characterised the Brazilian banking sector for the past 20 years, the BNDES is the main source of long-term loans for enterprises. The bank provides, for instance, financing (without limit on the value of the investment) for the purchase of sugar/ethanol plant equipment that is manufactured nationally. Through this policy, between 2004 and 2008, the bank has contributed

---

40   Approximately US$ 9.9 billion at the exchange rate of January 2003.

41   Approximately US$ 96.5 billion at the exchange rate of January 2010.

42   See <www.bndes.gov.br>.

43   Milanez, Carvalcanti et al. 2010, p. 340.

44   Ibid., p. 342.

45   See <www.bndes.gov.br>.

to the modernisation of the industry in the state of São Paulo and its geographic expansion outside São Paulo, by extending a total of 23 billion reals.[46]

Second, the stability of the short-term operations of the sector is also a preoccupation of the state. Hence, through the *Programa de Apoio ao Setor Sucroalcooleiro* (Support Programme for the Sugar-Alcohol Sector, PAISS), the BNDES extends a line of credit to the sugarcane mill owners. It finances the stocking of ethanol with loans for working capital at nine percent annual interest for up to a maximum of 200 million reals, of which the first 50 million are given automatically, while the remainder require the approval of the BNDES.[47] In addition, between 2004 and 2009, the BNDES has provided financing for all kinds of transport and stocking equipment for close to 423 million reals.[48]

Third, and more importantly, the state has also contributed to the sector through mega-infrastructure projects for the national distribution of ethanol and its export abroad. In the mid-2000s, three competing infrastructure projects were put together to tackle the problems of the transport of ethanol from the producing regions – mainly in the west of the state of São Paulo, Goiás, Mato Grosso, Mato Grosso do Sul, and Minas Gerais – to its main market in the metropolitan regions of São Paulo and Rio de Janeiro, as well as to the ports for exports abroad. The main objective is to distribute ethanol through a transport network organised around ethanol pipelines connected to a system of motorways, railways, refineries, and ports. The first project was proposed and financed by the state-owned oil company, Petrobras, and administered by a public private partnership between Petrobras, Mitsui, and Camargo Corrêa. The ethanol pipeline would have two branches, one beginning in Goiás and going through Mato Grosso and Riberão Preto, the main producing region of São Paulo, and the other one beginning in Mato Grosso do Sul, and going through the south of São Paulo. Both branches would end in Petrobras's terminal at the port of São Sebastião. The project also includes the adaptation of Petrobras's installations to accommodate ethanol as well as connections of the pipeline with important rivers. The cost of the investment: US$1.2 billion.[49] The second project called *Uniduto* brought together the biggest private companies of the industry, Copersucar, Cosan, São Martinho, Santa Cruz, São João,

---

46   Milanez, Barros et al. 2008a, pp. 11, 13–14.

47   Interest rates in the banking sector in Brazil vary tremendously according to the type and size of the loans, but it is not rare for financial institutions to charge over 20 percent and up to 45 percent for short and medium-term corporate loans.

48   Milanez, Nyko et al. 2010, p. 93.

49   Ibid., p. 76.

and Bunge. The pipeline would cover 570 kilometres and service the traditional regions of the state of São Paulo, but would include connections to railways to transport the ethanol from the state of the centre-south of Brazil, and a deep-water off-shore terminal in Guarujá to facilitate large boat transporters. The cost of the investment: US$ 1billion, provided by the private sector.[50] The third and most ambitious project is the *Centro-Sul Transportadora Dutoviária*, which would cover 1,164 kilometres and connect most regions where sugarcane production and ethanol is in expansion. The ethanol pipeline would begin in Alto Taquari, deep into Mato Grosso, go through Goiás and São Paulo, and end in the port of Santos. The project is a private initiative of the Brenco group, one of the most important companies of the sector until it was recently bought by ETH Bioenergy of the Odebrecht group, and would require 2.7 billion reals.[51] The first and second projects merged in October 2010, Petrobras keeping 20 percent of the shares of the corporation and requiring that no other partner surpass that 20 percent, and negotiations between Petrobras and ETH Bioenergia are ongoing in order to integrate the three projects into one large transport and distribution network.

Fourth, the Brazilian state has supported the internationalisation strategy of Brazilian capital in the sector through several means. It has extended loans to developing countries, principally in Central America and Africa, to buy the Brazilian technology of ethanol processing mills.[52] In order to do so, the Brazilian state has used the BNDES, but also its access to international organisations and its diplomatic ties. For instance, together with the United States, the Inter-American Development Bank (IDB), the Organisation of American States (OAS) and the UN Foundation, Brazil has provided funding for feasibility studies in Haiti, the Dominican Republic, and El Salvador, which will assist governments in the establishment of public-private activities around the production of sugarcane ethanol. In addition, the Brazilian state also foresees the need to coordinate efforts with potential rivals. Hence on 20 August 2007, Brazil and the United States convened the US-Brazil biofuels steering group to advance cooperation on biofuels.[53]

Finally, complying with one of the most traditional roles of populist regimes, the Lula and Rousseff governments have sought to provide capital with class peace, instead of creating mechanisms that might contribute to increasing the

---

50   Ibid., p. 77.

51   Approximately US$ 1.5 billion at the exchange rate of the time, ibid., pp. 77–8.

52   In 2003, the installation of an ethanol mill cost between US$ 37 to 55 million.

53   Ministry of External Relations of Brazil 2007.

power and capacities of the working classes. In June 2009, using his privileged relationship with labour unions, President Lula was able to broker a deal, the *National Commitment to Enhance Working Conditions in the Sugarcane Sector*, between the unions representing sugarcane cutters and the plant owners to improve wages and working conditions in the sugarcane sector. The agreement addressed important grievances of sugarcane cutters, such as the need to combat the abuses of labour recruiters, as well as the practice of discounting the cost of transport to the field from the workers' salary, improvements to housing facilities for migrant workers, improvements to transparency in the way of assessing the amount of sugarcane cut by a worker, and the establishment of production targets in collaboration with unions. However the agreement is not legally binding as it only represents an attempt to establish a 'best practices' framework for the industry. The voluntary agreement, signed by 75 percent of the industry, is certainly in the interest of the industry to improve its image abroad.[54] The agreement should also not impact the productivity of the industry too much since it is estimated that production will be almost completely mechanised by 2014.

Since the end of the military dictatorship, Lula's party, the Partido dos Trabalhadores (the Workers' Party, PT) has been the principal party of the working classes. Electorally and politically, the PT has had to find ways to satisfy its electoral base. The Lula administration has tackled the issue in a typically neo-populist fashion. It has used its control of the state apparatus to create a series of measures that only partially address the needs of the organised sectors of the rural population. The anti-poverty conditional cash transfer programme *Fome Zero*, later replaced by *Bolsa Família*, provides families living below the line of poverty with a maximum of US$ 43 a month, and has been very rewarding for the PT in the electoral arena. Incidentally, this programme, by covering part of the cost of the reproduction of labour, contributes to provide a flexible and cheap rural labour force for the agricultural industry.

As for small peasant producers, Lula has increased funding for family farming and has sought to integrate them into the different agricultural commodity chains. In the case of sugarcane ethanol, in December 2004, the federal government created the *Programa Nacional de produção e Uso de Biodiesel* (the National Programme of Production and Use of Biodiesel, PNPB). The programme provides the reduction of federal taxes for up to 68 percent to enterprises that buy a minimum amount of the agricultural input from small producers, which is higher in the case of the poorest regions of Brazil, such as the northeast. In order to benefit from these reductions, enterprises

---

54   Altieri 2009.

have to apply for the 'social fuel stamp' given by the Ministry of Agricultural Development. The PNPB also facilitates credits for small producers that want to acquire equipment to integrate into the biodiesel commodity chain. Critics who have studied the application of the PNPB argue that the programme does not effectively give the means to peasant producers to collectively set up their own production infrastructure, but rather subordinates them to large agribusiness corporations operating in the sector.[55]

One of the arguments of the industry in favour of ethanol from sugarcane, repeated by Lula, and now Dilma Rousseff, at international forums, is that it is not using or diverting land from food production because sugarcane is planted on degraded pastures. This is only partly true, because 'degraded pastures' are often not so, but simply unused pastures. These 'degraded' pastures could thus be used for other purposes than planting sugarcane, namely agrarian reform. For instance, according to the Brazilian constitution, land that does not reach a certain level of productivity – very often, large properties where landlords put up a few heads of cattle per hectare – can be expropriated for agrarian reform. The properties that can be proven to have been acquired illegally are the other type of properties that can more easily be expropriated.

In the region of Pontal Paranapanema, in the extreme west of the state of São Paulo, these two types of properties were almost the norm, because the shady legal status of their property titles discouraged landlords from significantly investing in agricultural production.[56] The MST began organising landless families in the region in the mid-1990s. Even if the struggle was extremely difficult, and at times saw landlords use violence against the landless people, the movement managed to force the creation of numerous agrarian reform settlements. However, since the ethanol boom of 2004, the numbers of successful land occupations in the region has significantly diminished. Indeed, property expropriation for agrarian reform requires mobilisation from the rural poor and their allies and some political will on the part of the authorities. Since the legal status of several of the properties of the regions has not changed, the latter is what seems to be missing.

What has changed is the type of agricultural production on these estates. As sugarcane ethanol enterprises are not interested in fixing too much of their capital, they are falling back on renting land from (or establishing partnerships with) landowners for 80 percent of their sugar input.[57] Thus, traditional landlords are now able to cling to their property by renting out their

55   Fernandes, Welch and Gonçalves 2010, p. 808.
56   Ibid., p. 800.
57   Milanez, Barros et al. 2008, p. 19.

land to sugarcane ethanol producers or by planting sugarcane themselves. In either case, the state prefers to turn a blind eye to the legal status of the property, as long as it contributes to increasing the production of ethanol. As a result, whereas in 2003 sugarcane was being planted on an area occupying 71,095 hectares, as compared to 127,438 occupied by agrarian reform settlements, in 2008 the area occupied by sugarcane increased to 152,027 hectares. This 114 percent increase contrasts dramatically with the amount of land distributed to landless families in the region, which only increased by 10 percent during the same period.[58]

It could thus be said that the current production of ethanol, with the political support it gets from the state, is creating an environment in which traditional landlords, who had been the target of successful land occupations, are now able to avoid expropriation. These traditional landlords, who were the weakest link of the agrarian dominant classes, can now use the conjuncture to restructure their production and integrate themselves into the ethanol commodity chain in a longer-term perspective, thus avoiding further erosion of their power. The losers in this new environment are the landless families that instead of becoming food-producing smallholders with some degree of autonomy are left with the option of working as sugarcane cutters on the few estates that have not mechanised production, seeking employment in another agricultural sector, or migrating to the cities.

We've Got the Solution! Selling the Virtues of Sugarcane Ethanol

Marx (and Marxists after him) understood that the market is not a thing but a social relation. The market is not natural. It has to be created by human beings through their interactions with each other. Including in its ranks several ex-Marxists, the Lula government understood this insight. In collaboration with the private sector, the government argued for years that for sugarcane ethanol to have any kind of serious future it would have to become a global commodity. For that to happen, ethanol could not be restricted to the national market, but rather an international ethanol market would have to be created.

On the technical front, under both the Lula and Rouseff governments, the Department of Biofuels of the BNDES has taken the lead by participating in forums such as the Global Bioenergy Partnership, the Roundtable on Sustainable Biofuels, and the International Organisation for Standardisation.[59]

58   Fernandes, Welch and Gonçalves 2010, p. 800.
59   Milanez, Nyko et al. 2010, p. 344.

But the ethanol industry could not find a better ambassador than ex-President Lula himself, the world-famous former union leader and once 'radical opponent' of neoliberalism, the World Bank, and the International Monetary Fund. As president, Lula promoted ethanol from sugarcane in all the major international forums. Lula, as a public figure, was well positioned to sell the virtues of sugarcane ethanol, as a way of solving many of the development problems facing countries of the global South. On 5 July 2007, at the International Conference on Biofuels in Brussels, Lula presented the Brazilian case as a model to follow for developing countries that benefit from similar climatic conditions:

> I'm convinced that biofuels give us a historic opportunity to confront these dilemmas, allowing us to build a world of prosperity, solidarity and fairness that we all wish for... There are lessons to be learned from the Brazilian experience... We have created more than 6 million direct and indirect jobs, including jobs for small farmers in economically depressed areas. There has been significant generation of income, avoiding an exodus from rural areas and reducing the anarchic growth of our cities.[60]

Because of his personal and political trajectory – that of a poor shoe-shining boy, and later a union leader who fought against a brutal dictatorship – Lula can convincingly present himself abroad as a well-intentioned 'Third-Worldist' politician. In the same speech, he stated:

> [I]t is important to look at biofuels not so much through the eyes of a European citizen but through the eyes of a citizen of the world... Look at biofuels with an eye on the map of Africa, of South America, and Latin America. Look at the Asian countries that, in the first place, have land and sun, but aren't able to plant [biofuels] because they don't have financial resources and don't have access to the necessary technology... Now, look at the world and see that everyone – from the poorest country on Earth, from the poorest living person on this planet – has the technology to dig a small hole, 30 centimetres deep, and plant an oil-producing plant that could provide the energy they couldn't produce in the twentieth century.[61]

---

60   Silva 2007.
61   Ibid.

Nationally, although he also benefits from these attributes, Lula has had to tap into more deeply rooted symbolism. The nature of the state discourse, and particularly its form, is characteristic of the nationalist discourse of many other Latin American nation-states that have relied on natural resources (that is, ground rent) as their main source of wealth creation. Just like with the case of Venezuela and oil studied by Coronil, the state discourse on ethanol production rests on powerful national myths. The discourse speaks of a Brazil extremely blessed in natural resources, vegetation, soil, and climate: a country like no other in the world that should learn to master its exuberant environment. However, unlike Coronil's analysis of state discourse and management of the oil wealth by the Venezuelan state throughout the twentieth century, the Brazilian state discourse about ethanol is set in neoliberal times. In Venezuela, in clearly conventional rentier mentality, the state discourse on wealth was cast in terms of simply drawing the benefits directly from the ground.[62] The current Brazilian discourse in contrast emphasises competitiveness, know-how, and international prestige:

> Ethanol and food production are both offspring of the same revolution that in recent decades has transformed Brazil's countryside, thanks to the inventiveness of our researchers and the entrepreneurial spirit of Brazilian farmers. The revolution made Brazil a worldwide reference for tropical agricultural technology.[63]

This matter is not trivial. It is not simply a case of discourse masking or covering the real material 'relations of production'. The discourse about sugarcane ethanol contributes to producing conditions for the extended reproduction of capital in that sector, for it is essential that people, particularly investors, be it national or international, believe in this sector in order for it to exist and grow. And this is increasingly important as the growth of the sector will require it to raise capital through the stock market, transnational energy giants, and agribusiness joint ventures. State discourse is as fundamental to the production of ethanol as the relationship between capital and labour. In fact, the discourse is part and parcel of this relationship and is clearly on the side of capital. When Lula spoke at international forums, he was actively contributing to raising capital for the ethanol industry. State discourse is also essential domestically. It must tap into national myths, and the specific relationship that Brazilian nationalism has had with nature, for the state to be able to justify its billions of

---

62   Coronil 1997.

63   Silva 2008a.

dollars of investment in infrastructure building for the distribution of ethanol within the country, as well as for its export. Finally, it is also essential that all this be presented under a nationalist garb capable of concealing its clear class component. For the state nationalist discourse is necessary for the legitimation of the siphoning of important amounts of money from the state and the super-exploited rural workers, toward large capitalist firms.

Conclusion: The Bitter Taste of Sugarcane Ethanol

This case study about sugarcane ethanol has attempted to describe and explain the historical foundations upon which the industry has been built and the role that the state has had in its recent expansion. Like in other countries in Latin America, neoliberalism in Brazil was characterised by market liberalisation and deregulation, and privatisation of state corporations. However, neoliberal restructuring also allowed for the rise of certain capitalist sectors. Although processes of primitive accumulation or 'accumulation by dispossession' were crucial during the initial emergence of the ethanol industry, and to some extent remain important in the agricultural sector, it cannot be said that this concept encapsulates entirely what has been going on in the economy of the country overall. As this study of the ethanol sector suggests, the idea of accumulation by dispossession cannot even fully encompass the developments within the agricultural sector itself. An emphasis on the role of the state can contribute to exposing other critical processes at play.

A Weberian analysis *à la Evans* would celebrate the synergy between the state and industry that is evident in this study because the policies of the BNDES appear to be satisfying the needs of the ethanol industry by helping it to expand. It would also probably see the development bank as a 'pocket of efficiency' within the Brazilian bureaucracy. From this perspective, the Brazilian developmental state, through the BNDES, is choosing industries and orienting the economy for the general well-being and development of the nation. In contrast, my approach to the role of the state has sought to expose its class character, because the state chooses to benefit capital over working people. Although the state, through the BNDES, has been very active it is difficult to know if it has been taking the lead or has been following the demands of the industry. The infrastructure project is probably the only instance where the state took a leading role. What is clear however is that the state has not been able to impose anything on capital. It has not even tried to extract from it substantial concessions on labour conditions, only managing to get a non-binding 'good practices' agreement. This case study has shown, rather, that the state has been subservient to capital, providing it with much more than a 'good business environment'. Beyond the parameters of the developmental state debate, however, this chapter demonstrates that something resembling a 'national bourgeoisie' still exists. This does not however mean that it is 'national' in the sense of being opposed to the transnational bourgeoisie. Instead, providing further fuel to Chibber's argument, the national sugarcane ethanol industry goes so far as to form alliances with transnational capital, even if this might ultimately mean its own subordination. For the sugarcane industry, capital does not have a nationality. An examination of the Brazilian state's activities reveals that it is certainly preoccupied with supporting its national capital. At the same time, however, the state is courting international capital to invest in the ethanol sector, thereby paradoxically fostering the rise of future potential competitors.

The PT shifted a long way towards the centre of the political spectrum in order to win the presidential election of 2002. After two terms in office and a third one beginning under Rousseff, the case of the sugarcane ethanol industry suggests that it has gone even further towards the right, becoming something like the party of the 'national bourgeoisie' by orienting its policies toward the support of 'national' fractions of the ruling class. The unintended consequence of this policy orientation has been to allow for the survival of more traditional sectors of the ruling class, such as the traditional landlords, who have linked up with agribusiness. More ironically, this process has happened at the expense of the landless movement in the sugarcane regions, a long-time class ally of the PT. On the labour front, in a very emblematic way, the PT is also the perfect neo-populist party. By establishing a kind of class peace through its control of the leadership of the union movement, PT governments manage to redistribute at least part of the wealth to popular sectors through cash transfer programmes and fiscal incentives without infringing upon the interests of national and transnational capital. The PT is, in this sense, the perfect instrument for a neo-corporatist class comprise. However, this class compromise resembles only superficially the slightly more substantive compromise established during the ISI period. The neoliberal era, post-Washington consensus or not, has not allowed for substantial workers' rights or welfare conditions. The neo-corporatist compromise under neoliberalism is restricted by its need to facilitate market competition.

During Lula's presidency sugarcane ethanol was made into one of the engines of growth of the Brazilian economy. Dilma Rousseff, Lula's successor, has a very long history in the energy sector. It is highly improbable that sugarcane ethanol will lose its place within the development strategy of the current PT government. The economic and political interests behind ethanol production are strong enough to influence the state in various ways. Moreover, 2011 ended with an enormous 'surprise' for the ethanol industry. On 31 December 2011, the United States lifted its tariff on imported ethanol, which was until then 52 cents per gallon. The US market is now open for Brazilian sugarcane ethanol. Insiders probably already knew it for some time, as the industry and the state had been lobbying the US government for years in that direction. This was probably the word of mouth that circulated within ruling class circles in order to rally support for the billions of dollars invested in the ethanol transportation pipelines and export facilities. The Brazilian state and the sugarcane industry will surely now step up their international marketing strategy to attract capital investment to the sector and turn sugarcane ethanol into a global commodity. However, regardless of this latest development, in times of crisis it will take more than words to convince investors. Time will tell if sugarcane ethanol will be turned into the hen of the golden eggs or if like in the children's tale agribusiness will rip open the countryside, emptying it of what is at the origin of its wealth, its peasants and rural workers.

CHAPTER 11

From Global Capital Accumulation to Varieties of Centre-Leftism in South America: The Cases of Brazil and Argentina

Nicolas Grinberg and Guido Starosta

In the last decade there has been a broad political and ideological shift to the left in the South American continent. Yet different types of political economy regimes can be discerned within this general common trend. A relatively widespread consensus has emerged that presumes that there are two varieties of centre-left administrations in office in the region. Mainstream analyses distinguish countries where a 'responsible left' governs (usually seen to include Brazil, Chile under Bachelet, and Uruguay), from countries where old style 'populism' is in control of the national state (in particular, Argentina, Venezuela, Ecuador, and Bolivia).[1] While the former have retained the 'prudent' macroeconomic policies of the 1990s (albeit combined with better social policies characterising 'second generation' reforms), the latter have relapsed into the 'classic' Latin-American populist vice of 'anti-private-initiative' state interventionism.[2] By contrast, some left-wing commentators conceive that distinction as one between formally centre-left but substantively 'neoliberal' governments, and more genuinely 'progressive' ones.[3]

Finally, other radical observers have been more sceptical about the existence of any real substantive change whatsoever in the political forms prevailing in South America.[4] These scholars have pointed to the need to distinguish between *rhetoric* of social change and *actual policies implemented.* Such scholars have argued that many leftist intellectuals and analysts have succumbed uncritically to the symbolic acts through which centre-left governments have accessed state power (essentially, an anti-neoliberal discourse). But in substance, most of these centre-left administrations continue to reproduce

---

1   *The Economist* 2006; Bremmer 2006.
2   This is also the view of international financial institutions. See, for example, the critique of the Inter-American Development Bank's flagship report *The Politics of Policies* in Charnock 2009.
3   Klein 2006; Chomsky 2006.
4   Petras and Veltmeyer 2005.

neoliberalism, even if with a 'human face'. Not much is offered, however, in terms of an actual explanation of the undeniable differences among the centre-left administrations prevailing in South America, which the two previously mentioned approaches do (rightly) note. In other words, these analyses that lump together all current South American centre-left administrations as 'neo-liberalism with a human face', do not shed much light on the reasons why such an allegedly revamped neoliberalism has taken a more modern centre-left guise in some countries, while assuming a more classic Latin American populist shape in others.

The present chapter challenges all those ways of approaching the diverse modalities assumed by the South American turn to the left in the past decade, on the grounds that they fail to uncover the essential material basis that is differentially expressed in each type of political regime. In other words, most positions in the debate fail to offer solid foundations for the comparative political and ideological analysis of the *economic forms* of these national processes of capital accumulation. Instead, they posit the different political and ideological forms that *mediate* the economic content as constituting in and of themselves the ground or foundation for the comparison between the 'varieties of centre-leftism' in South America.

In contrast to the aforementioned approaches, and by way of empirical illustration, here we offer a materialist inquiry into the respective varieties of centre-leftism in Brazil and Argentina. In order to do this, we rely on two main methodological insights from the Marxian critique of political economy.[5] First, we argue that the qualitatively specific *national* form taken by capitalist development in a particular country should be seen as expressing the determinations of the essentially *global* unity of the accumulation process on a world scale. Secondly, we grasp the particular *political forms* prevailing in each country as a necessary mode of existence and motion of the *economic content* of capital accumulation. Armed with these two insights, the article further submits that capital has been accumulating in Brazil and Argentina under the same specific form, namely: through the appropriation of the extraordinary mass of social wealth existing in those national spaces under the form of ground rent. From this starting point, the article then explores the commonalities and also singularities under which the same specific form of capitalist development has unfolded in these countries, and explains why this qualitatively identical content has recently given rise to diverse political forms within a broader trend of a shift to the centre-left. In a nutshell, we show

---

5   In our general approach to the critique of political economy, we follow the reading of *Capital* originally developed by Juan Iñigo Carrera (2007b; 2008a).

that the differences between the so-called modern social democracy prevailing in Brazil and the classic populist regime in power in Argentina stem from
the respective patterns of appropriation of ground rent by industrial capital
that have developed in each country to mediate the recent boom of primary
commodities. In turn, the country-specific modalities of channelling ground
rent into capital's profitability in the recent phase of economic expansion are
shown to have developed out of the respective forms taken by the ground rent
transfer mechanisms during the neoliberal period in each country, as the latter eventually clashed with their own immanent limits and entered into crisis.

On the Content and Form of Social Reproduction in its Capitalist Form

This section lays out the general determinations that underpin our inquiry into
the variety of political forms that have emerged in Brazil and Argentina as part
of the broader 'shift to the left' in South America. For reasons of space, we
can only offer a brief presentation of the main tenets of our general framework for the study of capitalist development.[6] The central issue at stake is the
'inner' connection between what outwardly appear as two sets of differentiated aspects of capitalist production: the economic and the political, and the
global and the national.

In a nutshell, our approach takes the intrinsic unity of the capitalist world
market as the starting point of the investigation. In our view, changing patterns of *national* differentiation are concrete forms that express the contradictory dynamics of the *global* accumulation process. In turn, the specific *political
forms* prevailing in each country are the expressions of the movement of the
economic forms taken by global capital accumulation in each national space
of valorisation. These two insights are grounded in the more general characteristics of the capitalist mode of production discovered by Marx through the
critique of political economy.

The historical specificity of capitalist production derives from the private
and independent form taken by human labour. In this historically specific
form of the human-life process, the social character of labour is represented as
an objective attribute of its product, namely, the value-form, which determines
useful objects as commodities.[7] Social relations thus take the alienated form

---

6   Similarly, reasons of space prevent us from any in-depth critical engagement with alternative
    approaches other than in passing references or comments.

7   Marx 1976, p. 132.

of powers of the product of labour, and human beings become determined as personifications of those objectified forms of social mediation; in its simplest form, as 'representatives of ... commodities'.[8]

This indirect form in which the unity of social labour is established is fully developed when it becomes capital. Subsumed under the capital-form, the production of surplus value – in short, the formally boundless quantitative progression of the reified 'social nexus' – becomes the content of social life.[9] In this more concrete form as self-valorising value, the materialised social relation does not simply formally mediate the material life-process of human beings, but actually becomes inverted into the very alienated subject of the process of social reproduction and its expansion *in its unity*: the material metabolism of society takes the inverted form of the accumulation of the *total social capital*.[10] In other words, in capitalist society the process of human metabolism is characterised by an automatism subject to laws, whose motion obviously takes shape through the conscious action of individuals, but whose general unity is unconsciously established 'behind their backs'. The 'law of value' is the succinct term that refers to the unity of the determinate forms of movement assumed by this alienated mode of existence of social life in all its concrete complexity.

In the process of renewal of the conditions for its self-valorisation, the total social capital produces and reproduces commodity owners as members of antagonistic social classes.[11] In its simplest determination, the class struggle is thus the most general direct social relation between collective personifications of commodities (such as a political form of social relations), which mediates the reproduction of the indirect relations of capitalist production through the generalised commodity-form (thereby determined as the economic form of social relations).[12] Although a necessary form taken by the reproduction of the total social capital, the antagonistic character of the class relation disrupts the fluidity of the former's valorisation. The establishment of the general unity of social labour must therefore take shape through a further objectified form of social mediation, the state, which confronts commodity owners (the personifications of money-as-capital and of the commodity labour-power), as an apparently external power with the authority and capacity to establish the

---

8   Ibid., pp. 178–9.
9   Ibid., 1976, pp. 251–7.
10   Ibid., 1976, p. 763.
11   Ibid., pp. 723–4; Marx 1978, p. 185.
12   Kicillof and Starosta 2007; Iñigo Carrera 2008a.

overall direct regulation of their antagonistic social relations.[13] The state thus develops as the most concrete political form that embodies the direct organisation of the unity of the conditions of social reproduction in its alienated capital-form. That is, the state is the concrete form of the essentially indirect social relations through the valorisation of capital. By virtue of this content, the state becomes the *general political representative of the total social capital*. In brief, capitalist social relations exist as differentiated into economic forms (the autonomised movement of capital-commodities on the market) and political forms (class struggle and the state). The latter, far from enjoying 'autonomy' (relative or otherwise), are the necessary mode of realisation of the contradictory content of the economic mode of existence of capitalist social relations. In other words, class struggle and state policies are not to be conceived of as independent, self-subsisting factors that externally modify or influence the workings of the law of value. Instead, they need to be grasped as necessary modes of motion through which the law of value further unfolds beyond the strictly economic forms immediately springing from the indirect nature of the social relations of capitalist production.

Now, as an expression of its inherently self-expansive nature, this fetishised social relation is global in content and national only in form.[14] This means that it is the self-valorisation of value on a global scale, or global accumulation on the level of total social capital, that constitutes the immanent end in the world market.[15] It follows from this that neither class antagonism nor its expression in the concrete form of state policies *determine* the modality and course of accumulation within each national space of valorisation. Instead, those nationally-differentiated political forms mediate the unfolding of the underlying formal and material unity of the inherently contradictory dynamics of the accumulation of the total social capital at the global scale. Moreover, the immanent content of these global dynamics is not one of 'imperialism' or 'dependency' (that is, a *direct political relation* between states, another mediating *form*), but determined by the production of (relative) surplus value on a world scale.[16]

In sum, the global aspect of capital accumulation should not be viewed as a given external context, which blocks or facilitates the more or less successful integration of abstractly autonomous national economies into the world market. Rather, the movement of capital is intrinsically global, and the unequal

13   Iñigo Carrera 2008b.
14   Iñigo Carrera 2008a, p. 134; Marx 1973, pp. 227–8; Clarke 2001.
15   Smith 2006, p. 193.
16   Burnham 1994 and Howe 1981 have made this point forcefully.

or uneven differentiation of national spaces is merely a manifestation of the contradictory character of the worldwide unfolding of the law of value. This eminently unconscious and crisis-ridden social process gives rise to changing constellations of the international division of labour and, as a consequence, to evolving developmental potentialities for each national space that mediates the production of relative surplus value by the total social capital across the globe.[17] The latter is, in sum, the general economic content that is realised in the political form of state policies (domestic and foreign) and class conflict, albeit 'behind the backs' of the antagonistic actions of the personifications involved (that is, social classes and their diverse political organisations, political elites, and/or state managers).

As is recognised by virtually all accounts of the history of capitalist development in South America, and more broadly Latin America, the original subsumption of these territories to the global accumulation of capital was based on the production of agricultural (and/or mining) commodities for the world market. As Marx remarks in *Capital*, the establishment of this 'classic' modality of the international division of labour was determined by the production of relative surplus through the system of machinery of large-scale industry.[18] In effect, the exceptional natural conditions prevailing in many of these territories allowed for a greater productivity of agricultural labour, thereby resulting in the cheapening of means of subsistence and a lower value of labour-power. However, this form of subsumption of South American territories into the global circuits of accumulation was ridden with a contradiction: if, on the one hand, the total social capital enhanced its valorisation by reducing the value of labour-power, on the other this was partly offset by the drain of surplus value,

---

17   For an elaboration of the implications of this point for the comprehension of the differentiation of the respective developmental trajectories in Latin America and East Asia, see Grinberg and Starosta 2009.

18   See Marx 1976, pp. 579–80. On the change in the modalities of the international division of labour as expressions of the transformations in the capitalist labour process, see the reflections by Ceceña 1990. In other words, the *material basis* of the forms of the international division of labour is to be found in the changing modalities of the real subsumption of labour to capital, and not in the international political relations between states or in the economic relations established in the circulation process by individual capitals (Iñigo Carrera, 2008a). This means that the *concrete subject* of the establishment of the international division of labour is the global total social capital, and not the particular national fragments of capital from 'imperialist' countries or transnational corporations. In the same vein, the international division of labour is not the result of the subordination of the 'periphery' to the dynamics of accumulation of the 'centre' (as in World-System and Dependency theories).

otherwise available for capital's appropriation, flowing into the pockets of domestic landowners in the form of ground rent.[19] Capital was thus driven to overcome this barrier to its accumulation capacity by reshaping those spaces of valorisation in order to recover part of that surplus value, through the establishment of an 'antagonistic association' with local landowners over the appropriation of ground rent. From being simply a source of cheap raw materials and means of subsistence, those territories became also determined as sources of ground rent recovery for global industrial capital. To the extent that primary commodities produced there have been consumed overseas, ground rent has constituted an inflow of social wealth. As we shall see in the next section, the developmental trajectory of these countries has been determined by the historical course of this modality of capital accumulation.[20]

---

19   Ground rent is surplus value potentially appropriated by landowners due to their differential and absolute *monopoly* over non-reproducible natural conditions of production that, respectively, increase labour productivity in the primary sector or allow production altogether. Effectively, primary production exhibits a specific characteristic that distinguishes it from industrial production. Unlike industrial commodities, the commercial prices of primary commodities are regulated by those marginal conditions of production that need to be used to satisfy solvent demand. Competition over the use of non-marginal lands, where production costs are lower, transforms potential surplus profits into ground rent paid to the landowner. Likewise, when successive applications of capital of a given size, each yielding different output, need to be undertaken on plots of land already under production to satisfy solvent demand, non-marginal portions of capital also yield surplus profit, even those applied to worst-quality lands. Competition by individual capitals also transforms these surplus profits into ground rent. Both the *extensive* and *intensive* types of *differential* rent spring from the monopoly by landowners over portions of the planet that yield a different output, and thus profits, for capitals of similar magnitude. Their existence is a concrete form of realisation of the equalisation of the rate of profit among individual capitals. Moreover, since owners of marginal lands would not allow their productive use by capital without also receiving rent in exchange, commercial prices of primary commodities must rise further above the price of production (i.e. the price that covers for normal production costs and average profits) corresponding to the output of worst-quality land (or, more precisely, lowest-yielding portions capital) in order to include a rent springing from the *absolute* monopoly by landowners of a non-reproducible means of production. Unlike *differential* ground rent, the magnitude of the rent of *absolute* monopoly varies not according to soil quality (or location) but to landowners' bargaining power *vis-à-vis* productive capital (Marx 1981, pp. 779–823, 882–907; Iñigo Carrera 2007a, pp. 11–14; Grinberg 2014).
20   Iñigo Carrera 2008a, pp. 150–6.

From Import Substitution Industrialisation (ISI) to the Debt Crisis

The accumulation of capital through the recovery of ground rent has taken a variety of economic and political forms; all of them have involved the mediation of the nation-state. As noted above, these diverse state-forms have not autonomously determined the pattern of industrialisation and economic development in the Latin American national spaces of accumulation. Rather, they have mediated their specific reproduction by channelling ground rent out of landowners' pockets and creating the conditions necessary to allow its appropriation by industrial capital. The process of import substitution industrialisation (ISI) consolidating in most primary commodity producing countries between the 1930s and 1950s, and reaching its peak during the 'commodities boom' of the 1970s, has been the most paradigmatic and developed politico-economic form through which this specific modality of capital accumulation has come about. In general terms, two types of policy-created mechanisms, indissolubly united, gave shape to the Latin American process of ISI as form of accumulation through ground rent recovery.[21] First, policies such as exchange rate overvaluation, taxes on primary commodity exports and state control over their domestic and international trade intervened in the turnover cycle of agrarian capital and separated from it a portion of ground rent. (See figure 11.1 for the evolution of Argentinian and Brazilian exchange rates relative to their purchasing power parity.) All of these policies transferred a portion of ground rent to privately-owned industrial capitals by setting domestic prices of raw materials below their international levels, and, in the case of the overvaluation of the currency, by reducing the local price of foreign exchange for specific imports and the remittance of profits abroad.[22] These policies also transferred a portion of ground rent to the state not only directly (through the monopoly/control of foreign exchange markets and commodity trade or the taxation of raw material exports), but also indirectly (through the payment of relatively high import taxes and other related duties with an overvalued currency). Second, other policies allowed for the appropriation of the

---

21   On the identification of these policies as a form of channelling ground rent into industrial capital in general, we draw on Iñigo Carrera 2007c. He originally developed the approach for the accumulation of capital in Argentina. For the Brazilian experience, see Grinberg 2014.

22   Competitive pressures have passed the 'discount' from exporters to agrarian capitalists and from these onto landowners and from internationally- to domestically-traded commodities.

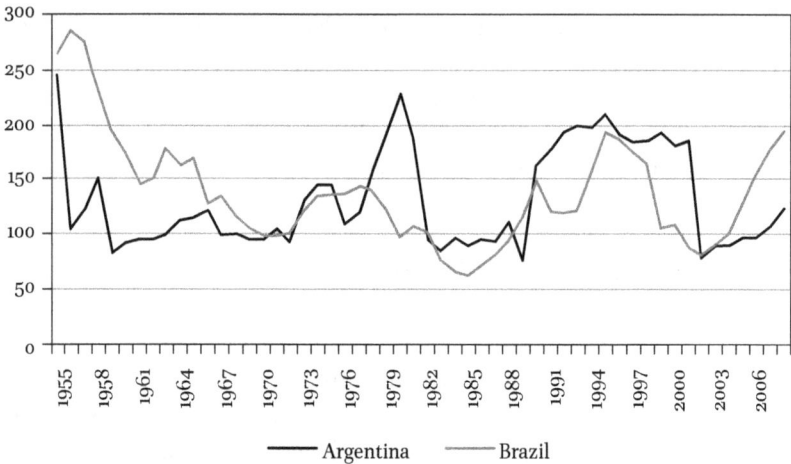

FIGURE 11.1   *Fluctuations of exchange rates around their purchasing power parity.*
                Source: Iñigo Carrera 2007; Grinberg 2014.

separated portion of ground rent by industrial capital either through market
mechanisms or direct state actions.[23] These included: the differentiated protection of domestic markets (which was stronger for final products than for
inputs and machinery); the provision of services, industrial inputs, and credit
at subsidised rates by state-owned companies and banks; the regulated expansion of domestic markets through their activities (for instance, the purchase
of locally produced goods at inflated prices and an oversized workforce); and
direct subsidies. (See figure 11.2 for the evolution of Argentinian and Brazilian
ground rent relative to different forms of surplus value.)

Hence, these ISI-promoting policies did not constitute a model of development implemented to solve an external problem (such as the supposed
decreasing terms of trade) or as a response to the emerging power of the urban
working classes, as argued by structuralist and orthodox writers respectively.
Rather, they were the political expression of a form of capital accumulation
based on the appropriation/recovery by industrial capital of a portion of the
ground rent available in these national economies. So were the populist, both
the nationalistic and developmentalist versions, and the authoritarian regimes
that, in the historical unfolding of the process, gave shape to those state forms.

Now, between the end of World War II and the mid-1970s, the amount of
ground rent available in these national spaces of accumulation increased

---

23   What is said here for industrial capital holds, *mutatis mutandis*, also for commercial
      capital.

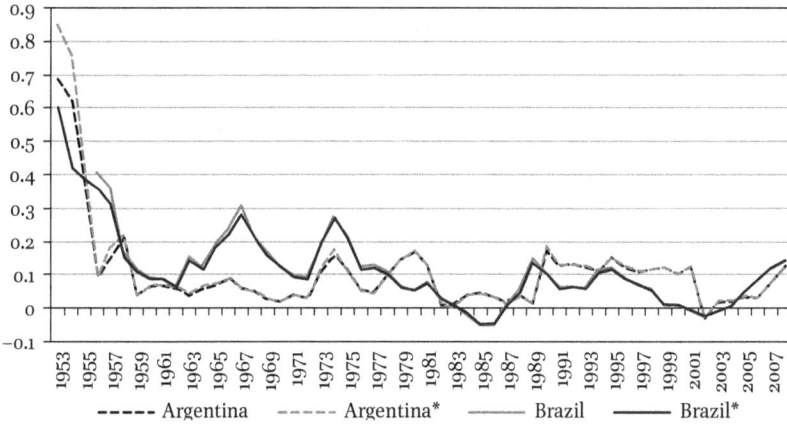

FIGURE 11.2   *Ground rent relative to total surplus value.*
Source: Iñigo Carrera 2007; Grinberg 2014.
Notes: Arg & Bra = ground rent in total surplus value
Arg* & Bra* = ground rent appropriated by others than landowners relative to
total surplus value appropriated by others than landowners.

strongly and remained, on average, sufficient to sustain the expanded reproduction of industrial capital there. The fast expansion of the global economy
was then sustaining world demand for raw materials, especially those of agrarian origin. Under these conditions, Latin American economies grew rapidly
while the ISI process widened and deepened. Employment and real wages
increased substantially, especially in the industrial sector.

Yet, the reproduction of the process of capital accumulation in the region
rested on inherently contradictory bases. In the first place, in order to recover
ground rent, industrial capital had to open and close its valorisation cycle in
these countries' domestic markets. As a consequence, these had to remain
protected to a degree conditioned by the amount of ground rent available to
sustain local industrial production. Indeed, unable to produce for world markets, and thus compete with those industrial capitals that had engendered the
spaces of accumulation where large amounts of ground rent arise, the scale of
accumulation of capital operating there became limited to the size of domestic markets. With a scale of accumulation below world market norms, the use
of cutting-edge technology remained restricted. Moreover, policies maximising the appropriation of ground rent by industrial capital (i.e. exchange rate
overvaluation) reinforced this restriction further. Hence, industrial capital's
accumulation capacity there became dependent on the evolution of the
ground rent available to compensate for the ever-growing difference between
local and world market production costs, in turn resulting from the difference

between local and world market scales of production and their impact upon technological profiles and, thus, levels of labour productivity. Nevertheless, foreign-invested industrial capital, which accelerated its entrance in these types of economies after the mid-1950s and dominated the most dynamic industrial sectors thereafter, managed in this way to valorise normally while recycling obsolete, and often already amortised, equipment. In the second place, by lowering the domestic prices of primary commodities, the forms of appropriation of ground rent by social subjects other than landowners also restricted the intensive and extensive application of capital to primary production and, thus, its growth and that of the available ground rent.[24]

Throughout the mid-to-late-1970s, these contradictory dynamics led to crisis. After the short-lived 1972–5 commodities 'boom', the prices of raw materials entered into a long period of contraction (in the case of oil, the decline began in 1981). This contraction was apparent thereafter in the relatively slow increase, or even absolute decline, of the amount of ground rent available for appropriation in the Latin American spaces of accumulation. Industrial capital then began to rely, or significantly increase its reliance, on a second source of extraordinary social wealth to complement normal surplus value extracted from the domestic working classes, namely, overproduced capital in the form of (external) credit. (See figure 11.3 for the evolution of net inflows of foreign loanable capital to Argentina and Brazil.) This source of extraordinary social wealth was not only qualitatively more unreliable than the ground rent, but also quantitatively more unstable. In effect, though the former has been expanding worldwide ever since (as a way of postponing the general crisis of overproduction), its expansion has not been constant. On the contrary, it has taken the form of an alternation of periods in which fictitious capital, and consequently the global supply of credit, expanded rapidly and sustained world social consumption, with periods in which the opposite occurred, as was the case during much of the 1980s and early 1990s.[25] The process of 'state-led' ISI would then enter into a deep crisis.

Neoliberalism in South America

In general terms, with the combined mass of ground rent and net loanable capital (credit) inflows stagnating/contracting, or simply growing more slowly than their requirement by capital, the previously developed scale of indus-

---

24   Iñigo Carrera 2008a.
25   Ibid.; Brenner 2006b.

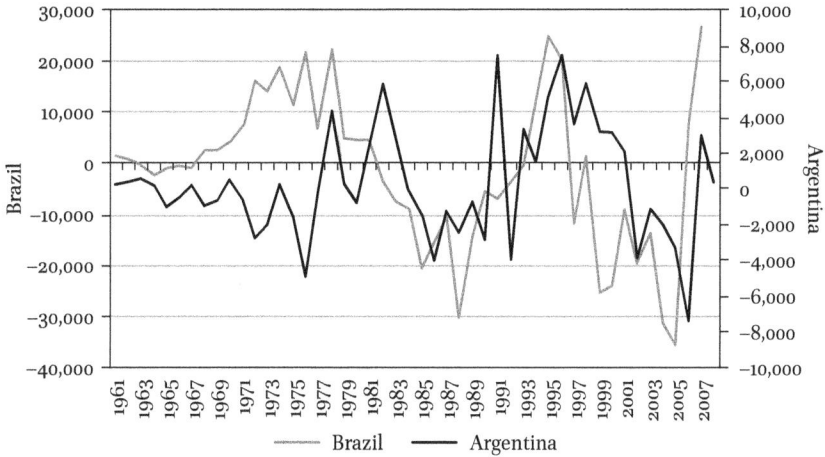

FIGURE 11.3 *Net inflow of external credit in million US$ 2004.*
Source: Iñigo Carrera 2007; Grinberg 2011.
Note: For Argentina only includes public sector external debt.

trial production could not be sustained any longer. Policies that had been transferring these resources to industrial capital, thus sustaining its profitability, then slowly reversed into neoliberal programmes inspired by the so-called Washington Consensus. Import tariffs were sharply, though not universally, reduced while several state-owned enterprises were privatised (or closed altogether) and public sector employment and welfare expenditures were 'rationalised', thus eliminating some of the main forms of ground rent transfer to, and appropriation by, industrial capital. State policies supporting the process of ISI (such as the combination of an overvalued currency and market protection, subsidised state-bank loans, and tax credits) became thereafter increasingly selective and limited. Industrial capital remained, nevertheless, largely producing for protected domestic markets and, after the large-scale privatisation programme of the 1990s, began to compete with capital invested in previously state-provided public-utility services and industrial inputs in the bid to appropriate ground rent.

Inevitably, without the necessary resources to compensate for the ever-growing productivity gap, industrial value-added collapsed and GDP growth stagnated during large parts of the post-1980 period. The demand for labour-power, especially in the manufacturing sector, suffered accordingly. Unemployment then mounted and real wages decreased substantially, thus creating another source of extraordinary surplus value available to compensate for the low level of labour productivity resulting from the reduced scale of production: the sustained payment of labour-power below its value. (See figures 11.4, 11.5, and 11.6

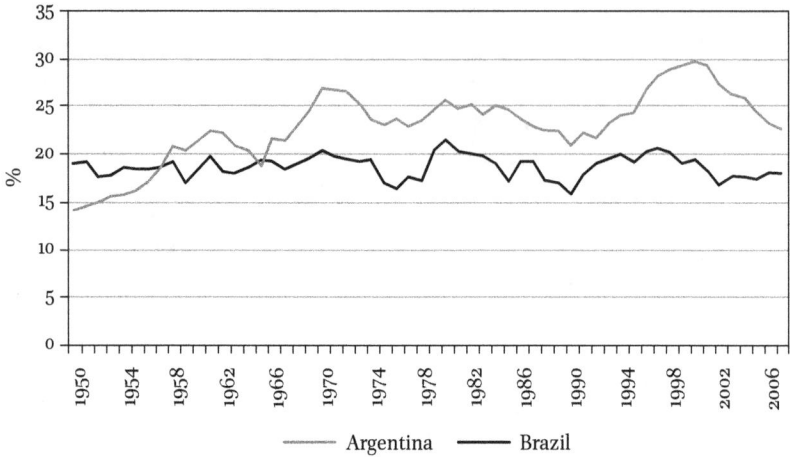

FIGURE 11.4   *Labour productivity relative to US levels.*
Source: Iñigo Carrera 2007; Grinberg 2011.

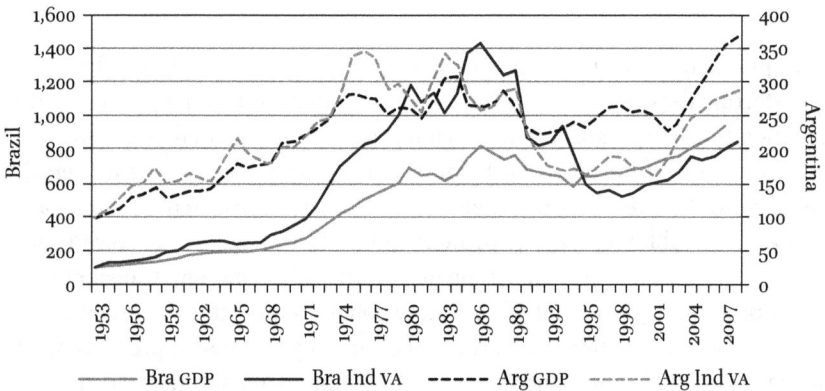

FIGURE 11.5   *GDP and industrial value-added (1953=100).*
Source: Iñigo Carrera 2007; Grinberg 2011.

for the evolution of Argentinian and Brazilian labour productivity relative to
US levels, growth processes and industrial wages, respectively.)

Yet, between 1993 and 1998 both the supply of credit and the amount of
ground rent experienced a worldwide recovery, and so did the process of capital accumulation in most of the Latin American countries where it was heavily
supported by them. These resources, together with the funds collected through
the privatisation of state-owned companies (which accelerated during the
1990s), became the bulk of the social wealth used to support the profitability

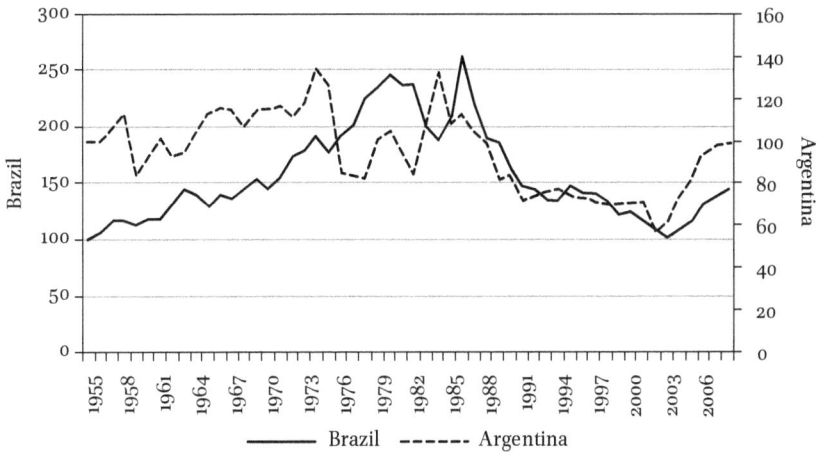

FIGURE 11.6   *Real industrial wages (1955=100).*
Source: Iñigo Carrera 2007; Grinberg 2011.

of industrial capital. The ensuing economic recovery, however, could not be represented politically by national-populist governments, as had been the case in most pre-1980 periods of ground rent expansion. On the one hand, it was far from being substantial or capable of sustaining significant expansions of industrial production and employment and, consequently, real wage gains. On the other hand, the extended use of foreign loans and the privatisation of state-owned assets at fire-sale prices to sustain the process of capital accumulation clashed with the deeply-embedded nationalistic ideology of Latin American populist movements, for which national autonomy from international finance capital and state ownership of firms in strategic sectors were paramount. Furthermore, the 1990s marked (through the dismantling of most forms of social security, the reduction in public-sector employment, and the increase in the price of public services after their privatisation) the acceleration of the process of differentiation of the productive attributes of the working class (the skills and concomitant conditions of reproduction), which resulted from the development of increasingly automated and computerised technologies. Right-of-centre governments, with their 'modernising' ideology, were much better suited than left-of-centre ones to undertake and realise these developments, especially when the 'heterodox' policies of the second half of the 1980s ended in hyperinflation and massive declines in real wages.

In contrast to the developmentalist stage of import substitution industrialisation, the neoliberal period became characterised by the appropriation of ground rent, and its complementary sources of extraordinary wealth, by only a restricted portion of industrial capital. Crucially, that controlled by foreign-owned companies, which remained protected from external competition, and/or receiving state subsidies (for instance, the all-important automobile companies in Argentina, Brazil, and Venezuela), those directly associated with natural resource exploitation, and the privatised service sector (including banks). The latter was 'naturally' protected from external competition, benefited from lax regulatory frameworks and, in some cases, also received state support. Service sector companies, such as energy and telecommunications providers, were among the most concentrated industrial capitals in the world; hence their power to become one of the main partners of landowners in the appropriation of the South American ground rent. The overvaluation of the national currency became, again, the predominant form of ground rent transfer and appropriation by social subjects other than landowners.[26]

The 1993–8 recovery, however, was neither sufficiently strong to reverse the deterioration produced by the severe contraction of the previous period, nor long-lasting. By the end of the decade, a new deceleration in credit supply expansion became apparent in the decline of the growth rate of the global economy and, therefore, of the demand for raw materials and the Latin American ground rent. This global slowdown also resulted in the reduction of the amount of loanable capital available to Latin America, especially to South American countries, which transformed the substantial net inflow of the previous years into large outflows. Without these sources of extraordinary social wealth, the process of capital accumulation in the region entered a new period of economic hardship. In some cases, like Argentina, sharp and violent economic contraction manifested itself in deep political crises. In other cases, such as Brazil, economic problems came about through less intense political confrontations. In all cases, strong wage contractions compensated for the fall in the amount of ground rent and foreign loans available to sustain capital's valorisation. Yet, through 2003–4, these difficulties began to recede. The global economy was then entering a new period of credit-fuelled growth, which resulted in the strengthening of the demand for raw materials and, to a lesser extent, the positive inflow of loanable capital to developing countries. The next two sections will analyse the singularities of the Brazilian and Argentinean experiences during the post-2003 period of rapid growth, while

---

26   In Mexico and the rest of the Caribbean Basin capital accumulation was then taking a new, different form. Since the mid-1980s, capital has valorised there through the production of industrial commodities for world markets using the relatively cheap and disciplined local workforce for simplified activities as an appendage of the increasingly automated machinery or in manual assembly operations. See Grinberg 2010.

also paying attention to the immediately preceding period in order to show the intrinsic unity of the two.

Brazil: From the 'Letter to the Brazilian People' to Lula's Second Term[27]

In 1998, international interest rates peaked, after increasing steadily since 1993. The increased cost and scarcity of credit was beginning to have a negative impact on global economic activity and, consequently, on the price of raw materials. Exporters of primary commodities began to feel the impact of the developments in the world economy in the same way as Asian exporters of 'industrial commodities' such as memory chips had done the previous year. Brazil was no exception to this trend. The substantial inflow of long-term debt, attracted at an unsustainably high cost, barely compensated for the massive outflow of 'hot-money'.[28] The difference between the two, however, was not enough to compensate for the large current account deficit, in turn worsened by the prevailing exchange-rate overvaluation. Central Bank international reserves fell sharply, even when privatisation funds peaked, potentially increasing the amount of foreign exchange that could be used to support the overvaluation of the national currency, the Real. While the rate of economic growth in 1997 had been 3.1 percent, in 1998 the economy contracted by 1.1 percent.[29] Labour market conditions worsened markedly, especially in the industrial sector, where they were already in poor shape. The Cardoso administration then took advantage of labour's weakened bargaining power to further

---

27 On the specific manifestations of processes of capital accumulation through ground rent recovery in Brazil since the 1990s we mainly draw on Grinberg 2011 and Grinberg 2013. For a long historical view and quantitative empirical evidence, see Grinberg 2011 and Grinberg 2014.

28 In late 1998, real interest rates on the Brazilian public debt skyrocketed to 35 percent. See Lopes 2003, p. 51.

29 Throughout this chapter, economic growth is measured in terms of the evolution of the GDP in domestic currency of constant purchasing power, i.e. time-series of nominal GDP deflated using the evolution of the relevant Consumer Price Index (CPI). This is a more appropriate measure of the aggregate economic performance of a country than the conventionally-used GDP in constant prices of a base year. Although usually taken as an indicator of 'real' growth, the evolution of the latter is not an accurate measure of the expansion of the scale of a capitalist economy. Insofar as it is a *quantity* index, it can only capture the evolution of the material content of social wealth, i.e. *use-value* production, but is incapable of measuring the latter's evolution in its capitalist *value-form*.

the programme of labour market reform through flexibilisation.[30] Indeed, the organised labour movement was particularly hard hit during the 1990s neo-liberal 'restructuring', when formal employment in the industrial sector contracted by 30 percent.[31]

By the end of 1998, the pressure on the Brazilian economy became unbearable, even though the country received massive financial and political support from a consortium led by the International Monetary Fund (IMF).[32] Governments in such large states as Minas Gerais, Rio de Janeiro, and Rio Grande do Sul declared a moratorium on the service of their debts with the Federal administration, weakening the fiscal stance of the state even further.[33] Although the IMF argued against it, fearing that it would trigger a region-wide currency and banking crisis, exchange-rate devaluation was the first move of incumbent president Fernando Henrique Cardoso after securing his re-election in late 1998.[34] After four-and-a-half years, the exchange-rate targeting regime was replaced by one targeting the inflation rate, as part of a new understanding with the Fund. There is no doubt that the timing of the devaluation helped Cardoso's re-election. It is doubtful, however, that his main rival, Workers' Party (PT) leader Luiz Inácio Lula Da Silva, would have been able to administer the further wage contraction that would result from the deterioration of the economic conditions of the Brazilian process of capital accumulation.[35]

Cardoso's second term in office (from January 1999 to December 2002) was concurrent with a period of global economic slowdown. In 1999, net loanable capital outflows from Brazil became significant for the first time since the early 1990s. Part of these outflows was financed with a portion of the foreign exchange reserves accumulated during the previous years when credit was abundant. Most of the rest was paid with a portion of the value of labour-power and of normal surplus value. International primary commodity prices also dropped sharply, negatively affecting the size of the Brazilian ground rent. Nevertheless, economic growth during Cardoso's second term was, on average, as strong as during his first four years in office. As ever before, growth during this period resulted from, and reproduced, the specifically limited, essentially unchanged mode of capital accumulation that had characterised the Brazilian economy.

30   Novelli and Galvão 2001–2, pp. 24–5; Marshall 2004.
31   Pochmann 2008, pp. 65–77.
32   The contribution amounted to around US$ 41 billion. See Novelli and Galvão 2001–2, p. 16.
33   Amann and Baer 2000, p. 1817; Abreu 2008, p. 438.
34   Lopes 2003; Amann and Baer 2000, pp. 1817–28; Abreu 2008, pp. 439–40.
35   See Bethell and Nicolau 2008, pp. 263–4, on the 1998 general elections.

First, industrial wages had fallen significantly during the second part of the 1990s and dropped a further 5.2 percent yearly on average during 1999–2003, thus partly compensating capital for the effect of a contracting ground rent on its profitability. The post-1998 devaluation of the exchange rate had led to an inflationary process with which wages could not catch up fully. The disarticulated trade union movement was incapable of offering sufficient resistance. In 2003, the year before they began to recover, average real wages in manufacturing were already 24 percent below their 1998 level and only 37.5 percent of the level of 1986, at the peak of the newly established civilian government. Second, there was underutilised productive capacity in the industrial sector, largely built up and financed during the previous period of relatively abundant ground rent and large loanable capital inflows (1994–8). Third, the exchange rate was at purchasing power parity during 1999–2000 and became undervalued (15 percent average) in 2001–2. Until early 2002, the currency of Argentina – the largest market for Brazil's durable-consumer goods exports – was kept strongly overvalued. Despite Argentina's economic recession, this over-evaluation helped expand the market for Brazilian industrial commodities and partly compensated for the contraction of domestic demand.[36] Indeed, in 2003, economic growth in Brazil stalled, as the Argentine currency became itself massively undervalued. Fourth, the inflow of foreign capitals searching for cheap industrial and public sector assets in Brazil helped sustain the economy's import capacity (and expand the scale of accumulation).

Through 2002, the globally integrated cycle of capital accumulation began to turn around. Stimulated by the prevailing low interest rates, credit markets in the advanced industrialised economies were finally regaining liquidity. Nevertheless, when the presidential election was held in late 2002, the Brazilian economy confronted another 'currency' crisis.[37] Although the situation would begin to change in the following period, the availability of loanable capital for 'developing' countries was still at its lowest levels in many years. So were the international prices of primary commodities. As in 1994 and 1999, the candidates of the incumbent right-of-the-centre Partido da Social Democracia Brasileira (Brazilian Social-democratic Party, PSDB) and the leftist PT contended for the presidency. This time, however, the context was markedly different. Cardoso's administration was highly compromised by the continuing fiscal adjustment programme, the fall in real wages and the emerging 'currency' crisis. It would have found it hard to continue with the fiscal adjustments without

---

36   Amann and Baer 2000, p. 1818.

37   See Abreu 2008, pp. 444–7, on the 2002 currency crisis. Abreu, however, partly attributes the turmoil to the prospects of a PT victory in the upcoming elections.

the backing of trade unions and social movements, which were the PT's main sources of support. Moreover, Cardoso's party, the PSDB, could hardly be transformed into a political organisation that would administer the post-2002 strong recovery of the ground rent, even if led by its left wing. The political forms of the process of capital accumulation would change in order to express and mediate its economic transformations. In the 2002 elections, Lula was finally successful in his fourth attempt to win the presidency, defeating PSDB's candidate, ex-dependency theory economist, José Serra. As always, corporate media support was a key factor in the election's result.[38]

Lula's electoral manifesto, however, was far less radical than the one the PT defended when it had been founded in 1980, at the highest point of expansion of the Brazilian process of capital accumulation through ISI. Indeed, when in the final stages of the campaign Lula was blackmailed by the incumbent authorities, the mainstream press, and the IMF, to reassert his neoliberal credentials, he not only radically softened his stance on economic policy, but also wrote the infamous 'Letter to the Brazilian People' claiming he would honour Brazil's foreign debt commitments and continue with the economic legacy left by the Cardoso administration.[39] Lula also distanced himself from the various social movements and radical left groups that had formed and supported the PT, such as the Movimento dos Trabalhadores Sem Terra (Landless Workers' Movement, MST), which had grown considerably since the 1970s. The PT leadership also took pains to differentiate itself from the trade union movement, the original backbone of the party.[40] Moreover, to reassure the business sector of his intentions, Lula recreated the populist inter-class alliance of the 1950s by picking José Alencar as deputy, a well-known businessman, ex-Honorary President of the conservative Partido da Frente Liberal (Liberal Front Party, PFL), and current member of the Brazilian Republican Party, which is closely related to the rapidly growing Evangelical Church.[41] The fact that openly neoliberal economists formed Lula's first economic policy-making team, including

---

38   Oliveira 2006, p. 12; Bethell and Nicolau 2008, pp. 274–5.

39   Abreu 2008, pp. 448–9 suggests that Lula's change of opinion regarding an IMF bail-out involved 'subtle games' that made him 'feel constrained to publicly pledge to honour the general terms of the agreement'.

40   On the changes in the Brazilian rural sector, including the fall in employment, see Valle Silva 2008, pp. 485–7.

41   On the PT's strategic change and Lula's electoral victory, see Panizza 2004; Bethell and Nicolau 2008, pp. 275–7; Abreu 2008, pp. 446–9.

the incumbent president of the Central Bank, shows that his makeover was far from a simple electoral trick.[42]

In practice, the new Lula administration fulfilled its latest campaign promises. With the ground rent only slowly recovering and loanable capital outflows growing, the adjustment of the public sector budget went further than it did during Cardoso's second term. Foreign lenders were not fully willing to finance the service of Brazil's external liabilities, most of it indirectly falling on the state through its domestic borrowing from economic agents issuing debt instruments in international markets. Primary budget surpluses had to be expanded in order to pay an increasingly large portion of the interest services on the massive public debt. The Brazilian state was then paying one of the world's largest interest rate premiums (11.2 percent on average in real terms above the cost of the US government debt during 2002–5) and was still unable to fully finance its debt-servicing requirements.[43] As noted, growth remained weak during the first years of Lula's tenure.

In 2004, however, Brazilian economic growth accelerated to levels not experienced for many years. Indeed, during 2004–8, before the credit crunch rocked global markets, the Brazilian economy expanded at a yearly average of seven percent while industrial value added grew by five percent annual average. The strong recovery of international primary commodity prices, together with substantial output increases, yielded a solid expansion of the ground rent available for appropriation, notably after 2005. Moreover, in 2006 the flow of loanable capital reversed once more and large net inflows became the norm thereafter.

As many times before, the national currency became increasingly overvalued to allow capital to directly appropriate a portion of the enlarged ground rent. Portraying it as a policy to target (control) inflation, itself resulting from its own reserve accumulation strategy and the increasingly expansionary fiscal and credit policies, the Central Bank kept interest rates at relatively high levels, even when international liquidity was rising and global interest rates were falling. As interest rates set by the Central Bank to control inflation also directly affect the return of public sector bonds, this policy has attracted large sums of 'hot money' in the form of loans to the Brazilian state.[44] Hence, in practice, like in the 1990s, the Central Bank has, through its interventions to sterilise the monetary expansion resulting from these inflows of loanable capital, borrowed foreign-exchange resources indirectly, at internationally high interest

42   Oliveira 2006, pp. 12–13.
43   See Saad-Filho and Morais 2005, pp. 19–20; Abreu 2008, pp. 452–3, on the orthodox fiscal and monetary policies implemented by the first economic team of Lula's government.
44   See Arestis et al. 2011 on inflation 'targeting' and exchange-rate policy in Brazil.

rates, increased their supply and thus kept their domestic price low, and the national currency overvalued, despite the prevailing free-floating exchange-rate regime. In 2008, the degree of overvaluation of the Real already reached 93 percent and helped channel a portion of the expanding ground rent equivalent to 14 percent of total surplus value available for appropriation in the national economy to social subjects other than landowners, notably industrial capital. As exchange-rate overvaluation, as well as market protection, strengthened thereafter, the portion of the ground rent transferred through this policy also increased, even if its absolute amount decreased in the context of falling prices of primary commodities.

The expansion of the ground rent not only manifested itself in the expansion of the process of capital accumulation, as industrial capital managed to appropriate directly a portion of the enlarged rent through exchange-rate overvaluation. It also resulted in the increase of state resources. To begin with, a portion of ground rent was, in the first instance, appropriated by the state through import taxes paid with an increasingly overvalued currency. Second, the expansion of economic activity allowed by the increased ground rent enlarged fiscal revenues in general. The new conditions required still another change in the direction of public policies. The first economic team, dominated by conservatives, was then partly replaced by a more 'developmentalist' group of policy-makers. Finance Minister Antonio Palocci, from the PT's right wing, was replaced by ex-Marxist economist Guido Mantega, while ex-guerrilla member and future President Dilma Rousseff was appointed chief of staff. Nevertheless, the commitment to sustain a 'strong' and 'stable' currency – the euphemisms used ideologically to defend the overvaluation of the currency – remained state policy. Ex-Bank Boston president and PSDB member Henrique Meirelles continued in his position as head of the Central Bank.[45]

Economic and social policies thus became increasingly expansionist and began to regain some developmentalist features. Interest rates on loans from the state bank were cut while their supply expanded. The protection of local industrial production was reinforced. Economic growth proceeded strongly while public sector expenditures increased, including those in infrastructure and social welfare.[46] The latter were not only needed to compensate for some of the negative consequences of the previous decade's market reforms

---

45   See Morais and Saad-Filho 2011 on the limited policy shift during Lula's second term in office. See Abreu 2008, pp. 453–4, on the relaxation of monetary policy in 2004. See also Oliveira 2006, p. 10, on policy continuity.

46   See Morais and Saad-Filho 2011, pp. 34–6, on economic and social policies. See Hall 2008; Hunter and Borges Sugiyana 2009, p. 47, on social policies specifically.

related to the conditions of reproduction of labour-power, but also to create or strengthen the political conditions needed for the normal reproduction of the process of capital accumulation under its new economic forms. These new social policies also contributed to the enlargement of the domestic markets for consumer goods. Foreign policies also recovered some of their past characteristics. This change not only came about through a new reaffirmation of Brazil's international leadership, but also through its alliance with Mercosur partners in rejecting the United States' free-trade projects for the region.[47] Both were necessary for the Brazilian state to sustain and, eventually, reinforce the protection of the markets where capital realised the appropriation of the ground rent.[48] Hence, the shift in foreign policy ought to be understood as nothing more than a political (and ideological) form of realisation of the expansion of the ground rent and, thus, an expression of the limited process of capital accumulation in Brazil. Finally, in 2007, at the peak of the expansion of ground rent, the government launched the Growth Acceleration Programme to improve, much like the Second National Development Plan during the 1970s commodities 'boom', the provision of social infrastructure.[49]

As the industrial sector expanded, employment growth accelerated. In 2004, industrial wages began to enjoy strong real-term increases. Necessary for the normal reproduction of labour-power, this process came about through the revitalisation of the trade union movement. In contrast to the defensive actions of the 1980s and the relative passivity of the 1990s, when the 'state-led' ISI process entered into a deep crisis and neoliberal reforms re-shaped it, respectively, the 2000s saw a revival of offensive trade union struggles. Strikes gained in participation, though not in frequency, and became focused on advances rather than on defending existing rights and payment arrangements. Traditional private sector and state-controlled industries such as metal-mechanics, petroleum, construction, and postal services increasingly became the locus of struggles. Moreover, the process of real wage increases also realised through changes in the relationship between trade unions and mainstream political parties. The fragmented labour movement that had unsuccessfully opposed neoliberal reforms under the Cardoso administration largely aligned in support of Lula's government.[50] Yet, despite the gains enjoyed in the industrial sector, economy-wide average wages failed to show any significant recovery and remained stagnant at the 2003 level, which was around 30 percent below

47   See Morais and Saad-Filho 2011, p. 37, on Brazil's foreign policies.
48   Grinberg 2010.
49   Schaller 2008.
50   Boito and Marcelino 2011.

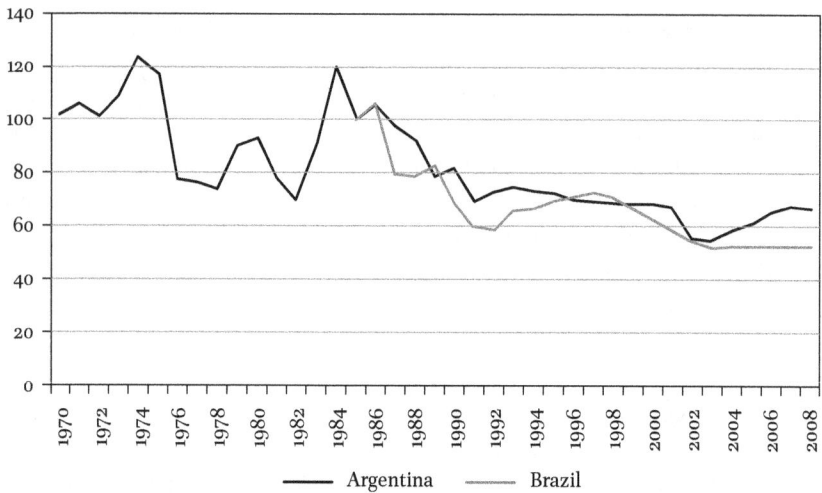

FIGURE 11.7   *Economy-wide real wages (1985=100).*
                Source: Iñigo Carrera 2007; Grinberg 2011.

that of 1997. (See figure 11.7 for the evolution of economy-wide real wages.) Nevertheless, in contrast to the 1990s, as total employment increased substantially, as well as minimum wages and related social-security payments, economic growth resulted in noticeable improvements in the conditions of reproduction of both low-skilled manual workers and the under/unemployed.[51]

As was the case during the 1970s commodities boom, the strong post-2003 expansion of the ground rent and the consequent improvement in the performance of the Brazilian economy created the impression that, after the fine tuning of the 1990s, Brazil was posed finally to realise all of its untapped potential.[52] This impression, however, might be misleading. This strong growth did not result from the 'reforms' introduced during Cardoso's administration and reinforced during Lula's, as argued by some authors.[53] But neither was the economic expansion the result of the corrections that the latter introduced to the course set during Cardoso's terms of office (tighter fiscal policy and flexible exchange rates), as other authors claimed.[54] Despite all the changes in its

---

51   Morais and Saad-Filho 2011, p. 36.
52   Some financial sector gurus even include it in a group of selected developing economies that in the immediate future will supposedly eclipse most of the current richest countries in the world; the so-called BRIC countries of Brazil, Russia, India, and China.
53   See, for example, Roett 2010 and Edwards 2010.
54   See, for example, Barros de Castro 2008.

political and ideological forms since the early 1990s, and the impressive post-2003 growth performance, the underlying structure of the Brazilian economy has not experienced any substantive transformation. Capital has continued accumulating in Brazil mainly by producing for 'politically' or 'naturally' protected domestic (or regional) markets. Capital has still compensated its higher production costs (compared to international norms), resulting from the low level of labour productivity, by appropriating a portion of ground rent, complemented with inflows of loanable capital and the payment of labour-power below its value. Moreover, though significantly enlarged after 2006, the ground rent has been sufficient to support only a relatively mild process of reindustrialisation. In 2008, after five years of rapid industrial expansion, manufacturing value-added and wages were, in real terms, still around 55–60 percent of the 1986 values. Moreover, despite growing strongly after 2003, Brazilian GDP and GDP per capita were in 2008 only 5.5 percent and nine percent of US levels, respectively. In 1980, they had been 8.7 and 17 percent, respectively, before the ground rent available for appropriation became unable to sustain an extended ISI process.[55]

Argentina: From '*Qué se Vayan Todos*' to Cristina Fernández de Kirchner (CFK)

As we have seen in the discussion above, public sector foreign debt was a crucial additional source of social wealth sustaining capital accumulation during the 1990s across South America. During that period, the particular modality of transferring ground rent (and also of channelling loanable capital) into industrial capital's profits in the region mainly revolved around the overvaluation of the currency. Argentina was no exception. On the contrary, it could be argued that the political forms taken by this process in Argentina actually made it the paradigmatic case of the way in which this mode of capital

---

55 Grinberg 2011, p. 197. After 2008, as the global economy slowed, Brazilian economic growth decelerated sharply. GDP growth went down to four percent yearly average during 2009–12, with most of this growth occurring in 2010 when the economy expanded by 10.8 percent. As international primary commodity prices fell from peak levels in the aftermath of the global 'credit crunch', the Brazilian ground rent was affected negatively. Industrial value added thus decreased by 1.53 percent annual average during that period. Yet, real wages in the sector increased 1.26 percent average, thus resulting in a fall in the rate of profit of industrial capital.

accumulation clashed against its own immanent limits.[56] The overvaluation of the national currency was the product of the Convertibility Plan, which legally fixed the exchange rate of the Argentine Peso to the US dollar at a level that did not reflect its international purchasing power. As elsewhere, the increasing requirements of hard currency by the Central Bank were covered by spiralling international loans. Coupled with a wider process of liberalisation of foreign trade, this form of appropriation of ground rent would result in the virtual disappearance of the more complex industrial activities (with the exception of those sectors like automobile final assembly, which remained strongly protected despite the liberalising rhetoric), mass bankruptcy of small-sized industrial capitals, and, therefore, the acceleration of the growth of the surplus population.[57]

As global accumulation expanded without any apparent limit, the multiplication of fictitious capital flowed into Argentina in the form of additional foreign loans that sustained the ever-growing needs for international reserves entailed by the increasingly strong overvaluation of the currency. More specifically, the peculiarity of the Argentine case during the 1990s springs from the way in which the state, through a series of lifelines that international financial institutions offered to one of their best 'pupils' (partial re-negotiations of the foreign debt and new loans), managed to extend the legally-created fiction of the strong peso despite the post-1997 slowdown of global accumulation – hence of the flow of ground rent and private loanable capital. The result of this was the continuous reproduction of this modality of transferring ground rent to industrial capital but at the cost of a prolonged recession that would stretch into the following decade. On the one hand, in the context of declining primary commodity prices, the overvaluation of the currency affected the normal valorisation of agrarian capital, thereby limiting output growth in the sector and thus the size of ground rent. On the other, with a contracting ground rent available for appropriation, the overvaluation of the peso hurt the profitability

---

56   On this specific form of capital accumulation in Argentina since the 1990s we mainly draw on Iñigo Carrera 2006. For a long historical view and quantitative empirical evidence, see Iñigo Carrera 2007c.

57   However, the content of this process has not been one of de-industrialisation. Rather, at stake in those years was an intensification of the concentration and centralisation of those industrial capitals that did survive (Grigera 2011). In fact, by cheapening imports, the overvaluation of the currency acted as a vehicle for the renovation of means of production, whose result was a period characterised by the relative growth of the productivity of labour. On the latter point, see Dachevsky 2011.

of industrial capital in general and thus social production beyond the agrarian sector.[58] This situation was further complicated by the legal restrictions that the 'convertibility' regime posed to a reduction of real wages via inflation, as a way to compensate for the fall in ground rent. Moreover, as the previous section showed, the latter was the path that Brazil followed after 1998, with the result of undermining the competitiveness of Argentina's exports even further. The effects were devastating: between 1997 and 2001 manufacturing value-added plummeted by 17 percent in real terms[59] and the rates of unemployment and underemployment respectively reached 17.4 percent and 15.6 percent by 2001.[60]

This situation, hanging as it did on the ability of the national state to continuously replenish the international reserves of the Central Bank through an ever-greater expansion of international loans, could obviously not last for long. In effect, as public foreign debt went up to over 58 percent of the GDP in 2001, it became increasingly apparent that the Argentine state had become an insolvent debtor.[61] Eventually, as the so-called dot.com crisis hit the world economy, the credit crunch dried up the prospect of procuring desperately needed additional loans. This could only mean that the country had to declare default on its foreign debt, and that it ended up in a huge banking crisis, as a run on the dollar ensued to which the state responded by locking in bank deposits (a large proportion of which were denominated in US dollars).

The unfolding of this economic content, however, clashed with the general political forms that the accumulation of capital was assuming up to that point: the presidency of De La Rua as part of the Alianza coalition.[62] In a democratic context, the outbreak of the economic crisis and the associated worsening of the conditions of reproduction of the working class could only develop if the labour movement stood still in the face of the negative consequences that this process would bring, precisely at a moment when after many years of relative acquiescence, trade union struggles were showing signs of reawakening

---

58   Iñigo Carrera 2007c.
59   Azpiazu and Schorr 2010a.
60   Arceo et al. 2008, p. 40.
61   Iñigo Carrera 2007c. pp. 84, 292.
62   Iñigo Carrera 2006. The Alianza coalition came to power after winning the 1999 elections ahead of Duhalde's Peronist candidacy. The latter represented the sheer continuity with Menem's prior administration, whose legitimacy had dwindled in the face of widespread accusations of corruption and, more importantly, the prolonged recession dating from 1998. However, the actual programme and policies implemented by De La Rua hardly differed from Menem's, i.e. they entailed a new round of neoliberal structural adjustment.

since 1999–2000.[63] The Alianza administration, with a social base in the petty bourgeoisie and the more 'skilled' (usually non-unionised) sections of the working class, was incapable of disciplining workers and their trade union representatives and even less able to deal with the increasingly militant struggles of the organised movement of the unemployed – the *piqueteros* – that had flourished during the 1990s as a response to neoliberal structural adjustment programmes.[64] Additionally, the coalition in power, which up to that point had made a key policy of the explicit commitment to meet all its foreign debt obligations and to sustain the prevailing parity of the peso to the US dollar, was not equipped ideologically to declare the insolvency of the state that would inevitably follow suit.

These economic developments thus necessitated a transformation in the forms of general political representation of the accumulation of capital, which could only unfold through the mediation of a profound political crisis. Although on previous historical occasions capital had resolved the development of similar crises through the state's deployment of direct political coercion over, hence repression of, the working class (such as through a military dictatorship), since the 1980s the simple 'silent yoke of economic coercion' of a massive (and rapidly expanding) relative surplus population would suffice to enforce discipline on wage-workers. The unfolding of the economic crisis could therefore take place through democratic political forms. Eventually, a broad popular insurrection in December 2001, in which the petty bourgeoisie and the different sections of the working class coalesced under the slogan '*Que se vayan todos!* (Out with them all!)', forced the resignation of the incumbent president De la Rua and led to the fall of the Alianza administration two years before their term of office finished.[65] After twelve tumultuous days in late 2001, in which the country successively had four interim presidents and formally declared the default on a substantial part of its foreign debt, the Legislative Assembly eventually appointed Duhalde, the leader of the Peronist party in the province of Buenos Aires who was also a member of the Senate, as caretaker president on 1 January 2002. While assuming the presidency on the basis

---

63   Piva 2009; Iñigo Carrera and Cotarelo 2003.

64   See Castorina, this volume. By more skilled workers we specifically mean those doubly free individuals whose only commodity, labour-power, embodies more complex productive attributes vis-à-vis direct production (factory or industrial) workers.

65   This is only part of the story. The democratic popular insurrection was not the only form of direct action that emerged as a response to the economic crisis. In the more deprived areas of the Greater Buenos Aires, the dominant form of struggle by those poorer sections of the working class was the looting of shops (Iñigo Carrera 2006).

of a 'pro-industry' and 'anti-finance' rhetoric, Duhalde's provisional administration actually channelled the unfolding of a deep crisis that would lead to a significant scrapping of productive capital, a dramatic fall in real wages and the further expansion of un- and under-employment.

As usual, capital shoved the burden of the crisis onto the working class. As the combined rates of unemployment and underemployment reached about 50 percent in May 2002, real wages plummeted.[66] Crucial in this process was the abandonment of the Convertibility Law in early 2002, which led, in a short period after the exchange rate was allowed to float freely, to a pronounced devaluation of the national currency. From an overvaluation of almost 100 percent before the crisis, the local currency would end up experiencing an *undervaluation* of about 30 percent in 2002 (it was still around 20 percent in 2004). This strong devaluation triggered a considerable rise in the domestic prices of internationally tradable commodities (food prices rose on average 45 percent in 2002 and 17 percent in 2003), with which wages did not catch up.[67] The rate of profit in the manufacturing sector thus experienced a drastic rise during the worst part of the prolonged recession – going from a meagre 0.3 percent in 2001 to 8 percent in 2002.[68]

As a leading figure of the Peronist Party, and in contrast to De la Rua, Duhalde had a political weapon at his disposal that would, at first, allow him to navigate through those stormy economic and political circumstances, namely the control over trade unions. Duhalde was thus able to impose and maintain the needed passivity of the labour movement despite the dramatically negative consequences on the workers' conditions of reproduction that his own adjustment policies would bring about. In addition, his crisis-management strategy involved a combination of a vast extension of unemployment benefits, to alleviate the growing pauperism of the working class, with the heavy hand of repression of the more militant elements of the *piquetero* movement.[69] Thus, Duhalde's right-wing populism came to be the adequate political form to mediate the reproduction-through-crisis of the specific form taken by capital accumulation in Argentina.

However, Duhalde's tenure turned out to be shorter-lived than originally planned. As the effects of the crisis unfolded, it soon became clear that the initial alleviatory measures taken to deal with the growing poverty of the relative surplus population would turn out to be insufficient in a context of high

---

66   CENDA 2004.
67   Iñigo Carrera 2005, p. 102.
68   Iñigo Carrera 2007c, p. 97.
69   Svampa 2008, p. 84.

inflation and rapidly expanding unemployment. This led to an intensification of the struggle of unemployed workers but also to its repression by the state. Eventually, the assassination of two workers by the police led to a political scandal that shook the foundations of Duhalde's legitimacy. The forthcoming elections were brought forward.[70] Despite coming second in the first round, left-of-centre Peronist Néstor Kirchner was appointed as president after openly neoliberal Carlos Menem, who had been in office during 1989–99, withdrew from the second voting round in the face of a certain defeat.

Kirchner came to office in late May 2003 on the basis of an anti-neoliberal discourse that postulated a break with the Washington Consensus-style policies of the 1990s. Many critical commentators have noted the mostly rhetorical nature of that alleged break, which in practice involved a great amount of substantive continuity with the neoliberal past, both at the level of his economics (unchanged industrial structure and forms of integration into the world market) and his politics (low-intensity democracy, a strong presidentialism based on a 'decisionist' tendency to govern by decree, recourse to old-style clientelism).[71] Kirchner's adoption of a critical line on neoliberalism is seen in many of those accounts as a political and ideological strategy to co-opt and demobilise the spirit of the 2001–2 popular mobilisations, while reproducing the essence of the old politico-economic order in a superficially altered guise.[72] The success of this strategy is in turn considered as having been facilitated by a fortuitous favourable international economic context, in which rising prices of primary commodities provided the state with the resources needed to deploy this populist strategy of co-option.[73] In other words, in this view the populist turn to the left is seen as the joint product of the external relations between an abstractly self-determining political and ideological strategy and an enabling international economic context.

By contrast, we claim that Kirchner's centre-left populism should be seen as the political and ideological form assumed by the renewed expansion of the specific modality taken by accumulation in Argentina as, on the one hand, the flow of ground rent into the country started to recover and, on the other, the forced exit of the Convertibility regime led to a change in the modalities of its appropriation by industrial capital.

---

70   Dinerstein 2003.

71   For instance, see the analyses of Borón 2008 and Petras and Veltmeyer 2005.

72   See, for example, Svampa 2008; Zibechi 2011a; Bonnet 2007.

73   Petras and Veltmeyer 2005.

In effect, already during the election campaign, and more clearly when Kirchner started his mandate, the economy was showing signs of recovery; from the first trimester of 2003 real GDP started to grow again and unemployment was receding, standing at just below 20 percent after reaching a peak of almost 25 percent in May 2002.[74] Initially, this recovery was sustained mainly on one economic foundation: the dramatic fall of real wages that had taken place in 2002. This increased exploitation of the working class thereby translated into a greater cost-competitiveness for local individual capitals, both in domestic and foreign markets. Coupled with the effective market protection from foreign competition derived from the resulting undervalued exchange rate, domestic manufacturing production began to experience a new phase of growth. At first this took the form of a timid resuscitation of import substitution industrialisation, as productive capacity, which had remained idle during the late 1990s, became profitable in the new economic conditions. Moreover, the undervalued currency also boosted Argentine exports, which experienced a notable increase from 2003 as well, although remaining mainly of natural resource-based or agri-business origin.[75]

The devaluation of the currency did not simply boost exports, especially of primary commodities. More importantly, it removed what during the Convertibility regime had constituted a specific barrier for the extensive and intensive application of capital in the primary sector. The resulting expansion of agrarian production thus reversed the previous decline of the flow of ground rent into the national space of capital accumulation. After reaching a low point in 2002, total ground rent more than doubled a year later.[76] From then onwards, this initial expansion of the flow of ground rent further multiplied due to the recovery and later rocketing of the international prices of primary commodities and the associated expansion of production. In 2007, the mass of ground rent was more than four times greater than the rock-bottom levels of 2002. With this source of extraordinary social wealth quickly expanding, Argentina enjoyed an unprecedented period of strong economic growth. The manufacturing sector experienced a notably strong expansion as well. Unemployment thus fell below 10 percent in early 2008.[77] As a result of the consequent

---

74   CENDA 2004, p. 28.

75   Ibid., p. 11; Iñigo Carrera 2007c, p. 102; Azpiazu and Schorr 2010a, p. 126ff.

76   Iñigo Carrera 2008c.

77   This downward trend in the rate of unemployment has continued in more recent times, albeit at a considerably slower pace and with the proportion of those in *formal* employment virtually stagnant at approximately 35 percent since 2008. Moreover, the poor

mitigation of the disciplinary effects of the surplus population, economy-wide real wages reversed their downward path and by mid-2006 recovered to their pre-crisis levels. Nevertheless, in 2008, even after experiencing a slight growth, they were still significantly below both their historic peak of 1973–4 and the average of the expansive years of the first incarnation of the ISI in 1960–75. As in Brazil, industrial workers with formal employment contracts enjoyed a much stronger recovery in their payment conditions during this period. This was indeed needed to reproduce – however limitedly from a long-term perspective – the productive attributes of the workforce at the core of the modern ISI process after being depleted during the 1990s.[78] This recovery of employ-

---

economic performance during 2012 reversed the trend and unemployment started to rise again, reaching 7.9 percent in early 2013 (one percentage point above the level of late 2011). More generally, the evolution of GDP also shows a decelerating trend after 2008. Between 2003 and 2007, the average rate of growth of GDP was 9.25 percent while manufacturing value-added grew at an average rate of 8.5 percent. In the period 2008–12, GDP growth was actually slightly negative (–0.32 percent), and even more so was manufacturing value-added (–2.16 percent). Note that these latter figures, based on the value of GDP expressed in domestic currency of constant purchasing power (see footnote 33 above), contrast significantly with the more 'optimistic' measurement of the recent evolution of the Argentine economy based on the conventional method of estimation of real GDP. Thus, according to the latter method, whilst the compound annual rate of growth was 8.8 percent between 2003 and 2007, it decreased to 5.1 percent in the period 2008–12, which is substantially below the levels of the first five years, although still considerable in view of the global slowdown. As for manufacturing value-added, from a compound rate of growth of nine percent in the period 2003–7 it went down to 4.8 percent between 2008 and 2012. Thus, the widespread conventional view overstates the dynamism of the Argentine economy since 2008. Moreover, an additional comment is in order regarding these latter estimates. Official statistics on GDP growth measured in constant prices after 2007 are a contentious issue due to Nestor Kirchner's administration's political meddling in the national statistics institute (INDEC for its Spanish acronym) and subsequent 'change in the calculation method' of the consumer price index (CPI), which grossly underestimates the actual inflation rate. According to most critical commentators, due to technical issues relating to the method of estimation of GDP, the distortion of the CPI reacts on the accuracy of data on the evolution of aggregate output, overestimating its rate of growth.

78   This diverging trend continued after 2007. While the real growth of economy-wide wages stalled in the more recent period, industrial wages continued recovering. The section of the working class that has fared the worst under Kirchnerism has been that of public sector employees (even worse than those in informal employment in the private sector), whose real wages never fully recovered from their collapse during the crisis of the Convertibility regime and have been actually falling since 2009, thus largely accounting

ment and real wages in the industrial sector was considerable enough to take concrete political form through the recomposition and strengthening of the (historically Peronist) trade union movement. The latter became one of the central pillars sustaining the Kirchner administration and, therefore, of the left-populist political and ideological turn in the form of the state.

As in other South American countries, the shift to the centre-left must be seen as the political and ideological form that mediated this period of expanded accumulation of capital revolving around the appropriation of a portion of ground rent.[79] The specifically nationalistic-populist element of the Argentine case is to be found, however, in the peculiar *forms* that the transfer of ground rent to industrial capital adopted after the pronounced devaluation of the currency in 2002. Unlike the cases of, say, Chile and Uruguay, the magnitude of ground rent (coupled with stronger previous industrial development), was significant enough to make possible a revival of the ISI process. But unlike the case of Brazil discussed earlier, the prevailing modality of channelling this extraordinary mass of social wealth into the valorisation of industrial capital would involve a greater number of the policy instruments characteristic of the 'classic' populist form of the state.

In contrast to the apparently depoliticised transfer mechanisms that prevailed during the 1990s (primarily, the overvaluation of the currency), the strong devaluation of the Argentine peso meant that the channelling of ground rent into the accumulation of industrial capital could only develop through more interventionist state policies. This formed the second pillar of the left-populist transformation of the state. In particular, from 2002 onwards, export taxes were reintroduced after a decade in which they virtually disappeared as a policy instrument. Although initially set by Duhalde at a relatively low level that did not even compensate for the strong undervaluation of the currency, export taxes were gradually increased by the Kirchner administration. In the case of soya (the star export commodity), they reached 35 percent in late 2007 while the exchange rate returned to its parity.[80] Moreover, export taxes

---

for the stagnation of the average real wage in recent years. As of late 2012, public sector wages were 40 percent below their 2001 levels.

79   Grinberg 2010.

80   Since 2007, with an annual inflation rate consistently over 20 percent (with the exception of 2009, when the recession that hit the Argentine economy lowered it to between 15 and 18 percent) that more than compensated for the administered nominal devaluation of the exchange rate, the national currency became increasingly overvalued again. Thus, by late 2012 the Argentine peso was standing about 70 percent over its purchasing power parity. This policy-induced increasing overvaluation of the national currency has been the response of the CFK administration to the rocketing of primary commodities' prices since

were not the only classic populist policy-making instrument that reappeared. The Kirchner administration resurrected other interventionist measures that mediated the channelling of ground rent into industrial capital, among them: direct state control of domestic food prices; subsidised rates of public utilities and public transport; credit at negative interest rates; and, more generally, fiscal expansionism (e.g. through public works) riding on the general bonanza in public finances resulting from both growing revenues (themselves the upshot of unprecedented high growth rates and of new income sources for the state: the aforementioned export taxes); and a substantial reduction of the burden of debt servicing as a consequence of the restructuring of public debt defaulted on in late 2001.[81] This fiscal expansion also included measures aimed at putting a break on and mitigating (*without abolishing*) the tendency for labour-

---

2007. More specifically, it has been a relatively less confrontational way of mediating a larger transfer of the growing ground rent to industrial capital in the face of the government's failed attempt to pass a law that raised export taxes in 2008. The latter strategy clashed with the strong political opposition of landowners who, after five years of unprecedented prosperity, enjoyed the material base to sustain a long 'lock-out' that eventually made CFK's administration back down from its proposal to increase taxes on the export of primary commodities (Iñigo Carrera 2008c). However, the shift to currency overvaluation as an alternative modality of transferring ground rent accelerated the development of the contradictory economic foundations on which CFK's 'left populism' rested. On the one hand, it weakened the international competitiveness of domestic industrial capital, especially of those smaller firms that had resurged after the 2002 devaluation and that had been greatly contributing to the expansion of employment. The tendency for import substitution industrialisation and the associated recovery of real wages became increasingly difficult to sustain, thus progressively undermining the material basis of the political alliance that had been supporting the government (the official trade union confederation experienced a new split, as happened in the 1990s). On the other hand, the overvaluation of the domestic currency fuelled unprecedented levels of capital flight (for instance, via profit remittance) which, between 2007 and 2011, amounted to almost US$ 80 billion. In this context, compounded by a shortage of domestic fuel production which rebounded in a spiralling oil and gas import bill, typical balance of payments difficulties historically characterising ISI processes in Argentina soon started to resurface. Without access to international loans like Brazil, the government responded in 2011 with ever-stricter controls over the foreign exchange market. So far, in a context of still-high international prices of primary commodities, coupled with a relatively more overvalued Brazilian currency, the contradictions of capital accumulation in Argentina have found 'room to move' and an open economic and political crisis does not seem imminent.

81   In the first couple of years after the 2001 crisis, public finances also directly benefited from the purchase of labour-power considerably below its value. In effect, in 2002 and 2003, public sector real wages fell by 21 and seven percent, respectively; see Iñigo Carrera 2005.

power to be sold below its value. Thus, social assistance programmes greatly increased in depth and extension during the Kirchner administration.[82]

This feature of Kirchnerist populism became even more notable under the administration of his wife and successor Cristina Fernández de Kirchner (CFK) since 2007. CFK instituted far-reaching social policies among which the implementation of a universal child benefit and the re-nationalisation of the pension system stand out.[83] Although usually presented by the government and its supporters as epoch-making ruptures with the neoliberal past of the previous decade, their impact has remained rather modest. Indeed, they are an attempt to improve the conditions of reproduction of the relative surplus population (and retired workers) without uprooting its determination as superfluous vis-à-vis the specifically limited needs of the form of capital accumulation prevailing in Argentina.

A final economic foundation underlying the left-leaning populist form of the state under Kirchnerism concerns the fate of the public debt on default since 2001. Indeed, after the devaluation of the currency, public foreign debt rocketed and reached over 70 of the GDP.[84] Quite literally, foreign debt had become simply impossible to service. In these circumstances, the expanded reproduction of industrial capital in Argentina itself came to depend on a restructuring of the debt that would of necessity entail a substantive write-off. In effect, after three years of international negotiations an agreement was eventually reached in 2005, which, in what represented the greatest write-off of sovereign debt in history up to that point, took public foreign debt down to 19.2 percent of GDP.[85] But this economic content could only develop by being politically and ideologically mediated through an assertion of national autonomy by the Argentine state vis-à-vis the 'predatory' demands of global financial capital. The centre-left populist turn taken by the reproduction of ground-rent-based accumulation in Argentina thus acquired a further nationalistic edge,

---

82   Svampa 2008, p. 84.

83   CENDA 2010.

84   Arceo and Wainer 2008; Iñigo Carrera 2007c.

85   The write-off amounted to 65.6 percent of total capital plus overdue interests over the portion of the debt actually eligible for the swap and 46.6 percent over total public debt. On this process, see Arceo and Wainer 2008. Note, however, that the diminished burden of public foreign debt is not simply the result of the write-off but also of *dutiful repayments* after the default. Ironically, and in contrast to its neoliberal predecessor, the left-populist government is actually using the expanding ground rent to pay the foreign debt back. This move is reconciled with its nationalistic ideology by euphemistically referring to the meeting of financial obligations as a '*política de desendeudamiento*' (policy of debt reduction).

which appeared as antagonistic to the globalising interests of international financial institutions.[86]

In sum, as much as in Brazil and the rest of South America, the shift to the centre-left in Argentina has been the political and ideological expression of the reproduction of the same modality of capital accumulation that has prevailed throughout its history in a context of rapidly expanding ground rent flowing into the national space of valorisation. However, despite its apparently dramatic increase, this recovery of ground rent has been insufficient to recreate the scale of the first incarnation of ISI. The limits to this 'neo'-populist developmentalism have been of the same nature as those mentioned above regarding Brazil. The revival of industrial production has been rather narrow and shallow in Argentina as well. In fact, it has not gone far beyond a weak 'primary ISI' phase: both the sectoral composition of manufacturing GDP and the pattern of international insertion have not significantly altered in relation to the neoliberal 1990s. It has been led by a handful of branches; most of them are natural resource based. Real wages are still considerably below their 1960s–70s levels.

Conclusion: Argentina and Brazil's Shift to the Left in Comparative Perspective

Both in Argentina and Brazil there has been a resurgence of many of the classic transfer mechanisms of ground rent to industrial capital, and therefore it is possible to observe a certain revival of 'old-style' ISI state policies such as the introduction of export taxes on primary commodities, protection of domestic markets, the provision of services, industrial inputs, and credit at subsidised rates by state-owned companies and banks, etc. As a consequence, the political regime has left behind the openly neoliberal shape assumed during the 1990s and shifted to the centre-left. Yet, even if there has been an associated resurgence of domestic industrial production in both countries, the increase in ground rent to 1970s levels has taken place in a completely different context from the first incarnation of ISI between 1930 and 1975: one in which the productivity gap with world market standards that ground rent needs to cover has increased dramatically. The potentialities for this limited form of industrialisation have been therefore more modest than in the past. Although still present in the contemporary forms of the state in both Argentina and Brazil, the popu-

---

86   This apparent antagonism in part explains the demonisation of Kircherism by financial capital's representatives in the bourgeois media (e.g. *The Economist, Financial Times*, etc.).

list tendencies of the political regimes that have channelled the recent economic expansion have thereby been more moderate than their paradigmatic modalities during the Peron and Vargas administrations.

However, even if more timid in both countries, this revived populism has been more marked in Argentina than in Brazil. Our claim is that the reasons for this are to be found mainly in the forms of appropriation of ground rent by capital prevailing in each country in the recent past. First, whereas in Argentina the main mechanism has been taxes on commodity exports combined with subsidies of all sorts (hence a more 'interventionist' or 'politicised' form of channelling ground rent into the accumulation of industrial capital), in Brazil the main mechanism has been a strongly overvalued currency (hence, a form of transfer of ground rent that appears to occur without direct state action, but rather as the 'spontaneous' product of 'free market forces'). Moreover, the lower level of labour productivity and higher wages prevailing in the Argentine industrial sector vis-à-vis the Brazilian one have resulted in more active forms of domestic market protection in the former in order to allow the appropriation of ground rent by capital, most markedly after 2006, when Argentina's exchange rate began to become overvalued again.

Second, in Brazil the inflow of loanable fictitious capital has complemented the transfer of ground rent since at least 2005–6. Genuine cancellations of foreign debt taking place during 1999–2004 had been a condition for reestablishing the net inflow thereafter. These processes could only be realised with a more moderate type of neopopulism vis-à-vis the one prevailing in Argentina, where there has been no considerable renewed inflow of loanable capital since the default in 2001. Thus, the Lula and Dilma administrations had to maintain a more market-friendly institutional and ideological climate in order to mediate the renewed inflow into the country in the last five or six years. By contrast, the Kirchner and Fernández de Kirchner administrations not only faced objectively drier credit conditions after the default, but also had to personify the actual renegotiation of a substantial write-off of foreign public debt in order to sustain the reproduction of ground-rent-fed accumulation. The political and ideological forms of the accumulation process have therefore acquired a more pronounced nationalistic shape in Argentina (especially visible, for instance, in the tenser relationship that the Argentine government had been maintaining with international financial institutions like the IMF).

Finally, the modality of appropriation through the combination of exchange-rate overvaluation and selected market protection in Brazil has maximised the portion of ground rent appropriated by foreign capitals at the expense of the resurgence of smaller domestic capitals, crucially as it involved the multiplication of profits when remitted abroad. This form of accumulation has limited employment creation. Real wages in Brazil have thus stagnated more than in Argentina. The mediating role of the organised working class as an active political subject in the expanded reproduction of capital has differed accordingly, with a greater political recomposition of the (traditional) trade union movement in Argentina. This trend also has contributed to the consolidation of a more moderate form of populism in Brazil.

In sum, the specific incarnations of Brazilian and Argentine left-leaning neopopulism have been the necessary political and ideological forms mediating the respective courses of the process of capital accumulation in each country, which, although sharing a common general determination in the transfer of ground rent into industrial capital, have nonetheless taken different concrete economic forms in the last decade. As we have seen, it is this divergence in the movement of the economic content of social relations that has shaped the varieties of centre-leftism prevailing in these two South American countries in the recent past.

CHAPTER 12

The Three Dimensions of the Crisis[1]

Claudio Katz

Since the banking debacle in 2008, there have been numerous signs that capitalism is experiencing a systemic crisis. The upheaval reflects more than just the collapse of the financial sector or the exhaustion of a regime of accumulation; rather it is at once a social, geopolitical, and environmental crisis. But what are the links between these different phenomena? What are the relationships between the various imbalances at play? This chapter seeks to clarify these connections, drawing a distinction between the conjunctural, structural, and historical aspects of the upheaval, aiming to highlight how these different crises are intertwined.

The first section analyses the immediate causes of the tremor, investigating how financial hypertrophy, the overproduction of commodities, and escalating trade imbalances have created short-term tensions. The second section addresses the structural causes of the crisis, based on the transformations of capitalism during the neoliberal period of the last twenty years. It argues that the changes that have taken place under capitalism during this period have produced unique imbalances, both in the sphere of demand and in the rate of profit. The third section puts forward several hypotheses regarding possible outcomes, describing which reforms are likely to resolve structural contradictions and which are likely to prolong them, particularly regarding whether the world economy is entering a deflationary context or inflationary context. I also challenge here both the neoliberal and Keynesian interpretations of the upheaval. The conclusion investigates the historical scope of the crisis, putting special emphasis on the dramatic consequences of environmental destruction, and it explains why global warming poses a threat to civilisation that is comparable to other destructive tendencies of capitalism. I conclude with an analysis of the prospects of a new anti-capitalist popular project rooted in eco-socialism.

---

1   This essay is a shorter version of "Three Dimensions of Crisis" published at www.lahaine.org/katz on 2 May 2010. Translated from Spanish by Shana Yael Shubs and Ruth Felder.

Overproduction and Trade Imbalances

The current crisis erupted in the US financial sphere in mid-2007, when it became clear that there were great difficulties paying off subprime loans. Loans granted to non-creditworthy borrowers first swelled the list of high-risk operations and then triggered an avalanche of arrears. The holes that appeared in small US banks spread to the large institutions and eventually shook the entire international system. In late 2008, the bankruptcy of Lehman Brothers unleashed a large-scale collapse, creating a widespread sense of impending breakdown. This impression diminished after massive state relief was granted to the bankrupt institutions. After the bailout, some economists proclaimed the end of the crisis. But instability persists, which is conjuncturally related to tensions created by over-accumulated capital, over-produced commodities, and uneven exchange.

The current crisis has unleashed the most important global recession of recent decades, with enormous contractions in production in the United States, Europe, and Japan. This regression hit bottom in the middle of 2009, but the rebound to recovery is not complete. Credit has not returned, consumption remains contracted, and the lack of investment persists. This conjuncture is reflected in a very popular remark: 'Wall Street prospers while ordinary people suffer'.[2]

The overall performance of the global economy continues to be determined by developments in the three central regions that produce two-thirds of the global GDP. Economic growth in the poorest and most dependent peripheral countries in Africa, Asia, and Latin America has scant impact upon the overall level of productive activity. Yet these nations have been shaken once again by an external phenomenon with dramatic domestic impacts. They suffer from reduced exports, remittances, and international aid. But most striking is the magnitude of certain social tragedies, such as the spread of hunger produced by higher food prices.

What is principally new about the crisis is the emergence of a third bloc of countries, led by the so-called BRICS (Brazil, Russia, India, and China), which oscillate between the two traditional poles of centre and the periphery. The lesser impact of the financial crisis upon these countries has renewed the debate about coupling, decoupling, or recoupling these regions to the world economy. There is widespread interest in the future of China, in particular. The new Asian power kept itself afloat during the crisis, although growth rates have been below average compared to recent years. Nonetheless China still

---

2   Reich 2010.

sustains a level of economic growth that will result in the doubling of its GDP every eight years. But it remains to be seen if it will manage to shift toward greater domestic consumption, thereby reducing exports, as expected by some analysts.[3]

However, the process of capitalist restoration in China has created massive agricultural, social, and demographic imbalances. In tandem with the privatisations and deregulation, inequality has risen dramatically such that it is now the second most unequal country in Southeast Asia. What is particularly striking is that old absolute poverty in rural areas has been replaced by a new social polarisation in the cities, which has already reached Latin American proportions, along with the consolidation of forms of exploitation based on unemployment, the loss of union rights, and the deterioration of working conditions (especially for domestic migrants). Meanwhile, a new class of multimillionaires is gaining power.[4] So while intermediate economies such as China are still on their feet, they do not replace the driving force of the Triad (United States, Europe, and Japan).

The global crisis has resulted in a highly uneven economic performance, evident in rising unemployment. The destruction of jobs continues at a furious pace in all the advanced economies, and the ILO estimates that only in a context of high global growth could the level of employment begin to recover by 2013. For the first time in 26 years, the unemployment rate in the United States has reached double digits, and in some European countries like Spain, it is already approaching 20 percent. These unemployment levels limit reactivation, erode purchasing power, and crush 'consumer confidence' in economies that rely on credit.

In a likely repeat of what happened in previous recessions, the recent fall of the GDP has tended to destroy more jobs than those that are created in the subsequent recovery. In the United States, five percent growth of GDP would be needed in order to decrease the unemployment rate by just one point. Following the last setback (2001–3), it took four years to get back to the previous average. An underlying problem is the impact of labour flexibilisation and the segmentation of the labour market. These regressive transformations have resulted in widespread, ruthless competition for low-quality jobs. This continuing deterioration of the labour market constitutes the most nefarious aspect of the current crisis, intensifying the poverty of marginalised sectors

---

3   Llach 2010.

4   52 percent of manufacturing has already been privatised, and the percentage of goods regulated by market prices jumped from three percent (1978) to 98 percent (2003). The number of trillionaires went from zero (2003) to 260 (2009) (Hart-Landsberg 2010).

of the US population. The same lack of jobs in Europe has already reached a dramatic average unemployment rate of 10 percent. The lack of work has also emerged as major news in Japan, which for decades maintained its employment level above the OECD average.

Unemployment is a direct effect of the over-production that prevails in the current contractionary phase of the capitalist cycle. The mass of products introduced to the market far exceeds the demand for them. This type of excess is present in all the periodic crises of a system based on competition for profits. The unemployed are the first victims of this imbalance, as the lack of jobs increases along with the amount of unsold products. This mass of excess creates a high level of industrial inactivity, which in turn further stimulates unemployment. The utilisation rate in US industry was 68 percent last year, at its lowest level since 1948. Excess capacity especially affects the housing sector, several branches of industry (machinery, buildings, fibre optics) and their counterparts in all the services (hospitality, tourism).[5] In the automobile industry, unsellable stocks have multiplied significantly, in an area that registered significant increases in its productive capacity in recent decades given the entry of Asian firms.[6] The current volume of over-capacity has surpassed that recorded during the Southeast Asian crisis of 1997, when the overproduction of computers, microchips, and fibre optics led to searing devaluations. But currency depreciation – as a way to mitigate excess production – has been limited due to the global nature of the crisis.

The plethora of commodities on the market is a result of global competition to produce growing masses of products with low wages and ever lower costs. In the frantic race to introduce new goods, supply has become divorced from demand, causing major imbalances. There is a frenzied search for consumers that runs up against insurmountable limits to absorption. The drastic processes of privatisation, deregulation, and liberalisation over the last three decades have fostered this onslaught of unsellable commodities. The rise in global trade above production reinforces global competition, and productivity growth exceeding wage increases hinders the realisation of goods. Only a vigorous recovery of income and consumption will enable the eventual absorption of this excess production. But this scenario is not expected to occur any time soon due to severe global imbalances.

The current crisis includes a new imbalance in the relationship between the United States and China: the over-consumption, under-saving, and under-investment of the former coexist with the low consumption, over-saving,

---

5   McNally 2008.

6   Vessillier 2009.

and over-investment of the latter. At one end of the pole, the United States imports a large part of the goods made in China, where there is a very low level of domestic consumption in comparison with the magnitude of investment. China controls its public finances, avoids the convertibility of its currency, restricts the leveraging of its banks, and places limits on household debt. But these protections at the financial level do not extend to trade, where a high degree of dependency upon foreign demand prevails. This is why overproduction leads to Chinese industry's considerable overcapacity, which in recent decades has been structured around exports. While the average wage remains stagnant, the soaring investment rate – close to 40 percent of the GDP – has developed around the export economy.[7]

In recent years, the asymmetries created by the US trade deficit (and its credit gaps), faced with China's exportable surplus (with its resulting excess capital) have grown more extreme. US households have gone into debt in order to consume products manufactured (and financed) by China, in a circuit fed by transnational companies. These companies have played a strategic mediating role between the two markets and are now grappling with the consequences of a severe constriction of the US market.

These differences also started to spread within the East Asian trading bloc, a region in which China is now the principal employer. Indeed, China functions like an assembly shop for parts made in neighbouring countries (for example, in the electronics, machinery, and telecommunications industries). Thus the Asian power's trade surplus with its Western partners coexists with trade deficits with its regional suppliers. China has increased these advantages with the recent signing of a free-trade agreement with its East Asian partners. It is reproducing the unequal division of labour by purchasing basic goods and selling manufactured goods, while it absorbs the bulk of foreign investment and favours its own capitalists (with subsidies and regulations), to the detriment of foreign competitors. The dependence of all the lesser economies of the region – economies that had already lost significant margins of monetary and exchange rate autonomy during the 1997 crisis – is thus reinforced.[8]

But this kind of imbalance is also evident in other parts of the world. Within the European Union, similar asymmetries are very apparent. The crisis has brought into relief the polarisation between those European countries with trade surpluses and those with trade deficits. This fracture was initially softened when the Euro was adopted following prior devaluations. In this way, some economies had a certain reserve of competitiveness at their disposal

---

7   Loong Yu 2009.
8   Jetin 2009; Bello 2010; Seongin 2008.

for several years. But there is an unevenness that illustrates the considerable heterogeneity in the European Union that can no longer be obscured.[9] Large trade and finance imbalances also played a part in the Mexican crisis (1994), the Brazilian crisis (1999), the Russian Crisis (1998), and the Argentinean crisis (2001), and triggered the great spiral of devaluations and trade adjustments that followed the Southeast Asian upheaval (1997). Creditors' lack of confidence in economies that finance their imports with large public or private debt triggers periodic runs against the financial instruments and currencies of deficit countries. But the big news now is the spread of these tensions to the United States and the European countries, which had accumulated large imbalances in recent years.

The capitalist economy always functions with sectoral, regional, and global imbalances. There are problems with supply, prices, and production volumes, both between different branches of production and in multiple spheres of consumption at the national level. These tensions become more significant for purchases and sales between trading countries with very different productivity levels. Under the rule of competition, these differences necessitate periodic adjustments, which are paid for by the oppressed classes. In the current crisis, the principal imbalances affect the major powers and will demand sacrifices of the people in these regions. But the severity of the accumulated imbalances and the global entanglement of capital with varied origins make the mitigation of these differences very complex.

Until now, establishment economists have made generic calls to reduce trade and financial imbalances between countries by 'rebalancing' global accounts. One starting point for this solution would be a simultaneous increase in US savings and Chinese consumption in order to slow down the addiction to excessive consumption in the US and stimulate reticent Asian spending. A weakening of the dollar and strengthening of the yuan would speed up this correction.[10] But, in reality, it is not easy to resolve this imbalance. The profits brought to transnational companies by the process of neoliberal globalisation have been based on these asymmetrical exchanges. While high domestic consumption facilitated the recovery of US hegemony, the strength of China's export sector sustained its transition to capitalism. A US shift to savings and an Asian turn to domestic spending would seriously jeopardise this framework.

Overcoming global imbalances entails much more than trade and financial policy adjustments. It requires politico-strategic changes that come up against resistance from the global economy's principal actors. Even though the model

---

9   Önaran 2009; Husson 2010; Castro 2010.

10   Ferguson 2009; Krugman 2009c.

of US consumption financed by Chinese suppliers has been seriously affected by the crisis, there are no clear alternatives to this framework. The United States cannot go back to a policy of domestic savings without impairing its global leadership, and China cannot replace the leading power as the driving force of global consumption. The US giant is no longer in a position to dictate the terms of a rebalancing to its principal partner, but neither does its counterpart have sufficient strength to impose its own agenda. This contradiction creates the series of conflicts that conventional economists explain in terms of disagreements about tariffs, exchange rates, and interest rates. They do not connect these economic imbalances to the social inequalities that benefit capitalists on both sides.

Neoliberalism: A New Stage of Capitalism

The current crisis takes on a different scale if we consider it as a part of the neoliberal period as a whole. In this case, the short-term imbalances caused by over-accumulated capital, over-produced commodities, and asymmetrically exchanged goods are inscribed in more significant structural imbalances. These contradictions determine the underlying causes of the crisis, which have been created by tensions accumulated over two decades. These imbalances are made manifest in the sphere of demand and in the behaviour of the rate of profit in a new stage of capitalism.

Since the mid-1980s, neoliberal globalisation has introduced significant changes to how the system works, stemming from the attack carried out by power-holders on the social conquests won by the working class in the post-WWII era. This attack has led to the deterioration of working conditions in the advanced countries and further impoverishment in the periphery, in a context of capital expansion into new sectors (privatisations, education, health, pensions) and new territories (the former socialist countries). Capitalism has begun to operate in a context of increasing trade, financial, and productive globalisation. This change was encouraged by the information revolution, which made the use of computers in economic activity widespread, modifying the forms of manufacturing, selling, and consuming goods. This same innovation offered banks a new basis for managing finances.

It is important to highlight that these transformations were implemented in a political context of union retreat and the ebb of anti-capitalist ideas. Neoliberal ideology – propagated by the corporate media – came to be disseminated at unprecedented levels.[11] Other characterisations of this same process emphasise the importance of the attack by employers and distinguish between the economic influence of globalisation and the political and ideological impact of neoliberalism.[12] They describe how the large corporations took advantage of the major international differences in jobs and wages to maximise their profits. These inequalities were used to introduce new forms of employer control into the labour process, which business owners were able to impose with threats to relocate their firms to other countries.

This analysis is sometimes contested on the grounds that the new model has not managed to bring about significant increases in productivity and is highly vulnerable to financial bubbles.[13] Such analysts claim that the influence of transnational companies is undermined by their excessive concentration and by the instability they create by draining resources away from the rest of the economy. Questions are also raised about the inability of neoliberalism to drive sustained growth as a result of the erosion of state regulatory mechanisms that it has created.[14] But none of these authors deny that we find ourselves in a new period; rather, the debate centres on its degree rather than its existence. Those who consider that the current model is less stable than its predecessor do not question its dominance. This agreement is much more important than controversies about the degree of coherence or the type of contradictions present in the current context.

Regardless of the assessments of its future, it is clear that neoliberalism has brought about a substantial change in the dynamics of capitalism. Accepting these changes allows us to analyse their correlates in the crisis. The new imbalances have different features from their twentieth-century counterparts. These include financial hypertrophy, but also the mechanisms of securitisation, derivatives and leveraging created over two decades of finance internationalisation, banking deregulation, and corporate management dictated by the stock markets. The same is true for the over-production of commodities. Unlike what was previously the case, current surpluses are global in nature due to the race to reduce costs by putting plants in countries with low salaries and high rates of labour exploitation. The asymmetries between China and the United States characterise a very different period from that of the classic post-war stage (1945–73) and the rupture of this framework (1973–82), which

---

11   Katz 2003.

12   McDonough 2003; 2008.

13   O'Hara 2002; 2004.

14   Kotz 2003.

preceded the current period (1982–). How should we analyse the contradictions in this new stage?

Emphasizing the Qualitative

Many analysts have tried to clarify the current imbalances by determining if, indeed, a new long wave of economic growth is underway. Some consider that this upward movement has been apparent since the 1990s. As evidence for this trend, they present high rates of growth in those activities led by transnational companies in a range of productive sectors and geographical areas.[15]

The opposing thesis rejects this analysis and presents evidence of low average growth worldwide, along with political assessments of global disorder and a lack of hegemonic leadership. Based on this description, analysts infer that the downward trend, which goes back more than forty years, will continue.[16]

But the debate becomes bogged down here, as it turns out to be just as difficult to demonstrate the return of the flourishing post-war period, as it is to demonstrate that there has been a continual state of decline. The signs of an upward trend contrast with the intensity and recurrence of short-term crises in recent decades. But the opposing thesis of a persistent downturn makes this fall seem endless and ignores the impact of neoliberalism on the restructuring of capital.

The discussion is more conceptual than it is empirical, as there is no universally indicative data on the nature of a period. Average high growth does not have the same meaning in the late twentieth century as it does for the middle of the next century or the beginning of the twenty-first. The same is true for the different regions. An annual five percent GDP growth is considered high for the United States but very low for China.

As I have explained elsewhere, distinguishing between the concepts of stage and phase may help to clarify the problem. I identify the first notion with a different functioning of the system and the second with a predominant tendency for economic growth or stagnation over the medium term.[17] Instead of strictly associating both phenomena with long waves, I emphasise that the existence of a new phase is not directly correlated with productive growth. We can thus assert that the post-war era has been completely superseded, without giving rise to another overall period of economic vigour. What is important is the existence of a qualitatively different dynamic and not the predominance of high levels of activity.

---

15   Martins 2007; Dos Santos 2005.

16   Wallerstein 2004, chapter 26.

17   Katz 2003.

The existence of a neoliberal stage is partially independent of the rate of production. Over the last two decades, the dynamics of accumulation have been substantially modified, without resulting in a clear pattern of change in GDP growth rates. A very heterogeneous context has developed, with sharp regional and sectoral inequalities that combine prosperity and stagnation, and the forms the crisis take are essentially determined by this unprecedented framework.

The imbalances in the neoliberal period are different from the tensions that flourished in the 1960s and the 1970s with the exhaustion of the welfare state. They are contradictions that arise from new problems and are not remnants of previous tensions. Those who interpret the 2008–10 crisis as one more wave of the turbulence the world economy has experienced in the last four decades see continuities where there were ruptures. They do not see that the crisis in the Keynesian model ended with the rise of neoliberalism, which launched a new framework that created different imbalances.

It is important to note these particularities in order to avoid the simplification of merely associating neoliberalism with stagnation. The current model has created new turbulence because it has also involved the partial return of accumulation. If the system had languished, the imbalances produced would be different.

The new structural contradictions are being processed in two spheres: the realisation of the value of commodities and the valorisation of capital. These contradictions have a simultaneous impact on both demand and profitability at a scale that exceeds the periodic tremors of the conjuncture.

Crisis of Realisation

The imbalances in the sphere of consumption are highly conspicuous. By cutting salaries, expanding unemployment, and increasing poverty, neoliberalism eroded people's incomes, which affected workers' purchasing power. This created obstacles to realising the value of commodities, and led to a re-emergence of difficulties realising the surplus value that capitalists extract from wage earners.

Many authors have explained how this contradiction grew during neoliberalism. They consider that a model of permanent abuse with respect to the lives of the masses must necessarily result in a smothering of demand. The benefits gained by capitalists by reducing costs have deleterious effects on purchasing power.[18] Other analysts describe in what ways this imbalance distinguishes current capitalism from its predecessor. While the Fordist model included sig-

---

18   Wolfson 2003; Kotz 2008.

nificant wage increases as productivity increased, the neoliberal framework is based on prioritising competition to reduce wage costs, creating a wide gap between increases in production and purchasing power.[19]

Over the last two decades, this fracture has become dramatically evident in the misery of the Third World and the scourge of hunger. In the most plundered regions of the planet, the deterioration in people's incomes has had devastating effects. This regressive situation has had harsh impacts upon the malnourished in Africa, Asia, and Latin America. Hunger has increased relentlessly over the last two decades and currently affects 1.2 billion people. Neoliberal capitalism has amputated the basic source of subsistence for one-sixth of the world's population. According to IMF estimates, the current financial crisis alone is responsible for another 53 million people falling into extreme poverty, causing the death of 1.2 million children from 2010 to 2015.[20]

But this decline in consumption has not been the most pervasive element in the rest of the world, nor is it the central characteristic of the current model. Rather, this framework has counterbalanced decreased demand with a range of mechanisms.

First, it stimulated massive consumption in the developed countries. Those who benefited came not only from the sectors that profited from the suffering of the masses, that is, the upper and middle classes; lower classes benefited, too, from the availability of luxury goods. This consumerism differs from the mass consumption that enlarged the basket of essential goods during the postwar boom. This new spending pattern replaced the former purchases of essential goods with more volatile spending patterns, adapted to the shortening of product life cycles.

Neoliberal competition strengthened the production of goods that are vulnerable to the accelerated obsolescence of manufacturing processes. With enormous expenditures squandered on advertising, consumers are encouraged to dispose of purchased products before the end of their useful lives. This compulsion makes demand more vulnerable, as it loses the greater stability present in the Fordist model of consumption. This new purchasing framework has spread along with the extraordinary growth of social polarisation (especially in the United States). Instead of the increase in demand being linked to improvements in the income of the masses, the level of consumption is now linked to debt.

This new pattern of consumption is also frequently related to household assets. In this case, purchases are induced by the wealth accumulated by

19   Navarro 2010.
20   La Nación 2010.

households in the form of investments in bonds or stocks. The prices of these paper assets have more influence on consumption than wages. This is why the factors that affect 'consumer confidence' have become so tied to the fluctuations of the different financial markets. The amount of goods purchased by the masses increases during periods of stock market and real estate appreciation and decreases in times of financial loss or panic. This relation explains the large impact of the recent financial crisis upon US consumer behaviour.[21]

The realisation crisis created by neoliberalism was contained with household debt. This counterweight allowed purchasing power to be maintained, despite wage stagnation, increases in precarious work, and the spread of unemployment. Workers drew on credit relief, and this flow of credit kept consumption levels from collapsing completely. But as this increase in liabilities reached astronomical figures, wage earners were transformed into debt-riddled clients. The burden of loan payments coexists with the hardships created by the exploitation of labour. With these compensatory mechanisms, demand has been kept active in a context of declining wages.

Furthermore, this consumption is based on a highly polarised distributive structure at the global level. The wealthiest five percent of the world's population currently earns 114 times more than the poorest five percent. Advertising expenditures are highly representative of this situation, with 75 percent of such expenses concentrated in eight countries in North America and Europe.[22] The meagre participation of 80 percent of the planet's inhabitants in just 14 percent of total private consumption also illustrates the limited nature of this demand.[23]

This gap is a central feature of the framework that has prevailed in recent decades. While globalisation has made the over-production of goods and the over-abundance of capital widespread, neoliberalism has intensified socio-geographic disparities. This global polarisation has deepened the segmentation of consumption, sharpening the potential intensity of global imbalances in the ability of capitalists to realise profits.

But these fault-lines in the global system of production and consumption have been papered over in different ways. At a global level, there was a growth in demand over the last several decades, along with the entry of capital into the former 'socialist countries' and the intermediate economies. Significant segments of the population were thus able to move up a notch on the consumption scale, surpassing their former status as purchasers of basic goods.

---

21   Joshua 2009.

22   Katz 2003.

23   Migone 2007.

In some highly populated countries (such as China and India), a new middle class has been created, which is beginning to consume more sophisticated commodities.

Just as the production of capital goods balanced out the under-consumption cycles in the nineteenth century, new forms of purchasing have moderated the potential fragility of demand introduced by neoliberalism. The mechanisms of indebtedness, financialisation, and consumerism play a compensatory role, similar to that played by the markets for capital goods in early capitalism. These counterweights have so far prevented an explosion of realisation imbalances.

Crisis of Valorisation

The behaviour of the rate of profit is another structural contradiction in the current framework. The development of this variable may have been undermined in recent decades by the spread of new technology, which reduces the relative importance of living labour that is the basis for the creation of surplus value appropriated by capitalists.

This process reproduces the tendency inherent to accumulation to erode the rate of profit as investment reduces the proportion of immediate labour incorporated into goods relative to the dead labour that is already embodied in factories, machinery, or raw materials.[24] The dynamic of accumulation increases the organic composition of capital, which in turn tends to shrink the rate of profit based on the surplus value extracted from wage earners. Several analysts have emphasised this origin of the crisis as being rooted in imbalances in valorisation recreated by neoliberalism.[25]

There have been three signs of this increase in the organic composition of capital in recent decades. First, there were very significant increases in investment in the Asian economies, which became the new global factory for contemporary industry. The high rates of exploitation based on low wages (especially of migrant workers from rural areas) made the average level of investment in China extremely high in relative terms. This degree of capitalisation explains why situations of industrial over-capacity have flourished to such an extent in this country, while global trade contracts.[26]

Second, the same increase in the amount of machinery relative to labour is evident in all the regions and sectors associated with the activity of transnational companies. These companies have taken the lead in increasing

---

24   This process is analysed in the case of Argentina by Féliz in this volume.
25   Carchedi 2009; Harman 2009a.
26   Hart-Landsberg 2010.

productivity, especially by means of an intense computerisation of the production process.

This technological revolution brought with it growing turbulence and resulted in severe crises (such as the stock market crash of the dot-coms at the beginning of the 2000s). The impact of information technology upon the average rate of productivity in the leading economies has been the subject of major debate amongst economists. But regardless of the scope of this transformation, there is no doubt that it has brought about a reduction in the surplus value directly created by living labour.

The third sign of this process is the loss of jobs created by the growing incorporation of capital-intensive technology. The devastating increase in unemployment is the visible manifestation of this change. As automation becomes more widespread, job losses during each recession exceed the subsequent creation of new jobs. With the new technology, the recruitment of workers becomes consistently cheaper per unit of capital invested.

All analyses of unemployment in the United States point out this structural problem, which creates a growing need to increase the GDP in order to maintain the pace of job creation. Some assessments emphasise that it is not only the recession that has caused this loss of jobs. Automation has also made 5.6 million jobs disappear since 2000, and the increase in productivity has kept new wage earners from finding jobs in factories.[27]

These three processes – high foreign investment by transnational corporations, the information revolution, and structural unemployment – have increased the organic composition of capital, resulting in a relative deterioration of the rate of profit. However, many researchers emphasise that this level of profitability has remained high since the mid-1980s.[28] Other studies describe how this reorganisation has been more significant in companies operating at the transnational scale relative to firms acting only at the national level. The rate of profit rose and split into two, with different margins in the two types of corporation.[29]

These assessments indicate that the recovery of the rate of profit that has accompanied neoliberalism is still in effect, despite all the domestic processes of accumulation that pressure this variable to fall. Just as with the realisation imbalances, the forces that counteract the declining valorisation of capital have slowed down this descent. This is another key contradiction in the current model that continues to develop beneath the surface. This counterweight was

---

27   Aversa 2010; Goodman 2010.

28   Moseley 2009; Valle 2009; Husson 2009a.

29   Caputo 2009.

accomplished, above all, with the increased rate of exploitation. Very strong wage stagnation was created by labour flexibilisation, unemployment, and the high levels of poverty within large segments of the population. Herein lies the essence of neoliberalism, and the evidence of this attack is overwhelming.

The declining cost of raw materials has been another factor compensating for the fall in the rate of profit, with a more contradictory trajectory. Throughout most of the neoliberal stage, this depreciation was significant, but this tendency has begun to be reversed in the period 2005–10.

Uneven behaviour has also been displayed in the devalorisation of obsolete capital, which constitutes the main counterweight to the tendency of the rate of profit to fall. Under neoliberalism, there was an opposite process of state relief for bankrupt businesses and a reorganisation of the least competitive firms. Overall, there was a significant cleansing of capital, which resulted in depreciations of constant capital and a weeding out of obsolete companies.

The succession of bankruptcies and mergers is illustrative of this process. Unlike the classic capitalism of the liberal era, in the current period the state intervenes directly in weeding out companies. Many firms have been nationalised and reorganised before being reprivatised. The sequence of capital valorisation-revalorisation takes place with this same state mediation. There is a great deal of debate about the magnitude of this process, but all evidence indicates that it has been of sufficient importance to maintain the recovery of business profits over the last two decades.[30]

This rise also confirms that all the financial bubbles that occurred during this stage were fed by real increases in employers' profits. The 2008–10 crisis caused these profits to crash, and the losses suffered by the banks and the stock exchanges suggest that companies' balance sheets will be in the red. But this kind of short-term drop has been present throughout the cycles of the neoliberal period thus far, without affecting the structural recovery of profitability. The great unknown about the current crisis is whether these counterweights will come to an end. The answer to this question requires an analysis of different scenarios.

Scenarios and Alternatives

It is very difficult to predict how long neoliberalism will be able to put off the detonation of its structural contradictions. But delaying these outcomes will surely lead to even more severe upheaval.

---

30   Post 2005.

Orthodox and Heterodox Views

Debates about the crisis have commanded the attention of all economists. In the early months after the collapse of the subprime mortgage market in 2008, a major collapse seemed imminent, but the reprieve in 2009 has moderated this impression. Amongst Marxists, there are different predictions about the scale of the crisis and whether collapse was imminent.[31] Neoliberals, for their part, have already put aside their initial bewilderment and once again spout the mythology of eternal capitalism. They believe this system will thrive once again after correcting the flaws that triggered the temporary financial collapse of 2008–10.[32]

But fables like this have lost credibility. It is clear that the magic of the market cannot spontaneously overcome the turbulence in the economy. Moreover, it is no longer so easy to conceal the terrible social suffering that accompanies these convulsions. As adjustments become ever harsher, the neoliberal message loses its justification, finds less of an audience and becomes more pragmatic. Heterodox economists also exonerate capitalism, with their proposals to regulate finance and supervise the banks. They attribute the crises exclusively to the lack of control over finance, and they suggest rectifying this ineffectiveness with regulations and penalties for speculative operations. They consider that these rules will allow the economy to get back on track if functional separations in financial activity can be reinstated with a certain priority for state banks. Other proposals include the dismantling of large banks and a limit to operations that would reduce the importance of institutional investors in the mechanisms of patrimonial capitalism.[33] At the peak of the crisis, these measures were discussed in presidential summits. There were discussions about reforming the IMF to reassert its supervisory role over international financial capital. There have also been discussions about introducing a Tobin tax in order to limit the upsets caused by the staggering mobility of circulating funds.[34] But with the relief that has followed the state rescue, these proposals have fallen out of favour with the upper echelons of power. Calls for regulation are still on the agenda, but nobody is interfering with the continued preeminence of financial liberalism. The prohibition of banking havens has taken a back seat, along with the promised elimination of bonuses for managers.

---

31   Panitch and Konings 2008 expect that it will be of limited scope, and Brenner 2009 believes it will bring about a major collapse.

32   A justification of this sort is offered by Sorman 2009.

33   Orlean 2010; Ghymers 2009; D'Arista 2009.

34   Krugman 2009a; 2009b; Stiglitz 2009; Lavagna 2009.

The institutional reform promoted by Obama is a light version of the original initiative, as is the version of the Tobin tax that Brown proposed in England. However, the mere intention to introduce certain restrictions on the banks' activities has invited a great deal of pressure from Wall Street, which continues to block a project to limit the size of institutions and make the risks involved in complex securities operations transparent. There are also proposals to introduce some protection for small bond-holders and grant power to shareholders in order to limit the premiums paid to managers.

But to date, there has been little willingness on the part of the US establishment to implement these changes. Some heterodox theorists question the government's powerlessness to respond to these pressures. They speak out against Wall Street's callousness and Washington's corruption, but they do not investigate the reasons that led to a replacement of the beloved post-war model with liberal deregulation. They especially ignore the role of competition between the banks themselves in the predominance of this course of action. This competition is characteristic of capitalism and consistently undermines government regulations. The very growth of business stimulates this deterioration as the pursuit of new sources of credit intensifies. Neither are the capitalist determinants of the bank hypertrophy acknowledged by the analysts that fetishise regulations and ignore the social foundation of these norms. As they assume that the state is a neutral institution at the service of society (and not of the dominant classes), they envision the regulations as an equitable umbrella that protects the community (without favouring the powerful).

In the generic praise for future financial regulations, it is never made clear who will benefit or be harmed by these rules. What is left out is that, if they benefit the bankers, they will not entail significant changes; and if they benefit other sectors (such as industrial sectors), they will unleash a competitive battle for the resulting restructuring of financial power. The Keynesians that are most amenable to using state power to tame the worst excesses of capitalism have resigned themselves to the regressive workings of capitalism. Not only do they legitimise the influence of the bankers, but they also accept the rampant growth of unemployment. This attitude positions them very far away from the 'euthanasia of the rentier' and very close to conservative viewpoints. Their support for state rescues of the banks is an example of this adaptation.

This outlook offers a contemporary version of the macro-economic strategies that both Keynesian and neo-classical economists adopted in the post-war period. These convergences reappeared later, with regulations adapted to free-market principles and anti-cyclical policies fashioned to suit neoliberal criteria.

Humane Capitalism?

Other heterodox currents disagree with this convergence and propose a progressive remodelling of capitalism by reducing inequality. They call for a reversion of the Anglo-Saxon model in favour of a social democratic framework that would replace financial neoliberalism with a relaunching of production. Some versions of this approach suggest immediately introducing measures to protect the groups most affected by the crisis (stopping evictions, increasing unemployment insurance, introducing a universal minimum income), along with social reforms (especially in health and education) that would allow the destroyed welfare state to be restored. Others propose rebuilding the spirit of labour and the mixed-economy strategy.[35] These perspectives do not hide their nostalgia for the framework that crashed in the 1970s. Rather, they call for its resuscitation without explaining the causes for its failure. They question at once both liberalism and collectivist management, emphasising that both experiments have failed. But they forget to add that the social democratic strategy was tested on a very large scale over most of the twentieth century. It is unclear why they do not include this framework as one of the great frustrations of the last century. Many of these currents share the hope of humanising capitalism. They believe that this system will lose its brutality as reforms sensitise the elites that rule the system.[36] But these kinds of calls never find an echo among top government officials. These leaders tend to adapt the system to the changing needs of the dominant classes. They push for limited social improvements in times of great popular discontent and revoke these reforms when resistance subsides. The same thing happens with financial regulations. Capitalism incorporates some controls that it then abandons when tensions dissipate.

What makes the development of a 'humane capitalism' impossible is the ongoing competition for profit. The pursuit of this unattainable objective leads to the squandering of the population's drive for transformation. A system based on the exploitation of people by people cannot be humanised, as it infringes upon the basic principle of coexistence between individuals. While competition prevents the creation of cooperative relationships, the lust for profit imposes a ruthless culture of social climbing, selfishness, and social Darwinism. These pillars of the system also explain the periodic recreation of regulated and liberal frameworks. When the principle of profitability is affected by the former, a traumatic move to the latter begins, and in opposite conditions, the reverse tendency holds sway.

---

35   Blackburn 2008; Boyer 2008; Hobsbawn 2009.
36   Ricupero 2009.

The compulsion of the rulers to attack workers constitutes an intrinsic feature of capitalism, and not a defect exclusive to the Anglo-Saxon model. The
conservative conduct displayed by the social democrats when they are in government is strong evidence of this dynamic. The only thing that can limit the
abuses of the rulers is social resistance by the oppressed and the development
of anti-capitalist political strategies. Many radical analysts who question the
superficial fixes to the same structure of domination challenge the conventional heterodox view. They point out the depth of the current crisis, emphasising its numerous impacts and objecting to the simple call for regulations. They
believe the 2008–10 crash has jeopardised the entire regime of accumulation
established by neoliberalism.[37] This approach correctly assesses the magnitude of the tremor, but it does not explain the connections that exist between
this framework and its capitalist pillars. The current upheaval is doubly powerful: it affects the structures of neoliberalism at the same time as it undermines
its capitalist foundations. It is an error to divorce these two facets, generically
alluding to the systemic nature of the crisis without specifying its capitalist
nature. When we emphasise the capitalist nature of the crisis, we also bring
up the necessity of a socialist option. Capitalism is not based on harmonious
relations between civil society and the state, which could be improved by per-
fecting one or the other. It is a regime based on the private ownership of the
means of production and the exploitation of waged labour, which can only be
eradicated with initiatives to build socialism.

Ecological Crisis and the Need for Anti-Capitalist Alternatives

If we refer to a range of terms and descriptions without mentioning how the
nature of the crisis is inherent to tendencies within the capitalist mode of
production, it becomes impossible to understand the significance of the crisis. When we emphasise the capitalist nature of the crisis, we also bring up
the necessity of a socialist option. Capitalism is a regime based on the private
ownership of the means of production and the exploitation of waged labour,
which can only be eradicated with initiatives to build socialism. Socialism is a
project that must be reconstructed from below, with experiences that open up
anti-capitalist horizons. The meaning of this objective has raised many questions since the collapse of so-called real socialism. This collapse created great
scepticism about the possibility of developing a society that can overcome the

---

37   Guillén 2009; Kregel 2009a; 2009b.

miseries of capitalism. But the reappearance of the crisis puts this option back onto the table.

Even the fanatic defenders of the current order recognise that today, capitalism has lost the attraction it had regained after the implosion of the USSR. I have explained elsewhere why this collapse sealed the failure of an experiment that was incompatible with a genuine socialist project. I have also indicated to what extent it is essential to reconstitute this objective upon new democratic and revolutionary pillars.[38] The challenge is to adapt socialism to take into account a new type of cataclysm that threatens contemporary society – the imminent threat of climate disaster – that transcends the usual imbalances of capitalism.

Climate Change: Failed Agreements and Green Capitalism

The dramatic impact of global warming is now recognised even by the sceptics, who for years played down the severity of the problem. Pollution has forced presidents, ministers, and business executives to discuss how to reduce the emission of greenhouse gases and how to replace fossil fuels.[39] The dominant classes address the issue in the face of worsening droughts, tsunamis, floods, hurricanes, and higher river levels. The very notion of climate change – which suggests a gradual transformation of the environment – does not convey the rapid destruction of biodiversity. In recent years, melting Arctic glaciers and higher water levels along the coast of Southeast Asia have brought about a sharp rise in environmental degradation. Many agree that after a certain point, these transformations will have irreversible effects.[40] Carbon dioxide emissions are 44 percent higher than the volume of gases the planet can reabsorb. This excess is creating an increasingly large ecological footprint. The quantity of resources needed to reproduce life and absorb waste doubled between 1961 and 2005. Currently, it is equivalent to 1.2 planets, and by 2030 it is estimated that two planets will be required to sustain current levels of consumption. Other calculations of this biocapacity to reproduce the conditions of life report even more alarming findings.[41] It is completely false to attribute

---

38   Katz 2004.

39   For an example of this shift from scepticism to concern, see Friedman 2009.

40   Tanuro 2009a; Bellamy Foster 2009b.

41   One measure in global hectares suggests a slide from 2.7 global hectares (gha) (13.2 billion gha for 6.3 billion inhabitants) in 1990 to 2.1 gha in 2009. This measure is used to measure the extent of the planet's destruction. Amin 2009; La Nación 2009.

this degradation to 'human irresponsibility', 'the neglect of nature', or 'scientific manipulations'. The environmental crisis is the consequence of a social system grounded in the desire for profit. For more than 200 years, competition for profit has led to the destruction of natural resources without affecting the continuity of accumulation. This reproduction is now threatened.

Capitalist development relies on an energy matrix based on the burning of non-renewable resources (first coal, then oil), which, along with deforestation and the emission of greenhouse gases, has led to global warming. The use of the natural environment as a mere input for accumulation has led to the gradual destruction of this environment. The very dynamics of valorisation lead to the violation of the limits of nature. Capitalism unfolds with all-consuming strength, promoting unlimited growth, while ignoring energy constraints and material limitations. This plunder has been very apparent in the use of oil. In just one century (1930–2030), most of the reserves of this fuel will have been squandered. This system of profitability also led to ruling out the development of solar energy, which would have protected nature. When coal and oil began to run out, nuclear energy became the preferred replacement, with potentially even more catastrophic effects.

Neoliberalism has breathed new life into capitalism by stimulating the over-production of commodities based on the increasing use of raw materials. The liberalisation of trade, the globalisation of transport, the implementation of just-in-time production, and increased urbanisation have intensified the excessive use of natural resources. This degradation has occurred in the race to boost productivity by reducing costs, increasing the speed of capital circulation and shortening product life-cycles.[42]

Capitalism treats nature like an externality, whose cost must be reduced without regard for the consequences. It absorbs growing quantities of all resources, ignoring their potential scarcity. But as it cannot function without material underpinnings, this destruction affects its own continuity.[43] The leading governments have been debating a way out of this ecological degradation for years. But all possible agreements have been blocked by the leading powers' invariable refusal to bear the cost of mitigating the disaster. They cannot agree on a goal for reducing global warming (avoiding temperature increases of 0.7 to two degrees Celsius above temperatures in 1850). At the current rate of emissions, even more dramatic scenarios are possible (four to six degrees) if a commitment to reduce the generation of harmful gases is not signed.

---

42   Chesnais 2008a; 2008b; Dierckxsens 2007.

43   Vega Cantor 2009; Antunes 2009.

The recessive impact of the global crisis is seen by many economists as an opportunity to begin this reduction, taking advantage of the drop in the level of activity. But nobody can find a way to reach an agreement among the advanced countries, which create 70 percent of the world's pollution and bear historical responsibility for the planet's environmental degradation. To rescue the banks, the leading powers agreed on swift bailouts, but they do not show the same urgency to save the planet. The meeting in Copenhagen ended worse than expected, with a total lack of objectives or timelines for reducing emissions. Nor was it agreed how an eventual agreement would be distributed, financed, or monitored. The only agreements were on mechanisms for information exchange. The big problem with this paralysis lies in the fact that remaining below two degrees of warming cannot be achieved without planning. It requires initiatives that no government is willing to put in place.[44]

The United States remains committed to transferring the disaster to the periphery, heightening climate injustice. The greatest impacts of the environmental disaster have for years been borne by the countries with the least responsibility in the matter. Large droughts and extensive pollution strike the countries that consume the least. But as was evident in the Katrina catastrophe, disasters can also hit the developed countries, and they especially affect the poor. The imperial policy of transferring a planetary problem to the periphery is unlikely to succeed. The United States blocks all global agreements for one simple reason: with just five percent of the global population, it uses 25 percent of the world's oil resources. It does not agree to bear its rightful share of cutbacks. It has thwarted UN conferences (1992) and refused to ratify the first agreement to limit emissions (Kyoto 1997). The Northern giant sometimes establishes alliances with Europe and Japan against the intermediate economies, and at other times, it experiments with the opposite tactic.

Obama seems determined to regain the ground lost by Bush to his rivals in the triad in the race to develop green technology. Since the United States will sooner or later have to implement some form of initiative, it is preparing to act as global arbiter. The way in which Obama is engaging in talks illustrates his degree of continuity with his predecessors. He stopped flirting with a range of ecological initiatives and, like his predecessors, supported the lobby of the 25 US coal-producing states. Unlike the European Union, the United States does not even limit emission increases. The environmental calamity has traditionally been ignored by orthodox economists, who are unable to understand these disturbances. Unlike scientists, who have followed the develop-

---

44   For an account of the meeting in Copenhagen, see Tanuro 2009b and Vivas 2009.

ment of the problem closely, they oscillate between denial and scepticism. They cannot perceive environmental degradation as they exclude nature from their approach to the economy. Neoclassical theorists consider that the environment functions as the basis for an unlimited circulation of commodity flows. Hence, they do not acknowledge the existence of a conflict between the valorisation of capital and its material basis. Instead of recognising the contradictions between these two dimensions, they imagine a spontaneous compatibility that would allow unrestricted growth. Orthodox economists assume that the market can resolve any ecological anomaly, and since their reasoning looks at the short term, they are unconcerned about future upsets. They also ignore environmental issues due to a basic moral insensitivity to the human tragedies of the periphery.[45]

Neoliberals deal with environmental degradation with the same vulgar optimism they have shown with respect to the financial crisis. They assume that both processes are transitory and will be spontaneously overcome with some balance between supply and demand. But if the cross between these two variables has not been sufficient to overcome the relapses in the economy, it is unclear how they might provide a remedy to the environmental catastrophe. Neoliberals deal with environmental degradation with the same vulgar optimism they have shown with respect to the financial crisis. They assume that both processes are transitory and will be spontaneously overcome with some balance between supply and demand. But if the cross between these two variables has not been sufficient to overcome the relapses in the economy, it is unclear how they might provide a remedy to the environmental catastrophe.

Most heterodox economists expect solutions to come from some technological achievement. Hopes are mainly riding on new uses of nuclear energy and genetically modified food. With Malthusian arguments, they attribute ecological degradation to population growth or to mistaken models of industrialisation.[46] A very popular version of this approach proposes reducing pollution by converting to electric automobiles, overlooking the exacerbation of the problem created by the very manufacturing of these vehicles.[47] The race in pursuit of green technologies, however, also acts as a source of pollution. Furthermore, this competition stimulates the multiplication of sorcerers' apprentices experimenting with risky innovations. This improvisation

---

45   Bellamy Foster 2009a.
46   Gray 2009.
47   Sachs 2009.

introduces additional threats to the terrible cost of maintaining the social system that has given rise to the environmental collapse.

Keynesians agree with their neoliberal adversaries in trying to find a way out of the ecological labyrinth by means of green capitalism. The main mechanism they envision is an emissions market that would penalise polluters and reward environmental protectors. The most ingenuous versions of this proposal assert that it would be free to implement. They assume that it will not require excessive investment nor reduce growth. The most cautious, however, contend that this success will depend on overcoming disagreements between the powers that prevent the implementation of environmental bonds.[48] It is clear that a credit market of this kind would lead to an increase in global polarisation. If every country exchanged commitments to environmental preservation in proportion to its financial strength, the developed economies would tend to ignore the problem, unloading it onto the periphery. This is the aim of triad capitalists, along with an intention to slow down the industrialisation of some dependent countries in order to convert them into a garbage dump for metropolitan factories.

The effective realisation of any project of environmental capitalism faces other, greater obstacles. It would require some global form of organising investment in order to penalise energy-consuming sectors in favour of conserving sectors, and it would need to reorient finances toward green technology credit. An international tax policy of eco-fees would also have to be introduced to encourage the transition toward some consumption norm that would replace current habits with a measure of green selectivity. The barriers to the implementation of such strategies are countless. The most obvious impediment is the lack of a global power able to impose such cooperative policies on rival companies in the leading powers. Nor is it simple to create the conditions of profitability necessary for the magnitude of investment required for such a shift. Capitalism has seen several large-scale mutations in the past, but for the moment, the conditions for such a shift are nowhere in sight.[49]

Environmental Collapse and the Crisis of Civilisation

The environmental collapse is of a greater scale than the conjunctural tremors (typical of accumulation) and the structural crises (specific to each stage of capitalism). This is why it is not equivalent to the financial crash of 2008–10,

---

48   Krugman 2009d holds the former position, and Stiglitz 2010 and Giddens 2009, the latter.
49   Husson 2009b.

or to the imbalances created by neoliberalism over the last two decades. The historic scope of the environmental disaster is measured by its impact on the future of human society. If global warming continues to expand the ecological footprint, it could unleash a disaster that would leave all known upheavals in its wake. The devastation of nature does not only create further social deterioration; it introduces a form of erosion that could destroy the pillars of collective life.

All processes of valorisation are intrinsically destructive of the environment and affect the material foundations of economic reproduction. The compulsion to compete always infringes upon the limits of the environment, but it has never threatened the pattern of growth in effect over the last two centuries to such an extent. The foundations of this framework have become severely weakened. The magnitude of the environmental upheaval has made it common to identify it with a crisis of an era or a crisis of civilisation. Both terms allude to two elements of the problem: its magnitude and its multiplicity. When the potential consequences of the disaster are highlighted, the former predominates, and when the convergence of the climate crisis and the financial upheaval (or the food tragedy) stands out, the latter prevails. Different characterisations of the civilisational crisis tend to emphasise one aspect or another. But they all highlight the threat that affects the very survival of the human species. In this sense, the environmental disaster shares similarities with the possibility of human destruction that emerged with the appearance of nuclear arms.

The ecological disaster is civilisational because it involves secular contradictions. Moreover, it shows destructive tendencies that elude the control of those who benefit from the current regime. The capitalists themselves cannot manage the effects created by the primacy of profits over any other social parameter. This 'zombie' behaviour illustrates how the monstrosities of the system overwhelm its own creators. The continuity of capitalism may result in an irreversible disaster.[50] Historical crises have always implied the enormous destruction of resources. Capitalism was born destroying the surrounding civilisations and has never been able to avoid great cataclysms. It developed over the seventeenth and eighteenth centuries with the plunder of primitive accumulation and the expropriation of the peasants. It brought a terrible level of devastation to native peoples, who suffered from the conquerors' appetite for muscles, blood, and gold. The largest massacre of the population in history took place during this period. During the colonial era, the system spread with the crime of slavery, which brought about the regression of the African

---

50   Harman 2009b; Klein 2009.

continent and blocked the endogenous development of all regions subordinated to the metropoles. Ultimately, capitalism matured over the last century with the tragedy of two world wars, causing the death of millions of individuals in the greatest organised massacre ever suffered by humans.

The environmental disaster can be inscribed in this series of major collapses, which have accompanied every period of capitalism. Nobody knows the magnitude of the current danger, just as the different tragedies of the past could not be foreseen either. But taking these precedents into account, warnings about a possible environmental catastrophe are not exaggerations.[51]

This historico-ecological crisis is interwoven with the conjunctural financial crash and with the structural tensions of neoliberalism, but it develops at its own pace. It processes imbalances that are not subject to the periodicity of either short cycles or long fluctuations. Only in their culmination might ecological tensions have direct connections with the immediate imbalances in accumulation or the tensions of the conjuncture. But some links are already taking shape as a result of two effects of neoliberal globalisation: the over-production of commodities and the under-production of the supplies necessary to sustain the new scale of global productivity. The shortage of supplies is becoming apparent in numerous sectors, reflecting the cumulative destruction of the environment. But some links are already taking shape as a result of two effects of neoliberal globalisation: the over-production of commodities and the under-production of the supplies necessary to sustain the new scale of global productivity. The shortage of supplies is becoming apparent, reflecting the cumulative destruction of the environment. The scale of this problem is unknown for now, but the exhaustion of natural resources brought about by excess production is already indicative of the severity of the current imbalance. This combination of excess production and scarce resources introduces a splintering of unpredictable consequences for the dynamics of accumulation. The classic imbalances of realisation and valorisation begin to act upon a seriously damaged natural platform.

But these intersections between the conjunctural, structural, and historical crises do not dilute the different dynamics of these imbalances and their processing at different rates. The convulsion of capitalism is multiple, and its diverse aspects have not merged. It is true that the financial crash reflects a failure of capital, interwoven with signs of environmental disaster. However, this process unfolds as a tendency that has not yet translated into a temporal convergence of the three upheavals. Will the 2008–10 financial tremors mark the beginning of this convergence?

---

51   Chesnais, no date.

For now, it is only a hypothesis. The environmental catastrophe continues to stalk capitalism like a brewing threat. It runs parallel to the conjunctural crises of finance, production, and trade, which have not detonated the structural imbalances of neoliberalism. Contemporary capitalism is affected by a varied succession of upheavals that unfold without fusing into one convergent crisis.[52] The tendency toward this convergence is an explosive ingredient in all the crises of recent decades, but it has not occurred as capitalism finds ways to periodically recreate itself following large upsets. A fusion of these critical points could occur, for example, if the current recession lasts, not only preventing a range of different resolutions to the financial collapse, but also leading to the burial of neoliberalism. An even larger-scale convergence could occur if a large environmental disaster – like the melting of the Arctic ice caps – has a major impact on the pace of economic activity. A fusion of these critical points could occur, for example, if the current recession lasts, not only preventing a range of different resolutions to the financial collapse, but also leading to the burial of neoliberalism. An even larger-scale convergence could occur if a large environmental disaster – like the melting of the Arctic ice caps – has a major impact on the pace of economic activity.

Conclusion

Resolving the environmental problem with different versions of green capitalism is the only future envisioned by neoliberals, Keynesians, and many currents of ecological activism. These latter currents hope to raise awareness among capitalists in order to compel them to protect the environment in their own best interest. They assume that large business owners and bankers will eventually understand that respect for nature is crucial to the continuity of their companies. With this hope, many environmental NGOs sugar-coat green business, without challenging the incompatibility of environmental protection and the supremacy of profits.

This position prevents them from engaging in meaningful struggle to defend nature, as pleading with capital leads to self-deception. The owners of the world do not need advice from their victims about how to manage their rule. It is useless to request them to be more reasonable, and to be aware of their long-term interests. The plunder of nature does not come from ignorance. It simply obeys the objective destruction imposed by a system driven by

---

52 The temporal dissonance between the different contradictions that are damaging capitalism was conceptualised by Bensaïd 1995.

competition for the benefits of exploitation. Instead of heeding requests from ecological reformism, the dominant classes face the problem with the same criteria with which they face any other obstacle stemming from accumulation. They seek to transfer the bill to the workers and demand sacrifices from the rest of society, as if they themselves had no responsibility for the disaster. The principal message from the orthodox economists in the face of the environmental disaster is a general call for adjustment measures in order to fund, with greater unemployment (and perhaps less production), a conversion to green technology. They demand compliance so that employers will come up with the investments necessary for this shift. But these measures imply that profits will remain unaffected and that the solutions will come from using the same recipes that stimulated pollution.

Other defenders of the current order propose inducing economic degrowth and the absolute contraction of consumption in order to stop the destruction of nature. But they overlook the existence of progressive alternatives. It is perfectly feasible to develop models of selective growth, which prioritise the creation of social goods to the detriment of non-essential commodities. Moreover, this process would enable the gradual replacement of non-renewable fuels with solar energy. This shift could even begin by reducing the manufacturing of products that harm the environment and decreasing private-sector consumerism. The clearest example of this shift would be a progressive replacement of individual automobiles with collective means of transportation.

The most interesting proposals are put forward by eco-socialist theorists. They have shown that there is no need to reduce the standard of living of the population if the meaning of goods is redefined, differentiating essential from non-essential products and creating information systems that replace advertising. These initiatives are part of a vision of greater social control over resources and of popular selection of production and consumption alternatives, along with the establishment of democratic forms of global planning. These ideas envision a socialist realm of responses to the environmental disaster.[53] This approach is also in opposition to neo-developmentalist proposals, which downplay the gravity of environmental issues in intermediate economies, presenting them as a problem for the core countries. Those that espouse such proposals reject all limitations on extractive mining, farming with pesticides, or polluting industrialisation. They try to turn a blind eye to the calamities these activities create in the poorest segments of the population. Several critical authors have also pointed to the need for a radical change in the prevailing ideology if we are to replace anthropocentric utilitarianism with a bio-centric

---

53   Lowy 2009.

vision that recognises the rights of nature. They base their vision on the concept of 'good living' developed by the continent's native peoples.[54]

But it is important to situate these proposals in the context of the historical crisis of capitalism, as any dissociation from this pillar prevents our understanding of the origin of current dangers and their eventual solutions. This is why the anti-capitalist consciousness beginning to gain influence in environmentalist mobilisations is critical. At the Copenhagen summit, more than 100,000 people mobilised to demand the adoption of measures that would defend nature. Many young people from all over the world participated in the marches, which included direct challenges to the bailout for financiers. 'If the climate were a bank, it would have already been rescued', chanted the demonstrators.[55]

This anti-capitalist tone is the most promising element of the current battle. Ideas like this were at the forefront of the 2010 summit in Cochabamba (Bolivia), which brought together a significant number of activists from 42 countries. It was resolved to demand a drastic reduction in emissions (50 percent between 2013 and 2020), to create an International Climate Justice Tribunal, to implement a global referendum in defence of nature, and to demand transfers from developed countries to the periphery to pay off the climate debt. The eco-socialist perspective is starting to be embodied in popular movements and political proposals.

---

54   Acosta 2010.
55   Castedo and García 2010.

CHAPTER 13

Revolution against 'Progress': Neo-Extractivism, the Compensatory State, and the TIPNIS Conflict in Bolivia

Jeffery R. Webber

> Marx says that revolutions are the locomotive of world history. But perhaps it is quite otherwise. Perhaps revolutions are an attempt by the passengers on this train – namely, the human race – to activate the emergency brake.
>
> WALTER BENJAMIN[1]

In the two and a half months that passed between mid-August and late-October of 2011, the Bolivian government of Evo Morales entered into its worst crisis to date. From a high of 70 percent popularity in January 2010, Morales had plunged by mid-October 2011 to an average 35 percent approval rating across the major cities of La Paz, El Alto, Cochabamba, and Santa Cruz.[2] The President's green light to a decades old project to build a highway connecting Villa Tunari (in the department of Cochabamba), north to San Ignacio de Moxos (in the department of Beni), through the indigenous territory and national park known as TIPNIS (Territorio Indígena del Parque Nacional Isiboro-Sécure), was the catalyst of crisis in this instance. Beginning on 15 August, lowland indigenous movements – in alliance with fractions of the highland indigenous movement, and later with the support of the urban labour movement – launched a 600-km, 65-day march of protest from Beni to La Paz to prevent the construction of the highway. The march, after having been denounced by state managers as an imperialist conspiracy, and violently repressed en route by police forces on 25 September, eventually forced the Morales government to capitulate to its demands, at least temporarily. There would be no road through TIPNIS. The bureaucratic leader of the principal highland indigenous peasant confederation (CSUTCB), Roberto Coraite, a prototypical steward of MAS interests embedded in a popular organisation, embarrassed the government by calling the lowland indigenous protesters 'savages'.[3] But the political fallout would

---

1 Quoted in Löwy 2005, pp. 66–7.
2 *Página Siete* 2011j.
3 *Página Siete* 2011a.

run deeper still. The Minister of Defence, Cecilia Chacón, resigned in disgust at the police repression of unarmed protesters on 25 September. The highest echelons of the regime, Evo Morales and Vice-President Álvaro García Linera, sought to distance themselves from the police raid once it proved unpopular, allowing Chief of Staff and Minister of the Interior Sacha Llorenti to take the hit for the team.[4,5] A masista peasant leader outed as an adherent of old-school modernisation theory. Two high profile ministers gone. A president and vice-president scrambling in the dark for convenient scapegoats. Encapsulating the tenor of the times, the so-called Pact of Unity, an eclectic coalition of various urban and rural social movements and trade unions that had lent support to the MAS at different junctures since 2004, has imploded. It was reduced from 11 pillar organisations to merely three at its last national assembly in November 2011, as a consequence of key lowland indigenous groups and urban labour confederations leaving en masse after having been denounced as traitors and forces of the opposition by government officials.[6] The TIPNIS conflict is the most recent, and in some ways most intense, expression of the class contradictions – or 'creative tensions' as government functionaries prefer[7] – underlying the development model of reconstituted neoliberalism introduced by the Morales government after its assumption of power in January 2006.[8] How did we get here?

Revolutionary Moments and Bureaucratic Stagnation

Evo Morales was elected as Bolivia's first indigenous president in December 2005 on the heels of a revolutionary epoch. Left-indigenous insurrection shook the city streets and countryside over the first five years of this century. Two neoliberal presidents were overthrown through mass extra-parliamentary mobilisation in under two years – Gonzalo Sánchez de Lozada in 2003 and Carlos Mesa in 2005. A counter-power from below emerged in opposition to the capitalist state, in which the popular classes 'practiced that democracy that we have always wanted: direct, participatory, without intermediaries, in

---

4 *Página Siete* 2011a.

5 Stefanoni 2011.

6 *Pagina Siete* 2011i; 2011k.

7 García Linera 2011b.

8 I defend the idea that the Morales administration represents a project of reconstituted neo-liberalism at some length in Webber 2011b. I develop this thesis further at a later point in the present essay.

assemblies and councils, in the plazas, the streets, the unions, the communities, the families, and the territories, deliberating, deciding, and executing what we had decided'.[9] The cycle of left-indigenous revolt was a combined liberation struggle for emancipation from the endemic and systematised racial oppression of the indigenous majority as well as their intricately intertwined class exploitation and subordination to imperialism through the racialised form that capitalism assumed in the Bolivian context.[10]

American imperialism had been militarily overextended in Iraq and Afghanistan at the time. It had also been financially weakened through the debilitation of the International Monetary Fund and World Bank on the entirety of the world stage, but particularly in Latin America, where there emerged simultaneously alternative lines of credit through oil-rich Venezuela, under the presidency of Hugo Chávez. Neoliberalism had been devastated ideologically in South America in the wake of the steep recession of 1998–2002. Heads of state had been overthrown through revolts in Ecuador and Argentina. Centre-left governments in neighbouring states were asserting relative autonomy from the US Empire, even as they encountered frequent challenges domestically through class struggle from below, and to their left. The monotonous routine of neoliberal impositions over the preceding two decades was now in question. Discussion of anti-capitalism on the road blockades, in communal assemblies, in poor neighbourhoods, and in union halls was now imbued with an intensity that accompanies the sense of real possibility.

The Bolivian right had retreated to its parochial geographical heartland, namely the departments of Santa Cruz and Tarija, and could offer no alternative political platform to the entirely discredited neoliberal orthodoxy first introduced in 1985. Moreover, they had lost their links in the military. The social bases for the reproduction of their doctrine of free markets had eroded beneath their feet, tested as that ethos had been against the fire of Bolivian reality. The figurative rising tide that would lift all boats failed to materialise. Instead, orthodox economics meant poverty, inequality, unemployment, and dispossession. What is more, had there been a genuine possibility of a military coup in the face of left-indigenous encroachments on the reigning power structures, this would have occurred during the crisis of June 2005, when Mesa was clearly on his way out and key figures of the far-right in Congress wanted to assume power directly and avoid elections at any cost. The right was evidently unable to garner sufficient support within the military to carry out their plans.

---

9   Colectivo Manifiesto 2011, p. 286.

10   See Webber 2011c.

As Álvaro García Linera – current Vice-President of Bolivia, and erstwhile revolutionary Marxist – has explained, the 2000–5 period represented a genuine revolutionary epoch in Bolivia.[11] The late French Marxist Daniel Bensaïd summed up in a singular phrase the theorisation of such a historical moment in the works of Lenin and Trotsky: 'It is defined by an interaction between several variable elements in a situation: when those above can no longer govern as they did before; when those below will not tolerate being oppressed as they were before; and when this double impossibility is expressed by a sudden effervescence of the masses'.[12] Despite its impressive capacity to mobilise and its far-reaching anti-capitalist and indigenous-liberationist objectives, however, the left-indigenous bloc lacked a revolutionary party that might have provided the leadership, strategy, and ideological coherence necessary to overthrow the existing capitalist state and rebuild a new sovereign power rooted in the self-governance of the overwhelmingly indigenous proletarian and peasant majority. As a consequence, the fallout of the extraordinary mobilisations and profound crisis of the state witnessed during the gas war was not a revolutionary transformation but a shift in popular politics from the streets and countryside to the electoral arena, as elections were moved up to 18 December 2005.

Electoral Sclerosis and Missed Opportunities

'When Morales entered office', Forrest Hylton, one of the preeminent historians of modern Bolivia, has suggested, 'the lowland right in Santa Cruz, Beni, Pando, and Tarija was weak, divided, and disorganised. Had Morales pressed his political weight to full advantage by mobilising the movements that brought him to power, he might have had the field to himself, much as Chávez has [in Venezuela]'.[13] The approach actually adopted by the Morales government, however, was to limit any substantive confrontation with the economic power of the eastern lowland bourgeoisie, thus providing the oxygen for the right's slow political rearticulation, and eventually its capacity to destabilise the Morales regime through extra-parliamentary street violence and racist thuggery. Over time, the right obstructed the functioning of the Constituent Assembly (2006–8), orchestrated a massacre of indigenous peasants (September 2008), and

---

11   García Linera 2006.
12   Bensaïd 2002.
13   Hylton 2011, p. 245.

launched an unsuccessful coup attempt (October 2008). It is notable, however, that none of this destabilisation occurred on any significant scale until
two years into the Morales administration. As Hylton points out, 'between
the time the Assembly was designed and concluded, the government showed
its reluctance to rely on direct action from below and its willingness to make
backroom concessions, to the right. As the massacre in Pando – the circumstances of which remain murky – demonstrated, in September 2008, such
caution did not restrain the racist violence of the right, or prevent bloodshed,
although the rightwing rampage may well have hastened the failed coup plot of
October 2008, and the popular ratification of the new Constitution in January
2009'.[14] Indeed, for Hylton, the Morales regime ultimately 'gave the right an
opening through which it reconstituted itself as the arbiter of the limits of
social change'.[15] Even as the Morales administration gifted the extreme right
with an enviable opportunity for ascent, the latter managed to self-destruct
soon after its rebirth. The massacre of peasants loyal to the government –
carried out by right-wing paramilitaries in the department of Pando in
September 2008 – morally repulsed most of Bolivian society, and the extreme
articulations of the autonomist right wing of the lowland departments – Beni,
Pando, Santa Cruz, and Tarija – suffered massively as a result.

Even as the new right was reduced to playing a pathetic younger brother to
its orthodox older sibling of the 1980s and 1990s, it nonetheless managed to
sap the energies of the social left in 2008 and 2009. Despite numerous sectoral
disputes with the government across many different economic sectors, the
popular classes in 2008 and 2009 had been consumed by the battle against the
proto-fascist forces of the right, and thus no independent political organisation to the left of Morales had even begun to take shape. It was precisely in
this vacuum that Morales faced re-election. On 6 December 2009, Evo Morales
won a decisive mandate for a second term in office with an astonishing 64 percent of the popular vote.[16] The turnout was close to 90 percent.[17] This latest
electoral victory marked the peak of a wave of successes in the polls, including
67 percent support for his administration in the recall referendum of 2008,

---

14   Ibid.
15   Ibid.
16   This article draws from sections of my book: see Webber 2011b. The sources for data on
      economic and social trends touched on in this article are cited more comprehensively in
      the book, and their significance is explained at much greater length.
17   *The Economist* 2009.

and 61 percent approval of the new constitution in a popular referendum held on 25 January 2009.[18]

The December 2009 elections represented the most profound level of institutional consolidation in the apparatuses of the state for any political force in recent Bolivian memory. Morales is the first president in Bolivia to be re-elected in successive terms, and the first to win with a larger percentage of votes when elected for a second term.[19] For the first time since the 1952 National Revolution, a party won a massive majority, and control of both houses of the legislature, providing the Movement Towards Socialism (MAS) with the power, among other things, to reconfigure the reactionary judiciary. The MAS controls 25 of 36 Senate seats, and 82 of 130 seats in the House of Deputies.[20]

Morales also made important gains in the departments of the *media luna*, the heartland of the country's autonomist right wing. In Tarija, Morales actually won a majority of votes, and in Beni, Pando, and Santa Cruz, he increased his support substantially. Most importantly in this regard, he won 41 percent of the popular vote in the department of Santa Cruz, the principal axis of the eastern bourgeois bloc.[21] In the departmental elections for governors, mayors, and departmental assemblies held on 4 April 2010, moreover, the tide continued to turn in favour of the MAS. Of the nine governorships, the MAS won six (Chuquisaca, La Paz, Cochabamba, Oruro, Potosí, and Pando) and lost three to right-wing oppositions (Tarija, Santa Cruz, and Beni). This represented a significant shift from merely three MAS governorships (Chuquisaca, Potosí, and Oruro) in the 2005 departmental elections. What is more, the race was tight in Tarija and Beni, and reasonably close in Santa Cruz. The winning opposition won 49, 53, and 43 percent to the MAS's 44, 38, and 40 percent, in Tarija, Santa Cruz, and Beni respectively.[22] In the wake of this decisive victory, Morales embraced a fevered rhetoric of 'communitarian socialism' at home, coupled with denunciations of capitalism as the principal enemy of nature abroad. It is unsurprising on one level, then, that confusion as to what Morales represents continues to run the gamut of the political spectrum.

---

18   See Stefanoni 2010; and, on the recall and constitutional referendums, see Rossell 2009.

19   Borón 2009.

20   Rojas 2009.

21   Stefanoni 2010. For a discussion of the origins and trajectory of the eastern bourgeois bloc, see Webber 2010a.

22   For the election results, see Corte Nacional Electoral 2010. For the April 2010 departmental elections, the position historically known as 'prefect' was changed to 'governor'.

Murky Waters

'Bolivia's indigenous-cum-socialist revolution in the high Andes has made the country a close ally of Venezuela's Hugo Chávez, and a natural friend of poncho-wearing well-wishers in the west', writes John Paul Rathbone in the *Financial Times*. 'At the same time, its almost Thatcherite approach to public finances, combined with soaring prices for its gas and mineral exports, has won it praise from the International Monetary Fund'.[23] Leaning heavily on the first sentiment, while tirelessly ignoring the second reality, the most militant – not to say theocratic – supporters of Morales on the international left, have cleaved themselves to even the most romantic self-images of the government in La Paz.

'Bolivia's economy [sic] policy has been "nationalised" and is no longer dictated by the IMF or Washington', Australian socialist Frederico Fuentes argues. Furthermore, the Morales government has taken important 'steps towards decolonising the state', and there is 'little doubt that the Bolivian masses are in a far superior position to where they were five or ten years ago'.[24] For Fuentes, the Morales government represents 'the broad aspirations of Bolivia's indigenous majority', and the official refrain issued from the Presidential Palace in La Paz – that this is a 'government of social movements' – is to be taken literally – 'important advances have been made by the social movements precisely because they decided to move from resistance to power'.[25] The popular classes are in the driver's seat. But a steely, realistic tone is then assumed. Fuentes acknowledges that there is 'still a long struggle ahead'. In one memorable passage he both falsely attributes to me the notion that socialism can be achieved in one miraculous moment, and then plants the equally fantastical idea, if only in implicit form here, that even if Bolivia is not yet socialist, it is on the long road in that direction: 'Yet one feels that none of this will be enough for Webber who would prefer they abandon their route [to socialism?] in favour of an imaginary one in which socialism is installed overnight'.[26] More surprising is that these views find an echo in recent interventions made by Canadian socialist intellectual and activist, John Riddell.[27] Riddell recog-

---

23   Rathbone 2010.
24   Fuentes 2011c.
25   Fuentes 2011b. See also my extensive response: Webber 2011a.
26   Ibid. Fuentes 2011c.
27   In addition to the earlier translation and editing of seven volumes of documents of the Communist movement in the era of the Russian Revolution, Riddell has just completed the mammoth translation and editorial introduction of *United Front: Proceedings of the Fourth Congress of the Communist International.* See Riddell 2012. His writings on Bolivia,

nises that 'Bolivia remains capitalist, and that a socialist transformation is not underway',[28] but insists that the country never entered into a revolutionary situation and that there were no prospects for a transition to socialism in 2000–5, nor are there any today, or presumably in the foreseeable future. Imperialism and the domestic right amount to virtually insurmountable obstacles.

Thus, against a very low bar of expectations, we can celebrate 'the real achievements, the gains [the government] has made against formidable odds', and prioritise 'support of Bolivia's positive moves towards national sovereignty, social progress, and effective action on global warming'. Symptomatically, for Riddell, as for Fuentes, social movements are embodied in, and expressed through, the government of the MAS – 'despite all strains, the tie between social movements in Bolivia and the Morales government has not been broken'. Pointing to what he understands to be my misreading of the political-economic terrain in this regard, Riddell writes, 'Webber's counterposition of the masses and the MAS leadership fails to acknowledge their close relationship'.[29] Elsewhere, in a less-considered formulation, Riddell goes so far as to claim – albeit with a host of important caveats – that '[t]he government of Bolivia headed by President Evo Morales can indeed be viewed as a "workers'" government' of the type discussed by the German revolutionary Clara Zetkin and the Communist International (Comintern) in the early 1920s'.[30] 'In Western radical and intellectual circles', the anthropologist Roger N. Lancaster has observed, 'a distinct moral cycle has revolved around every Third World revolution: unrealistic, romantic, and Rousseauian images dominate the first stages of that cycle; antagonism, despair, and feelings of betrayal dominate the later ones'.[31] In the readings of Bolivia offered by Fuentes and Riddell we witness an immaculate inversion; fatalistic despair is embraced in the face of the impossibility of revolutionary transformation in the 2000 to 2005 period, followed by a Rousseauian optimism for the prospects of ever-deepening change under the leadership of Evo Morales.

---

however, do not reveal a similar commitment to careful scholarship or precision, relying narrowly as they do on selective readings from the oeuvre of Frederico Fuentes, the Vice-President Álvaro García Linera, and the authorised biographer of Evo Morales, Martín Sivak. Riddell nonetheless also engages in a comradely and thoughtful critique of some of my recent articles and writings. My book, *From Rebellion to Reform in Bolivia*, appears in the references, but the content of Ridell's critique does not suggest a close reading of that text. See Riddell 2011a.

28   Riddell 2011a.
29   Riddell 2011b.
30   Riddell 2011a.
31   Lancaster 1988.

An appraisal of the TIPNIS conflict and the wider dynamics of racialised class struggle under reconstituted neoliberalism in Bolivia should, I want to argue, undermine the basis of such views. If I am correct, it does not make sense to speak of the consistent clashes between popular classes and the state as 'errors' committed by the Morales administrations, but rather as systematic expressions of the necessary class commitments daily reproduced in the administration of the capitalist state during a phase of reconstituted neoliberalism.

TIPNIS in Context

Much of the debate around TIPNIS has been curiously ahistorical. One example of this problem is straightforwardly evident in the frequent claims that the lowland indigenous resistance march of 2011 – however legitimate some of its concerns – was largely conducted in the interests of the 'green imperialism' of Western environmental NGOs, and a destabilisation campaign against Morales, run by elements of the domestic right, and funded and directed by USAID.[32] Unless we attribute divine foresight to US imperialists, the logic of such accounts is difficult to marry with the historical facts of mobilisations of lowland indigenous peoples that long predated the emergence of the MAS and Evo Morales, of course, and thus we are asked to forget they ever existed.

Most importantly, we are to disregard the recent precedent of 700 men and women, from largely the same indigenous groups involved in the 2011 conflict, marching 400 miles from Trinidad to La Paz in 1990. The 'march for territory and dignity', as it was called, gained massive popular support and, against the wishes of the neoliberal government of Jaime Paz Zamora, won

---

32   These are roughly the unsubstantiated assertions made – with different emphases in different moments – by the Morales government and sympathetic journalists and analysts over the course of the conflict. In English, one example of this genre is Fuentes 2011a. There is no doubt that American imperialism has played a critical role in Bolivian dynamics for much of the twentieth century, and into the twenty-first. I discuss the topic at length in *From Rebellion to Reform in Bolivia* as well as a host of other articles. Nonetheless, the arguments for a decisive role by American imperialism in this conflict have relied mainly on conjecture, and the recycling of assertions made by government officials to undermine the indigenous march. It is at least curious to note – given the government's claims of an active conspiracy behind the march – that very shortly after the seeming resolution of the TIPNIS conflict, the Morales administration normalised relations with the United States after three years of dispute. See *Pagina Siete* 2011m.

legal recognition for TIPNIS as an indigenous territory.[33] Another victory of the 1990 march was the establishment of a 'red line', after which point further settlement by commercial farmers, loggers, and rich peasants seeking to accumulate more land for production would be prohibited, so as to maintain the capacity of predominantly non-capitalist indigenous communities inhabiting the area to reproduce their cultural, economic, environmental, and spiritual ways of life. Just as importantly, evocations of categories such as 'indigenous', 'the masses', 'the people', and 'the peasantry' are employed with abundance on all sides, with precious little empirical attention paid to the class interests associated directly or indirectly with 'development' in the TIPNIS. It makes sense to begin our discussion, therefore, by positioning the debate within the context of transformations in Bolivia's rural class structure in recent decades.[34]

Rural Class Structure

At the outset of the twenty-first century the rural class structure in Bolivia is characterised by a dramatic concentration of land in the hands of a few, on the one hand, and a sea of poor – often landless – peasants on the other. *Haciendas* (large-landholdings) dominate 90 percent of Bolivia's productive land, leaving only 10 percent divided between mostly indigenous peasant communities and smallholding peasants.[35] Roughly 400 individuals own 70 percent of productive land while there are 2.5 million landless peasants in a country with a total population of nine million.[36] Most of the peasants are indigenous, with 77 percent of rural inhabitants self-identifying as such in the 2001 census.[37] Bolivia's rural structure prior to the 1952 National Revolution was dominated by large landholdings in which 'neo-feudal' social relations predominated, 'based on established modes of colonial extraction and exploitation in the countryside'.[38] Pre-revolutionary Bolivia had the highest inequality of land concentration in all of Latin America, with 82 percent of land in the possession of four percent

---

33   Albó 1996. Ironically, one of the best – sympathetic, even celebratory – accounts of the march can be found in a book co-authored by Vice-President Álvaro García Linera. See García Linera et al. 2006.

34   My discussion here draws upon Webber 2011b, pp. 26–30.

35   Chávez and García Linera 2005, p. 65.

36   Enzinna 2007, p. 217.

37   Romero Bonifaz 2005, p. 40.

38   Hylton and Thomson 2007, p. 59.

of landowners.[39] As the nationalist-populist revolutionary process of 1952 unfolded, mass direct-action tactics and independent land occupations orchestrated by radicalised peasants in Cochabamba, La Paz, and Oruro, and to a lesser extent in northern Potosí and Chuquisaca, challenged this rural class structure profoundly.[40] The new revolutionary government of the MNR was forced to enact the Agrarian Reform Law of 1953 in response to the pressure from below. Forced labour was made illegal and *haciendas* in the *altiplano* (La Paz, Oruro, Potosí) and the valleys (Cochabamba, Chuquisaca, Tarija) were divided and the land redistributed, creating a new smallholding peasantry in large sections of these departments. The MNR, though, was never a socialist party. Its interests coincided with the radical peasants only insofar as the MNR saw the breakup of semi-feudal agrarian modes of production as a prerequisite for establishing and developing a dynamic capitalist agricultural sector with ample state support. The geographic fulcrum for capitalist agriculture in Bolivia became the eastern department of Santa Cruz, beginning shortly after the revolution. Santa Cruz was relatively uninhabited at the time of the revolution and was largely unaffected by the agrarian reform. Over the next several decades it became the most dynamic centre of capitalist agriculture in the country, producing cotton, coffee, sugar, and timber for export; the department also spearheaded the reconcentration of land in the hands of a few that eventually spread again throughout much of the rest of the country, reversing, through complex legal and market mechanisms, many of the reforms achieved in the National Revolution. With the onset of neoliberalism in the mid-1980s, the agro-industrial dominance of Santa Cruz was solidified. Bolivian neoliberalism emphasised the orientation of agriculture toward exports for external markets. Transnational corporations and large domestic agricultural enterprises based in Santa Cruz led this intensified insertion into the global economy. The traditional peasant economy was increasingly displaced in various parts of the country as large agro-industrial enterprises solidified control and focused increasingly on a few select commodities, soy in particular. In 1986, 77 percent of the total land area under cultivation was devoted to the production of cereals, fruit, vegetables, and tubers in which small-peasant production predominated. By 2004, this area had been reduced to 48.2 percent. By one estimate, in 1963 peasant production represented 82.2 percent of the total value of agricultural production in the country, whereas by 2002 peasant production

---

39   Eckstein 1983, p. 108.
40   Dunkerley 1984, p. 67.

accounted for only 39.7 percent of total production, and agro-industrial capitalist production accounted for 60.3 percent of the total.[41]

Of the approximately 446,000 peasant production units remaining in the country today, 225,000 are located in the *altiplano* departments of La Paz, Oruro, and Potosí, 164,000 in the valley departments of Cochabamba, Chuquisaca, and Tarija, and only 57,000 in the eastern lowland departments of Santa Cruz, Beni, and Pando. Capitalist relations of production now predominate in the eastern lowlands and are increasingly displacing small-scale peasant production in the valleys and *altiplano*, although the latter continues to be the most important form of production in the *altiplano*.[42] Of the 2,118,988 hectares of land cultivated in Bolivia in 2004, 59 percent were in the eastern lowland departments. These departments were home to 96 percent of industrial crop production (cotton, sugarcane, sunflowers, peanuts, and soy), 42 percent of production of vegetables (beans and tomatoes), and 27 percent of fruit production (mainly bananas and oranges). These eastern departments furthermore accounted for 73.3 percent of national cattle ranching, 36.3 percent of pig farming, and 37.8 percent of poultry production. Finally, 60.1 percent of the timber extracted from Bolivian forests came from Santa Cruz, Beni, and Pando.[43] Large agro-industrial capitalists dominate in this part of the country. In the valley departments, small and medium capitalist enterprises account for most of the agricultural sector. These departments play a significant role in ranching. They account for 60.3 percent of poultry production, 48 percent of pig farming, and 18.5 percent of Bolivian cattle ranching. The rural *altiplano*, on the other hand, is still dominated by small peasant producers and indigenous communities. This region accounts for only 19 percent of total cultivated land in Bolivia, and its contribution to national ranching is limited to the sheep and llama sectors.[44] The rural population is diminishing throughout the country as processes of semi-proletarianisation and proletarianisation accelerate with the gradual extension of capitalist relations of production into all corners of the country. Beginning in the early 1970s, migrant semi-proletarians provided the workforce for sugarcane and cotton harvests while for the rest of the year they maintained small plots of their own land in the departments from which they primarily traveled – Cochabamba, Potosí, and Chuquisaca. Between 1976 and 1996, the rural population as a proportion of the total population fell

---

41   Ormachea Saavedra 2007, pp. 29–32.

42   Ibid., p. 33.

43   Ibid., pp. 33–4.

44   Ibid., p. 34.

from 59 percent to 39 percent.[45] This exodus has to do with two interrelated developments in the agricultural sector. On the one side, peasant production has been living through a prolonged crisis. Peasant families are increasingly unable to reproduce themselves and must supplement their farming income by selling their labour-power, whether in the countryside or in the cities. In the *altiplano*, small-scale peasant producers and indigenous communities are experiencing diminishing productive capacities of their soil, the division of land into smaller and smaller plots (*minifundios*) as families grow in size from generation to generation, the migration of young people to cities, and an acute absence of new technologies, making competition with foreign suppliers to the domestic Bolivian markets impossible.[46] Meanwhile, in the dynamic centre of agro-capitalism in the eastern lowlands, technical innovation and modernisation has led to more capital-intensive forms of agricultural production and consequently a paucity of employment opportunities even as industries expand.[47] As capitalist social relations increase their reach the differentiation of the peasantry into rich, medium, and poor peasants also intensifies. Survey data from 1988 suggested that 76 percent of peasantry were poor peasants, meaning they did not have the means to reproduce their family labour-power based on the income generated from their land and were obligated to sell their labour elsewhere on a temporary basis. Medium peasants constituted 11 percent of the peasantry when defined as peasant family units fundamentally based on family labour with the ability to reproduce that labour without selling their labour-power elsewhere. Rich peasants – those who regularly made a profit after reproducing their family and their means of production, purchased the labour of poorer peasants, and utilised modern technology – constituted 13 percent of the peasantry.[48] This process of differentiation within the peasantry has only accelerated since that time, with the transformation of some rich peasants into commercial farmers in specific regions of the *altiplano* and valley departments.[49]

---

45   Pacheco Balanza and Ormachea Saavedra 2000, p. 9.
46   Ibid., p. 19.
47   Ibid., pp. 31–2.
48   Ormachea Saavedra 2007, pp. 27–8.
49   Ibid., p. 28.

REVOLUTION AGAINST 'PROGRESS': THE TIPNIS CONFLICT IN BOLIVIA   315

Stratification of the Peasantry and the Class Dynamics in TIPNIS

Under the government of Evo Morales, despite an uplifting discourse which valorises the poorest of peasants, actual agro-industrial production with fully capitalist social relations has expanded from 79 percent of total agricultural production in the country to 82 percent. Whereas in 2005–6 small peasant production accounted for 25 percent of total production in the *altiplano* and valley regions, by 2008–9 this figure had dropped to 21.6 percent. While state support has been offered to agro-industrial soya producers and ranchers in the eastern lowlands, small-scale peasant production in the western highlands has been abandoned by the state.[50] How are these wider rural class dynamics relevant to TIPNIS? The park encompasses 1,200,000 hectares of territory, the bulk of which is in the northern section, in the department of Beni. Northern TIPNIS is inhabited principally by three indigenous groups – the Mojeños-Trinitarios, the Chimanes, and the Yuracarés. Southern TIPNIS, which borders the Chapare, a coca-producing region in the department of Cochabamba, is inhabited principally by Quechua and Aymara peasants – also known as 'colonizadores', or 'colonisers' – who migrated to the area from the western *altiplano* in different waves since the 1970s.[51]

The MAS government maintains the position that the construction of the highway to run through TIPNIS was intended to benefit all inhabitants of the region, above and beyond any material interests specific to particular groups. 'All sides in the dispute want greater development and improved access to basic services', Fuentes writes, in an echo of the government's line. 'The issue at stake is how the second poorest country in the Americas, facing intense pressure from more powerful governments and corporate forces, can meet the needs of its people while protecting the environment'.[52] A closer analysis, rooted in a Marxist – rather than populist – conceptualisation of the peasantry, how-ever, reveals the fact that certain groups would benefit from highway devel-opment at the expense of others. A zero-sum game developed, reflecting the usual growing class stratification within the peasantry under capitalist social relations, a process of differentiation mystified by pro-government, populist discourse that treats the peasantry as a homogeneous social class.

---

50   Ormachea Saavedra 2011a.

51   For the most lucid account of the region of which I am aware, see Orozco Ramírez et al. 2006, pp. 29–117. Ironically, the title of the book translates as 'We are the toy-things of nobody', a notion that does not square well with García Linera's position today, that they are indeed the toy-things of imperialism, NGOs, and the domestic right.

52   Fuentes 2011a.

In particular, a significant and growing lawyer of the Aymara and Quechua peasants in the region can be classified as rich in the schema developed above – that is, they accrue profits as a direct result of surplus appropriation through the work of salaried labourers. As rich peasants they also have growing motivations for expanding accumulation through the expropriation of further land. Geographically, to one side, we find possibilities of expansion into the department of Santa Cruz. But this would imply incursions into the inhabited lands of other Aymara-Quechua migrant peasants, or the small, medium, and large capitalist agricultural and ranching expanses that make up the agro-industrial sector of that department. This is not something the MAS government has been willing to contemplate.

On the other side, that is in TIPNIS to the north, we encounter the largely non-capitalist social relations of the Mojeños-Trinitarios, Chimanes, and Yuracarés – that is, communities based on collective self-reproduction through small-scale agricultural activities, the extraction of forest resources, and artisanal production. Increasingly, layers of these indigenous communities are forced into semi-proletarian status through the process Marx called 'primitive accumulation',[53] as they are compelled to sell their labour for part of the year to ranchers, timber barons, and the rich layer of the *cocalero*, or coca-growing peasantry.[54] As Guillermo Almeyra has perhaps understood better than anyone, the maintenance of an extractivist economy of natural resource extraction and capitalist agriculture geared toward export under the MAS government, has necessarily meant repeated clashes with the hunger for land expressed by poor and landless peasants, as well as those indigenous communities rising up in defence of forests, natural resources, water, and biodiversity.

Almeyra asks us to consider the legal and economic logic underpinning the current system that allows a few managers of a transnational mining or natural gas company operating in Bolivia today to gravely affect the environment of everyone without a care in the world, while 10,000 indigenous inhabitants of TIPNIS, with a non-capitalist mode of production, confront the full force of the law and defamation by the government when they seek to defend their values and ways of life against highway construction. This highway construction, far from being a neutral force for the 'development' of all, would destroy the integrity of their territory, and would allow for the destruction of their norms and modes of living.[55]

---

53   See part eight of Marx 1977.
54   Ormachea Saavedra 2011.
55   Almeyra 2011d.

Linking Local Class Dynamics to Brazilian Sub-Imperialism

Such are the class dynamics at play on a local scale, but it would be a mistake to see this micro-rhythm as the only propeller behind the highway. The plan for road development is, in fact, one small part of a much more ambitious regional integration project driven by Brazilian capital and the Brazilian state, known as the Initiative for the Integration of the Regional Infrastructure of South America (IIRSA). While opening up Bolivia's northern savannah region to further capitalist expansion, the TIPNIS highway would also crucially provide an integral link in an international north-east-to-south-west trade corridor, allowing Brazilian commodities from the western expanses of that country to reach pacific ports in northern Chile, via Bolivia.[56] The details of the project were established on 4 August 2008, in an agreement signed by representatives of the Administradora Boliviana de Carreteras (Bolivian Administrator of Highways, ABC), the Brazilian construction company OAS, and the massive Brazilian development bank, the Banco Nacional de Desarrollo Económico y Social (BNDES). The price of construction was established at $US 415 million, 80 percent of which BNDES would provide to the Bolivian government as a loan, provided that a Brazilian company – ultimately OAS – be rewarded the contract.[57]

Large swathes of Bolivian popular society have found protesters' accounts of the highway project more persuasive, it seems, than the government's crude equivocations concerning the 'development' the highway would bring, as well as the by now all-too-familiar, and all-too-easy defamation of the marchers as manipulated tools, or useful idiots, of western NGOs, American imperialism, and the domestic far-right. More compelling, to many, have been the protesters' understandings, rooted in a history of indigenous struggle for self-determination in the area, as well as class analysis tied to the diametrically opposed interests of different social groups imbricated in the region's dynamics. The interests of Brazilian sub-imperialism are almost self-evident. Domestically, there are the open alliances established between the government and agro-industrial soya producers in the eastern lowlands, particularly those in Santa Cruz, and financial capital, as expressed in the booming banking sector. These bourgeois groups have traditionally played an intermediary role in South American rhythms of capital accumulation, articulating with the wider interests of Brazilian sub-imperialism. The soya producers are vehemently opposed

---

56   EIU 2011, p. 11.

57   *Página Siete* 2011g. For an interesting theorisation and empirical discussion of Brazilian sub-imperialism in South America, see Flynn 2007, pp. 9–27.

to authentic agrarian reform for obvious material reasons. Meanwhile, as noted, within the increasingly class-stratified peasantry, a rich layer of *cocaleros*, a central social component of the government's rural base, has emerged with expansionary interests for coca production that could be satisfied in the TIPNIS without encroaching on large landholdings through authentic agrarian reform elsewhere in the country. Poorer layers of the peasantry in the TIPNIS, an amalgam of increasingly dispossessed indigenous communities, could serve as wage labour in coca production for richer peasants as they already have in larger numbers each year.

Moreover, the illegal activities of narcotrafficking and logging are not easily separable from the legal endeavours of finance, coca growing, and agro-industry, not to mention construction and real estate, particularly in the cities of Cochabamba and Santa Cruz, where dirty money is made clean. The narcos and timber barons, with ties to the state through various channels of corruption, are also in line to benefit from easier access in and through TIPNIS.

Finally, directly from the mouth of the Minister of Hydrocarbons and Energy for the government of Evo Morales, we learned of the possibility of expansive hydrocarbon reserves within TIPNIS region. Exploration for, and confirmation of, such riches would be vastly simplified with highway development and dispossession of uppity, partially non-capitalist indigenous social formations still presiding in the area.[58] Thus any comprehensive understanding has to link the issue of TIPNIS development with the interests of petroleum multinationals, and consider the ties between these multinationals and the Bolivian state. Likewise, this overarching dynamic that frames developments in the TIPNIS ought to be linked theoretically to the expanding literature on the new extractivism in Latin America and the associated theorisation of the 'compensatory state'.

Compensatory States and the New Extractivism

If the prominent Uruguayan political ecologist Eduardo Gudynas never offers a satisfying critique of capitalism in his analytical interventions on the 'new extractivism' of centre-left governments in South America, he does, at a minimum, understand the role played by the Morales regime within the logic of endless accumulation and expansion inherent in the world system as it is

---

58   For a brief sketch of some of these material interests in TIPNIS development, see Prada Alcoreza 2011.

currently organised.[59] In 2010 and 2011, South America achieved an average growth rate of 6.4 percent, with Paraguay hitting 15 percent, Argentina 9.2 percent, and Uruguay 8 percent. After a dip in 2009, Bolivia's economy picked up again to 4.1 percent in 2010, and grew at 5 percent in the first semester of 2011. A set of unique regional dynamics in South America over the last decade, related to patterns of accumulation elsewhere in the world market (notably high rates of growth in China), has set off a concerted shift towards the acceleration of mining, oil and gas extraction, and agro-industrial monocrop cultivation throughout the continent. In other words, the uneven mutations of the ongoing economic crisis on a world scale have not resulted in low growth rates on an aggregate level across South America – at least not yet. Similar to the period normally described as 'neoliberal', massive multinational corporations are deeply imbricated in the extension of extraction at the heart of this primary-commodity-led growth everywhere in the region. Those cases in which centre-left regimes have entered into joint contracts between state-owned enterprises and multinationals and negotiated relatively higher royalties and taxes on these extractive activities, are no exception. Skimming from the rent generated, many South American governments have established what Gudynas terms 'compensatory states', whose legitimacy rests on the modest redistribution achieved through the priming of, often already existing, cash-transfer programmes to the extremely poor, without touching the underlying class structure of society. Indeed, the very reproduction of these political economies depends upon states prioritising the maintenance and security of private property rights and juridical environments in which multinationals can profit.

Because the legitimacy function of relatively petty handouts runs on the blood of extraction, the compensatory state increasingly becomes a repressive state, on behalf of capital, as the expansion of extraction necessarily accelerates what David Harvey calls accumulation by dispossession, and the variegated forms of resistance it regularly spawns.[60] In the representative case of

---

59   Gudynas 2012.

60   Geographer David Harvey's concept of accumulation by dispossession is an elaboration of Marx's 'primitive accumulation'. Marx writes of those epoch-making 'moments when great masses of men are suddenly and forcibly torn from their means of subsistence, and hurled onto the labour-market as free, unprotected and rightless proletarians. The expropriation of the agricultural producer, of the peasant from the soil is the basis of the whole process. The history of this expropriation assumes different aspects in different countries, and runs through its various phases in different orders of succession, and at different historical epochs'. See Marx 1977. For Harvey, Marx rightly highlighted these processes of capital accumulation 'based upon predation, fraud, and violence', but incorrectly

the TIPNIS in Bolivia, the steamrolling of the rights to self-governance of indigenous communities resisting highway construction through their territory illustrates the coercive wing of the compensatory state in action. Indigenous self-government in Bolivia is to be defended by Morales, it would seem, only when the claims are to territories marginal to the state's development project.

The compensatory state co-opts and coerces in response to such signs of opposition, and builds an accompanying ideological apparatus to defend multinationals – an ideology in which communities of resistance are vilified as internal enemies acting in concert with the interests, or even in the pay of, various instruments of imperialism. The discursive gestures of state officials, of course, safely set to one side the obvious imperial character of the dispossessing activities of multinational corporations – now called 'partners' rather than 'bosses' in development – within the matrix of the new extractivism. The logic of the new-extractivism has its particular expressions in the Bolivian case. In terms of natural gas extraction, it pays to remember that in the first administration of Gonzalo Sánchez de Lozada (1993–7), the Bolivian state attempted to extend the area designated for gas exploration and exploitation to approximately thirteen million hectares. When this initiative was defeated through indigenous resistance in different areas of the Amazon, the multinational petroleum corporations were forced to concentrate on their mega-gasfields in the south of the country, above all in the department of Tarija. At the end of 2011, however, Morales had taken up the defeated mantle of Sánchez de Lozada, and proposed the extension of gas exploration and exploitation to roughly twelve million hectares – an area four times as great as that in 2009. Of this area, close to fifty percent was conceded entirely to multinationals. New government measures introduced in 2012 will likely amplify significantly this area, bringing the level of extraction of gas in the country to unprecedented levels.[61] Likewise, in mining, spokespeople for the Morales government have announced initiatives for the large-scale expansion of mining activities beyond those in the traditional zones of the *altiplano*, or the western high plateau, where mining has been underway since the colonial era. Much of this new mining will involve opening new frontiers into the Amazon.[62] Similar to other cases of dispossession from Mexico to Chile, the geographies being

---

imagined them to be exclusively features of a 'primitive' or 'original' stage of capitalism. With the concept of accumulation by dispossession, Harvey wants to point rather to the continuity of predatory practices that have risen dramatically to the surface once again in the era of neoliberalism. See Harvey 2003, p. 144.

61   Gandarillas Gonzales 2012, pp. 29–31.

62   Ibid., p. 30.

encroached upon in Bolivia for extending gas and mineral extraction, together with the growth of agro-industrial production (the majority of which is soya production under the control of Brazilian capital), include protected areas of biodiversity and indigenous territories which are currently among the last regions of the country relatively free of industrial and commercial activity, and which are, at the moment, governed by ecologically sustainable economies. It is the logic of accumulation by dispossession at the heart of this tripartite process – mining, gas, and agro-industry – that has generated the TIPNIS conflict, and which is likely to generate many more social conflicts into the future. It used to be the case that the theoreticians of the Latin American left opposed enclave economies ruled by the interests of multinational capital and argued instead for building paths toward socialist revolution; but today, the likes of Fuentes are dangerously reversing this axiomatic point of departure, accepting as the parameters of transformation the crumbs dispensed by a compensatory state, which in Fuentes's vision of the world appears capable of regulating capitalism, a mode of production that can be benevolent if only the government is on the side of 'the people'.

Assessing the Politics of the TIPNIS March

It was against this backdrop of Brazilian sub-imperialism, intensifying domestic class struggles over the Morales government's accumulation strategies, and the contradictions of the new extractivism and its compensatory state that a march of 65 days' duration emerged. The march was backed by 12 lowland and highland indigenous organisations, the most important of which were the lowland Confederation of Indigenous Peoples of Bolivia (CIDOB), and a highland organisation, CONAMAQ. This context helps to explain how the march was able to grow from 500 people at its outset to 2,500 people *en route*, with additional mass expressions of support in the form of thousands upon thousands taking to the streets in solidarity in the cities, including a general strike called for by the Bolivian Workers Central (COB), in the wake of fierce repression of unarmed protesters on 25 September 2011.[63] The campaign of defamation and violence orchestrated by the government ultimately proved unsuccessful. The popularity of the president plummeted. Ministers resigned. And the decision on the highway – ostensibly 'non-negotiable' in August – was reversed by October.

---

63   *Página Siete* 2011b; 2011c; 2011d; 2011e; 2011f.

It is true that there were opportunistic interventions by reactionary forces in the course of events, as is natural in any such scenario. We do not yet know the extent of US involvement, or of the far-right from the eastern lowlands. It is safe to assume, however, that they attempted infiltration. What is interesting, though, is that it appears from initial evidence that it was less the extreme right of the eastern lowlands that attempted to milk the conflict for all it was worth than the centre-right, under the guise of the Movimiento Sin Miedo (Movement without Fear, MSM), erstwhile allies of the government. The MSM is the political vehicle of former La Paz Mayor Juan del Granado. Granado is the first oppositional figure to emerge with even a remote hope of presenting a realistic electoral challenge to Morales. It is also true that two of the 16 demands put forth by the TIPNIS march against the highway were deeply problematic in different ways – one endorsed the UN-REDD initiative (Reduced Emissions from Deforestation and Forest Degradation), which would essentially place the preservation of forests in the hands of foreign capital, and the other called for the total closure of natural gas extraction from Aguaragüe, from which 90 percent of the gas currently sold and consumed in Bolivia is extracted. But these demands can be criticised without refuting the central problematic of the struggle, its essentially just nature, and its overwhelming character as an expression of the self-organisation and self-activity of an oppressed and exploited people defending their life values against the imposition of the exchange value of capital. This is a revolt in the revolutionary, rather than conservative, tradition of anti-capitalist romanticism. 'The central feature of industrial (bourgeois) civilisation that Romanticism criticises', Michael Löwy has explained, 'is the *quantification of life*, i.e. the total domination of (quantitative) exchange-value, of the cold calculation of price and profit, and the laws of the market, over the whole social fabric ... the decline of all qualitative values – social, religious, ethical, cultural or aesthetic ones – the dissolution of all qualitative human bonds, the death of imagination and romance, the dull uniformisation of life, the purely "utilitarian" – i.e. quantitatively calculable – relation of human beings to one another, and to nature'.[64]

'In Venezuela, Bolivia, and Ecuador', sociologist William I. Robinson contends, 'prevailing state institutions have tried to constrain, dilute, and coopt mass struggles from below'. It is precisely this process which represents a key weakness in the face of authentic threats of right-wing and imperialist subversion, and counter-reform. 'The US and the right wing in Latin America have launched a counteroffensive to reverse the turn to the left', Robinson explains. 'The Venezuelan revolution has earned the wrath of Latin American and trans-

---

64   Löwy 1987, p. 892.

national elites, but Bolivia and Ecuador, and more generally, the region's social movements and leftist political forces are as much targets of this counter offensive as is Venezuela. In Chile, a right-wing neo-liberal party defeated the socialists in the elections in 2010; in Honduras, the army deposed the progressive government of Manuel Zelaya in a 2009 coup d'etat with the tacit support of Washington; and the US has expanded its military presence throughout the continent, including the installation of new military bases in Colombia, Panama, and Honduras'. "How best could the region's left defend itself? 'The Pink Tide governments will not be able to stave off this counteroffensive without mass support', Robinson rightly argues. 'And it may be that the only way to assure that support is by advancing a more fundamentally transformative project'.[65]

Reconstituted Neoliberalism

Such a necessary deepening of the process of change is hardly what can be said to be occurring in contemporary Bolivia. Indeed, after an initial period of hysteria from the mainstream social sciences and concomitant euphoria from sections of the left, a slightly clearer picture about what has and has not happened in Bolivian political economy since 2006 is slowly coming to light in recent scholarly literature. For example, Kenneth M. Roberts and Steven Levitsky, two dominant figures in American political science, from Cornell and Harvard respectively, recently situated Bolivia's economic policies, alongside those of Argentina and Ecuador, in a 'heterodox' camp between the 'orthodox' free market policies of Brazil, Chile, Uruguay, and Peru, and the 'statist' policies of Venezuela.[66] In the same edited volume, Raúl Madrid points out that while the Bolivian government frequently engages in 'radical, even incendiary, rhetoric' its 'economic and social policies . . . have not represented a dramatic break with the past'.[67] 'Despite its periodic criticisms of capitalism', Madrid argues, 'the government has not sought to carry out a transition to socialism or change the existing pattern of development', an argument substantiated by the fact that the economy remains 'focused largely on the export of natural resources', under the control of foreign capital, and that 'the government has largely respected private property and has sought to encourage private investment'.[68]

---

65   Robinson 2011.
66   Levitsky and Roberts 2011.
67   Madrid 2011, p. 240.
68   Ibid., p. 248.

The government has 'eschewed radicalism in social policy as well, focusing instead on deepening or broadening policies that were enacted by previous governments', while in the area of agrarian reform, the government's 'initiative, which it enacted in 2006 after protracted struggle in the Senate, is largely in keeping with the land reform principles laid down in the Sánchez de Lozada administration's 1996 land reform measure'.[69]

Roberto Laserna, a prominent academic advocate of neoliberalism in Bolivia, poses a question: 'What has changed in the last few years?' His answer: 'A lot, if one observes the process in terms of its discourses and symbols and maintains a short-term perspective. But very little if one is attentive to structural conditions and observes the economic and social tendencies with a longer-term view'.[70]

'New economic policies have not signalled a dramatic shift towards a new economic model', write Amy Kennemore and Gregory Weeks, in an article on recent developments in Bolivia and Ecuador, 'but rather a pragmatic way for centre-left governments to better capture capitalist surplus in the exploitation of natural resources'.[71] 'The Morales government has gone to enormous effort to demonstrate that it guarantees private property', writes the critical Bolivian anthropologist Pablo Regalsky, 'while at the same time seeking to maintain its social base'.[72] Even in the domain of hydrocarbons (natural gas and oil) policy, where there is little dispute that the most far-reaching reforms have occurred under Morales, the early Marxist critiques of the 'nationalisation' of 2006 have now been more widely acknowledged as essentially correct. For example, geographer Brent Z. Kaup recently called it a 'neoliberal nationalisation'. In a certain superficial sense 'it technically returned physical control of Bolivia's natural gas to the state', but 'the space opened up for private investment in the hydrocarbon sector in the 1980s and 1990s still exists. Transnational firms still extract the majority of Bolivia's natural gas, and most of it is still sent to more profitable export markets'.[73]

---

69   Ibid., pp. 249–50.
70   Quoted in Robinson 2011.
71   Kennemore and Weeks 2011, p. 278.
72   Regalsky 2010, p. 48.
73   Kaup 2010, p. 135.

Endorsements from the IMF and World Bank

It should not be surprising that the latest reports on Bolivia by the International Monetary Fund, released earlier this year, are full of praise for Bolivia's 'solid macroeconomic performance in recent years', rooted in 'prudent macroeconomic policies', garnering 'record-high net international reserves' for the Bolivian state.[74] After IMF officials met with Bolivian state managers, the former group happily reported that the latter were 'keen to keep macroeconomic equilibrium'.[75] Another IMF report this year raises further doubt as regards Fuentes's claims that economic policy has been 'nationalised' under Morales. In 2009, the document notes, IMF authorities met with Bolivian managers and 'praised the Bolivian authorities for their sound macroeconomic management', but also advised the government to engage in the 'gradual withdrawal of fuel subsidies'.[76] The report goes on to explain that '[t]he authorities attempted to eliminate fuel subsidies upfront [in December 2010], but this measure was reversed in the face of social unrest'.[77] What the IMF is referring to here, in typical prosaic fashion, is the government's attempt to eliminate fuel subsidies late last year in line with IMF requests, and the concomitant explosion of popular protest – the *gasolinazo* – that rippled through the major cities of the country, forcing the government ultimately to back down.[78] The Morales administration remains to this day determined to reintroduce some version of the legislation that would abolish the subsidies.[79] The World Bank also praises Bolivia's macroeconomic management. Representatives of the bank have been meeting with state managers throughout 2011 in preparation for the drafting of a Country Partnership Strategy (CPS) that will guide the bank's activities in the country for the 2012–15 period. Thus far, the bank has 13 active investment projects in Bolivia, totalling a commitment of just under $US 445 million.[80]

---

74   IMF 2011a.
75   Ibid.
76   IMF 2011b.
77   Ibid.
78   On the revolt, see *The Economist* 2011; Zibechi 2011b; 2011b; Guillermo Almeyra 2011a; 2011b; 2011c.
79   *Página Siete* 2011; 2011h.
80   See World Bank, *Bolivia – Country Brief,* accessed online on November 16, 2011.

New Currents of Radical Social Theory

'In recent months', the Economist Intelligence Unit reported in September of
this year, 'MAS supporters have become more aware of the breach between the
revolutionary populist-socialist discourse of the president, Evo Morales, and
his government's more pragmatic policy course'.[81] An important reflection of
this new cognisance appeared in the form of a Collective Manifesto released
in June, which was signed by former MAS officials, leading social movement
activists, and radical intellectuals.[82] 'Today, the large majority of our people
basically find themselves in the same situation of poverty, precariousness,
and anguish in which they have always been', the manifesto reads. 'It would
seem that those who have improved are those that had always been well: the
bankers, transnational oil and mining companies, the smugglers, and the
narcotraffickers'.[83]

'The continuity of political party clientelism and extractive, export-oriented
development', Forrest Hylton points out, 'is the most remarkable feature of
the new order – the liberal capitalist model, albeit one slightly modified in
favour of national development, has survived. By Bolivian standards, it could
even be said to be thriving'. Indeed, for Hylton 'it is difficult to conceive of any
government channelling revolutionary dynamism into reformist sclerosis
more effectively than the Bolivian government's enthusiasm for mining and
resource extraction'.[84] Likewise, for Mexican radical Raquel Gutiérrez – who
lived in Bolivia between 1984 and 2001, and spent five of those years in jail
as a political prisoner – 'Evo has...led the reconstruction of the state along
liberal-capitalist lines as dictated by the World Bank...It is increasingly difficult to distinguish between the policies imposed by this so-called progressive government and those followed by previous neoliberal governments;
the rhetoric is different, but the results are largely the same. With resource
extraction so central to the financial stability of the government, people
and environments are simply expendable. Only disaster can emerge from
this'.[85] According to John Riddell, 'Webber and others who agree with him are
measuring the Bolivian government against an impossible standard, against

81   EIU 2011, p. 10.
82   Colectivo Manifiesto 22 de Junio 2011.
83   Ibid, p. 286.
84   Hylton 2011, p. 244.
85   Gutiérrez 2011, p. 277.

the ideal program of a hypothetical mass socialist movement'.[86] However, Riddell, like Fuentes, can offer no reasonable response to the Morales regime's ongoing commitment to fiscal austerity, low-inflationary growth, Central Bank independence, labour market 'flexibility', inconsequential agrarian reform (even the expansion of capitalist social relations in the countryside), vast accumulation of international reserves, low social spending, alliances with transnational capital across all sectors of the economy but particularly their dominance in natural resource extraction, export-oriented capitalism premised on low-wage, flexible labour, documented increases in rates of exploitation of the working class, and state investment amounting to only 32 percent of total investment, with a maximum official goal of 36 percent.[87] Riddell's argument, although more sophisticated in a theoretical sense than that of Fuentes, ultimately ends up sounding dangerously close to a revised version of TINA, there is no alternative. If one points to the real trends and contradictions in Bolivia's political economy, even after explicitly calling for opposition to any and all imperialist intervention – direct or indirect, overt or covert – as I have repeated at length in various writings, one is likely to receive a sharp reminder from the likes of Fuentes: 'Our role is not to tell the Bolivian masses from afar that they are doing it all wrong or that their process is not revolutionary enough; our priority must be to defend the gains of the Bolivian process and help to create the necessary space for its continued advance'.[88]

The implied lesson here is that it is not sufficient for activists and intellectuals in the global North to condemn and fight the imperialism of their governments: we must also close our eyes to contradiction, shut our mouths, and play the role of Evo's loyal soldiers abroad. International working-class solidarity, on this view, means parroting the communiques of the presidential palace in La Paz and aligning ourselves with Bolivian embassies in our countries. We must observe a stern silence as regards explosions of independent working-class, peasant, and indigenous resistance against the impositions of a reconstituted neoliberalism in Bolivia. Better still, when faced with a struggle like that in the TIPNIS, we are to tip our hats to their legitimate demands, while portraying the movement as largely a by-product of 'green imperialism'.

---

86   Riddell 2011b.
87   See Webber 2011b.
88   Fuentes 2011b.

The Social Consequences of Reconstituted Neoliberalism

Most of Morales's almost six years in office can be described, from an economic perspective, as high growth and low spending. Prior to the fallout of the worldwide economic crisis, which really started to impact the Bolivian economy in late 2008 and early 2009, the country's gross domestic product (GDP) had grown at an average of 4.8 percent under Morales. It peaked at 6.1 percent in 2008, and dropped to 3.4 percent in 2009, which was still the highest projected growth rate in the region. In 2010 the economy picked up again to 4.1 percent, and grew at five percent in the first semester of 2011. This growth was based principally on high international prices in hydrocarbons (especially natural gas) and various mining minerals common in Bolivia.

Government revenue increased dramatically because of changes to the hydrocarbons tax regime in 2006. But fiscal policy remained austere until the global crisis struck. Morales ran budget surpluses, tightly reined in inflation, and accumulated massive international reserves by Bolivian standards. Public investment in infrastructure, particularly road building, increased significantly, but social spending rose only modestly in absolute terms, and actually declined as a percentage of GDP under Morales. Fiscal policy changed in 2008 and 2009, as a consequence of a sharp stimulus package designed to prevent recession in the face of the global crisis. The social consequences of reconstituted neoliberalism have been almost no change in poverty rates under Morales, and deep continuities in social inequality. Both of these axes persist as monumental obstacles standing in the way of social justice in the country.

As Table 14.1 indicates, official poverty figures from the Bolivian government document a 6.8 percent decline in extreme poverty at the national level between 2002 and 2008, from 39.5 to 32.7 percent of the population. Extreme rural poverty rates drop more substantially, from 62.3 to 53.3 percent over the same period, and the biggest decrease occurs between 2007 and 2008, under the watch of Morales. Moderate poverty at a national level declined from 63.3 to 59.3 percent between 2002 and 2008, although it actually increased in 2007, before dropping less than one percentage point in 2008. These figures are the usual basis for social democratic defences of government progress. However, they hardly constitute a 'communitarian-socialist' redistribution of wealth, and need to be considered comparatively and against the backdrop of the anomalous 2002–8 commodities boom enjoyed by much of South America. For example, poverty reduction in Brazil and Argentina over the same period – when these countries were controlled by centre-left governments at best – was much more significant than the modest decline experienced in Bolivia.

TABLE 14.1   *Poverty and inequality indicators in Bolivia/ethnic-linguistic condition*, 2002–8*

Geog Area/Indicators	2002	2003/04	2005	2006	2007**	2008***
National						
Moderate Poverty (%)	63.3	63.1	60.6	59.9	60.1	59.3
Indigenous	71.0	70.1	67.9	69.3	66.5	n/a
Non-Indigenous	53.3	49.1	49.7	46.0	51.8	n/a
Extreme Poverty (%)	39.5	34.5	38.2	37.7	37.7	32.7
Indigenous	48.7	42.0	47.4	48.8	47.4	n/a
Non-Indigenous	27.5	19.4	24.2	21.3	25.2	n/a
Gini Index	0.6	n/a	0.54	0.53	0.51	n/a
Urban						
Moderate Poverty (%)	53.9	54.4	51.1	50.3	50.9	51.2
Indigenous	60.5	61.7	56.2	58.9	55.6	n/a
Non-Indigenous	48.1	43.7	46.0	42.1	46.9	n/a
Extreme Poverty (%)	25.7	22.9	24.3	23.4	23.7	22.0
Indigenous	31.6	29.0	29.4	31.1	29.0	n/a
Non-Indigenous	20.5	14.1	19.4	16.0	19.1	n/a
Gini Index	0.54	n/a	0.54	0.53	0.51	n/a
Rural						
Moderate Poverty (%)	78.8	77.7	77.6	76.5	77.3	74.3
Indigenous	81.9	80.7	80.8	80.4	78.9	n/a
Non-Indigenous	70.2	66.4	65.5	62.2	72.4	n/a
Extreme Poverty (%)	62.3	53.7	62.9	62.2	63.9	53.3
Indigenous	66.7	58.3	67.6	67.6	68.2	n/a
Non-Indigenous	50.1	36.4	45.2	42.8	50.6	n/a
Gini Index	0.63	n/a	0.66	0.64	0.64	n/a

Source: Derived from Unidad de Análisis de Políticas Sociales y Económicas (UDAPE)

  * 'Indigenous' classification here includes those who self-identify as indigenous, as well as those who may or may not identify as having indigenous origin, but who have spoken and understood an indigenous language since childhood.

  ** Preliminary figures

*** Estimated figures

Definition of Indicators:

Moderate Poverty – Percentage of the population situated below the poverty line which is calculated in relation to the minimum income necessary to satisfy basic necessities.

Extreme Poverty – Percentage of the population whose total income is so low that even if it was exclusively directed toward food it would be insufficient to satisfy minimum nutritional requirements.

Gini Index – Measure of income inequality in society, ranging from 0–1, where 0 is perfect income equality and 1 is perfect income inequality.

TABLE 14.2   *Bolivian distribution of national income*

Geog Area	Year	Quintile 1 Poorest	Quintile 2	Quintile 3	Quintile 4	Quintile 5 Richest
National	1999	1.3	5.9	11.5	20.2	61.2
	2007	2.2	6.4	11.7	20.1	59.7
Urban	1999	3.9	8.1	12.5	20.0	55.6
	2007	4.4	8.0	12.4	19.7	55.6
Rural	1999	1.2	3.9	9.3	19.4	66.1
	2007	1.4	5.5	10.7	18.6	63.8

Source: Derived from CEPAL, *Anuario estadístico de América Latina y el Caribe, 2010*. Santiago: CEPAL, 2011, p. 67.

Available figures for inequality are still less impressive. Table 14.2 shows how, in 2007, the richest 20 percent of the population continued to receive a whopping 59.7 percent of national income, while the bottom 20 percent received an astonishingly meagre 2.2 percent. Indeed, the concentration of income in 2007 was still roughly equivalent to what it had been in 1970.[89] In the latest *Human Development Report*, published annually by the United Nations Human Development Progamme, Bolivia is ranked as the 108th country in the Human Development Index (HDI). In another HDI index appearing in the same report, however, one that is adjusted for inequality, Bolivia falls 12 spots in the ranking.[90] 'Official rhetoric about communitarian socialism, accelerating the transition to socialism, and the like, used during and after the 2009 presidential campaign', Hylton suggests, 'is just that: rhetoric. Clientelismo and caudillismo continue to hold sway in political culture, even if the faces and parties of official politics have changed. The new political economy fits comfortably within the realm of liberal capitalism. Income and wealth are still intensely concentrated and are likely to remain so in the near future'.[91]

---

89   UNDP 2010, p. 8.
90   UNDP 2011, p. 136.
91   Hylton 2011, p. 247.

Conclusion

Even those Marxists, like Emiliano López and Francisco Vértiz, who insist on the differences between at least three emergent national development models in Latin America since the regional crisis of neoliberalism began in the late 1990s,[92] recognise that in the current world conjuncture, above and beyond their differences, each of these three models fall into line with a 'new international consensus' which assigns Latin America to the role of exporting natural resources. Such an insertion in the world market restores, if in novel ways, the role the region played historically in the geopolitical order at an international level.[93] More interestingly still, we need to seriously entertain the hypothesis recently advanced by José Seoane and Clara Algramati, that the particular logics of expression of the global crisis in the periphery of the world system is a radical deepening of processes of accumulation by dispossession.[94] That is to say, more specifically, between 2008 and 2011 we have witnessed a new cycle of commodification, appropriation, and assertion of control on the part of large capitals of a series of collective goods across the global periphery, but especially the commodification and appropriation of the common goods of nature. According to Seoane and Algramati there is still a direly insufficient consciousness of the scale and magnitude of this offensive, as well as the forces behind it. Reflecting on the trends of foreign direct investment (FDI) in Latin America since the world crisis began to unfold in 2008, we can at least begin to understand the necessity of further exploration of the issue. With the exception of 2009, when aggregate GDP across Latin America and the Caribbean momentarily dipped, the period between 2008 and 2011 witnessed record volumes of FDI in the region – depending on the year, an increase of between 70 and 130 percent compared to the average levels obtained between 2000 and 2005.

---

92   The first of these, according to this account, is that which maintains a clear continuity with the policies associated with the neoliberal ideal. In this group we encounter Mexico, Chile, Perú, Colombia, and large chunks of Central America. A second group of countries – which principally includes Argentina, Brazil, and Uruguay – is that which has adopted a national-popular rhetoric directed against international financial capital and certain domestic oligarchic sectors. In embracing such rhetorical positions, these countries have distanced themselves from the neoliberalism of the 1990s. Lastly, there are those countries – Bolivia, Ecuador, and Venezuela – with transitional projects. In this category, the rhetoric of anti-neoliberalism and anti-imperialism is more pronounced, and the positive position advanced by these governments is potentially anti-systemic.

93   López and Vértiz 2012.

94   Seoane and Algramati 2012.

In the mining sector, FDI in 2011 reached a record high of approximately $US 140 billion, a 40 percent increase on the figure for 2010 (already a massive year), and a 250 percent increase on the volume registered in 2003.[95] Seoane and Algramati stress the fact that, regardless of variations in political ideologies, most governments in the region appear intent upon deepening this model, and justifying it through the suggestion that it is a logical response to the instability of the global economy, the deceleration of growth on a global scale, and the possible impacts upon public budgets and trade balances, pillars of the preceding economic cycle. This relative commonality, furthermore, finds expression in projects such as the IIRSA, the supreme importance of which Fuentes cannot seem to understand.[96] IIRSA needs to be understood, according to Seoane and Algramati, in the context of this intensification of accumulation by dispossession in the areas of mining, gas, and agro-industry throughout the region. The priority of this public infrastructural project of regional integration is to facilitate the commercial export of raw commodities. IIRSA is, therefore, yet another expression of the increasing hegemony of the extractivist-export model of development, even if it is today cloaked in an ideological guise of neo-developmentalism and growing trade with China rather than the US.

In the face of this extractivist offensive, there has been a veritable wave of protest and social resistance emerging and developing at a regional level. A vast number of movements and struggles are calling into question the extractivist-export model and its attendant violence, looting, environmental devastation, and recolonisation in the form of multinational capital's power.[97] At the close of 2010, for example, one conservative estimate suggested at least 155 active mining conflicts across the region.[98] This is the wider imperial logic that needs to be understood in order to grasp its specific manifestations on a local scale in the context of TIPNIS. Discerning the players on all sides, and their descending relations of importance, is obviously a difficult and complex matter of investi-

---

95   Ibid.
96   IIRSA was launched in 2000 with the participation of 12 of South America's governments at the time. Brazil took the lead from the beginning in the initiative's planning and financing. With a current budget of just under $US 1 trillion, the vision is to increase access to remote regions of South America and to spike energy-generation capacity through the construction of highways, railways, bridges, seaports, and waterways. See Friedman-Rudovsky 2012. I briefly discuss the role of Brazilian sub-imperialism acting in and through IIRSA in the original article to which Fuentes is responding.
97   Seoane and Algramati 2012.
98   Delgado Ramos 2012, p. 4.

gation that requires the development of a series of research agendas that has only been touched on cursorily here.

Shifting from wider intellectual concerns to immediate questions of praxis, the first priority of activists in the global North should be to oppose imperialist intervention of any sort in the determination of the Bolivian process. This means, concretely, opposition under any circumstances to imperialist-backed destabilisation campaigns against Morales. But the political situation is too complicated to end our discussion at that stage. Our first allegiance ought to be with the exploited and oppressed themselves, rather than any leaders or governments who purport to speak in their name in an uncomplicated way. This is as true of the TIPNIS struggle of 2011 as it was of the miners' struggles of 2006 in Colquiri; the popular urban revolts against a right-wing governor in Cochabamba in late 2006 and early 2007; the strikes of miners, teachers, and health-care workers in May 2010; the general strike in the department of Potosí in August 2010; the peasant, worker, and community challenge to Japanese mining capital in 2010 at the San Cristóbal mine; and the popular rebellions against the elimination of fuel subsidies in December last year. The hope for Bolivia's future remains with the overwhelmingly indigenous rural and urban popular classes, organising and struggling independently for themselves, against combined capitalist exploitation and racial oppression, with visions of simultaneous indigenous liberation and socialist emancipation, as we witnessed on a grand scale between 2000 and 2005.

References

Abal Medina, Juan Manuel 2006, 'The Argentine Political Crisis and Necessary Institutional Reform', in *The Argentine Crisis and Argentine Democracy*, edited by Edward Epstein and David Pion-Berlin, Lanham, MD: Lexington Books.

Abreu, Marcelo de Paiva 2008, 'The Brazilian Economy, 1994–2004: An Interim Assessment', in *The Cambridge History of Latin America Volume IX, Brazil since 1930*, edited by Leslie Bethell, Cambridge: Cambridge University Press.

Abreu, Yoselyn and Cesar Espot 2006, 'Algunas consideraciones sobre la cogestión laboral en Alemania, España y Venezuela', *Gaceta Laboral* 12, 3: 29–46.

Achkar, Soraya 2007, 'Gestión participativa y socialismo del siglo XXI', in *Ideas Para Debatir el Socialismo del Siglo XXI*, edited by Magarita Lopez Maya, Caracas: Editorial Alfa.

Acosta, Alberto 2010, 'Hacia la declaración universal de los derechos de la naturaleza', *Agencia Latinoamericana de Informacion, 454*, 16 April, available at: <http://alainet .org/active/37414>.

Acosta, Vladamir 2007, 'El socialismo del siglo XXI y la Revolución Bolivariana. Una reflexión inicial', in *Ideas Para Debatir el Socialismo del Siglo XXI*, edited by Magarita Lopez Maya, Caracas: Editorial Alfa.

Agencia CTA 2009, 'El Estado debe tener una fuerte presencia ante la crisis', ACTA, CTA, Buenos Aires, 20 July, available at: <http://www.agenciacta.org.ar/article11669 .html>.

Agencias 2011, 'Sindicato de trabajadores de Alcasa fue denunciado ante la fiscalía', *Aporrea*, 2 February, available at: <www.aporrea.org/trabajadores/n175384.html>.

Albó, Xavier 1991, 'El Retorno del Indio', *Revista Andina*, 9, 2: 299–345.

—————— 1996, 'Making the Leap from Local Mobilization to National Politics', *NACLA Report on the Americas, March–April*.

Albrecht, Sonia 2006, '¿Opción socialista o trampa populista?', *Desarrollo humano e institucional en América Latina*, 47: 1.

Albro, Robert 2005, 'The Water is Ours, Carajo!: Deep Citizenship in Bolivia's Water War', in *Social Movements: A Reader*, edited by June C. Nash, Malden: Blackwell Pub.

Alcorta, Ludovico 1999, 'Flexible Automation and Location of Production in Developing Countries', *European Journal of Development Research*, 11, 1: 147–75.

Alexander, M. Jacqui and Chandra Talpade Mohanty (eds.) 1997, *Feminist Genealogies, Colonial Legacies, Democratic Futures*, New York: Routledge.

Ali, Tariq 2004, 'Venezuela: Changing the World by Taking Power', interview with Claudia Jardim and Jonah Gindin, available at: <http://venezuelanalysis.com/ analysis/598> (accessed August 5, 2011).

Almeyra, Guillermo 2011a, 'Bolivia: razones, intenciones, y métodas', *La Jornada*, 2 January.

———— 2011b, 'Bolivia: la cuestión de fondo', *La Jornada*, 9 January.

———— 2011c, 'Bolivia: hay alternativa a los aumentos', *La Jornada*, 16 January.

———— 2011d, 'Bolivia: Neodesarrollismo o alternativa al capitalismo', *La Jornada*, 16 October.

Altieri, Miguel A. 2009, 'The ecological impacts of large-scale agrofuel monoculture production systems in the Americas', *Bulletin of Science, Technology & Society*, 29, 3: 236–44.

Álvarez R., Victor, and Davgla Rodríguez A. 2007, *Guía teórico-práctica para la creación de EPS. Empresas de Producción Socialista*, Barquisimeto: CVG Venalum.

Álvarez, Víctor 2009a, '10 años de revolución el capitalismo ha crecido', *Últimas Noticias*, 21 June.

———— 2009b, *Venezuela: ¿Hacia Dónde va el Modelo Productivo?* Caracas: Centro Internacional Miranda.

Amann, Edmund and Werner Baer 2000, 'The Illusion of Stability: The Brazilian Economy Under Cardoso', *World Development*, 28, 10: 1805–19.

Amin, Samir 2009, 'Capitalism and the ecological footprint', *Monthly Review*, 61, 6, November, available at: <http://monthlyreview.org/2009/11/01/capitalism-and-the-ecological-footprint>.

Amsden, Alice 1989, *Asia's Next Giant: South Korea and Late Industrialisation*, London: Oxford University Press.

AN-DGIDL (Asamblea Nacional – Dirección General de Investigación y Desarrollo Legislativo) 2007, *Ejes fundamentales del proyecto de reforma constitucional. Consolidación del Nuevo Estado*, Caracas: AN-DGIDL.

Antillano, Andrés 2005, 'La lucha por el reconocimiento y la inclusión en los barrios populares: la experiencia de los comités de Tierras Urbanas', *Revista Venezolana de Economía y Ciencias Sociales*, 11, 3: 205–18.

Antunes, Ricardo 2009, 'Introducción', *La crisis estructural del capital*, Caracas: Ministerio del Poder Popular.

———— 2013, 'Trade Unions, Social Conflict, and the Political Left in Present-Day Brazil: Between Breach and Compromise', in *The New Latin American Left: Cracks in the Empire*, edited by Jeffery R. Webber and Barry Carr, Lanham, MD: Rowman and Littlefield.

Aporrea 2009, 'Víctor Álvarez: en 10 años de revolución el capitalismo ha crecido', available at: <http://www.aporrea.org/actualidad/n136931.html>.

———— 2010, 'Se realizó foro convocado por aporrea.org: la situación post 26 de septiembre y la propuesta de una corriente de izquierda radical', available at: <http://www.aporrea.org/actualidad/n170290.html>.

────── 2011, 'ALCASA no es más que la expresión muy pequeña de lo que pasa a nivel político en el país. Entrevista con los trabajadores de ALCASA Oswaldo León, Alcides Rivero, Cruz Barreto y Manuel Figuera (VIDEOS)', *Aporrea*, 25 May, available at: <www.aporrea.org/trabajadores/n181549.html>.

────── 2012, '¡Chávez con la clase obrera! ¡La derecha endógena y la oposición con las transnacionales!', *Aporrea*, 2 March, available at: <http://www.aporrea.org/trabajadores/a139521.html>.

Arbona, Juan M. and Benjamin Kohl 2004, 'City Profile – La Paz-El Alto', *Cities*, 21, 3: 255–65.

Arceo, Enrique 2006, 'El fracaso de la reestructuración neoliberal en América Latina. Estrategias de los sectores dominantes y alternativas populares', in *Neoliberalismo y sectores dominantes. Tendencias globales y experiencias nacionales*, edited by Eduardo M. Basualdo and Enrique Arceo, Buenos Aires: CLACSO.

Arceo, Nicolás and Andrés Wainer 2008, 'La crisis de la deuda y el default. Los distintos intereses en torno a la renegociación de la deuda pública', Documento de Trabajo Nro. 20, Buenos Aires: FLACSO.

Arceo, Nicolás, Ana Paula Monsalvo, Martín Schorr and Andrés Wainer 2008, *Empleo y salarios en Argentina. Una visión de largo plazo*, Buenos Aires: Capital Intelectual.

Arestis, Philip, Fernando Ferrari-Filho and Luiz Fernando de Paula 2011, 'Inflation Targeting in Brazil', *International Review of Applied Economics*, 25, 2: 127–48.

Arze, Carlos 2000, *Crisis del sindicalismo boliviano: consideraciones sobre sus determinantes materiales y su ideologia*, La Paz: CEDLA.

Astarita, Rolando 2001, 'Ciclos Económicos en la Argentina de los noventa', *Revista Herramienta*, 16, available at: <http://www.herramienta.com.ar/revista-herramienta-n-16/ciclos-economicos-en-la-argentina-de-los-noventaciclos-economicos-en-la-argentina-de-los-noventa>.

ATE-INDEC 2008, 'Índice de precios al consumidor IPC-GBA del año 2007: ejercicio alternativo ante la imposibilidad del cálculo del IPC-GBA debido a la intervención del INDEC', Buenos Aires: Junta Interna / Comisión Técnica ATE-INDEC.

Auty, Richard 1986, 'Resource-based Industrialisation and Country Size: Venezuela and Trinidad and Tobago', *Geoforum*, 17, 3: 325–38.

Auyero, Javier 2000, *Poor People's Politics. Peronist Survival Networks & the Legacy of Evita*, Durham, NC: Duke University Press.

────── 2005, 'Protest and Politics in Contemporary Argentina', in *Argentine Democracy: The Politics of Institutional Weakness*, edited by Steven Levistky and María Victoria Murillo, University Park: The Pennsylvania State University Press.

Aversa, Jeanine 2010, 'Por qué es tan difícil reducir el desempleo', *La Nación*, 2 February, availableat:<http://www.lanacion.com.ar/1228559-por-que-es-tan-dificil-reducir-el-desempleo>.

AVN and MinCI (Agencia Venezolana de Noticias and Ministerio de Comunicación e Información) 2011, 'Consumo de kilocalorías del venezolano supera suficiencia energética de la FAO', *Minci*, 28 April, available at: <www.minci.gob.ve/noticias-minci/1/204560/consumo_de_kilocalorias.html>.

Azpiazu, Daniel 1998, *La concentración en la industria argentina a mediados de los años noventa*, Buenos Aires: EUDEBA/FLACSO.

Azpiazu, Daniel and Martín Schorr 2010a, 'La industria argentina en la posconvertibilidad: Reactivación y legados del neoliberalismo', *Problemas del Desarrollo*, 41, 161: 11–139.

——— 2010b, *Hecho en Argentina. Industria y Economía. 1976–2007*, Buenos Aires: Siglo XXI Editores.

Azpiazu, Daniel and Nicolás Bonofiglio 2006, 'Nuevos escenarios macroeconómicos y servicios públicos', *Realidad Económica*, 224: 32–68.

Azzellini, Dario 2009, 'Venezuela's Solidarity Economy: Collective Ownership, Expropriation, and Workers Self-Management', *Working USA*, 12, 2: 171–91.

——— 2010a, 'Constituent Power in Motion: Ten Years of Transformation in Venezuela', *Socialism and Democracy*, 24, 2: 8–30.

——— 2010b, *Partizipation, Arbeiterkontrolle und die Commune. Bewegungen und soziale Transformation am Beispiel Venezuela*, Hamburg: VSA.

——— 2011a, 'De las cooperativas a las empresas de propiedad social directa en el proceso venezolano' in *Cooperativas y socialismo: Una mirada desde Cuba*, edited by Camila Piñeiro Harnecker, Havana: Editorial Caminos.

——— 2011b, 'Workers' Control under Venezuela's Bolivarian Revolution', in *Ours to Master and to Own. Workers' Councils from the Commune to the Present*, edited by Immanuel Ness and Dario Azzellini, Chicago: Haymarket Books.

Azzellini, Dario, and Oliver Ressler 2006, *5 Fábricas. Control Obrero en Venezuela* (film), Caracas, Berlin and Vienna.

——— 2010, *Comuna Under Construction* (film), Caracas, Berlin and Vienna.

Banko, Catalina 2008, 'De la descentralizacion a la "nueva geometria del poder"', *Revista Venezolana de Economía y Ciencias Sociales*, 14, 2: 167–84.

Baptista, Asdrúbal 1997, *Teoría económica del capitalismo rentístico*, Caracas: IESA.

Baptista, Asdrúbal and Bernard Mommer 1987, *El Petroleo en el pensamiento económico venezolano: un ensayo*, Caracas: Ediciones IESA.

Barker, Colin, Alain Johnson and Michael Lavalette 2001, 'Leadership Matters: An Introduction' in *Leadership and Social Movements*, edited by Colin Barker, Alan Johnson and Michael Lavalette, Manchester: Manchester University Press.

Barrera, Facundo 2009, 'Estudio 1: La Asignación "Universal" a la Niñez. Los claroscuros de una medida positiva', *Informeiefe*, 153: 5–12, La Plata: Instituto de Estudios Fiscales y Económicos.

Barrientos, Stephanie 2001, 'Gender, Flexibility and Global Value Chains', *IDS Bulletin*, 32, 3: 83–93.

Barros de Castro, Antonio 2008, 'From Semi-stagnation to Growth in a Sino-centric Market', *Brazilian Journal of Political Economy*, 28, 1: 3–27.

Barrow, Clyde 2007, 'Ralph Miliband and the Instrumentalist Theory of the State: The (Mis) Construction of An Analytic Concept', in *Class, Power and the State in Capitalist Society*, edited by Paul Wetherly, Clyde Barrow and Peter Burnham, Basingstoke: Palgrave MacMillan.

Basualdo, Eduardo 2001, *Sistema político y modelo de acumulación en la Argentina*, Buenos Aires: UNQ-FLACSO-IDEP.

———— 2006a, *Estudios de historia económica argentina. Desde mediados del siglo XX a la actualidad*, Buenos Aires: FLACSO / Siglo veintiuno editores.

———— 2006b, 'Evolución de la economía argentina en el marco de las transformaciones de la economía internacional de las últimas décadas', in *Neoliberalismo y sectores dominantes. Tendencias globales y experiencias nacionales*, edited by Eduardo M. Basualdo and Enrique Arceo, Buenos Aires: CLACSO.

Basualdo, Eduardo M., Claudio Lozano and Martín Schorr 2002, 'Las transferencias de recursos a la cúpula económica durante la presidencia Duhalde. El nuevo plan social del gobierno', Working Paper presented at the National Assembly of FENAPRO, March, Buenos Aires.

Basualdo, Victoria, no date, 'La clase trabajadora durante la última dictadura militar argentina 1973–1983', *Memoria en las aulas*, Dossier 13, La Plata: Comisión Provincial por la Memoria.

———— 2010, 'Los delegados y las comisiones internas en la historia argentina: 1943–2007', in *La industria y el sindicalismo de base en la Argentina*, edited by Daniel Azpiazu, Martín Schorr, and Victoria Basualdo, Buenos Aires: Cara o Seca.

Baumol, William J. 1969, 'Macroeconomics of Unbalanced Growth', *The American Economic Review*, 57, 3/4: 415–26.

Baute, Juan Carlos 2009, 'Las cooperativas no desaparecerán', *Últimas Noticias*, 17 June, available at: <www.aporrea.org/poderpopular/n136615.html>.

BBC News 2005, 'Chávez Calls for Democracy at Work', reported by Ian Bruce, BBC, 17 May, available at: <http://news.bbc.co.uk/2/hi/business/4155936.stm>.

Belik, Walter and Luiz Fernando Paulillo 2001, 'O financiamento da produção agrícola brasileira na década de 90: ajustamento e seletividade', in *Políticas Públicas e Agricultura no Brasil*, edited by Sergio Leite, Porto Alegre: Editorial da Universidade/ UFRGS.

Bellamy Foster, John 2009a, 'Capitalism in Wonderland', *Monthly Review*, 61, 1, available at: <http://monthlyreview.org/2009/05/01/capitalism-in-wonderland>.

————— 2009b, 'The vulnerable planet fifteen years later', *Monthly Review*, 61, 7, available at: <http://monthlyreview.org/2009/12/01/the-vulnerable-planet-fifteen-years-later>.

Bello, Walden 2008, 'The Coming Capitalist Consensus', Foreign Policy in Focus, 24 December, available at: <http://www.fpif.org/articles/the_coming_capitalist_consensus>.

————— 2010, 'O neocolonialismo chines', *Institute for Policy Studies*, 10 March.

Benería, Lourdes 2001, 'Shifting the Risk: New Employment Patterns, Informalization, and Women's Work', *International Journal of Politics, Culture, and Society*, 15, 1: 27–53.

Bensaïd, Daniel 1995, *La discordance des temps*, Paris: Editions de la Passion.

————— 2002, 'Leaps! Leaps! Leaps!' *International Socialism*, 95, Summer, available at: <http://pubs.socialistreviewindex.org.uk/isj95/bensaid.htm>.

Berins Collier, Ruth and Samuel Handlin (eds.) 2009, *Reorganizing Popular Politics: Participation and the New Interest Regime in Latin America*, University Park: Pennsylvania State University Press.

Bethell, Leslie and Jairo Nicolau 2008, 'Politics in Brazil, 1985–2002', in *The Cambridge History of Latin America Volume IX, Brazil since 1930*, edited by Leslie Bethell, Cambridge: Cambridge University Press.

Bielschowsky, Ricardo 2009, 'Sesenta años de la CEPAL: estructuralismo y neoestructuralismo', *Revista Cepal*, 97: 173–94.

————— 2010, 'Sesenta años de la CEPAL y el pensamiento reciente', in *Sesenta Años de la CEPAL. Textos seleccionados del decenio 1998–2008*, edited by R. Bielschowsky, Buenos Aires: CEPAL-Siglo XXI.

Bina, Cyrus 1985, *The Economics of the Oil Crisis*, New York: St. Martin's Press.

————— 1989, 'Some Controversies in the Development of Rent Theory: The Nature of Oil Rent', *Capital and Class*, 39: 82–111.

————— 2006, 'The Globalization of Oil: A Prelude to a Critical Political Economy', *International Journal of Political Economy*, 35, 2: 4–34.

Blackburn, Robin 2008, 'The subprime crisis', *New Left Review*, 50, March–April, available at: <http://www.newleftreview.org/?view=2715>.

Blankenburg, Stephanie 2008, 'El Estado y la revolución. Reestatización del Banco del grupo Santander', *América XXI*, 41: 18–21.

Boito, Armando and Paula Marcelino 2011, 'Decline in Unionism? An Analysis of the New Wave of Strikes in Brazil', *Latin American Perspectives*, 38, 5: 62–73.

Bolpress 2005, 'El Alto otra vez de pie', 13 January.

Bonnet, Alberto 2002, 'Que se vayan todos. Crisis, insurrección y caída de la convertibilidad', *Revista Cuadernos del Sur*, 33: 39–70.

————— 2007, 'Kirchnerismo: el populismo como farsa', *Periferias*, 14 (primer semestre), 97–114.

————— 2008, *La hegemonía menemista*, Buenos Aires: Prometeo Libros Editorial.

———— 2009, '¿Por qué ganó Evo?', *Rebelión*, 8 December.

Bonnet, Alberto and Eduardo Glavich 1993, 'El huevo y la serpiente: Notas acerca de la crisis del régimen democrático de dominación y la reestructuración capitalista en Argentina, 1983–1993 (primera parte)', *Revista Cuadernos del Sur*, 16.

Bonnet, Alberto and Adrian Piva 2011, 'El estado en el kirchnerismo. Un análisis de los cambios en la forma de estado a partir de la crisis de 2001', in *La posconvertibilidad a debate*, edited by Juan Grigera, Buenos Aires: Imago Mundi.

Boron, Atilio A. 2006, 'The truth about capitalist democracy', *Socialist Register*, London: Merlin Press.

———— 2008, 'Promises and challenges: The Latin American left at the start of the twenty-first century', *The New Latin American Left: Utopia Reborn*, edited by Patrick Barrett, Daniel Chavez, Cesar Rodriguez-Garavito, London: Pluto Press.

———— 2009, 'Democracia y movimentos sociales en America Latina', *Revista Em Pauta* 19: 27–38.

Borras Jr., Saturnino M., Ruth Hall, Ian Scoones, Ben White and Wendy Wolford 2001, 'Towards a better understanding of global land grabbing: an editorial introduction', *The Journal of Peasant Studies*, 38, 2: 209–16.

Boyer, Robert 2008, 'Hoy el estado está en mejor posición para definir el futuro', *Página/12*, 29 December, available at: <http://www.pagina12.com.ar/diario/dialogos/21-117451-2008-12-29.html>.

Bradley, Keith and Alan Gelb 1983, *Worker Capitalism: The New Industrial Relations*, London: Heinemann Educational Books Ltd.

Braverman, Harry 1974, *Labor and Monopoly Capital: The Degradation of Work in the Twentieth Century*, New York: Monthly Review Press.

Bremmer, Ian 2006, 'Populist Resurgence in Latin America?', *Survival*, 48, 2: 5–16.

Brenner, Robert 1977, 'The origins of capitalist development: a critique of neo-Smithian Marxism', *New Left Review*, 104, 1: 25–92.

———— 1985, 'The Agrarian Roots of European Capitalism', in *The Brenner Debate. Agrarian Class Structure and Economic Development in Pre-industrial Europe*, edited by T.H. Aston and C.H.E. Philpin, Cambridge: Cambridge University Press.

———— 2006a, 'What Is, and What is Not, Imperialism?' *Historical Materialism*, 14, 4: 79–105.

———— 2006b, *The Economics of Global Turbulence*, London: Verso Books.

———— 2009, 'Un análisis histórico-económico de la actual crisis', *Sin Permiso*, 22 February, available at: <http://www.sinpermiso.info/textos/index.php?id=2385>.

Bruce, Ian 2005, 'Venezuela promueve la cogestión', BBC, 19 August, available at: <news.bbc.co.uk/hi/spanish/business/newsid_4167000/4167054.stm>.

Bruschtein, Luis 2003, 'Todos debieron renunciar y Menem no fue la excepción', *Página/12*, 15 April, available at: <http://www.pagina12.com.ar/diario/elpais/1-20137-2003-05-15.html>.

Brusco, Valeria, Marcelo Nazareno and Susan C. Stokes 2004, 'Vote Buying in Argentina', *Latin American Research Review*, 39, 2: 66–88.

Bruton, Henry J. 1998, 'A Reconsideration of Import Substitution', *Journal of Economic Literature*, 36, 2: 903–36.

Burawoy, Michael 2003, 'For a Sociological Marxism: The Complementary Convergence of Antonio Gramsci and Karl Polanyi', *Politics and Society*, 31: 193–261.

Burnham, Peter 1994, 'Open Marxism and Vulgar International Political Economy', *Review of International Political Economy*, 1, 2: 221–31.

Bustamente, Rocio, Elizabeth Peredo and María Esther Udaeta 2005, 'Women in the "Water War" in the Cochabamba Valleys', in *Opposing Currents: The Politics of Water and Gender in Latin America*, edited by Vivienne Bennett, Sonia Dávila-Poblete and María Nieves Rico, Pittsburgh: University of Pittsburgh Press.

Butrón Oporto, Mariana and Jorge Miguel V. Rosales 2003, *La Población en el Municipio Cercado de Cochabamba*, Cochabamba: ASDI/UMSS.

Cairncross, Frances 2001, *The Death of Distance: How the Communications Revolution is Changing our Lives*, Boston: Harvard Business School Press.

Calvo, Guillermo, Alejandro Izquierdo and Eduardo Talvi 2003, 'Sudden Stops, the Real Exchange Rate and Fiscal Sustainability: Argentina's Lessons', NBER Working Paper Series, 9828, Cambridge, MA: National Bureau of Economic Research.

Cammack, Paul 1991, 'Brazil – the Long March to the New Republic', *New Left Review*, 190: 21–58.

Campbell, Martha 2002, 'Rent and Landed Property', in *The Culmination of Capital. Essays on Volume III of Marx's Capital*, edited by Martha Campbell, and Geert Reuten, New York: Palgrave.

Canitrot, Adolfo 1981, *Orden social y monetarismo*, Estudios CEDES, Buenos Aires.

Caputo, Orlando 2009, 'La crisis actual de la economía mundial: una nueva inter-pretación teórica e histórica', *XI Encuentro Internacional sobre Globalización y Problemas del Desarrollo*, Havana, 2–6 March.

Carchedi, Guglielmo 2009, 'The return from the grave, or Marx and the present crisis', *International Socialism*, 7 July, available at: <www.isj.org.uk>.

Cardoso, Fernando Henrique 1977, 'The Originality of a Copy: CEPAL and the Idea of Development', *CEPAL Review*, 4: 7–38.

Cardoso, Fernando Henrique and Enzo Faletto 1969, *Dependencia y desarrollo en América Latina*, Mexico: Siglo XXI.

Carlson, Chris 2012, *Oil or Class Structure? Underdevelopment and Oil Dependence in Venezuela*, Latin American Studies Master's Thesis, Madison: University of Wisconsin.

Castañeda, Jorge G. 1994, *Utopia Unarmed: The Latin American Left after the Cold War*, New York: Vintage Books.

Castedo, Antía and Bernat García 2010, 'Perder la calle, ganar el discurso', *El País*, 8 January, available at: <http://elpais.com/diario/2010/01/08/sociedad/1262905201_850215.html>.

Castells, Manuel 2006, 'The Network Society: From Knowledge to Policy', in *The Network Society*, edited by Manuel Castells and Gustavo Cardoso, Washington: Center for Transatlantic Relations.

Castorina, Emilia 2012, 'Crisis and Recomposition in Argentina', in *The New Latin American Left: Cracks in the Empire*, edited by Jeffery R. Webber and Barry Carr, Lanham, MD: Rowman and Littlefield.

Castro, Jorge 2010, 'Alemania cada vez más inclinada hacia la demanda extra-europea', *Clarín*, 14 March, available at: <http://edant.clarin.com/diario/2010/03/14/opinion/0-02159013.htm>.

Ceceña, Ana Esther 1990, 'Sobre las diferentes modalidades de internacionalización del capital' *Problemas del Desarrollo*, 21, 81: 15–40.

CELS 2004, 'Plan jefes y jefas de hogar: derecho social o beneficios sin derechos?' Buenos Aires: CELS.

CENDA 2004, 'Las consecuencias económicas del Sr. Lavagna. Dilemas de un país devaluado', WP 1, Buenos Aires: Centro de Estudios Para el Desarrollo Argentino.

——— 2010, *La anatomía del nuevo patrón de crecimiento y la encrucijada actual. La economía argentina en el período 2002–2010*, Buenos Aires: Centro de Estudios Para el Desarrollo Argentino.

CEPAL 1969, *El pensamiento de la CEPAL*, Santiago de Chile: Editorial Universitaria.

Chang, Ha Joon 1993, *The Political Economy of Industrial Policy*, Basingstoke: Macmillan.

Charnock, Greig 2009, 'Why do Institutions Matter? Global Competitiveness and the Politics of Policies in Latin America', *Capital and Class*, 33, 2: 67–99.

Chávez Frías, Hugo 2008, *El Poder Popular*, Caracas: MinCI.

——— 2012, *Propuesta del Candidato de la Patria Comandante Hugo Chávez para la Gestión Bolivariana Socialista 2013–2019*, available at: <www.chavez.org.ve/Programa-Patria-2013-2019.pdf>.

Chávez, Walter, and Álvaro García Linera 2005, 'Rebelión Camba: Del dieselazo a la lucha por la autonomía', *El Juguete Rabioso*, January.

Chesnais, Francois 2008a, 'La récession mondiale: moment, interprétations et enjeux de la crise', *Carré Rouge*, 39: 3–14.

——— 2008b, 'Les origines communes de la crise économique et de la crise écologique', *Carre Rouge*, 39: 15–20.

——— no date, 'Socialisme ou barbarie: les nouvelles dimensions d'une alternative', *Contretemps*, available at: <http://www.contretemps.eu/lectures/socialisme-barbarie-nouvelles-dimensions-dune-alternative>.

Chibber, Vivek 2004, 'Reviving the Developmental State? The Myth of the "National Bourgeoisie"', in *Socialist Register 2005. The Empire Reloaded*, edited by Leo Panitch and Colin Leys, London: The Merlin Press.

Chilcote, Ronald 1990, 'Post-Marxism: The Retreat from Class in Latin America', *Latin American Perspectives* 17: 3–24.

Chomsky, Noam 2006, 'Latin America Declares Independence', *International Herald Tribune*, 3 October, available at: <http://www.chomsky.info/articles/20061003.htm>.

Ciccantell, Paul 1994. *Firms, States and Raw Materials in the Capitalist World Economy: Aluminum and Hydroelectricity in Brazil and Venezuela*, Unpublished PhD Dissertation: University of Wisconsin Madison.

———— 2000, 'Globalisation and Raw Materials-Based Development: The Case of the Aluminium Industry', *Competition and Change*, 4: 273–323.

Ciccariello-Maher, George 2007, 'Dual Power in the Venezuelan Revolution', *Monthly Review*, 59, 4, September: 42–56.

Clarke, Simon 1984, 'Alternative Models of Co-operative Production', *Economic and Industrial Democracy* 5: 97–129.

———— 1988, *Keynesianism, Monetarism and the Crisis of the State*, Aldershot: Edward Elgar.

———— 1991, 'State, Class Struggle and the Reproduction of Capital', in *The State Debate*, edited by Simon Clarke, London: Macmillan.

———— 2001, 'Class Struggle and the Global Overaccumulation of Capital', in *Phases of Capitalist Development. Booms, Crises Globalizations*, edited by Robert Albritton, Makoto Itoh, Richard Westra and Alan Zuege, Basingstoke: Palgrave.

CNE 2004, *Elecciones Regionales Octubre 2004*, available at: <http://www.cne.gob.ve/regionales2004/>.

———— 2008, *Divulgación Elecciones Regionales 2008*, available at: <http://www.cne.gob.ve/divulgacion_regionales_2008/index.php?e=11&m=06&p=00&c=00&t=00&ca=00&v=02>.

Coatsworth, John H. 2005, 'Structures, Endowments and Institutions in the Economic History of Latin America', *Latin American Research Review*, 40, 3: 126–44.

Colburn, Forrest D. 1992, *Latin America at the End of Politics*, Princeton: Princeton University Press.

Colectivo Manifiesto 22 de Junio 2011, 'For the Recuperation of the Process of Change for the People and with the People', *Dialectical Anthropology*, 35, 3: 285–93.

Coletti, Claudinei 2006, 'Neliberalismo e burguesia agrária no Brasil', *Revista Lutas y Resistências*, 1: 131–45.

Collier, Ruth Berins and David Collier 1991, *Shaping the Political Arena: Critical Junctures, the Labor Movement And Regime Dynamics in Latin America*, Princeton: Princeton University Press.

Collins, Jane 1993, 'Gender, Contracts and Wage Work: Agricultural Restructuring in Brazil Sao-Francisco Valley', *Development and Change*, 24, 1: 53–82.

Comninel, George, 1987, *Rethinking the French Revolution: Marxism and the Revisionist Challenge*, New York: Verso.

Coronil, Fernando 1997, *The Magical State. Nature, Money and Modernity in Venezuela*, Chicago: University of Chicago Press.

Corte Nacional Electoral, 'Resultados: Elecciones departamentales y municipales 2010', available at: <http://www.cne.org.bo/>.

Cova, Andres 2009, 'Mibam triplico en un año numero de empresas con cupo de aluminio', *El Nacional*, Caracas, 23 May.

Crespo Flores, Carlos 1999, *La guerra de los pozos*, Cochabamba: CERES.

——— 2001, *La concesión de La Paz a los cinco años; elementos para una evaluación*, available at: <http://www.aguabolivia.org>.

——— 2002, 'Water Privatization Policies and Conflicts in Bolivia – The Water War in Cochabamba (1999–2000)', PhD Thesis, Oxford Brookes University.

Crespo Flores, Carlos, Omar Fernández Quiroga and Carmen Peredo 2004, *Los regantes de Cochabamba en la Guerra del Agua*, Cochabamba: CESU-UMSS.

CTA de los Trabajadores 2009a, '22 de abril. Día Nacional de Lucha. Los trabajadores no vamos a pagar la crisis', 15 April, available at: <http://www.cta.org.ar/base/article12136.html>.

——— 2009b, 'Acciones en todo el país. 7 de agosto: Jornada Nacional de Movilización de la CTA', 4 August, available at: <http://www.cta.org.ar/base/article13220.html>.

Cufré, Martín 2008, 'El gobierno promulgo la ley que termina con el régimen de jubilación privada. Sello y firma para el final de las AFJP', *Página/12*, 12 October 2008, Buenos Aires, available at: <http://www.pagina12.com.ar/diario/economia/2-116412-2008-12-10.html>.

Curia, Eduardo 2007, *Teoría del modelo de desarrollo de la Argentina: las condiciones para su continuidad*, Buenos Aires: Galerna.

CVG-Alcasa 2005, 'Presidente de CVG Alcasa Ratifica el Arranque de la Linea V', *Cogestión: Todo el Poder para los Trabajadores*, 8 March.

——— 2011, *La hoja de aluminio*, 28 April, 49, 28.

D'Arista, Jane 2009, 'Limitar el apalancamiento', *Página/12*, 26 May, available at: <http://www.pagina12.com.ar/diario/economia/2-125588-2009-05-26.html>.

Dachevsky, Fernando 2011, 'Echale la culpa al yuyo: la enfermedad holandesa y los límites de la industria argentina', *El Aromo*, 60, May/June: 30–31.

Damián, Araceli, and Julio Boltvinik 2006, 'A Table to Eat on: The Meaning and Measurement of Poverty in Latin America', in *Latin America after Neoliberalism: Turning the tide in the 21st century*, edited by Eric Hershberg and Fred Rosen, New York: The New Press.

Damill, Mario, Frenkel, Roberto and Maurizio, Roxana 2003, 'Políticas macroeconómi-
cas y vulnerabilidad social, La Argentina en los años noventa', *Serie Financiamiento
del Desarrollo*, 13, Santiago de Chile: CEPAL.

Damill, Mario, Roberto Frenkel and Martín Rapetti 2005, 'La deuda argentina: Historia,
default y reestructuración', *Nuevos documentos CEDES*, 16, Buenos Aires: CEDES.

Deere, Carmen 2005, 'The Feminization of Agriculture? Economic Restructuring in
Rural Latin America', *United Nations Institute for Social Development*, Occasional
Paper 1, available at: <www.unrisd.org/publications/opgp1>.

Di Giminiani, Daniele 2007, '¿Que es la nueva geometría del poder?', *Aporrea*,
23 August, available at: <www.aporrea.org/actualidad/a40153.html>.

Dierckxsens, Wim 2007, 'Política económica en la transición al socialismo del siglo
XXI', *World Social Forum*, Nairobi.

Dinerstein, Ana C. 2003, 'Power or Counter Power? The dilemma of the Piquetero
Movement in Argentina post crisis', *Capital & Class*, 81: 1–7.

———— 2008, 'The Politics of Unemployment: Employment Policy, the Unemployed
Workers Organizations and the State in Argentina (1991–2005)', NGPA Research
Paper Number 9.

Dinerstein, Ana Cecilia, L. Melina Deledicque and Daniel Contartese 2008, 'Notas de
investigación sobre la innovación organizacional en entidades de trabajadores
desocupados en la Argentina', *Realidad Económica*, 234: 50–79.

Document 1 2009, 'No votes contra el pueblo', Otro camino para superar la crisis,
Buenos Aires.

Dolan, Catherine and John Humphrey 2000, 'Governance and Trade in Fresh Vegetables:
The Impact of UK Supermarkets on the African Horticulture Industry', *Journal of
Development Studies*, 37, 2: 147–76.

Dornbusch, Rudiger and Sebastian Edwards 1991, *The Macroeconomics of Populism in
Latin America*, Chicago: University of Chicago Press.

Dos Santos, Theotonio 2005, 'El renacimiento del desarrollo', América Latina en
Movimiento, 3 May, available at: <http://alainet.org/active/22609&lang=es>.

Dosman, Edgar J. 2001 'Los mercados y el estado en la evolución del 'manifiesto' de
Prebisch', *Revista de la CEPAL*, 75: 89–105.

Draper, Hal 1990, 'The Myth of Lenin's "Concept of the Party"', available at: <http://
www.marxists.org/archive/draper/1990/myth/index.htm>.

Duménil, Gérard and Dominique Lévy 2006, 'Argentina's Unsustainable Growth
Trajectory: Center and Periphery in Imperialism at the Age of Neoliberalism', Draft
Paper, PSE-CNRS.

Dunkerley, James 1984, *Rebellion in the Veins: Political Struggle in Bolivia, 1952–1982*,
London: Verso.

———— 1993, 'The Crisis of Bolivian Radicalism', in *The Latin American Left: From the
Fall of Allende to Perestroika*, edited by Barry Carr and Steve Ellner, London: Latin
America Bureau.

—— 1998, *Pacification of Central America*, London: Verso.

Dunn, Bill 2004, *Global Restructuring and the Power of Labour*, New York: Palgrave Macmillan.

—— 2009, 'Myths of Globalisation and the New Economy', *International Socialism Journal*, 121, winter, available at: <www.isj.org.uk/?id=509>.

Eckstein, Susan 1983, 'Transformation of a "Revolution from Below": Bolivia and International Capital', *Comparative Studies in Society and History*, 25, 1: 105–35.

EIU 2011, *Bolivia: Country Report, London: Economist Intelligence Unit*, September.

ECLAC 2003, *Economic Survey of Latin America and the Caribbean*, Santiago: Economic Commission for Latin America and the Caribbean (ECLAC).

—— 2011, *Preliminary Overview of the Economies of Latin America and the Caribbean*, Santiago: Economic Commission for Latin America and the Caribbean (ECLAC).

—— 2012a, *Economic Survey of Latin America and the Caribbean*, Santiago: Economic Commission for Latin America and the Caribbean (ECLAC).

—— 2012b, *Social Panorama of 2012*, Santiago: Economic Commission for Latin America and the Caribbean (ECLAC), Briefing Paper, available at: <http://www .eclac.org/cgi-bin/getProd.asp?xml=/prensa/noticias/comunicados/9/48459/ P48459.xml&xsl=/prensa/tpl-i/p6f.xsl&base=/tpl-i/top-bottom.xsl>.

Edwards, Sebastian 2010, *Left Behind: Latin America and the False Promise of Populism*, Chicago: University of Chicago Press.

Egan, Darren 1990, 'Toward a Marxist Theory of Labour-Managed Firms: Breaking the Degeneration Thesis', *Review of Radical Political Economics*, 22, 4: 67–8.

El Informador 2011, 'Reyes Reyes es el Resumen de Lasluchas del Pueblo Larense', 24 April, available at: <http://www.elinformador.com.ve/noticias/lara/politica/ reyes-reyes-resumen-luchas-pueblo-larense/37403>.

El Universal 2009, 'Autoridades de Alcasa afirman que la empresa está operativa', *Economía*, 2 March, by Sailú Urribarrí Núñez, available at: <http://www.eluniversal .com/2009/03/02/eco_art_autoridades-de-alcas_1286764.shtml>.

—— 2010, 'Chávez ordenó reducir exportación de materias primas', *Economia*, 17 May, available at: <http://www.eluniversal.com/2010/05/17/eco_art_chavez- ordeno-reduci_1903844.shtml>.

—— 2014, Capital accumulation and ground-rent in Brazil: 1953–2008, *International Review of Applied Economics* (forthcoming).

Ellner, Steve 2006, 'Las estrategias "desde arriba" y "desde abajo" del movimiento de Hugo Chávez', *Cuadernos del Cendes*, 23, 62: 73–93.

—— 2008a, *Rethinking Venezuelan Politics*. Boulder, CO: Lynne Reiner.

—— 2008b, 'Las tensiones entre la base y la dirigencia en las filas del chavismo', *Revista Venezolana de Economía y Ciencias Sociales*, 14, 1: 49–64.

Elson, Diane 1996, 'Appraising Recent Developments in the World Market for Nimble Fingers', in *Confronting State, Capital and Patriarchy: Women Organising in the*

Process of Industrialisation, edited by Amrita Chhachhi and Renée Pittin, Basingstoke: Macmillan, in association with the Institute of Social Studies.

Enzinna, Wes 2007, 'All We Want is the Earth: Agrarian Reform in Bolivia', in *Socialist Register 2008: Global Flashpoints, Reactions to Imperialism and Neoliberalism*, edited by Leo Panitch and Colin Leys, New York: Monthly Review Press.

Epstein, Edward 2003, 'The Piquetero Movement of Greater Buenos Aires: Working Class Protest During the Argentine Crisis', *Canadian Journal of Latin American and Caribbean Studies*, 28, 55/56: 11–36.

Epstein, Edward and David Pion-Berlin (eds.) 2006, *Broken Promises? The Argentine Crisis and Argentine Democracy*, Lanham, MD: Lexington Books.

Escalante, Hector 2009, 'PDVSA Industrial firma memorando para construir fábrica de medidores eléctricos', available at: <http://www.radiomundial.com.ve/node/192248>.

Estévez, Hector 2011, 'La pelea a cuchillo del PSUV en las empresas básicas de Guayana', *Aporrea*, 31 January, available at: <www.aporrea.org/regionales/a116778.html>.

Etchemendy, Sebastián 2005, 'Old Actors in New Markets: Transforming the Populist/Industrial Coalition in Argentina, 1989–2001', in *Argentine Democracy: The Politics of Institutional Weakness*, edited by Steven Levistky and María Victoria Murillo, University Park: The Pennsylvania State University Press.

Etchemendy, Sebastián and Ruth Collier 2007, 'Down but Not Out: Union Resurgence and Segmented Neocorporatism in Argentina: 2003–2007', *Politics and Society*, 35, 3: 363–401.

Etchemendy, Sebastián and Vicente Palermo 1998, 'Conflicto y concertación: gobierno, congreso y organizaciones de interés en la reforma laboral del primer gobierno de Menem', *Desarrollo Económico*, 37, 148: 559–90.

Evans, Peter 1995, *Embedded Autonomy. States and Industrial Transformation*, Princeton: Princeton University Press.

Evans, Peter, and Leandro Wolfson 1996, 'El estado como problema y como solución', *Desarrollo Económico*, 35, 140: 529–62.

Fajnzylber, Fernando 1983, *La industrialización trunca de América Latina*, Santiago de Chile: Centro de Economía Transnacional.

———— 1990, 'La industrialización en América Latina: de la caja negra al casillero vacío', *Cuadernos de la CEPAL*, 60.

Farber, Samuel 2006, *The Origins of the Cuban Revolution Reconsidered*, Chapel Hill, NC: University of North Carolina Press.

———— 2011, *Cuba since the Revolution of 1959: A Critical Assessment*, Chicago: Haymarket Books.

Faria, Vilmar E. 1978, 'Desarrollo económico y marginalidad urbana: los cambios de perspectiva de la CEPAL' *Revista Mexicana de Sociología*, 40, 1: 9–29.

Farthing, Linda 1991, 'The New Underground', *NACLA Report on the Americas*, 25: 18–23.

Feitlowitz, Marguerite 1998, *A Lexicon of Terror: Argentina and the Legacies of Torture*, New York: Oxford University Press.

Féliz, Mariano 2007, 'A Note on Argentina, its Crisis and the Theory of Exchange Rate Determination', *Radical Review of Political Economics*, 39, 1: 80–99.

———— 2008, 'Jubilaciones: ¿ volver al '93 o crear un verdadero sistema de previsión social?', *Prensa de Frente*, 29.

———— 2009a, 'Crisis cambiaria en Argentina', *Problemas del Desarrollo. Revista Latinoamericana de Economía*, 40, 158: 185–213.

———— 2009b, 'Frente a la economía política del capital, la economía política de la clase trabajadora: Alternativas populares ante la crisis capitalista en Argentina', *Herramienta Web*, 2, Buenos Aires.

———— 2010, 'Crisis mundial e impacto sobre la economía de Argentina', *Revista académica Plustrabajo*, 1, 1: 111–125, Centro de Estudios para el Desarrollo Laboral y Agrario (CEDLA).

———— 2011, *Un estudio sobre la crisis en un país periférico. La economía argentina del crecimiento a la crisis, 1991–2002*, Buenos Aires: Editorial El Colectivo.

Féliz, Mariano and Emiliano López 2010a, 'La dinámica del capitalismo periférico posneoliberal-neodesarrollista. Contradicciones, barreras y límites de la nueva forma de desarrollo en Argentina', *Herramienta. Revista de debate y crítica marxista*, 45.

———— 2010b, 'Políticas sociales y laborales en la Argentina: del Estado "ausente" al Estado posneoliberal' in *Pensamiento crítico, organización y cambio social*, edited by Mariano Féliz, Melina L. Deledicque, Emiliano López, and Facundo Barrera, Buenos Aires: Editorial El Colectivo.

Féliz, Mariano and Ernesto Pablo Pérez 2004, 'Conflicto de clase, salarios y productividad. Una mirada de largo plazo para la Argentina', in *La economía Argentina y su crisis (1976–2001): visiones institucionalistas y regulacionistas*, edited by Robert Boyer and Julio César Neffa, Buenos Aires: Miño y Dávila.

———— 2007, '¿Tiempos de cambio? Contradicciones y conflictos en la política económica de la posconvertibilidad', in *Salidas de crisis y estrategias alternativas de desarrollo. La experiencia argentina*, edited by Robert Boyer and Julio C. Neffa, Buenos Aires: Editorial Miño y Dávila.

Féliz, Mariano, Emiliano López and Lisandro Fernández 2010, 'Estructura de clase, distribución del ingreso y políticas públicas. Una aproximación al caso argentino en la etapa post-neoliberal', *VI Jornadas de Sociología de la UNLP*, 9–10 December, Universidad Nacional de La Plata, La Plata, Argentina.

Ferguson, Niall 2009, 'El matrimonio entre China y EEUU no podía durar', *Clarín*, 28 December, available at: <http://edant.clarin.com/diario/2009/12/28/opinion/o-02108884.htm>.

Ferm, Nora 2008, 'Non-Traditional Agricultural Export Industries: Conditions for Women Workers in Colombia and Peru', *Gender and Development*, 16, 1: 3–26.

Fernandes, Bernardo Mançano, Welch, Clifford Andrew and Elienaí Constantino Gonçalves 2010, 'Agrofuel Policies in Brazil: Paradigmatic and Territorial Disputes', *Journal of Peasant Studies*, 37, 4: 793–819.

Fernandes, Sujatha 2010, *Who Can Stop the Drums? Urban Social Movements in Chávez's Venezuela*, Durham, NC: Duke University Press.

Fernández Terán, Roberto 2003, *FMI, Banco Mundial y Estado neocolonial: Poder supra-nacional en Bolivia*, La Paz: Plural.

Ferreres, Orlando (ed.) 2005, *Dos siglos de economía argentina. 1810–2004*, Buenos Aires: Editorial El Ateneo.

Figuera, Manuel 2011, 'Dictadura sindical en Alcasa', *Aporrea*, 28 May, available at: <www.aporrea.org/trabajadores/a124125>.

Filho, José Juliano de Carvalho 2001, 'Política Agrária do Governo FHC', in *Políticas Públicas e Agricultura no Brasil*, edited by Sergio Leite, Porto Alegre: Editorial da Universidade/UFRGS.

Flynn, Matthew 2007, 'Between Subimperialism and Globalization: A Case Study in the Internationalization of Brazilian Capital', *Latin American Perspectives*, 34, 6: 9–27.

Freire, Paulo 1970, *Pedagogy of the Oppressed*, New York: Continuum.

Frenkel, Roberto 2005, 'Una política macroeconómica enfocada en el empleo y el creci-miento', *Revista de Trabajo*, Año 1, Buenos Aires: Nueva época.

Friedman, Thomas 2006, *The World is Flat: The Globalized World in the Twenty-First Century*, London: Penguin.

———— 2009, 'Un ataque preventivo vale la pena', *La Nación*, 16 December, available at: <http://www.lanacion.com.ar/1212237-un-ataque-preventivo-que-vale-la-pena>.

Friedman-Rudovsky, Jean 2012, 'The Bully from Brazil', *Foreign Policy*, 20 July, available at:<http://www.foreignpolicy.com/articles/2012/07/20/the_bully_from_brazil?page=full>.

Fuentes, Frederico 2011a, 'Bolivia: NGOs Wrong on Morales and Amazon', *Bolivia Rising*, 25 September.

———— 2011b, 'Government, Social Movements, and Revolution in Bolivia Today: A Response to Jeffery Webber', *International Socialist Review*, 76, March–April, avail-able at: <http://www.isreview.org/issues/76/debate-bolivia.shtml>.

———— 2011c, 'Separating Fact from Fantasy in Bolivia: Review of *From Rebellion to Reform in Bolivia*, by Jeffery R. Webber', *Alborada: Latin America Uncovered*, 19 August.

Gandarillas Gonzales, Marco A. 2012, 'La ampliación de las fronteras extractivistas en Bolivia', *América Latina en Movimiento, March: 29–31*.

Ganz, Marshall 2000, 'Resources and Resourcefulness: Strategic Capacity in the Unionization of California', *American Journal of Sociology*, 105, 4: 1003–62.

García Linera, Álvaro 2004, 'The "Multitude"', in *Cochabamba! Water War in Bolivia*, edited by Oscar Olivera and Tom Lewis, Cambridge, MA: South End Press.

—— 2005, 'El descencuentro de dos razones revolucionarias: Indianismo y marxismo', *Barataria*, 1: 4–14.

—— 2006, 'State Crisis and Popular Power', *New Left Review*, II, 37 (January–February): 73–85.

—— 2011b, *Las tensiones creativas de la revolución: La quinta fase del proceso del cambio, La Paz: Vicepresidencia del Estado Plurinacional*.

García Linera, Álvaro, Marxa Chávez León, and Patricia Costas Monje 2006, *Sociología de los movimientos sociales en Bolivia: Estructuras de movilización, repertories culturales y acción política*, La Paz: Oxfam.

García-Guadilla, María Pilar 2008, 'La praxis de los consejos comunales en Venezuela: Poder popular o instancia clientelar?', *Revista Venezolana de Economía y Ciencias Sociales*, 14, 1: 107–24.

Garza Toledo, Enrique de la, and Araceli Almaraz 1998, *Estragias de modernizacion empresarial en Mexico: Flexibilidad y control sobre el proceso de trabajo*, Mexico: Rayuela Editores.

Gereffi, Gary, and Miguel Korzeniewicz (eds.) 1994, *Commodity Chains and Global Capitalism*, Westport, CT: Greenwood.

Ghymers, Christian 2009, 'Una visión europea', *XI Encuentro Internacional sobre Globalización y Problemas del Desarrollo*, Havana, 2–6 March.

Gibson, Edward 1996, *Class and Conservative Parties: Argentina in Comparative Perspective*, Baltimore: Johns Hopkins University Press.

—— 1997, 'The Populist Road To Market Reforms: Politics and Electoral Coalitions in Argentina and México', *World Politics*, 49, 2: 339–70.

Gibson, Edward and Ernesto Calvo 2000, 'Federalism and Low-Maintenance Constituencies: Territorial Dimensions of Economic Reform in Argentina', *Studies in Comparative International Development*, 35, 3: 32–55.

Giddens, Anthony 2009, 'El clima definirá otra economía', *Clarín*, 17 March, available at: <http://edant.clarin.com/diario/2009/03/17/opinion/o-01878682.htm>.

Gill, Lesley 2000, *Teetering on the Rim: Global Restructuring, Daily Life, and the Armed Retreat of the Bolivian State*, New York: Columbia University Press.

Gill, Stephen 1995, 'Globalization, Market civilization and Disciplinary Neoliberalism', *Millennium – Journal of International Studies*, 24, 3: 399–423.

Gills, Barry, Joel Rocamora and Richard Wilson 1993, *Low Intensity Democracy: Political Power in the New World Order*, London: Pluto Press.

Gindin, Sam 2001, 'Turning Points and Starting Points: Brenner, Left Turbulence and Class Politics', in *Socialist Register 2001: Working Classes, Global Realities*, edited by Leo Panitch and Colin Leys, London: Merlin Press.

Golbert, Laura 2004, '¿Derecho a la inclusión o paz social? Plan Jefes y Jefas de Hogar Desocupados', *Serie Políticas Sociales*, 84, Santiago de Chile: CEPAL.

Gómez, Marcelo 2000, 'Conflictividad laboral y comportamiento sindical en los '90: transformaciones de clase y cambios en las estrategias políticas y reivindicativas', *Seminario "Mercado de trabajo e intervención sindical"*, Buenos Aires: Programa de Estudios Sociales Internacionales/IDES.

Goodman, David and Michael Redclift 1981, *From Peasant to Proletarian. Capitalist Development and Agrarian Transitions*, Oxford: Basil Blackwell.

Goodman, Peter 2010, 'La pesadilla americana de vivir sin trabajo por años', *Clarín*, 22 February, available at: <http://www.ieco.clarin.com/economia/pesadilla-americana-vivir-trabajo-anos_0_212978737.html>.

Gowan, Peter 1999, *The Global Gamble. Washington's Faustian Bid for World Dominance*, London: Verso.

Gramsci, Antonio 2000, *The Gramsci Reader*, edited by David Forsacs. New York: New York University Press.

Graña, Juan M. 2007, 'Distribución funcional del ingreso en Argentina, 1935–2005', Documento de Trabajo, 8, Buenos Aires: Centro de Estudios sobre Población, Empleo y Desarrollo (CEPED).

Grandin, Greg 2004, *The Last Colonial Massacre: Latin America in the Cold War*, Chicago: University of Chicago Press.

Gray, John 2009, 'Planeta en riesgo', *La Nación*, 15 November, available at: <http://www.lanacion.com.ar/1199591-planeta-en-riesgo-la-hora-de-las-soluciones-realistas>.

Green, Duncan 2003, *Silent Revolution: The Rise and Decline of Market Economics in Latin America*, London: Latin American Bureau.

Greider, William 1997, *One World, Ready or Not: The Manic Logic of Global Capitalism*, New York: Simon & Schuster.

Grigera, Juan 2009, 'Right-wing Social Movements? The Argentinean "Development Model" in Question', *Historical Materialism 6th Annual Conference*, 27–9 November, London.

——— 2011, 'La desindustrialización en la Argentina: Agresión a la manufactura o reestructuración capitalista?' in *El país invisible. Debates sobre la Argentina contemporánea*, edited by Alberto Bonnet, Buenos Aires: Ediciones Continente.

Grinberg, Nicolas 2008, 'From the "Miracle" to the "Lost Decade": Intersectoral Transfers and External Credit in the Brazilian Economy', *Brazilian Journal of Political Economy*, 28, 2: 291–311.

———— 2010, 'Where is Latin America Going? "FTAA or 21st Century Socialism"?', *Latin American Perspectives*, 37, 1: 185–202.

———— 2011, 'Transformations in the Korean and Brazilian Processes of Capitalist Development between the mid-1950s and the mid-2000s: The Political Economy of Late Industrialisation', PhD thesis, London School of Economics and Political Science.

———— 2013, 'The Political Economy of Brazilian (Latin American) and Korean (East Asian) Comparative Development: Moving beyond Nation-centred Approaches', *New Political Economy*, 18, 2: 171–97.

Grinberg, Nicolas and Guido Starosta 2009, 'The Limits of Studies in Comparative Development of East Asia and Latin America: The Case of Land Reform and Agrarian Policies', *Third World Quarterly*, 30, 4: 761–77.

Grindle, Merilee 2003, 'Shadowing the Past? Policy Reform in Bolivia, 1985–2002', in *Proclaiming Revolution: Bolivia in Comparative Perspective*, edited by Merilee Grindle and Pilar Domingo, London: University of London.

Gudynas, Eduardo 2012, 'Estado compensador y nuevos extractivismos: Las ambivalencias del progresismo sudamericano', *Nueva Sociedad*, 237, January–February: 128–46, available at: <http://www.nuso.org/upload/articulos/3824_1.pdf>.

Guillen, Arturo 2009, 'En la encrucijada de la crisis global', *Agencia Latinoamericana de Informacion*, 18 June, available at: <http://alainet.org/active/31072>.

Gurrieri, Adolfo 1983, 'Technical Progress and its Fruits: The Idea of Development in the Works of Raúl Prebisch', *Journal of Economic Issues*, 17, 2: 389–96.

Gutiérrez, Raquel 2011, 'Competing Political Visions and Bolivia's Unfinished Revolution', *Dialectical Anthropology*, 35, 3: 275–7.

Hall, Anthony 2008, 'Brazil's *Bolsa Família*: A Double-Edged Sword?', *Development and Change* 39, 5: 799–822.

Hanieh, Adam 2009, 'Hierarchies of a Global Market: The South and the Economic Crisis', *Studies in Political Economy*, 83: 61–84.

Hardt, Michael and Antonio Negri 2000, *Empire*, Cambridge, MA: Harvard University Press.

———— 2002, 'Globalizzazione e democrazia', *Hortus Musicus*, 10: 26–31.

———— 2004, *Multitude*, Cambridge, MA: Harvard University Press.

Harman, Chris 2009a, 'The slump of the 1930s, and the crisis today', *International Socialism*, 121, 2 January, available at: <http://www.isj.org.uk/index.php4?id=506&issue=121>.

———— 2009b, *Zombie capitalism*, London: Bookmarks.

Harnecker, Marta 2005, 'On Leftist Strategy', *Science and Society*, 69, 2: 142–152.

———— 2006, *Reconstruyendo la izquierda*, Editorial El Viejo Topo.

———— 2008a, *Reconstruyendo la Izquierda*, Mexico: Siglo Veintiuno Editores.

———— 2008b, *Transfiriendopoder a la Gente*, Caracas: Centro Internacional Miranda.

Hart-Landsberg, Martin 2010, 'China, capitalist accumulation and the world crisis', *XII International Conference of Economists on Globalization*, Havana, 2–6 March.

Harvey, David 1982, *The Limits to Capital*, London: Verso.

——— 2003, *The New Imperialism*, New York: Oxford University Press.

——— 2005, *A Brief History of Neoliberalism*, Oxford: Oxford University Press.

——— 2006, *Spaces of Global Capitalism*, London: Verso.

——— 2009, '¿Estamos realmente ante el fin del neoliberalismo?', *Herramienta. Revista de debate y crítica marxista*, 41, available at: <http://www.herramienta.com.ar/revista-herramienta-n-41/estamos-realmente-ante-el-fin-del-neoliberalismo>.

Hein, Wolfgang 1980, 'Oil and the Venezuelan State', in *Oil and Class Struggle*, edited by Petter Nore and Terisa Turner, London: Zed Press.

Hellinger, Daniel 2008, 'Changes in the Andean Subsoil: Why the Venezuelan, not the Chilean Model', Paper presented at the seminar *Changes in the Andes*, Brown University, Providence, RI, 12–13 February.

Hirschman, Albert 1968, 'The Political Economy of Import-Substituting Industrialization in Latin America', *The Quarterly Journal of Economics*, 82, 1: 1–32.

Hite, Amy 2002, 'Globalization Restrained: Thwarted Privatizations of the Venezuelan Guayana Region's Basic Industries', Unpublished paper, Tulane University: Latin American Studies Program.

——— 2004, 'Natural Resource Growth Poles and Frontier Industrialisation in Venezuela', *Studies in Comparative International Development*, 39, 3: 50–75.

Hobsbawm, Eric 1994, *The Age of Extremes: The Short Twentieth Century 1914–1991*, London: Penguin.

——— 2009, 'Socialism has failed. Now capitalism is bankrupt. So what comes next?' *The Guardian*, 10 April, available at: <http://www.guardian.co.uk/commentisfree/2009/apr/10/financial-crisis-capitalism-socialism-alternatives>.

Holloway, John 2002a, 'Argentina: Que se vayan todos!' *Herramienta 20*, VII, Winter: 71–6.

——— 2002b, *Change the World Without Taking Power*, London: Pluto Press.

——— 2004, '¿Dónde está la lucha de clases?' in *Clase=Lucha. Antagonismo social y marxismo crítico*, edited by John Holloway, Buenos Aires: Editorial Herramienta.

Houtzager, Peter P. 1998, 'State and Unions in the Transformation of the Brazilian Countryside, 1964–1979', *Latin American Research Review*, 33, 2: 103–42.

Howe, Gary Nigel 1981, 'Dependency Theory, Imperialism, and the Production of Surplus Value On a World Scale', *Latin American Perspectives*, 8, 3–4: 82–102.

Humphrey, John 2007, 'The Supermarket Revolution in Developing Countries: Tidal Wave or Tough Competitive Struggle?', *Journal of Economic Geography*, 7, 4: 433–50.

Hunter, Wendy and Natasha Borges Sugiyana 2009, 'Democracy and Social Policy in Brazil: Advancing Basic Needs, Preserving Privileged Interests', *Latin American Politics and Society*, 51, 2: 29–58.

Husson, Michel 2009a, 'Le dogmatisme n'est pas un marxisme', *Nouveau Parti Anticapitaliste*, 8 August, available at: <http://www.npa2009.org/content/le-dogmatisme-n percent E2 percent 80 percent 99est-pas-un-marxisme-par-michel-husson>.

——— 2009b, 'Un capitalisme vert est-il posible?' *Contretemps*, 1 January, available at: <http://hussonet.free.fr/capivert.pdf>.

——— 2010, 'Europe: la refondation ou le chaos', *Hussonet*, March, available at: <http://hussonet.free.fr/epohi10.pdf>.

Hylton, Forrest 2011, 'Old Wine, New Bottles: In Search of Dialectics', *Dialectical Anthropology*, 35: 243–7.

Hylton, Forrest and Sinclair Thomson 2007, *Revolutionary Horizons: Past and Present in Bolivian Politics*, London: Verso.

Hyman, Richard 2007, 'How Can Trade Unions Act Strategically?' *Transfer: European Review of Labour and Research*, 13, 2: 2193–210.

IDEF-CTA 2002, 'El nuevo plan social de Duhalde. Los ganadores de la devaluación y la pesificación', Working Paper, Buenos Aires: Central de los Trabajadores Argentinos.

IMF 2011a, *Bolivia: Public Information Notice (PIN) No. 11/65*, Washington, DC: International Monetary Fund, 27 May.

——— 2011b, *Bolivia: IMF Country Report No. 11/124*, Washington, DC: International Monetary Fund, 2 June.

Iñigo Carrera, Juan 2002, 'The Historical Reason of Existence of the Capitalist Mode of Production and the Determination of the Working Class as a Revolutionary Subject', Unpublished paper, Centro para la Investigación como crítica práctica, available at: <http://www.cicpint.org/>.

——— 2005, 'Argentina: Acumulación del Capital, Formas Políticas y la Determinación de la Clase Obrera como Sujeto Revolucionario', *Razón y Revolución*, 14: 87–109.

——— 2006, 'Argentina: The Reproduction of Capital Accumulation through Political Crisis', *Historical Materialism* 14, 1: 185–219.

——— 2007a, *La formación económica de la sociedad argentina. Volumen I. Renta agraria, ganancia industrial y deuda externa. 1882–2004*, Buenos Aires: Imago Mundi.

——— 2007b, *Conocer el capital hoy. Usar Críticamente El Capital*, Buenos Aires: Imago Mundi.

——— 2007c, *La formación Económica de la Sociedad Argentina*, Buenos Aires: Imago Mundi.

———— 2008a, *El Capital: Razón Histórica, Sujeto Revolucionario y Conciencia*, Buenos Aires: Ediciones Cooperativas.

———— 2008b, 'Acerca del carácter de la relación base económica – superestructura política y jurídica: la oposición entre representación lógica y reproducción dialéctica', paper presented at XIV Jornadas de Epistemología de las Ciencias Económicas, Faculty of Economic Sciences, University of Buenos Aires, 2–3 October 2008.

———— 2008c, 'Terratenientes, retenciones, tipo de cambio, regulaciones específicas: Los cursos de apropiación de la renta de la tierra agraria 1882–2007', Documento de Trabajo Junio/08, *Centro para la Investigación como Crítica Práctica*, Buenos Aires, Argentina.

Iñigo Carrera, Nicolás and María Celia Cotarelo 2003, 'Social Struggles in Present Day Argentina', *Bulletin of Latin American Research*, 22, 2: 201–13.

Instituto Nacional de Estadisticas (INE), 2012, 'Resumen de Indicadores Socio-demográficos', March, available at: <www.ine.gov.ve/documentos/Social/IndicadoresSocioeconomicos/Resumen_ISD .pdf>.

Iranzo, Consuela and Thanali Patrayo 2002, 'Trade Unionism and Globalization: Thoughts from Latin America', *Current Sociology*, 50, 1: 57–74.

James, Daniel 1990, *Resistencia e integración. El peronismo y la clase trabajadora argentina 1946–1976*, Buenos Aires: Editorial Sudamericana.

Jemio, Luis Carlos and María del Carmen Choque 2003, *Employment-Poverty Linkages and Policies: The Case of Bolivia*, Discussion Paper no.11, Geneva: ILO.

Jessop, Bob 2010, 'What Follows Neo-Liberalism? The Deepening Contradictions of US Domination and the Struggle for a New Global Order', in *Political Economy and Global Capitalism. The 21st Century, Present and Future*, edited by Robert Albritton, Bob Jessop, and Richard Westra, London: Anthem Press.

Jetin, Bruno 2009, 'The crisis in Asia: An over-dependence on international trade or reflection of 'labour repression-led' growth regime?' *International Seminar: Marxist analyses of the global crisis*, Amsterdam, International Institute for Research and Education, 2–4 October, available at: <http://www.iire.org/fr/iire-activities-mainmenu-30/22-courses-at-iire/179-international-seminar-marxist-analyses-of-the-global-crisis.html>.

John, Di, Jonathon 2005, 'Economic Liberalization, Political Instability, and State Capacity in Venezuela', *International Political Science Review*, 26, 1: 107–24.

Jones, Mark P. and Wonjae Hwang 2005, 'Provincial Party Bosses: Keystone of the Argentine Congress', in *Argentine Democracy: The Politics of Institutional Weakness*, edited by Steven Levistky and María Victoria Murillo, University Park: The Pennsylvania State University Press.

Joshua, Isaac 2009, 'Capitalism: fin d'epoque?' *Contretemps*, 1.

———— 2010, 'Crisis económica: se acerca la hora de la verdad', *Viento Sur*, 2 February, available at: <http://www.vientosur.info/articulosweb/noticia/?x=2750>.

Kabeer, Naila 1999, 'Globalization, Labour Standards, and Women's Rights: Dilemmas of Collective (in) action in an Independent World', *Feminist Economics*, 10, 1: 3–35.

Kalantzis, Yannick 2004, 'Estudio de la crisis argentina: ¿por qué deberíamos concentrarnos en el desempeño exportador', in *La economía Argentina y su crisis (1976–2001): visiones institucionalistas y regulacionistas*, edited by Robert Boyer and Julio César Neffa, Buenos Aires: Miño y Dávila.

Karl, Terry Lynn 1997, *The Paradox of Plenty*, Berkeley: University of California Press.

Katz, Claudio 2003, 'Capitalismo contemporáneo: etapa, fase y crisis', *Ensayos de Economía*, 13, 22: 36–68.

——— 2004, *El porvenir del socialismo*, Buenos Aires: Herramienta e Imago Mundi. Caracas: Monte Avila.

——— 2007, 'Socialist Strategies in Latin America', *Monthly Review*, 59, 4: 25–41.

——— 2011, 'Los atolladeros de la economía latinoamericana', *Herramienta Web*, 10 December, available at: <http://www.herramienta.com.ar/revista-web/herramienta-web-10>.

Katz, Claudio, Maristella Svampa, Hugo Calello, Ezequiel Adamovsky and Eduardo Lucita, 2008, 'Otra vía para superar la crisis', *Página/12*, 30 May, available at: <http://www.pagina12.com.ar/diario/economia/2-105111-2008-05-30.html>.

Katz, Elizabeth 2003, 'The Changing Role of Women in the Rural Economics of Latin America', in *Current and Emerging Issues for Economic Analysis and Policy Research – CUREMIS II, vol. 1: Latin America and the Caribbean*, edited by Benjamin Davis, Rome: FAO.

Kaup, Brent Z. 2010, 'A Neoliberal Nationalization? The Constraints on Natural-Gas-Led Development in Bolivia', *Latin American Perspectives*, 37, 3: 123–38.

Kay, Cristóbal 1998, 'Estructuralismo y teoría de la dependencia en el período neoliberal, Una perspectiva latinoamericana', *Nueva Sociedad*, 158: 100–19.

Kennemore, Amy and Gregory Weeks 2011, 'Twenty-First Century Socialism? The Elusive Search for a Post-Neoliberal Development Model in Bolivia and Ecuador', *Bulletin of Latin American Research*, 30, 3: 267–81.

Ketelaars, Sofie 2008, '"You Block the Road, I Give you Something", Political Clientelism in Relation to Democracy and Citizenship in Gran Buenos Aires', Argentina, Master Thesis, Utrecht University.

Kettell, Stephen 2006, 'Circuits of Capital and Overproduction: A Marxist Analysis of the Present World Economic Crisis', *Review of Radical Political Economics*, 38, 24: 24–44.

Kicillof, Axel and Guido Starosta 2007, 'Value form and class struggle: A Critique of the Autonomist Theory of Value', *Capital and Class*, 92: 13–40.

Kirchner, Néstor and Torcuato DiTella 2003, *Después del Derrumbe*, Buenos Aires: Ed. Galerna.

Klein, Herbert S. 2003, *A Concise History of Bolivia*, Cambridge: University of Cambridge Press.

Klein, Naomi 2006, 'Latin America's Shock Resistance', *The Nation* on-line, 26 November, available at: <http://www.thenation.com/article/latin-americas-shock-resistance>.

———— 2009, 'Capitalism, Sarah Palin style', *The Progressive*, August, 73, 8, available at: <http://www.progressive.org/kleino809.html>.

Klubock, Thomas 1998, *Contested Communities: Class, Gender, and Politics in Chile's El Teniente Copper Mine, 1904–1951*, Durham, NC: Duke University Press.

Kohl, Benjamin 2004, 'Privatization Bolivian Style: A Cautionary Tale', *International Journal of Urban and Regional Research*, 28: 893–908.

Kornblihtt, Jorge 2006, 'Seguimos perdiendo' *Aromo*, 28, May.

Kotz, David 2003, 'Neoliberalism and the social structure of accumulation theory of long-run capital accumulation', *Review of Radical Political Economics*, 35, 3: 263–70.

———— 2008, 'Contradictions of economic growth in the neoliberal era: Accumulation and crisis in the contemporary U.S. economy', *Review of Radical Political Economics*, 40, 2: 174–88.

Kregel, Jan 2009a, 'Regulaciones para después de la crisis', *Página/12*, 26 May, available at: <http://www.pagina12.com.ar/diario/economia/2-125588-2009-05-26.html>.

———— 2009b, 'Taming the bond market vigilantes: Gaining policy space', XI Encuentro Internacional sobre Globalización y Problemas del Desarrollo, Havana, 2–6 March.

Krugman, Paul 2009a, 'Los dilemas de nacionalizar', *Clarín*, 7 March, available at: <http://edant.clarin.com/diario/2009/03/07/elmundo/i-01872095.htm>.

———— 2009b, 'Es hora de reflotar la tasa Tobin', *Clarín*, 28 November, available at: <http://edant.clarin.com/diario/2009/11/28/elmundo/i-02050415.htm>.

———— 2009c, 'El peligroso juego que practican los chinos', *La Nación*, 17 November, available at: <http://www.lanacion.com.ar/1200744-el-peligroso-juego-que-practican-los-chinos>.

———— 2009d, 'Solución a la vista', *La Nación*, 8 December, available at: <http://www.lanacion.com.ar/1209097-solucion-a-la-vista>.

La Nación 2009, 'La humanidad ya demanda un planeta y medio: Consume y contamina en un año lo que a la naturaleza le lleva 18 meses producir y degrader', *La Nacion*, 24 November, available at: <http://www.lanacion.com.ar/1203576-la-humanidad-ya-demanda-un-planeta-y-medio>.

———— 2010, 'Crece en el mundo la pobreza extrema: Duro informe del FMI y el Banco Mundial', *La Nación*, 24 April, available at: <http://www.lanacion.com.ar/1257758-crece-en-el-mundo-la-pobreza-extrema>.

Lacabana, Miguel, and Cecilia Cariola 2005, 'Los bordes de la esperanza: nuevas formas de participación popular y gobiernos locales en la periferia de Caracas', *Revista Venezolana de Economía y Ciencias Sociales*, 11, 1: 21–41.

Lafaber, Walter 1993, *Inevitable Revolutions: The United States in Central America*, second edition, New York: W.W. Norton and Company.

Lancaster, Roger N. 1988, *Thanks to God and the Revolution: Popular Religion and Class Consciousness in the New Nicaragua*, New York: Columbia University Press.

Lander, Edgardo 1996, 'The Impact of Neoliberal Adjustment in Venezuela, 1989–1993', *Latin American Perspectives*, 23, 3: 50–73.

Lascano, Marcelo R. 2001, *La economía argentina hoy. Un análisis riguroso de un país en crisis*, Buenos Aires: Editorial El Ateneo.

LASFRC 2002, 'Resolution of Argentina's Financial Crisis', Latin American Shadow Financial Regulatory Committee Meeting, 5 May, Washington: American Enterprise Institute for Public Policy Research, available at: <http://www.aei.org/article/15138>.

Laurie, Nina 2005, 'Establishing Development Orthodoxy: Negotiating Masculinities in the Water Sector', *Development and Change*, 36, 3: 527–49.

Lavagna, Roberto 2009, 'La crisis global reclama reformas no cosméticas', *Clarín*, 24 February, available at: <http://edant.clarin.com/diario/2009/02/24/opinion/0-01864915.htm>.

Lazarte, Jorge 1989, *Movimiento obrero y procesos políticos en Bolivia (Historia de la COB 1952–1987*, La Paz: Instituto latinoamericano de investigaciones sociales.

Lebowitz, Michael 2006a, *Build it Now: Socialism for the Twenty First Century*, New York Monthly: Review Press.

—— 2006b, 'The Politics of Beyond "Capital"', *Historical Materialism*, 14, 4: 167–83.

—— 2007, 'Venezuela: A Good Example of the Bad Left of Latin America', *Monthly Review*, 59, 3: 38–54.

—— 2010,*The Socialist Alternative: Real Human Development*, New York: Monthly Review.

Leiva, Fernando Ignacio 2008a, *Latin American Neostructuralism: The Contradictions of Post-Neoliberal Development*, Minnesota: University of Minnesota Press.

—— 2008b, 'Toward a Critique of Latin American Neostructuralism', *Latin American Politics and Society*, 50, 4: 1–25.

Lenin, Vladimir Illych 1968 [1917], *State and Revolution*, New York: International Publishers.

—— 1969 [1902], *What is to be Done?* New York: International Publishers.

Levistky, Steven and Victoria Murillo (eds.) 2005, *Argentine Democracy. The Politics of Institutional Weakness*, University Park: The Pennsylvania State University Press.

Levitsky, Steven 2003, *Transforming Labor-based Parties in Latin America. Argentine Peronism in Comparative Perspective*, Cambridge: Cambridge University Press.

—— 2005, 'Crisis and Renovation: Institutional Weakness and the Transformation of Argentine Peronism, 1983–2003', in *Argentine Democracy. The Politics of*

Institutional Weakness, edited by Steven Levitsky and Victoria Murillo, University Park: The Pennsylvania State University Press.

Levitsky, Steven, and Kenneth M. Roberts 2011, 'Latin America's "Left Turn": A Framework for Analysis', in *The Resurgence of the Latin American Left*, edited by Steven Levitsky and Kenneth M. Roberts, Baltimore: The John Hopkins University Press.

Levy, David L. and Daniel Egan 2003, 'A Neo-Gramscian Approach to Corporate Political Strategy: Conflict and Accommodation in the Climate Change Negotiations', *Journal of Management Studies*, 40, 4: 803–29.

Lewis, Collin 1999, 'Industry and Industrialisation: What Has Been Accomplished, What Needs to Be Done', *Economia*, 23: 7–25.

Lievesley, Geraldine and Steve Ludlam 2009, 'Introduction: A "Pink Tide"?' in *Reclaiming Latin America: Experiments in Radical Social Democracy*, edited by Geraldine Lievesley and Steve Ludlam, London: Zed Books.

Lindenboim, Javier and Claudia Danani (eds.) 2003, *Entre el trabajo y la política. Las reformas de las políticas sociales argentinas en perspectiva comparada*, Buenos Aires: Editorial Biblos.

Llach, Juan 2010, 'Preocupaciones globales', *La Nación*, 17 March, available at: <http://www.lanacion.com.ar/1244115-preocupaciones-globales>.

Llanos, Mariana 2004, 'From De la Rúa to Kirchner: the Beginning of a New Political Cycle in Democratic Argentina', in *The Argentine Crisis at the Turn of the Millennium: Causes, Consequences and Explanations*, edited by Flavia Fiorucci and Marcus Klein, Amsterdam: Center for Latin American Research and Documentation.

Lobato, Mirta and Juan Suriano 2003, *La protesta social en la Argentina*, Buenos Aires: Fondo de Cultura Económica.

Lobina, Emanuele 2000, 'Cochabamba – Water War', *Focus (Public Service International Journal)*, 7, 2: 1–6.

Loong Yu, Au 2009, 'Fin d'un modele ou naissance d'un nouveau modele', *Inprecor*, 555, November, available at: <http://orta.dynalias.org/inprecor/article-inprecor?id=825>.

Lopes, Francisco L. 2003, 'Notes on the Brazilian Crisis of 1997–99', *Brazilian Journal of Political Economy*, 23, 3: 35–62.

López, Emiliano and Francisco Vértiz 2012, 'Capital transnacional y proyecto nacionales de desarrollo en América Latina: Las nuevas lógicas del extractivismo neodesarrollista', *Herramienta*, 50, July, available at: <http://www.herramienta.com.ar/revista-herramienta-n-50/capital-transnacional-y-proyectos-nacionales-de-desarrollo-en-america-latin>.

Los Tiempos 2004, 'Bolivia perdería juicio por Aguas del Tunari', 20 November.

———— 2005, 'Concejo retira cupo laboral del directorio de Semapa', 6 October.

———— 2006, 'El Gobierno se compromete a condonar deudas de Semapa', 4 February.

Love, Joseph L. 1984, 'Economic Ideas and Ideologies in Latin America Since 1930', in *The Cambridge History of Latin America*, edited by Leslie Bethell, Volume 6, Cambridge: Cambridge University Press.

—— 2005, 'The Rise and Decline of Economic Structuralism in Latin America: New Dimensions', *Latin American Research Review*, 40, 3: 100–25.

Lovera, Alberto 2008 'Los consejos comunales en Venezuela: Democracia participativa o delegativa?', *Revista Venezolana de Economía y Ciencias Sociales*, 14, 1: 107–24.

Löwy, Michael 1987, 'The Romantic and the Marxist Critique of Modern Civilization', *Theory and Society*, 16, 6: 891–904.

—— 2005, *Fire Alarm: Reading Walter Benjamin's 'On the Concept of History'*, London: Verso.

—— 2009, 'Changement climatique: Contribution au débat', *Inprecor*, 553–4, September–October, available at: <http://orta.dynalias.org/inprecor/~18424d3d8c9 71c92802e52e8~/article-inprecor?id=783>.

Lozano, Claudio 2005, 'Los problemas de la distribución del ingreso y el crecimiento en la Argentina actual', Mesa Nacional CTA, CTA-IDEP.

—— 2006, 'Clandestinidad y precarización laboral en la Argentina de 2006', Instituto de Estudios y Formación, CTA.

—— 2007, 'Crecimiento y Distribución: Notas sobre el recorrido 2003–2007', Instituto de Estudios y Formación, CTA.

—— 2009, 'Apuntes sobre la coyuntura actual. El cambio de fase en la etapa económica: de la desaceleración al estancamiento', Report, Buenos Aires: Instituto de Estudios y Formación (IDEF-CTA).

Lucena, Hector 2007, *Lo Laboral en Tiempos de Transición*, Valencia: Universidad de Carabobo.

Lucita, Eduardo 2001, 'Cortando rutas, abriendo nuevos senderos. Desocupados, ocupados, "piqueteros": viejas y nuevas formas de lucha', *Cuadernos del Sur*, 32: 79–93.

Lukín, Tomás 2010, 'Operación ... Suplemento Cash', *Página/12*, 31 January, available at: <http://www.pagina12.com.ar/diario/suplementos/cash/17-4166-2010-01-31.html>.

Macdonald, Laura and Arne Rückert (eds.) 2009, *Post-neoliberalism in the Americas*, New York: Palgrave.

Madrid, Raúl 2011, 'Bolivia: Origins and Policies of the Movimiento al Socialismo', in *The Resurgence of the Latin American Left*, edited by Steven Levitsky and Kenneth M. Roberts, Baltimore: The John Hopkins University Press.

Mandel, Ernest 1968, *Introducción a la teoría económica marxista*, Buenos Aires: Carlos Pérez Editor.

Mann, Susan and James Dickinson 1978, 'Obstacles to the Development of Capitalist Agriculture, *Journal of Peasant Studies*, 5, 1: 466–87.

Manzano, Osmel and Francisco Monaldi 2008, 'The Political Economy of Oil Production in Latin America', *Economía*, 9, 1: 59–103.

Marea Socialista 2010, 'En CVG ALCASA, Trabajadores derrotan golpe de Estado orquestado por la FBT (Movimiento 21)', *Aporrea*, 10 November, available at: <www .aporrea.org/endogeno/n169305.html>.

Marini, Ruy Mauro 1973, *Dialéctica de la dependencia*, México: Era.

──── 1979, 'El ciclo del capital en la economía dependiente', in *Mercado y dependencia*, edited by Ursula Oswald, México: Nueva Imagen.

Marshall, Adriana 2004, 'Labour Market Policies and Regulations in Argentina, Brazil and Mexico: Programmes and Impacts', Employment Strategy Papers No. 13, International Labour Office.

Martins, Carlos Eduardo 2007, 'Los impasses de la hegemonía de Estados Unidos: Perspectivas para el siglo XXI', in *Crisis de hegemonía de Estados Unidos*, edited by Marco A. Gandásegui, Argentina: Consejo Latinoamericano de Ciencias Sociales.

Marx, Karl 1973, *Grundrisse. Foundations of the Critique of Political Economy*, Harmondsworth: Penguin.

──── 1976, *Capital. Volume I*, trans. B. Fawkes, Harmondsworth: Penguin.

──── 1977, *Capital, volume I*, available at: <www.marxists.org/archive/marx/works/ 1867-c1/>.

──── 1978, *Capital. Volume 2*, trans. D. Fernbach, Harmondsworth: Penguin.

──── 1981, *Capital. Volume 3*, Harmondsworth: Penguin.

──── 1990, *Capital. A Critique of Political Economy. Vol. I*, London: Penguin Press.

──── 1991, *Capital. A Critique of Political Economy. Vol. III*, London: Penguin Press.

──── 2000 [1863], *Theories of Surplus Value (Volume IV of Capital)*, Prometheus Books.

Massaraat, Mohssenn 1980, 'The Energy Crisis: The Struggle for the Redistribution of Surplus Profit from Oil', in *Oil and Class Struggle*, edited by Petter Nore and Terisa Turner, London: Zed Press.

Massey, Doreen 2009, 'Concepts of space and power in theory and in political practice', *Documents D'Anàlisi Geogràfica*, 55: 15–26.

Matthews, Karine and Matthew Patterson 2005, 'Boom or Bust? The Economic Engine Behind the Drive for Climate Change Policy', *Global Change, Peace and Security*, 17, 1: 59–75.

Mayo, Peter 1999, *Gramsci, Freire, and Adult Education: Possibilities for Transformative Action*, London: Macmillan.

McDonough, Terrence 2003, 'What does long wave theory have to contribute to the debate on globalization?' *Review of Radical Political Economics*, 35, 3: 280–6.

──── 2008, 'Social structures of accumulation theory: The state of the art', *Review of Radical Political Economics*, 40, 2: 153–73.

McKenna, Tony 2009, 'Hugo Chávez and the PSUV in Light of the Historical Process in Venezuela', *Critique: Journal of Socialist Theory*, 37, 1: 121–34.

McMichael, Philip 2011, *Development and Social Change: A Global Perspective*, fifth edition, Thousand Oaks, CA: Sage Publications.

McNally, David 2006, *Another World Is Possible. Globalization and Anti-Capitalism*, updated and expanded edition, Winnipeg, MB: Arbiter Ring.

————— 2008, 'From financial crisis to world slump', *Historical Materialism Conference*, London, 7–9 November.

————— 2009, 'From Financial Crisis to World-Slump: Accumulation, Financialisation, and the Global Slowdown', *Historical Materialism*, 17, 2: 35–83.

McSherry, J. Patrice 2005, *Predatory States: Operation Condor and Covert War in Latin America*, Lanham, MD: Rowman and Littlefield.

MIBAM 2005, *Resumen Ejecutivo Sobre el Proceso de Cogestión en CVG Alcasa*, Caracas: Ministry for Mines and Basic Industry.

————— 2006, *Crónica y documentos del proceso de cogestión en CVG Alcasa*, vol. I, February/March, Caracas: Ministry for Mines and Basic Industry.

Michels, Robert 1962 [1915], *Political Parties: A Sociological Study of the Oligarchical Tendencies of Modern Democracy*, New York: Dover.

Migone, Andrea 2007, 'Hedonistic consumerism', *Review of Radical Political Economics*, 39, 2: 173–200.

Milanez, Artur Yabe, Barros, Nereida Resende and Paulo de Sá Campello Faveret Filho 2008, 'O perfil do apoio do BNDES ao setor sucroalcooleiro', *BNDES Setorial no. 28*, Rio de Janeiro, BNDES, available at: <http://www.bndes.gov.br/SiteBNDES/export/sites/default/bndes_pt/Galerias/Arquivos/conhecimento/bnset/set2801.pdf>.

Milanez, Artur Yabe, Carvalcanti, Carlos Eduardo de Siqueira, and Paulo de Sá Campello Faveret Filho 2010, 'O papel do BNDES no desenvolvimento do setor sucroenergético', in *O BNDES em um Brasil em Transição*, Brasilia, BNDES.

Milanez, Artur Yabe, de Sá Campello Faveret Filho, Paulo and Sergio Eduardo Silveira da Rosa 2008, 'Perspectiva para o etanol brasileiro', *BNDES Setorial no. 27*, Rio de Janeiro, BNDES, available at: <http://www.bndes.gov.br/SiteBNDES/export/sites/default/bndes_pt/Galerias/Arquivos/conhecimento/bnset/set2702.pdf>.

Milanez, Artur Yabe, Nyko, Diego, Garcia, Jorge Luiz Faria, and Carlos Eduardo Osório Xavier 2010, 'Logística para o etanol: situação atual e desafios futuros', *BNDES Setorial no. 31*, Rio de Janeiro: BNDES, available at: <http://www.bndes.gov.br/SiteBNDES/export/sites/default/bndes_pt/Galerias/Arquivos/conhecimento/bnset/set3102.pdf>.

MINCI 1999, *Constitution of the Bolivarian Republic of Venezuela*, Caracas: Ministry of Communication and Information.

Ministerio de Economía y Producción 2007, 'Lineamientos estratégicos para el desarrollo productivo de la Argentina', working paper, May, Buenos Aires.

Ministerio de Trabajo, Empleo y Seguridad Social 2005, 'Record de la negociación: colectiva en los últimos 14 años. Informe anual 2004', Buenos Aires: Subsecretaría de Programación Técnica y Estudios Laborales.

———— 2010, 'Comportamiento del empleo registrado en la actual etapa de recuperación económica. Encuesta de Indicadores Laborales. Datos del 2do trimestre de 2010', Buenos Aires: Subsecretaría de Programación Técnica y Estudios Laborales.

Ministry of External Relations of Brazil 2007, US-Brazilian Cooperation on Biofuels, Embassy of Brazil in London, 22 August, available at: <http://www.brazil.org.uk/press/pressreleases_files/20070822.html>.

Mitter, Swasti 1994, 'A Comparative Survey', in Women in Trade Unions: Organising the Unorganised, edited by Margaret H. Martens and Swasti Mitter, Geneva: ILO.

Molina, Jose 2004, 'The Unravelling of Venezuela's Party System: From Party Rule to Personalistic Politics and Deinstitutionalization', in The Unraveling of Representative Democracy in Venezuela, edited by Jennifer L. McCoy and David J. Myers, Baltimore: Johns Hopkins.

Mommer, Bernard 1998, 'The New Governance of Venezuelan Oil', WPM 23, Oxford: Oxford Institute for Energy Studies.

Monedero, Juan Carlos 2007, 'Sobre el Partido Socialista Unido de Venezuela: Potencialidades y Riesgos', in Ideas Para Debatir el Socialismo del Siglo XXI, edited by Magarita Lopez Maya, Caracas: Editorial Alfa.

Moody, Kim 1997, Workers in a Lean World, London: Verso.

Morais, Lecio and Alfredo Saad-Filho 2005, 'Lula and the Continuity of Neoliberalism in Brazil: Strategic Choice, Economic Imperative or Political Schizophrenia?' Historical Materialism, 13, 1: 3–32.

———— 2011, 'Brazil Beyond Lula: Forging Ahead or Pausing for Breath?', Latin American Perspectives, 38, 2: 31–44.

Moseley, Fred 1991, The Falling Rate of Profit in the Postwar United States Economy, London and New York: Macmillan Press/St. Martin's Press.

———— 2009, 'The U.S. economic crisis, causes and solutions', International Socialist Review, 64, March–April, available at: <http://www.isreview.org/issues/64/feat-moseley.shtml>.

MPD 2007, Proyecto Nacional Simon Bolivar, Primer Plan Socialista-PPS, Caracas: Ministerio del Poder Popular para la Planificacion y Desarrollo.

Nash, June 1979, We Eat the Mines and the Mines Eat Us: Dependency and Exploitation in Bolivian Tin Mines, New York: Columbia University Press.

Navarro, Vicenç 2010, 'Las causas de la crisis mundial actual', Redes Cristianas, 3 January, available at: <http://www.redescristianas.net/2010/01/03/las-causas-de-la-crisis-mundial-actualvicenc-navarro/>.

Neffa, Julio C. 2008, *La informalidad, la precariedad laboral y el empleo no registrado en la provincia de Buenos Aires*, Buenos Aires: CEIL-PIETTE/CONICET.

Negri, Antonio 1999, *Insurgencies: Constituent Power & the Modern State*, Missouri: University of Minnesota Press.

Nelson, Richard 1998, 'The Agenda for Growth Theory: a Different Point of View', *Cambridge Journal of Economics*, 22: 497–520.

Nelson, Richard R., and Sidney G. Winter 1982, *An Evolutionary Theory of Economic Change*, Cambridge, MA: Harvard University Press.

Newell, Peter and Matthew Patterson 1998, 'A Climate for Business: Global Warming, the State and Capital', *Review of International Political Economy*, 5, 4: 679–703.

Nicaragua Solidarity Network of Greater New York 2005, 'Bolivia: Protests Oust Water Company,' *Weekly News Update #781*, 16 January.

Novelli, José Marcos and Andreia Galvão 2001–2, 'The Political Economy of Neoliberalism in Brazil in the 1990s', *International Journal of Political Economy*, 31, 4: 3–52.

Novick, Marta 2001, 'Nuevas reglas del juego en Argentina, competitividad y actores sindicales', in *Los sindicatos frente a los procesos de transición política*, edited by Enrique De la Garza Toledo, Buenos Aires: CILAS/CLACSO/Asdi.

O'Donnell, Guillermo 1993, 'On State, Democratization and Some Conceptual Problems: A Latin American View with Glances at Some Postcommunist Societies', *World Development*, 21, 6: 1355–69.

O'Hara, Phillip 2002, 'A new financial social structure of accumulation in the US for long wave upswing?' *Review of Radical Political Economics*, 34, 3: 295–301.

———— 2004, 'A new transnational corporate social structure of accumulation for long wave upswing in the world economy?' *Review of Radical Political Economics*, 36, 3: 328–35.

Ocampo, José Antonio 1998, 'Cincuenta años de la CEPAL', *Revista de la CEPAL*, Special Issue: 11–16.

———— 2001, 'Raúl Prebisch', *REVISTA DE LA CEPAL* 75: 25–40.

Ohmae, Kenichi 1990, *The Borderless World*, New York: Harper Business.

Oliveira, Francisco de 2006, 'Lula in the Labyrinth', *New Left Review*, 42: 5–22.

Olivera, Oscar and Tom Lewis (eds.) 2004, *Cochabamba! Water War in Bolivia*, Cambridge, MA: South End Press.

Önaran, Ozlem 2009, 'Specificity of the crisis in Europe: Will national stimulus plans be enough in the absence of an EU coordinated response?' International Seminar: Marxist analyses of the global crisis, International Institute for Research and Education, Amsterdam, 2–4 October.

Opinión 2005a, 'Los trabajadores de Semapa paran rechazando un despido', 8 September.

———— 2005b, 'Semapa despide a 164 trabajadores pero promete comprar sus servicios', 20 October.

Orlean, André 2010, 'La crise moteur du capitalisme', *Le Monde*, 30 March, available at: <http://www.lemonde.fr/cgi-bin/ACHATS/acheter.cgi?offre=ARCHIVES&type_item=ART_ARCH_30J&objet_id=1119269>.

Ormachea Saavedra, Enrique 2007, *¿Revolución agraria o consolidación de la vía terrateniente? El gobierno del MAS y las políticas de tierras*, La Paz: CEDLA.

———— 2011a, 'El "Gasolinazo" desnudó la política agraria del gobierno del MAS', Nota de prensa, 12 January, La Paz: CEDLA.

———— 2011b, 'Marcha indígena por el TIPNIS: ¿Tensión creativa o contradicción de clase', Nota de prensa, 6 September, La Paz: CEDLA.

Orozco Ramírez, Shirley, García Linera, Álvaro and Pablo Stefanoni 2006, *'No somos juguetes de nadie . . . ': Análisis de la relación de movimientos sociales, recursos naturales, Estado y decentralización*, La Paz: Plural Editores.

Ortiz, Ricardo, and Martín Schorr 2007, 'La rearticulación del bloque de poder en la Argentina de la postconvertibilidad', *Papeles de trabajo. Revista electrónica del Instituto de Altos Estudios Sociales de la Universidad Nacional de General San Martín*, Año 1, 2, Buenos Aires.

Pacheco Balanza, Pablo and Enrique Ormachea Saavedra 2000, *Campesinos, patrones y obreros agrícolas: Una aproximación a las tendencias del empleo y los ingresos rurales en Bolivia*, La Paz: CEDLA.

Página Siete 2011a, *"Gobierno fracasa en todas sus estrategias contra indígenas"*, 20 October.

———— 2011b, 'Alianza de pueblos indígenas posibilitó el éxito de la marcha', 20 October.

———— 2011c, *'Marchistas levantaron carpas con el recuerdo de la represión'*, 20 October.

———— 2011d, 'Los marchistas aseguran que se quedarán hasta lograr su objetivo', 20 October.

———— 2011e, 'Indígenas no buscan "tumbar" al Gobierno de Evo Morales', 20 October.

———— 2011f, 'Un informe ambiental alerta sobre los efectos del camino', 20 October.

———— 2011g, 'La sospecha del sobreprecio salió de documentos oficiales', 20 October.

———— 2011h, 'Gobierno replantea eliminar subvención a los carburantes', 2 November.

———— 2011i, *'El Pacto de Unidad feneció y el movimiento indígena se rearma'*, 3 November.

———— 2011j, 'Aprobación a Evo baja al 35% en ciudades del eje troncal', 3 November.

———— 2011k, *'Rearticulan Pacto de Unidad sin la presencia de indígenas'*, 7 November.

———— 2011l, 'Gobierno eliminará subsidio si así lo decide la cumbre social', 12 November.

———— 2011m, 'Bolivia y EEUU deberán partir casi de cero en tres áreas clave', 13 November.

Página/12 2008a, 'El Senado rechazó el proyecto de las retenciones móviles', 17/7/2008, available at: <http://www.pagina12.com.ar/diario/ultimas/20-107977-2008-07-17 .html>.

———— 2008b, 'Marcha del espacio "Otro Camino". Por las retenciones y una canasta básica sin IVA', 11/7/2008, available at: <http://www.pagina12.com.ar/diario/ultimas/ 20-107656-2008-07-11.html>.

———— 2009, 'Por un "Blindaje Social" ante la crisis. La CTA convocó a un paro nacional el 27 de mayo', Página/12, 11/5/2009, available at: <http://www.pagina12.com.ar/ diario/ultimas/20-124716-2009-05-11.html>.

Palma, Gabriel 1978, 'Dependency: A Formal Theory of Underdevelopment or a Methodology for the Analysis of Concrete Situations of Underdevelopment?' *World Development*, 6, 7–8: 881–924.

Panitch, Leo and Martijn Konings 2008, 'US financial power in crisis', *Historical Materialism*, 16, 4: 3–34.

Panitch, Leo and Sam Gindin 2004, 'Global Capitalism and American Empire', in *Socialist Register 2004: The New Imperial Challenge*, edited by Leo Panitch and Colin Leys, New York: Monthly Review Press.

———— 2004, 'Global Capitalism and American Empire', in *Socialist Register 2004: The New Imperial Challenge*, edited by Leo Panitch and Colin Leys, London: Merlin Press.

Panizza, Francisco 2004, ' "Brazil Needs to Change": Change as Iteration and the Iteration of Change in Brazil's 2002 Presidential Election', *Bulletin of Latin American Research*, 23, 4: 465–82.

Parodi Solari, Jorge and Catherine M. Conaghan 2000, *To be a worker: identity and politics in Peru*, Chapel Hill: University of North Carolina Press.

Parot, Rodrigo 1998, 'Venezuela: Natural Resources and Public Enterprises', in *Resources, Industrialisation and Exports in Latin America: the Primary Input Content of Sustained Exports of Manufactures from Argentina, Colombia and Venezuela*, edited by Elio Londero and Simón Teitel, London: MacMillan.

Patroni, Viviana 2001, 'The Decline and Fall of Corporatism? Labor Legislation Reform in Mexico and Argentina during the 1990s', *Canadian Journal of Political Science*, 34, 2: 249–74.

———— 2008, 'After the Collapse: Workers and Social Conflict in Argentina', in *Global Economy Contested: Power and Conflict across the International Division of Labour*, edited by Marcus Taylor, London: Routledge.

Peralta Ramos, M. 2007, *Economía política argentina: poder y clases sociales (1930–2006)*, Buenos Aires: Fondo de Cultura Económica.

Perelman, Michael 2000, *The Invention of Capitalism: Classical Political Economy and the Secret History of Primitive Accumulation*, Durham, NC: Duke University Press.

REFERENCES

Pérez Sainz, Juan and Paul Zarembka 1979, 'Accumulation and the State in Venezuelan Industrialisation', *Latin American Perspectives*, 6, 3: 5–29.

Pérez, Julián 2006, 'Social Resistance in El Alto – Bolivia', in *Reclaiming Public Water: Achievements, Struggles and Visions from Around the World*, second edition, edited by Belén Balanyá, Brid Brennan, Olivier Hoedeman, Satoko Kishimoto and Philipp Terhorst Porto Alegre: Transnational Institute and Corporate Europe Observatory, available at: <http://www.tni.org/books/waterelalto.pdf>.

Pérez, Pablo Ernesto 2005, 'Los sospechosos de siempre. Los desocupados de larga duración en Argentina y su (in)empleabilidad', in *Desequilibrios en el mercado de trabajo argentino. Los desafíos en la postconvertibilidad*, edited by Julio C. Neffa, Buenos Aires: Editorial Trabajo y Sociedad.

Pérez, Pablo Ernesto and Mariano Féliz 2010, 'La crisis económica y sus implicancias sobre la política de empleo e ingresos en Argentina', *Revista Ser Social*, 12, 26: 31–58.

Perraton, Jonathan 2005, 'What's Left of "State Capacity"? The Developmental State After Globalisation and the East Asian Crisis', in *Global Encounters: International Political Economy, Development and Globalisation*, edited by Graham Harrison, London: Palgrave-MacMillan.

Petras, James 1990, 'Retreat of the Intellectuals', *Economic and Political Weekly*, 25, 38: 2143–9.

Petras, James and Henry Veltmeyer 2002, 'The Peasantry and the State in Latin America: A Troubled Past, An Uncertain Future', *Journal of Peasant Studies*, 29, 3–4: 41–82.

—— 2003, *Cardoso's Brazil: a Land for Sale*, Lanham, MD: Rowman and Littlefield Publishers.

—— 2005, *Social Movements and State Power: Argentina, Brazil, Bolivia, Ecuador*, London: Pluto.

Piñeiro-Harnecker, Camila 2009 'Workplace Democracy and Social Consciousness: A Study of Venezuelan Cooperatives', *Science and Society*, 73: 309–39.

—— 2010, 'Venezuelan Cooperatives: Practice and Challenges', unpublished paper held at 28th ILPC, March 15–17, Rutgers University.

Pinto, Aníbal 1970, 'Naturaleza e implicaciones de la "heterogeneidad estructural" de la América Latina', *El Trimestre Económico*, 37, 145: 83–100.

Piva, Adrián 2001, ' "La década perdida". Tendencias de la conflictividad obrera frente a la ofensiva del capital (1989–2001)', *Cuadernos del Sur*, 32: 55–77.

—— 2006, 'El desacople entre los ciclos de conflicto obrero y la acción de las cúpulas sindicales en Argentina (1989–2001)', *Revista Estudios del Trabajo*, 31: 23–52.

—— 2009, 'Vecinos, piqueteros y sindicatos disidentes. La dinámica del conflicto social entre 1989 y 2001', in *Argentina en Pedazos*, edited by Alberto Bonnet and Adrian Piva, Buenos Aires: Ediciones Continente.

Pochmann, Marcio 2008, *O Emprego no Desenvolvimento da Nação*, São Paulo: Boitempo.

Ponce, Aldo 2007, 'Unemployment and Clientelism: The *Piquetero* Movement', *Journal of Interdisciplinary & Multidisciplinary Research*, 1, 2: 1–24.

Post, Charles 2005, 'Ernest Mandel and the Marxian Theory of Bureaucracy', 26 July, *International Viewpoint*, available at: <http://internationalviewpoint.org/spip.php?article848>.

Postero, Nancy 2004, 'Neoliberal restructuring in Bolivia', *A Contracorriente* 2: 126–35.

——— 2005a, 'Indigenous Responses to Neoliberalism', *PoLAR: Political and Legal Anthropology Review*, 28, 1: 73–92.

——— 2005b, 'Neoliberal Restructuring in Bolivia', *A Contracorriente*, 2: 133.

Poulantzas, Nicos 1979, *Estado, Poder y Socialismo*, México: Siglo XXI.

Pozzi, Pablo 2008, *La oposición obrera a la dictadura (1976–1982)*, Buenos Aires: Imago Mundi.

Pozzi, Pablo and Alejando Schneider 1993, *Combatiendo al capital: Crisis y recomposición de la clase obrera Argentina (1985–1993)*, Buenos Aires: El Bloque Editorial.

Prada Alcoreza, Raúl 2011, 'La defensa de los derechos de la Madre Tierra en el TIPNIS', *La Época*, 14–20 August.

Prebisch, Raúl 1949, *El desarrollo económico de la américa latina y algunos de sus principales problemas*, Santiago de Chile: CEPAL.

——— 1951, 'Theoretical and Practical Problems of Economic Growth', Document E/CN UN 12/221, Mexico DF: United Nations-ECLAC.

——— 1961, 'Economic Development, Planning and International Cooperation', UN. II.G. 1961.6–8, Santiago de Chile: United Nations.

——— 1981, *Capitalismo periférico: crisis y transformación*. México: Fondo de Cultura Economica.

Prensa CVG-Alcasa 2007, *Aporrea*, 22 February, available at: <www.alcasa.com.ve/>.

Prensa de Frente 2005, 'Nuevas formas de construcción sindical' Boletín Quincenal (Buenos Aires), 29, 19 December, available at: <www.prensadefrente.org/pdfb2/index.php/a/2005/12/19/p879>.

——— 2009, 'Movimientos sociales y de desocupados pedimos audiencia al gobierno para el "diálogo"', press release, Buenos Aires, 24 July, available at: <http://www.prensadefrente.org/pdfb2/index.php/anuncios/2009/07/27/p4931>.

Prensa Frente Socialista de Trabajador (PFST) 2011, 'Vuelve Don Gato y su pandilla a cerrar los portones ya son mas de 5 días que este paro esta afectando las operaciones de la planta', *Aporrea*, 29 January, available at: <www.aporrea.org/trabajadores/a116676.html>.

Prensa Marea Socialista 2011, 'Entrevista al compañero trabajador Osvaldo León, militante del colectivo Control Obrero de ALCASA', *Aporrea*, 27 January, available at: <www.aporrea.org/trabajadores/n173806.html>.

Prensa Sidor 2011, 'Avanza constitución de Empresa Naviera Socialista del Orinoco', *Aporrea*, 16 May, available at: <www.aporrea.org/endogeno/n181020>.

Prensa UNETE 2011a, 'Electas 5 personas de la comunidad para integrar directiva de la EPS La Gaviota conjuntamente con los trabajadores', *Aporrea*, 15 January, available at: <www.aporrea.org/trabajadores/n173066>.

———— 2011b, 'UNETE llama a la clase obrera a seguir ejemplo de lucha de "La Gaviota"', *Aporrea*, 24 March, available at: <www.aporrea.org/trabajadores/n179633.html>.

———— 2011c, 'Trabajadores de Pescalaba participarán en la gestión de la empresa', *Aporrea*, 30 April, available at: <www.aporrea.org/trabajadores/n180038.html>.

Prensa CVG-Alcasa 2011, 'Alcasa activa conversaciones con Chinalco para ejecutar proyectos de adecuación tecnológica', *Aporrea*, 1 March, available at: <www.aporrea.org/trabajadores/n176022.html>.

Presencia 1999, 'Tarifas de agua subirán hasta en un 175 percent en Cochabamba', in *30 Días de Noticias*, edited by CEDIB, La Paz, Bolivia: CEDIB.

Prieto, Marina and Carolina Quinteros 2004, 'Never the Twain Shall Meet? Women's Organisations and Trade Unions in the Maquila Industry in Central America', *Development in Practice*, 14, 1/2: 149–57.

Provea 2011, *Venezuela: Una década de protestas 2000–2010*, Caracas: Provea, available at: <www.derechos.org.ve/pw/wp-content/uploads/Protestas2000-2010.pdf>.

Przeworksi, Adam 1985, *Capitalism and Social Democracy*, Cambridge: Cambridge University Press.

Purcell, Thomas 2011, 'The Political Economy of Venezuela's Bolivarian Cooperative Movement: A Critique', *Science and Society*, 75, 4: 567–78.

Raby, Diana 2006, *Democracy and Revolution: Latin America and Socialism Today*, London: Pluto Press.

Radice, Hugo 1999, 'Taking Globalisation Seriously', *Socialist Register 1999: Global Capitalism vs. Democracy*, edited by Leo Panitch and Colin Leys, London: Merlin Press.

Rameri, Ana, Tomás Raffo and Claudio Lozano, 2008, 'Sin mucho que festejar: radiografia actual del mercado laboral y las tendencias postconvertibilidad', *Instituto de Estudios y Formación*, 15 May, Buenos Aires: Central de los Trabajadores Argentinos.

Ramírez, Raphael 2006, 'Expert Meeting on Economic Diversification', Vienna: OPEC Secretariat, Energy Studies Department.

Ramos, Gian Carlo 2012, 'Extractivismo, fronteras ecológicas y geopolítica de los recursos', *América Latina en Movimiento*, March: 1–4.

Rapoport, Mario 2000, *Historia Económica, Política y Social de la Argentina (1880–2000)*, Buenos Aires: Macchi.

Rathbone, John Paul 2010, 'Bolivia: Where Thatcher Meets Che', *Financial Times*, 12 November.

Ray, Julie 2011, 'High Wellbeing Eludes the Masses in Most Countries Worldwide. Majorities in 19 out of 124 countries "thriving", mostly in Europe and the Americas', April, available at: <www.gallup.com/poll/147167/High-Wellbeing-Eludes-Masses-Countries-Worldwide.aspx>.

Raynolds, Laura T. 2001, 'New Plantations, New Workers: Gender and Production Politics in the Dominican Republic', *Gender and Society*, 15, 1: 7–28.

Razavi, Shahra 1999, 'Export-Orientated Employment, Poverty and Gender: Contested Accounts', *Development and Change*, 30: 653–83.

Reardon, Thomas, Jean-Marie Codron, Lawrence Busch, James R. Bingen and Craig Harris 2001, 'Global Change in Agrifood Grade and Standards: Agribusiness Strategic Responses in Developing Countries', *International Food and Agribusiness Management Review*, 2, 3: 421–35.

Regalia, Ida 1988, 'Democracy and Unions: Towards a Critical Appraisal', *Economic and Industrial Democracy*, 9, 3: 345–71.

Regalsky, Pablo 2010, 'Political Processes and the Reconfiguration of the State in Bolivia', *Latin American Perspectives*, 37, 3: 35–50.

Reich, Robert 2010, 'Wall Street salió a flote, pero la gente común, no', *Clarín*, 21 January, available at: <http://edant.clarin.com/diario/2010/01/21/opinion/0-02124068.htm>.

Reinaga, Fausto 1969, *La Revolución india*, La Paz: Ediciones PIB (Partido Indio de Bolivia).

Ricupero, Rubens 2009, 'De la crisis global surgirá un capitalismo mucho más humano', *La Nación*, 3 June, available at: <http://www.lanacion.com.ar/1135092-de-esta-crisis-global-surgira-un-capitalismo-mucho-mas-humano>.

Riddell, John 2011a, 'How Clara Zetkin Helps us to Understand Evo Morales', 18 September, available at: <http://johnriddell.wordpress.com/2011/09/18/how-clara-zetkin-helps-us-understand-evo-morales/>.

———— 2011b, 'Progress in Bolivia: A Reply to Jeff Webber', *The Bullet*, 9 May.

Riddell, John (ed.) 2012, *United Front: Proceedings of the Fourth Congress of the Communist International, 1922*, Leiden: Brill.

Rivera Cusicanqui, Silvia 1990, 'Liberal Democracy and Ayllu Democracy: The Case of the Northern Potosí Bolivia', *Journal of Development Studies* 26, 4: 97–121.

Rivero, Alcides 2009, *La coherencia de la FBT en Guayana*, available at: <http://www.aporrea.org/trabajadores/a112483.html>.

Roberts, Kenneth 1996, 'Neoliberalism and the Transformation of Populism in Latin America: The Peruvian Case', *World Politics*, 48, 1: 82–116.

———— 1998, *Deepening Democracy?: The Modern Left and Social Movements in Chile and Peru*, Stanford: Stanford University Press.

Robinson, William I. 2003, *Transnational Conflicts: Central America, Social Change and Globalization*, London: Verso.

———— 2008, 'Transforming Possibilities in Latin America', in *Socialist Register 2008: Global Flashpoints*, edited by Leo Panitch and Colin Leys, London: Merlin Press.

———— 2009, 'Transformative Possibilities in Latin America', *Socialist Register*, 44, 44: 1–19.

———— 2011, 'Latin America's Left at the Crossroads', *Al Jazeera*, 14 September.

Rodríguez, Octavio 2001, 'Prebisch: Actualidad de sus ideas básicas', *Revista de la CEPAL* 75: 41–53.

Rodríguez, P., María C., Hermelinda Mendoza de Ferrer and Arelis Vivas 2009, 'Articulación de los sistemas de acción social de cara al desarrollo endógeno en Venezuela. Una perspectiva de construcción sociológica', *Revista de Ciencias Sociales*, 15, 4: 668–80.

Roett, Riordan 2010, 'How Reform Has Powered Brazil's Rise', *Current History*, 109, 724: 47–52.

Rojas, Rosa 2009, 'Arrasa Evo Morales: Gana reelección y el MAS tiene mayoría en el Congreso', *La Jornada*, 7 December.

Roman, Richard and Edur Velasco Arregui 2013, 'Neoliberal Authoritarianism, the "Democratic Transition", and the Mexican Left', in *The New Latin American Left: Cracks in the Empire*, edited by Jeffery R. Webber and Barry Carr, Lanham, MD: Rowman and Littlefield.

Romero Bonifaz, Carlos 2005, 'Los territorios indígenas: Avances y dificultades teóricas y prácticas', *Barataria*, 1, 3.

Romero, Luis Alberto 2004, 'The Argentine Crisis: A Look at the Twentieth Century', in *The Argentine Crisis at the Turn of the Millennium: Causes, Consequences and Explanations*, edited by Flavia Fiorucci and Marcus Klein, Amsterdam: Center for Latin American Research and Documentation.

Rossell, Pablo 2009, 'El proyecto de Evo Morales más allá de 2010', *Nueva Sociedad*, 221, May–June: 23–32.

Rubinstein, A. Saul 2001, 'A Different Kind of Union: Co-Management and Representation', *Industrial Relations*, 40, 2: 163–203.

Rude, Christopher 2005, 'The Role of Financial Discipline in Imperial Strategy', in *Socialist Register 2005: The Empire Reloaded*, edited by Leo Panitch and Colin Leys, London: Merlin Press.

Russo, John and Sherry Linkin 2005, 'Introduction: What's New About New Working Class-Studies?' in *New Working Class Studies*, edited by John Russo and Sherry Linkin, Ithaca: ILR.

Saad-Filho, Alfredo 1993, 'A Note on Marx's Analysis of the Composition of Capital', *Capital and Class*, 50: 127–46.

———— 2005, 'The Rise and Decline of Latin American Structuralism and Dependency Theory', in *The Origins of Development Economics: How Schools of Economic Thought Have Addressed Development*, edited by Jomo K.S. y Erik S. Reinert, London: Zed Books.

—— 2011, 'Brazil beyond Lula: Forging Ahead or Pausing for Breath?', *Latin American Perspectives*, 38, 2: 31–44.

Sachs, Jeffrey 2009, 'Está naciendo un nuevo modelo de capitalismo', *Clarín*, 14 February, available at: <http://edant.clarin.com/diario/2009/02/14/opinion/0-01858675.htm>.

Sanabria, Harry 1999, 'Consolidating States, Restructuring Economies, and Confronting Workers and Peasants: The Antinomies of Bolivian Neoliberalism', *Comparative Studies in Society and History*, 41: 535–62.

Sánchez Gómez, Luis 2004, 'Directing SEMAPA: An Interview with Luis Sánchez-Gómez', in *Cochabamba! Water War in Bolivia*, edited by Oscar Olivera and Tom Lewis, Cambridge, MA: South End Press.

Sánchez Gómez, Luis and Philipp Terhorst 2005, 'Cochabamba, Bolivia: Public-Collective Partnership after the Water War', in *Reclaiming Public Water-Achievements, Struggles, and Visions from Around the World*, Second Edition, edited by Belén Balanyá, Brid Brennan, Olivier Hoedeman, Satoko Kishimoto and Philipp Terhorst, Porto Alegre: Transnational Institute and Corporate Europe Observatory.

Sándor John S. 2009, *Bolivia's Radical Tradition: Permanent Revolution in the Andes*. Tucson: University of Arizona.

Sartelli, Eduardo 2007, *La Plaza es Nuestra. El Argentinazo a la luz de la lucha obrera en la Argentina del siglo XX*, Buenos Aires: Ediciones ryr.

Sartelli, Eduardo, Fabián Harari, Marina Kabat, Juan Kornblihtt, Verónica Baudino, Fernando Dachevsky and Gonzalo Sanz Cerbino 2008, *Patrones en la ruta. El conflicto agrario y los enfrentamientos en el seno de la burguesía*, Buenos Aires: Ediciones ryr.

Schaller, Susan 2008, 'Lula's Growth Acceleration Program: The Best that Brazilian Government Funding Can Buy?' *Council on Hemispheric Affairs*, available at: <http://www.coha.org/lula%E2%80%99s-brazilian-growth-acceleration-program-the-best-that-government-funding-can-buy/>.

Schvarzer, Jorge 1998, 'Economic Reform in Argentina: Which Social Force for What Aims, in *What kind of Democracy? What kind of Market?: Latin America in the Age of Neoliberalism*, edited by Philip Oxhorn and Graciela Ducatenzeiler, University Park: The Pennsylvania State University Press.

Scott, James 1998, *Seeing Like a State*, Princeton: Princeton University Press.

Seidman, Gay, 1994, *Manufacturing Militance: Workers' Movements in Brazil and South Africa, 1970–1985*, Berkeley: University of California Press.

Selwyn, Ben 2007a, *Export Grape Production and Development in North East Brazil*, PhD Thesis, London: University of London.

—— 2007b, 'Labour Process and Workers' Bargaining Power in Export Grape Production, North East Brazil', *Journal of Agrarian Change*, 7, 4: 526–53.

—— 2008, 'Bringing Social Relations Back in: (Re) Conceptualising the "Bullwhip Effect" in Global Commodity Chains', *International Journal of Management Concepts and Philosophy*, 3, 2: 156–75.

———— 2009, 'An Historical Materialist Appraisal of Friedrich List and his Modern-Day Followers', *New Political Economy*, 14, 2: 157–80.

———— 2010, 'Gender, Wage Work and Development in North East Brazilian Export Horticulture', *Bulletin of Latin American Research*, 29, 1: 51–70.

———— 2012, *Workers, State and Development in Brazil: Powers of Labour, Chains of Value*, Manchester: University Press.

Seoane, José and Clara Algramati 2012, 'La ofensiva extractivista en América Latina: Crisis global y alternativas', *Herramienta*, 50, July, available at: <http://www .herramienta.com.ar/revista-herramienta-n-50/la-ofensiva-extractivista-en-america-latina-crisis-global-y-alternativas>.

Seongin, Jeong 2008, *Página/12–Cash*, 19 October.

Shaikh, Anwar 1991, 'Competition and Exchange Rates: Theory and Empirical Evidence', Working Paper, New York: New School for Social Research.

———— 1992, 'The Falling Rate of Profit as the Cause of Long Waves: Theory and Empirical Evidence', in *New Findings in Long Wave Research*, edited by Alfred Kleinknecht, Ernest Mandel and Immanuel Wallerstein, London: Macmillan Press.

Sierra Corrales, Francisco 2011, 'Lo que se está jugando en Guayana', *Aporrea*, 2 February, available at: <www.aporrea.org/regionales/a117561.html>.

Silva, Luiz Inácio Lula da 2007, *Speech by President of Brazil, Luiz Inácio Lula da Silva*, available at: <http://www.brazil.org.uk/press/speeches_files/20070705.html>.

———— 2008a, Speech by the President of Brazil, Luiz Inácio Lula da Silva, at the UN Food and Agriculture Organisation (FAO) Conference on World Food Security – Rome, 3 June, available at: <http://www.brazil.org.uk/press/speeches_ files/20080603.html>.

———— 2008b, *Statement by H.E. Luiz Inácio Lula da Silva, President of the Federative Republico of Brazil, at the General Debate of the 63rd Session of the United Nations General Assembly*, New York, 23 September, available at: <http://www.un.org/en/ ga/63/generaldebate/pdf/brazil_en.pdf>.

———— 2009, *Statement by H.E. Luiz Inácio Lula da Silva, President of the Federative Republico of Brazil, at the General Debate of the 64th Session of the United Nations General Assembly*, New York, 23 September, available at: <http://www.brazil.org.uk/ press/speeches_files/20090923.html>.

Silver, Beverly 2003, *Forces of Labour: Workers Movements and Globalization Since 1870*, Cambridge: Cambridge University Press.

Singer, Hans W. 1950, 'The Distribution of Gains Between Investing and Borrowing Countries', *The American Economic Review*, 40, 2: 473–85.

Smith, Neil 2006, 'The Geography of Uneven Development', in *100 Years of Permanent Revolution: Results and Prospects*, edited by Bill Dunn and Hugo Radice, London: Pluto.

Smith, Tony 2006, *Globalisation. A Systematic Marxian Account*, Leiden: Brill.

Sorman, Guy 2009, 'El sistema capitalista no muere, siempre rebota', *Clarín*, 28 October, available at: <http://edant.clarin.com/diario/2009/10/28/opinion/o-02028260.htm>.

Sparovek, Gerd 2003, *A Qualidade dos Assentamentos da Reforma Agrária Brasileira*, São Paulo: Páginas e Letras Editora e Gráfica.

Spraos, John 1980, 'The Statistical Debate on the Net Barter Terms of Trade Between Primary Commodities and Manufactures, *The Economic Journal*, 90, 357: 107–28.

Spronk, Susan 2013, 'Neoliberal Class Formation(s): The Informal Proletariat and "New" Workers' Organizations in Latin America', in *The New Latin American Left: Cracks in the Empire*, edited by Jeffery R. Webber and Barry Carr, Lanham, MD: Rowman and Littlefield.

Spronk, Susan and Jeffery R. Webber 2007, 'Struggles against Accumulation by Dispossession in Bolivia: The Political Economy of Natural Resource Contention', *Latin American Perspectives*, 34, 2: 31–47.

Spronk, Susan and Jeffery R. Webber, George Ciccariello-Maher, Roland Denis, Steve Ellner, Sujatha Fernandes, Michael A. Lebowitz, Sara Motta and Thomas Purcell 2011, 'The Bolivarian Process in Venezuela: A Left Forum', *Historical Materialism*, 19: 233–70.

Stallings, Barbara and Wilson Peres 2011, 'Is Economic Reform Dead in Latin America? Rhetoric and Reality Since 2000', *Journal of Latin American Studies*, 43, 4: 755–86.

Standing, Guy 1992, 'Do Unions Impede or Accelerate Structural Adjustment? Industrial Versus Company Unions in an Industrialising Labour Market', *Cambridge Journal of Economics*, 16: 327–54.

———— 1999, *Global Labour Flexibility: Seeking Distributive Justice*, New York: Palgrave Macmillan.

Stefanoni, Pablo 2010, 'Bolivia después de las elecciones: ¿a dónde va el *evismo*?', *Nueva Sociedad*, 225, January–February: 4–17.

———— 2011, 'Algunas claves del conflicto del TIPNIS', *Rebelión*, 2 October.

Stiglitz, Joseph 2002, *Globalization and its Discontents*, New York: Norton.

———— 2009, 'Un nuevo sistema de crédito es vital para frenar esta crisis', *Clarín*, 11 November, available at: <http://edant.clarin.com/diario/2009/04/11/elmundo/i-01895397.htm>.

———— 2010a, 'Obama ignora cómo ayudar a su clase media', *Clarín*, 11 March, available at: <http://edant.clarin.com/diario/2010/03/11/opinion/o-02156668.htm>.

———— 2010, 'Seguimos sin un acuerdo para salvar el planeta', *Clarín*, 8 January, available at: <http://edant.clarin.com/diario/2010/01/08/elmundo/i-02115497.htm>.

Stokes, Susan 2005, 'Perverse Accountability: A Formal Model of Machine Politics with Evidence from Argentina', *American Political Science Review*, 99, 3: 315–25.

Stratta, Fernando and Marcelo Barrera 2009, *El tizón encendido. Protesta social, conflicto y territorio en la Argentina de la posdictadura*, Buenos Aires: Editorial El Colectivo.

Svampa, Maristela and Sebastían Pereyra 2003, *Entre la ruta y el barrio. La experiencia de las organizaciones piqueteras*, Buenos Aires: Editorial Biblos.

Svampa, Maristella 2008, 'The End of Kirchnerism', *New Left Review*, 53, September/October: 79–98.

Swarcberg, Marina 2007, 'Strategies of Electoral Mobilization in Comparative Perspective: Lessons from the Argentine Case', paper presented at Congress of the Latin American Studies Association, Montréal, Canada, 5–8 September.

Sztulwark, Sebastián 2006, *El estructuralismo latinoamericano*, Buenos Aires: Prometeo.

Tabb, William K. 2009, 'Globalization Today: At the Borders of Class and State Theory', *Science and Society*, 73, 1: 34–53.

Tanuro, Daniel 2009a, 'Rapport sur le changement climatique et les taches anticapitalistes', *Inprecor*, 551–552, July–August, available at: <http://orta.dynalias.org/inprecor/article-inprecor?id=739>.

———— 2009b, 'Derrota en la cumbre, victoria en la base', *Viento Sur*, 108, 24 December, available at: <http://www.vientosur.info/articulosweb/noticia/index.php?x=2772>.

Taylor, Marcus 2009, 'The Contradictions and Transformations of Neoliberalism in Latin America: From Structural Adjustment to "Empowering the Poor"', in *Post-Neoliberalism in the Americas*, edited by Laura Macdonald and Arne Ruckert, Basingstoke: Palgrave Macmillan.

The Economist 2006, 'The Return of Populism', 26 April, available at: <http://www.economist.com/node/6802448>.

———— 2009, 'The Explosive Apex of Evo's Power: Bolivia's Presidential Election', 10 December.

———— 2011, 'Bolivia's Evo Morales: The Calle Gets Restive', 3 March.

Thomaz Junior, Antonio 2007, 'Não há Nada Novo sob o Sol num Mundo de Heróis (A Civilização da Barbária na Agroindústria Canavieiria)', *Revista Pegada*, 8, 2: 5–26.

Thompson, E.P. 1963, *The Making of the English Working Class*, London: Penguin.

Thrupp, Lori Ann 1995, *Bitter-Sweet Harvests for Global Supermarkets*, Washington, DC: World Resource Institute.

Trabajadores de CVG/Alcasa 2009, *Control Obrero*, Publicación de trabajadores de CVG/Alcasa, *Aporrea*, 16 September, available at: <www.aporrea.org/endogeno/a86731.html>.

Troudi, E. Haiman and Juan C. Monedero 2006, *Empresas de Producción Social: Instrumento para el Socialismo del Siglo XXI*, Caracas: Centro Miranda Internacional.

Ugarteche, Oscar 2012, 'Hasta dónde hay resilencia a la crisis global en América Latina (y cómo termina)', *Crítica y Emancipación*, 8: 23–37.

UNDP 2010, *The Changes Behind the Change: Inequalities and Social Mobility in Bolivia*, La Paz: United Nations Development Programme.

———— 2011, *Human Development Report 2011 – Sustainability and Equity: A Better Future for All*, New York: United Nations Human Development Programme.

VALEXPORT 2008, *Há 20 Anos Unindo Forças Para O Desenvolvimento Do Vale Do São Francisco E Da Fruticultura Brasileira*, Petrolina: VALEXPORT.

Valle, Baeza 2009, 'Una explicación de la gravedad de la actual crisis estadounidense', *XI Encuentro Internacional sobre Globalización y Problemas del Desarrollo*, Havana, 2–6 March.

Valle Silva, N. de 2008, 'Brazilian Society: Continuity and Change, 1930–2000', in L. Bethell (ed.), *The Cambridge History of Latin America Volume IX: Brazil since 1930*, Cambridge: Cambridge University Press.

Van der Linden, Marcel 2002, 'Globalizing Labour Historiography: The IISH Approach', Amsterdam: International Institute of Social History.

———— 2004, 'The "Globalization" of Labour and Working-Class History and its Consequences', *International Labour and Working-Class History*, 65: 136–56.

———— 2008, *Workers of the World*, Leiden/Boston: Brill.

Vega Cantor, Renan 2009, 'Crisis civilizatoria', *Herramienta*, 42, available at: <http://www.herramienta.com.ar/revista-herramienta-n-42/crisis-civilizatoria>.

Veltmeyer, Henry and Juan Tellez 2001, 'The State and Participatory Development in Bolivia', in *Transcending Neoliberalism: Community-Based Development in Latin America*, edited by Henry Veltmeyer and Anthony O'Malley, Bloomfield, CT: Kumarian Press.

Vergara-Camus, Leandro 2012, 'The Legacy of Social Conflicts over Property Rights in Rural Brazil and Mexico. Current Land Struggles in Historical Perspective', *Journal of Peasant Studies*, 39, 2: 197–222.

Vessillier, Jean Claude 2009, 'Automobile. La fin d'un cycle', *Inprecor*, 545–546, January–February, available at: <http://orta.dynalias.org/inprecor/article-inprecor?id=630>.

Viner, Jacob 1951, 'A economia do desenvolvimento', *Revista Brasileira de Economia*, 5, 2: 181–225.

Vivas, Esther 2009, 'El clima en jaque', *Diagonal Periodico*, 113, 11 November, available at: <http://www.diagonalperiodico.net/El-clima-en-jaque.html>.

Void Manufacturing 2009, 'Interview with James C. Scott', 17 December, available at: <http://voidmanufacturing.wordpress.com/2009/12/17/interview-with-james-c-scott/>.

Wade, Robert 2003, *Governing the Market: Economic Theory and the Role of Government in East Asian Industrialization*, Princeton: Princeton University Press.

Wallerstein, Immanuel 2000, 'A Left Politics for the 21st Century? Or, Theory and Praxis Once Again', *New Political Science*, 22, 2: 143–59.

———— 2004, *Capitalismo histórico y movimientos anti-sistémicos: un análisis de sistemas-mundo*, Madrid: Akal.

Webber, Jeffery R. 2010a, 'Carlos Mesa, Evo Morales and a Divided Bolivia (2003–2005)', *Latin American Perspectives*, 37, 3: 51–70.

———— 2010b, 'Review: Latin American Neostructuralism by Fernando Ignacio Leiva', *Historical Materialism*, 18, 3: 208–29.

———— 2011a, 'Fantasies Aside, It's Reconstituted Neoliberalism in Bolivia under Morales: A Rejoinder to Frederico Fuentes', *International Socialist Review*, 76, March–April, available at: <www.isreview.org/issues/76/debate-bolivia.shtml>.

———— 2011b, *From Rebellion to Reform in Bolivia: Class Struggle, Indigenous Liberation, and the Politics of Evo Morales*, Chicago: Haymarket Books.

———— 2011c, *Red October: Left-Indigenous Struggles in Modern Bolivia*, Leiden: Brill Academic Publishers.

Webber, Jeffery R., and Barry Carr (eds.) 2013, *The New Latin American Left: Cracks in the Empire*, Lanham: Rowman & Littlefield Publishers.

Weber, Max 1968, *Economy and Society*, Berkeley and Los Angeles: University of California Press.

Weeks, John 1981, *Capital and Exploitation*, London: Edward Arnold Publishers/ Princeton University Press.

Weisbrot, Mark, Rebecca Ray and Luis Sandoval 2009, 'The Chávez Administration at 10 Years: The Economy and Social Indicators', Washington: Center for Economic and Policy Research, available at: <http://www.networkideas.org/featart/feb2009/ Venezuela.pdf>.

Weitz-Shapiro, Rebeca 2008, 'Choosing Clientelism. Political Clientelism, Poverty and Social Welfare Policy in Argentina', Doctoral Thesis, Columbia University.

Williamson, John 1993, 'Democracy and the "Washington Consensus"', *World Development*, 21, 8: 1329–36.

Wilpert, Gregory 2007, *Changing Venezuela by Taking Power: The History and Policies of the Chavez Government*. London: Verso.

Winn, Peter 1986, *Weavers of the Revolution: The Yarur. Workers and Chile's Road to Socialism*, New York: Oxford University Press.

Wolff, Jonas 2007, '(De)Mobilizing de Marginalized: A Comparison of the Argentine *Piqueteros* and Ecuador's Indigenous Movement', *Journal of Latin American Studies*, 39: 1–29.

Wolfson, Martin 2003, 'Neoliberalism and the social structure of accumulation', *Review of Radical Political Economics*, 35, 3: 255–62.

Wood, Ellen Meiksins 1995, *Democracy against Capitalism: Renewing Historical Materialism*, Cambridge: Cambridge University Press.

———— 1999, *The Origin of Capitalism*, New York: Monthly Review Press.

Woods, Alan 2006, *The Venezuelan Revolution; A Marxist Perspective*, Delhi, India: Aakar Books.

World Bank no date, *Bolivia Country Brief*, available at: <http://www.worldbank.org/en/country/bolivia/overview>.

Wright, Erik Olin 2000, 'Working-Class Power, Capitalist-Class Interests, and Class Compromise', *American Journal of Sociology*, 105, 4: 957–1002.

——— 2010, *Envisioning Real Utopias*, London: Verso.

Wrigley, Neil and Michelle Lowe 2007, 'Introduction: Transnational Retail and the Global Economy', *Journal of Economic Geography*, 7, 4: 337–40.

Yashar, Deborah J. 2005, *Contesting citizenship in Latin America: The Rise of Indigenous Movements and the Postliberal Challenge*, Cambridge: Cambridge University Press.

Zibechi, Raúl 2006, 'Movimientos sociales: nuevos escenarios y desafíos inéditos', *OSAL*, 21: 221–30.

——— 2010, *Dispersing Power*, Oakland, CA: AK Press.

——— 2011a, 'La autonomía en las fauces del progresismo', *Herramienta*, available at: <http://www.herramienta.com.ar/revista-impresa-n-46>.

——— 2011b, 'Bolivia After the Storm', *Znet*, 6 April.

Index

accumulation *See: capital accumulation*
agriculture
    in Brazil
        sugarcane 217–230
        ethanol 220–223
        neoliberal restructuring of 220–221
austerity 5, 88, 327–328

Brenner, Robert 23, 206n60, 213n5, 218, 246n25, 288n31
BRICS 258n52, 274

Cardoso, Fernando Henrique 197n16, 200, 205n54, 207n56, 209
    Reforms under 251–255
capital *See also capitalism*, OCC
    finance 54n14r
    flight 59, 268n80
    foreign 54, 60, 89, 171, 179–180, 195–197, 201, 206, 213, 215, 323
    labour and 11, 14, 15, 17, 98–101, 117, 166, 263
    relations amongst capitals 79, 205–206, 213–214, 223, 226, 243–246
capitalism *See also* agrarian capitalism
    civil society and 79, 144, 291–292
    class-struggle and 11, 24, 33, 146, 161, 166–167, 305
    crises of 9, 31, 74, 84–85, 130n26, 273–279, 288, 291–292
    democracy and 15, 74–75, 78–79
    effect on political rights 15, 78
    historical specificity of 238
    as imperative 219
    labour and 6, 15–17, 53, 99, 101, 168, 206, 280, 285
    left intellectuals and 1, 6, 25, 85
    separation of 'political' and 'economic' in 144
    slavery and 297
Central America 4
Central de los Trabajadores Argentinos (CTA, Argentine) 57

Confederación General del Trabajo CGT 55–57, 65–66, 76n16, 79n25, 80, 95
Chavez, Hugo 120–121, 126–128, 130, 137, 154–156, 161
    administration/government of 137, 139, 141, 143, 147n24, 148, 163, 167, 180, 188–189
China 275–281
    trade with 62, 274–279
civil society
    capitalism and *See capitalism and civil society*
    conceptual problems of 123, 144
    and the state 17, 79, 123–125, 135, 144, 203, 214, 291
class
    exploitation 61–62, 69, 72, 74, 90, 290, 300
    formation 11, 16–17, 102
    abolition of 189
    identity and 102
    new working 12, 33–36, 117
    production-relations and 17–18, 22–23, 160, 189, 239–241, 315–316
    ruling 8, 14, 219, 234
    state and 20, 57, 141, 193, 201, 204–206, 210, 223–224, 234, 315, 317–318
    struggle 29–43, 49–50, 64n64, 67n79, 70, 141, 139–142, 165–173, 229, 239–240, 261–262, 304–306, 308–310
    working *See* also new working
        class 11–12, 101–104, 117, 279
coalitions
    working class 29–30, 41, 46, 303
    capitalist class 55, 80–81, 212, 222, 234, 317
    political 58, 65–66, 77, 79, 82, 95, 131, 203, 205, 223, 254 261–262, 268n80, 303
Cocalero (Bolivia) 316, 318
Cochabamba, Bolivia
    MAS and 307
    water war 37–42
Cogestion (co-management, Venezuela) 153–154, 164–165, 180–189

www.ingramcontent.com/pod-product-compliance
Lightning Source LLC
Chambersburg PA
CBHW060021030426
42334CB00019B/2121